"Asma Uddin, the preeminent defender of religious freedom for American Muslims, has for years been patiently explaining why her faith is no threat to non-Muslims. *When Islam Is Not a Religion* is an eloquent plea for tolerance, weaving astute legal analysis with a compelling personal story. Prejudice cannot survive her testimony."
—Tom Gjelten, Religion and Belief Correspondent, NPR

"Asma Uddin has written a terrific book. It is all at once a primer on the very American commitment to religious freedom, a history of the discrimination that Muslims in America have endured since 9/11 and a window into the life of a leading American Muslim intellectual. It is both deeply researched and a joy to read. I give it my highest recommendation."—Eboo Patel, author of *Out of Many Faiths*, founder and president of the Interfaith Youth Core

"A powerful book examining how modern discourse has tried to put Islam and Muslims into a small box of political identity. As Asma Uddin demonstrates, Islam is a vast corpus of ideas and Muslims incredibly diverse in the way they approach their faith. This book is a necessity at a time when American society is deeply divided. Perhaps in learning to recognize and appreciate the diversity within Islam, we can learn to transcend the differences we have with each other."
—Kamran Pasha, author of *Mother of the Believers* and *Shadow of the Swords*

"A powerfully written account of what is taking place in America today. With passion and power she shows us that oppression of religious rights of one group affects the rights of us all. The solution for the rising fear and hate of the other is an open and respectful dialogue. I learned a lot from this book and so will you! I highly recommend it!"—Farah Pandith, former Special Representative to Muslim Communities, U.S. State Department, and author of *How We Win: How Cutting-Edge Entrepreneurs, Political Visionaries, Enlightened Business Leaders, and Social Media Mavens Can Defeat the Extremist Threat*

"The freedom to practice and cultivate one's faith is the bedrock of America's founding principles. People have come to our country to escape religious persecution, but there has been a rising tide of discrimination right here at home. Ms. Uddin is a leader for religious freedom and calls our attention to the challenges facing First Amendment rights in the post-9/11 world."
—Senator Orrin G. Hatch (R-UT), former President
pro tempore of the United States Senate

"Uddin details the evolution over recent years of the shocking slander that one of the world's three Abrahamic faiths is not a religion; and therefore that its American adherents are not entitled to the protections enjoyed by citizens of all other faiths under the U.S. Constitution. Drawing on her extensive career, she examines the current landscape of the law. Even more, she describes the effect of bigotry and otherization on the human heart, calling on her experience as listener, feminist, mother and daughter."
—Meryl Chertoff, Executive Director of
the Aspen Institute Justice and Society Program

"A compelling examination of the nation's ongoing efforts to balance religious freedom with civil liberties—and where those efforts are falling short, particularly for Muslims but also for other non-majority communities. Uddin avoids heated rhetoric in favor of an insightful examination of modern-day Islam in the U.S. and worldwide, and argues persuasively that the United States' commitment to religious liberty must not be derailed by animus toward those who distort Islam and use it as a mechanism of intolerance, political terrorism and violence. If you want to think seriously about the future of freedom of religion, this is a must-read."—Gene Policinski, founding editor of *USA Today* and
COO of the Freedom Forum Institute

"I have been waiting for this book a long time. It is written by a young American scholar and lawyer who has fought for religious liberty for all, who also just happens to practice Islam. This is a must read for anyone who wants to understand religious freedom and how it relates to American Muslims. This could be the most important book written so far on the challenges Islam faces in the United States. You don't have to agree with everything but you should respect the thought process and the person writing it."
—Bob Roberts, Jr., founding pastor of Northwood Church, founder of Glocal.net, and author of *Bold as Love*

"In the age of Donald Trump, American Muslims face a graver threat to their religious freedom than any other group. Everyone who cares about American freedom should grasp the danger and rally to their cause. In her remarkable book, Asma Uddin explains how."
—Peter Beinart, Professor of Journalism and Political Science, City University of New York, CNN political commentator, and contributor to *The Atlantic*

"Asma Uddin's book explores a critical and unknown dimension of Islamophobia—the false claim that Islam is not a religion—as well as the danger of this claim to American religious freedom as we know it. It is required reading for anyone who cares about the future and health of our democracy."—Dalia Mogahed, coauthor of *Who Speaks for Islam? What a Billion Muslims Really Think*

"A must-read—especially for conservative Christians like me—to better understand the scope and the stakes of the religious liberty debate. I hope it starts a long-overdue conversation among believers. . . . It stands to be a landmark in the religious freedom discussion."
—Rod Dreher, author of the *New York Times* bestseller *The Benedict Option*

"This authoritative book thoroughly dissects the dynamics of religious freedom at the crossroads of U.S. Muslims, the Islamic faith, and U.S. national identity. A top expert in the field, Uddin demystifies some of the most 'hot-button' issues surrounding American Muslims and challenges all of us to think more critically about what it means to be 'American.' Uddin doesn't simply talk the talk with *When Islam Is Not a Religion*. She also walks the walk by using her personal experiences as a U.S. citizen, mother, and lawyer. This accessible piece of scholarship will empower Muslims and encourage people of various walks of life to move closer to the American motto—*E pluribus unum*—'out of many, one.'"
—Dr. Craig Considine, Rice University

when
islam is not
a religion

when islam is not a religion

INSIDE AMERICA'S FIGHT FOR RELIGIOUS FREEDOM

ASMA T. UDDIN

PEGASUS BOOKS
NEW YORK LONDON

WHEN ISLAM IS NOT A RELIGION

Pegasus Books, Ltd.
148 West 37th Street, 13th Floor
New York, NY 10018

First Pegasus Books hardcover edition July 2019

Interior design by Sabrina Plomitallo-González, Pegasus books

ISBN: 978-1-64313-131-3

10 9 8 7 6 5 4 3 2 1

Printed in the United States of America
Distributed by W. W. Norton & Company, Inc.

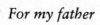

For my father

CONTENTS

INTRODUCTION

On Presidents Day 2019, I was invited to speak at the Museum of the Bible in Washington, DC, about our Founding Fathers' commitment to religious liberty for all. Part of a diverse panel, I was the Muslim speaker alongside the Jewish and Christian voices. The others spoke of George Washington; I focused on Thomas Jefferson.

"In the founding-era debates, there were two rival conceptions of the nation's identity," I said. "Preserving the Protestant status quo or guaranteeing individual rights regardless of religion." The Founders chose the latter. Jefferson in particular wanted to study other cultures and learn from their successes and failures. He made it a point to purchase a Qur'an, which he owned because it helped him better advocate for the acceptance and enfranchisement of Muslims in America.

Jefferson didn't know of any Muslims living in the US during his time (though recent research has revealed that almost 20% of the slaves in America were Muslims) but he still explicitly considered the rights of potential Muslim inhabitants of the nation. In fact, as scholar Denise Spellberg has noted, when the future, "imagined" Muslims figured into the Founders' debates, they served as a sort of litmus test or indicator of what America was meant to be.

"If you consider that anti-Muslim stereotypes at the time were entrenched and widespread," I said, "it's truly startling that Jefferson and others were able to move past them and imagine a day when Muslims would not only be welcome in America but also be afforded full and equal rights as American citizens."

No sooner had I finished my presentation than I had my first question, three of them rolled into one and shot at me with indignation. "Doesn't Islam believe in Sharia law and the oppression of women?

Why should we protect Muslims? After all, *they* don't protect the rights of religious minorities. What are Muslims doing to protect Christians?"

To some extent, I had known these questions were coming. I have spent the past decade working for religious liberty, and one of the most consistent features of that public advocacy is the claim that Muslims (and I as a Muslim) don't deserve religious liberty.

I'm not the only one to face these questions. David French, a columnist for the conservative *National Review*, is exasperated by the countless times he's "had the following conversation":

> I'll have just finished speaking to a church or a conference about the vital importance of American religious liberty, and some well-meaning, well-informed questioner will ask earnestly if all my words apply to Islam in the same way they do to Judaism or Christianity. When I say yes, the response is immediate. "But isn't Islam mainly a political system?" they'll ask. "Doesn't Sharia law violate the Constitution?"

The fear is that Muslims will use religious freedom to "destroy" and "take over" America. But that's not how our constitutional rights work.

* * *

Muslims are entitled to American religious liberty protections. America is home to great religious diversity, and our Constitution requires that the government protect that full range of diversity equally and fairly. The Constitution also envisions a society where we, as people, engage with each other's differences with respect. Every American, of every religion, or none, should protect religious freedom for people of all faiths—majority and minority faiths included. Among advocates, this concept is commonly referred to as "religious freedom for all."

Importantly, however, religious freedom for all is not about advocating a free-for-all. There are limits to religious freedom. The law starts by drawing a distinction between beliefs and actions. Americans can hold any belief they wish, unfettered from government interference. But when they express beliefs through actions, the government can restrict those actions.

Indeed, the government sometimes has really good reasons (which the law calls "compelling government interests") for stopping us from engaging in particular religious practices, and the law has standards in place to help strike the right balance between freedom and those government interests. The standard, or test, is called "strict scrutiny," and I mention it in various places throughout this book.

One common area where this test comes into play is national security. Some readers may be skeptical about a book advocating for religious liberty for Muslims because the first thing many people think of when they think of Muslims is, unfortunately, violence. We live in an age of global terrorism, with numerous incidents here in the US. Although terrorism is by no means the sole province of actors purporting to act on the basis of Islam, many Americans associate terrorism with Islam.

Another big concern for many Americans is "sharia"—a deeply misunderstood concept that recalls images of criminals being stoned or getting their hands chopped off, honor killings, child brides, and female genital mutilation. In these cases and every case where someone tries to justify an act on the basis of religion, the government can legally restrict the practice if the government meets the legal standard.

For example, in a case out of Florida where a Muslim woman refused to remove her face-covering veil for her driver's license photo, a court held that the Florida Department of Highway Safety and Motor Vehicles could revoke the woman's driver's license because the government had a compelling interest "in protecting the public against criminal activities and security threats." Facial images are necessary to law enforcement officers and help identify suspects quickly.

When someone's life is at risk, it's even easier for the government to show it has a "compelling interest" in restricting their religious freedom. For example, Jehovah's Witnesses' religious beliefs would deny their children life-saving blood transfusions, but American courts have held that their religious freedom is not protected. Adults can refuse these medical procedures but cannot deny them to their children when their children's lives are at risk. Similar concerns about health and safety come up in relation to Christian groups that believe in "faith healing" in lieu of medical care. Or parents who refuse to vaccinate their children because of religious objections (in Buncombe County, North Carolina, alone, "parents of 5.7% of kindergartners" claim a religious exemption from vaccinations, which led to a chickenpox outbreak in a local school in November 2018). In all of these cases, courts and legislators have to balance competing interests. Sometimes they get it right, sometimes they don't, but the standard still holds.

So, again, religious freedom for all does not mean a free-for-all. The American legal test does a very good job of balancing religious freedom with government interests. This book holds that standard up as the right one and does not advocate, in any way, that there be special exceptions to it—for Muslims or any other religious group. It asks only that the standard be applied equally and fairly to all faith groups.

* * *

"Why should we protect Muslims? After all, they don't protect the rights of religious minorities." I get this question a lot. By "they" the speaker is referring to Muslim-majority countries, and in many cases, to the authoritarian governments in those states. The comparison is faulty for a number of reasons. For one, it attempts to determine constitutional rights in America based on what's happening outside America. More specifically, it looks to autocratic states—places where everyone, Muslims included, have few rights—to define the scope of American liberty. In fact, what these critics don't realize is that in Muslim-majority states that restrict religious freedom, Muslims are the most frequent victims of the laws (not only because there are numerically more Muslims in those countries, but also because any Muslim who deviates from the state-sanctioned interpretation of Islam risks being punished by the state). The comparison is also deeply problematic because it tries to place on American Muslims the burden of actions they don't control or even influence.

Fearing *all* Muslims because *some* Muslims are doing abhorrent things also betrays an extreme ignorance of religion in general and Islam in particular. Muslims who use faith as a shield or justification for abhorrent behavior would not be the first to use faith—any faith—to do so. Religions are quite internally diverse; not all Muslims believe the same things or behave in the same ways. Religions are also rooted in culture (and, often, politics), so that many of the practices one might ascribe to Islam are intrinsically tied up with the culture in which some Muslims live.

Still, I understand the inclination. Especially if you don't know any Muslims personally (which is likely, since Muslims constitute only 1.1 percent of the US population), and generally think of Islam as foreign, your view of American Muslims will be colored by the actions of Muslims somewhere else in the world. As Yale historian Timothy Snyder explains, "You take people who are your neighbors and you define them not primarily as your neighbors and fellow citizens but primarily with some larger world community, all of whose members hold the same views." Snyder calls this process "denationalization."

Other vulnerable minorities have been denationalized in the past, but today Muslims are the target. Propagandists bent on generating fear and hatred of Muslims will use any evidence of any Muslim wrongdoing anywhere to demonize the entire religious community (I'll tell you more about them in chapter 2). And news headlines are regularly ablaze with the latest atrocity. When many Americans think of religious freedom in Islam, they think of the 2004 murder of Theo van Gogh, the Dutch filmmaker who made a film that criticized Islam, or the fiery protests in 2005 over the Danish cartoons mocking the Prophet Muhammad, or the deadly shooting at the *Charlie Hebdo* offices in France.

Together, these factors confirm for many critics that Islam is inherently incompatible with freedom and liberal values. But plenty of evidence contradicts this idea. For example, Daniel Philpott, a law professor at the University of Notre Dame, found that 11 out of 46 Muslim-majority states have little to no restrictions on religious freedom (countries like Kosovo, Djibouti, Albania, Mali, Senegal, and Sierra Leone). As Philpott notes, these countries may well have roots "in a particular form of Islamic theology or culture that embodies tolerance." Within the other 35 countries he looked at, Philpott notes that restrictions on religion fall into one of two patterns: Islamist or secularist. In the first case, governments use the law to promote and enforce a restrictive interpretation of Islamic law. But 32 percent of Muslim states that restrict religion basically use France as their model: they try to enforce a strict secularism by pushing religion (including Islam) out of the public square. The "secular repressive" pattern can be found in places like Uzbekistan, Algeria, pre-revolutionary Tunisia, and Turkey before the AKP party took power.

Philpott looked at government action. The Pew Forum on Religious and Public Life, on the other hand, surveyed individual Muslims living in Muslim-majority countries and found a variety of views on religious freedom. In a 2013 study, Pew found that "most Muslims around the world express support for democracy, and most say it is a good thing when others are very free to practice their religion." While many Muslims want their religious leaders to play some role in politics, "given a choice between a leader with a strong hand or a democratic system of government, most Muslims choose democracy." Most Muslims also think that religious freedom for people of other faiths is a good thing. "In 31 of the 38 countries where the question was asked, majorities of Muslims say people of other faiths can practice their religion very freely . . . And of those who share this assessment, overwhelming majorities consider it a good thing."

But there is a lot of room for improvement, and Muslim scholars and activists work every day to expand the scope of freedom. As the gentleman in the Presidents Day audience asked me so pressingly: "What are Muslims doing to protect Christians?" When I started rattling off the various initiatives underway in Muslim-majority states, he appeared taken aback.

Engage Pakistan, a nonprofit based in Lahore, Pakistan, battles laws that punish blasphemy or apostasy (the act of leaving a religion). Led by Arafat Mazhar, a devout Muslim millennial, the organization has spent years digging through classical Islamic texts and has found compelling evidence that Pakistan's blasphemy laws contradict these religious sources. In Egypt, Muslim activist Hossam Bahgat has spent decades working with religious scholars to undermine the religious justifications for antiblasphemy and anti-apostasy laws. In 2007, he found that government laws that punish apostasy have no religious bases. Based on his conversations with prominent religious leaders like the Grand Mufti of Egypt, Bahgat concluded that government officials "simply mak[e] up their own rules."

Lawyer and human rights activist Asma Jahangir, who passed away in February 2018, cofounded the Human Rights Commission of Pakistan and spent her entire adult life working for human rights. From 2004 to 2010, she served as the United Nations special rapporteur for freedom of religion or belief, appointed by the UN Human Rights Council to identify existing and emerging problems for religious freedom around the world. By all accounts, she was a fierce advocate.

The editor of the Pakistani newspaper, *Dawn*, called her "the guts-iest woman" in Pakistan. In 2007, Declan Walsh described her in *The Guardian* as "tower[ing] over Pakistan's human rights war."

Today, another Muslim, Ahmed Shaheed, holds the title of UN Special rapporteur for freedom of religion or belief. In that role, Shaheed continues Jahangir's contributions to religious freedom. He is joined by countless others. Muslim scholar Muhammad Hashim Kamali has produced detailed and precise scholarship on freedom of religion and free speech in Islam in his book series *Fundamental Rights and Liberties in Islam*. Muslim religious leaders, Abdullah Bin Bayyah and Hamza Yusuf, have since 2016 promoted global conversations around the Marrakesh Declaration through an organization called the Forum for Promoting Peace in Muslim Societies (or, Peace Forum). The declaration calls for a revival of the Islamic tradition of peaceful coexistence with other religious groups and a focus on Islamic theories of equal citizenship. Hundreds of religious figures from over 100 countries were party to the declaration, which also calls on activists and lawyers to implement these religious teachings in law. Sam Brownback, the US ambassador-at-large for international religious freedom in the Trump administration, has engaged with the Peace Forum ever since he took on the role; his first public appearance as ambassador was at the Forum's Alliance of Virtues conference in Washington, DC.

The Peace Forum gathering included prominent Christian and Jewish leaders, as well as members from persecuted communities in Muslim-majority states (such as Chaldean Catholics from Iraq). Pastor Bob Roberts was one of the American pastors in attendance. For years, Roberts has worked closely with Imam Mohamed Magid, who leads a 35,000-strong Muslim community in Northern Virginia. Together, Roberts and Magid "bring imams and pastors together to 'just hang out'"—and solve major world problems, like Christian and Muslim persecution in Pakistan, Nigeria, Sudan, Myanmar, Central African Republic, and elsewhere.

Among all this tremendous work are my own modest contributions. For the past decade I have advocated against blasphemy laws in Muslim-majority states. I helped develop and, for several years, was the primary attorney for the Legal Training Institute (LTI) in Southeast Asia and the Middle East and North Africa. The LTI worked with local partners to train advocates, lawyers, judges, religious leaders, journalists, and students in religious freedom law and principles. In that capacity, I helped bring a legal challenge against Indonesia's blasphemy law in 2010. Since then, I have continued to write and speak publicly about the injustices of blasphemy laws and ways to counteract them.

In doing this work, I recognize that there are serious problems with religious freedom across the world, and in many Muslim-majority states specifically. But the existence of these problems should not weaken the state of freedom in the United States. Muslims' rights in America cannot be dependent on the status of human rights abroad—we are talking about our Constitution, our fellow citizens, our neighbors. That is what this book is about.

* * *

Having addressed the first set of questions, I thought the crossfire was over. But just as I dared to settle back in my seat, a woman in the audience looked me straight in the eye, as if to stare me down: "Christians in America are being persecuted, too. Why do we keep talking about Muslims and not Christians?"

Rest assured that this book will talk about Christians—and Jews, Sikhs, Hindus, Buddhists; conservative religious believers and progressive religious believers, and non-believers, too. When I advocate for consistency in our application of religious freedom, I do so for everyone. In America today, politics tends to sway our support of other people's rights. We support those on "our side," people who further our political interests and oppose the "other side." But this book shows how politics is eroding our most fundamental rights—not just the rights of Muslims but the rights of Christians, too.

*   *   *

This book is divided into eight chapters, organized in two parts. Part 1 (chapters 1–5) looks at how many prominent Americans challenge any and all Muslim religious practice. This group argues that "Islam is not a religion," and that therefore "the First Amendment of the US Constitution does not protect Muslims." Part 2 (chapters 6–8) looks at how other prominent Americans want to protect Muslims only selectively. This group treats some Muslims favorably and others not. In all of these chapters, I argue that, while the threat to religious liberty is particularly acute for Muslims today, it exists for all Americans.

Chapter 1 gives you a snapshot of the problems facing religious liberty for Muslims in America today, with special focus on how and why people are arguing that "Islam is not a religion." Chapter 2 provides background on the origins of this argument and the broader range of anti-Muslim rhetoric. I expose the harmful words and harmful actions that deprive Muslims of psychological and physical security and threaten their human rights. I also consider other instances in US history when similar arguments were made with the same intention and effect against other religious groups.

Chapter 3 gives you the basic tools you need to understand religious liberty—legal theories, definitions, and standards. Many Americans talk about "religious liberty" but don't always know how courts figure out whether a religious practice can be protected or not. In this chapter, I also present recent empirical evidence about biases in judicial decision-making.

Chapter 4 looks at how the argument that "Islam is not a religion" shows up when Muslims try to build houses of worship and religious cemeteries. Chapter 5 takes a look at the so-called antisharia laws that have been proposed in forty-three states so far. I explain that sharia does not apply to non-Muslims (nor will it be used to force anyone to convert to Islam) and does not threaten American values. Chapter 6 looks at how national security policies criminalize Muslim religious exercise and force many Muslims to forego the public expression of their faith. I also discuss how protecting human rights strengthens, rather than weakens, national security. Chapter 7 examines how Muslim women experience unique burdens.

Beginning in Chapter 6, the book turns from more blatant attacks on Islam (mostly coming from the political Right) to subtler trends that threaten to erode Muslim religious identity in America (mostly coming from the Left). Chapter 6 introduces the problematic "good" versus "bad" Muslim dichotomy that inspires the US government's national security policy. This distinction makes being an outwardly religious Muslim a "bad" thing. Chapter 7 looks at how politics, media, and the beauty, fashion, and entertainment industries push an image of an "acceptable" Muslim. These trends in various ways secularize Muslim identity, making Islam "not a religion." Chapter 8 considers the effect of a secularized Islam on today's major debates about religious liberty and gay rights.

Of course, Islam is a religion and Muslims are entitled to American religious liberty protections. These are facts. Anyone with even a cursory understanding of Islam knows that Islam meets every definition of religion that scholars and linguists have come up with over the years. Islam's core obligations, or "pillars," are all squarely focused on charity and spiritual development (a declaration of faith, prayer, charity, fasting, pilgrimage).

These core foci do not preclude engagement with the political. Many religions have what scholars call political theology, or "ever-changing relationships between political community and religious order, in short, between power . . . and salvation." Commenting on

Christianity specifically, some Christian theologians have even said "there is no such thing as un-political theology." "There is consciously political theology, there is politically un-conscious theology, but there is no such thing as an un-political theology."

But whether it's Christianity or Islam or any other religion, just because a religion includes political beliefs doesn't mean that in every case a religious believer is free to implement those beliefs. As with every other religious liberty claim, a person is free to hold whatever beliefs they want, but their actions can be regulated. In the US constitutional context, religious behavior can and should be limited by the government when limitations are warranted. There is, as you know by now, a legal test that helps the state figure out when a limit is justified and when it is not.

Either way, a religion with political theology is still a religion. Regardless of whether a religious believer gets to implement his or her political theology, or whether a social majority disagrees with a religion's political implications, a religion with political theology is still a religion.

No accepted definition of religion includes political caveats. Consider, first, the dictionary definitions. The *Merriam-Webster Dictionary* defines religion as "the service and worship of God or the supernatural; commitment or devotion to religious faith or observance; a personal set or institutionalized system of religious attitudes, beliefs, and practices; . . . a cause, principle, or system of beliefs held to with ardor and faith." The *American Heritage Dictionary* and the *Online Etymology Dictionary* track this definition.

Scholarly definitions generally match up with the dictionary ones. Émile Durkheim, the primary architect of modern social science, defines religion as "a unified system of beliefs and practices relative to sacred things, that is to say, things set apart and forbidden—beliefs and practices which unite into one single moral community called a Church, all those who adhere to them." John Dewey, a founder of functional psychology, explained that "the religious is any activity pursued on behalf of an ideal end against obstacles and in spite of threats of personal loss because of its general and enduring value." Immanuel Kant said "religion is the recognition of all our duties as divine commands." When James Madison established the need for religious liberty in America, he defined religion as "the duty we owe the Creator."

Paul Tillich, an existentialist philosopher and Protestant theologian, wrote that religion is "the state of being grasped by an ultimate concern, a concern which qualifies all other concerns as preliminary, and a concern that in itself provides the answer to the question of the meaning of our existence."

These definitions are all illuminative. They give us a glimpse into the larger philosophical debate about what religion is, but ultimately, when it comes to protecting our rights under the US Constitution, the definition that matters is the legal one. Until 1961, the US Supreme Court used Madison's definition. More recently, Tillich's articulation has gained ascendancy. In chapter 3, I discuss the legal definition in more detail.

While the legal definition is the most important, I also share stories throughout this book of how Islam has enriched my and so many other Muslims' lives. I talk about the ways it gives our world meaning, helps us cope with tragedy, and inspires us to contribute positively to society—including defending the religious liberty of people of all faiths and none. I share these stories with the hope that the lived experience of religion (maybe we can call it the spiritual or "experiential" definition of religion) will help us connect as humans. Whether one adheres to a religion or not, all of us yearn to connect with greater truths. This shared yearning can compel us to protect each other, in the legal arena and in our everyday lives.

* * *

A word about terminology.

In this book, I use the phrase "religious freedom" and "religious liberty" interchangeably. The words "liberty" and "freedom" have different origins—the former comes from Latin, the latter from German and Old English—and some commentators note that the terms have carried different connotations in American political and cultural history. Freedom is the "capacity to do things in the world," whereas liberty is thought of as the absence of external restraints. During the American Revolution, "liberty" was the word of choice, but soon after the Declaration of Independence was signed, "freedom" became more common. More recently, the Tea Party has championed the return of "liberty." Ronald Reagan only used "freedom," but devout Reaganite Senator Ted Cruz prefers "liberty."

For purposes of this book, "religious freedom" and "religious liberty" both refer to our right to hold religious beliefs and engage in religious practice free from government interference.

I sometimes use "Islamophobia" to refer to anti-Muslim sentiments. *Merriam-Webster* defines the term as "irrational fear of, aversion to, or discrimination against Islam or people who practice Islam." *Oxford Dictionaries* defines it as "dislike or prejudice against Islam or Muslims, especially as a political force." The definitions are fairly straightforward, but in recent years, "Islamophobia" has become politically charged, with recurrent debates on whether it truly is "irrational" to fear Islam; whether Islamophobia is real; whether the term is designed to shut down criticism of Islam, etc. I discuss some of these debates in chapter 2, but I use the term purely out of a desire for coherence. Many resources on anti-Muslim prejudice use the term, and because I quote them, it makes sense for me to use the term from time-to-time, too.

I use "American Muslim" to refer to Americans of Muslim faith.

Unless I am quoting someone, I use the term "God" in place of "Allah," including in translations of the Qur'an. As the Wikipedia entry will tell you, "Allah . . . is the Arabic word for God in

Abrahamic religions . . . The word is thought to be derived by contraction from *al-ilāh*, which means 'the god,' and is related to *El* and *Elah*, the Hebrew and Aramaic words for God." Arab, Indonesian, and Maltese Christians use the term Allah, as do Arabic-speaking people of a variety of other religions, such as Babists, Baha'is, Mandaeans, and Mizrahi Jews.

Despite this wide usage of Allah across diverse religious faiths, in America's anti-Muslim discourse, speakers use Allah to conjure images of a wholly foreign (and wholly frightening) deity. The term is used intentionally in place of God to depict Muslims as fundamentally different from other believers in God (and Christians in particular). Understanding these negative connotations, I use the functionally equivalent God instead of Allah. As for theological debates about whether the Christian and Muslim God are the same or different, that is not relevant to this book's discussion.

Finally, I use interchangeably the terms "the Right" and "conservatives" and "the Left," "progressives" and "liberals." I know that in political discourse these terms don't always mean the same thing, but they are generally meant as equivalent in this book. I also acknowledge that our political identities often cannot be neatly divided between conservative and liberal, or between Republican and Democrat. Within each group, and sometimes across groups, there are subsets of political identities, which include, among others, solid liberals, disaffected Democrats, devout and diverse Democrats, core conservatives, country-first conservatives, social conservatives, and bystanders (the politically disengaged). There is also racial diversity within each group; for example, not all white Christians or white evangelicals are conservatives, and vice versa. In using broad terms like conservative and liberal, I do not mean to be simplistic, but do hope the book is simpler and easier to read.

PART I

||||||||||||||||||||||||||||||||||||||||||||||||||||||||||||||||||||||||||||||||||||||||||||||||||||||||

"Stop the Islamization of America."

*

"Congress shall make no law . . .
prohibiting the free exercise [of religion]"

Free Exercise Clause of the First Amendment,
US Constitution

CHAPTER 1

"ISLAM IS NOT A RELIGION."

Flames sweep through the construction site, illuminating early morning shadows in the still dark sky of August 28, 2010. The fire licks at the sides of the construction vehicles, engulfing one large earth-hauling machine and starting on three others. A passerby spots the flames and contacts the Rutherford County Sheriff's Office. The sheriff identifies the property as the future site of the Islamic Center of Murfreesboro. At 5:30 A.M., Imam Ossama Bahloul, and Planning Committee chair, Dr. Essim Fathy, arrive at the scene to a smoldering fire and the ominous odor of gasoline.

This was not the first time the Islamic Center has been attacked, nor would it be the last. In the following months and years, it would become clear that the billowing fire foreshadowed more fury to come. In this quiet Tennessee town, a deep-seated fear, almost hatred, was brewing. Neighbors would doubt neighbors, religious beliefs would be questioned, and political agendas would be manipulated and exposed.

Murfreesboro is located approximately thirty miles south of the capital, Nashville, in the middle of a state known as the buckle of the Bible Belt. The population of approximately 112,000 is made up mainly of white conservative Christians. When CNN correspondent Soledad O'Brien was in town filming a documentary about the mosque conflict, some residents described their town as a close-knit community based on faith. Murfreesboro has 140 churches and one mosque.

Part of the reason for this cohesion was that the Muslims of Murfreesboro were always careful to prioritize integration and strong relations with their Christian neighbors. They partnered with churches to convene interfaith exchanges, openly addressing any questions and concerns about Islam not just at these formal events but through potlucks and open houses. Mosque-goers recount never feeling estranged from their Christian neighbors.

The peace was not uniform—for years, the local newspaper, *The Rutherford Reader*, had published vehemently anti-Muslim and anti-immigrant pieces. One piece, "Islam and the Divine Deception," boldly proclaimed, "Islam is an ideology (as opposed to a religion)." But these proclamations were few and far between, and social cohesion was the assumed default. Until 2010, that is.

In 2009, the congregation had outgrown its prayer space for the fifth time in fifteen years. Each time, the congregation had to move: from a small apartment to a larger apartment to a garage to a medical office to a tight, 1,200-square-foot room with little ventilation. The men crowded in the main room, and women, who pray separately from men, had to use a nearby converted garage, with a closed-circuit TV giving them access to the prayer service in the main space. Many times, worshippers spilled out of the indoor space and had to pray in the parking lot. A new space was needed.

The mosque began its search for a construction site in March 2009 and soon identified a property at the outskirts of town. In December 2009, it purchased the land and posted a sign on the lot advertising it as the "Future Site of Islamic Center of Murfreesboro." Bahloul recounts the jubilant moment as "the homeless finding a new home."

But just a month later, on Martin Luther King Jr. Day, the sign announcing the center was vandalized with large purple spray-painted letters that screamed "Not WElcome" [sic]. The construction company graciously installed a new sign at no cost but that, too, was cut in half by vandals in June 2010—a grim prediction of a community soon to be torn asunder.

Despite these early indications of a brewing conflict, the mosque forged ahead, raising $600,000 from its members to fund the construction. In April 2010, the mosque sent the Regional Planning

Commission of Rutherford County a formal request for approval of their plans for the new site. At its monthly meeting in May, the commission unanimously approved the plans. Under county law, religious construction projects could be approved without a public hearing; all that was needed were the plans, the commission's approval of the project at a public meeting, and the advance advertisement of the meeting in a local newspaper. The process was tried and tested—other local, religious buildings, including the far larger World Outreach Church, had benefited from the streamlined process. To top it all off, federal law also mitigates zoning hurdles for religious institutions.

The Daily News Journal reported on the commission's approval with a small news update. But not all of Murfreesboro's citizens considered the happenings business as usual. When the commission next convened on June 17, 2010, they were met with more than 600 protestors, some dressed in American flag clothing, some with signs promoting Christian beliefs (one man wore a VOTE FOR JESUS T-shirt, another one wore an I LOVE JESUS hat). Other residents showed up in solidarity with their Muslim neighbors; one supporter held a sign proclaiming, "A bigot hiding behind a cross is still a bigot."

The opponents said they had not known of the mosque construction plans until after the plans were approved. They were fearful and angry:

> "Everybody knows they are trying to kill us. People are really concerned about this. Somebody has to stand up and take this country back."

> "They seem to be against everything that I believe in, and so I don't want them . . . in my neighborhood spreading that type of comment."

> "Our country was founded through the founding
> fathers—through the true God, the Father and Jesus
> Christ."

> "We have a duty to investigate anyone under the banner
> of Islam."

To add fuel to the fire, 2010 was a Tennessee State Senate election year. The Islamic Center controversy in Murfreesboro gained national attention when local Tea Party founder, Lou Ann Zelenik, a local Republican Party chair and hopeful candidate for the US House of Representatives, founded her campaign on anti-Islamic rhetoric. On June 14, 2010, she denounced the planned mosque as "an Islamic training center," saying that it is not a bona fide religious institution but instead had a political mission "to fracture the moral and political foundation of Middle Tennessee." She went on to proclaim, "Until the American Muslim community find it in their hearts to separate themselves from their evil, radical counterparts, to condemn those who want to destroy our civilization and will fight against them, we are not obliged to open our society to any of them."

Echoing Zelenik's doubts about Islam's status as a religion, the lieutenant governor of Tennessee, Tom Ramsey, publicly questioned whether Islam is "actually a religion, or is it a nationality, way of life, cult, or whatever you want to call it." Ramsey declared Islam "a violent political philosophy more than [a] peace-loving religion."

After the statements came the violence. Even as CNN was on the ground filming a segment about the proposed mosque, at least five rounds of gunshots were fired at the property. Bahloul's answering machine was riddled with death threats and obscene messages, including a bomb threat. Javier Alan Correa of Corpus Christi, Texas, called the Islamic Center from his cell phone and "left an expletive-laced message" ending with "On Sept. 11, 2011, there's going to be a bomb in the building." Correa later pled guilty to federal charges and was sentenced to "eight months of home detention and five years of federal probation."

In September 2010, four residents filed a lawsuit in chancery court to halt the building effort and nullify the construction permit. In *Estes v. Rutherford County Regional Planning Commission*, plaintiffs laid out a litany of grievances. They claimed the planning commission had failed to give adequate notice of the meeting where the mosque plans were approved (though the commission had done nothing different than usual with approving religious buildings). The construction project elevated risks to county residents, they said (though the risks were unspecified). And finally, the plaintiffs "have been and will be irreparably harmed by the risk of terrorism generated by proselytizing for Islam and inciting the practices of sharia law." At the heart of the complaint: Islam is not a religion, but rather a geopolitical system bent on instituting jihadist and sharia law in America. Because Islam is not a religion, the argument went, the mosque construction plans should not benefit from any of the county or federal laws that protected religious organizations.

On September 27, 2010, the judge, Robert Corlew II, held a public hearing for no apparent reason. At the hearing, he gave an open platform to the plaintiffs' attorney, the eccentric Joe Brandon Jr. His bright yellow tie and checkered shirt channeled the slapdash comedians from the 1950s or 1960s, except that Brandon's stage was an American courtroom. There, he badgered his witnesses with, "How can something be called a religion that promotes the abuse of women?" and "If they practiced sharia law, would you still consider it a religion?" Brandon spent six days trying to persuade the court that Muslims deserved no religious liberty protections because "these are the same people who flew jets into the World Trade Center on 9/11." He called as experts people who have developed careers out of spreading fear of Islam (I'll tell you more about these personalities in chapter 2).

Why did Corlew allow the theatrics to take place? Normally, Corlew had no patience for unruly conduct in his courtroom. But here, he not only asked for the hearing but also provided a platform for Brandon's theatrics, suggesting that the judge shared Brandon's anti-Muslim views and had deep misgivings about the mosque project.

The Murfreesboro case is notable as the first time anti-Muslim stereotypes were translated into the legal argument that "Islam is not a religion" and that therefore Muslims do not have religious liberty. The mosque, in this court case, was portrayed as part of a large-scale scheme to subvert the US Constitution. Islam's status as a major world religion was no longer incontrovertible—in twenty-first-century America, the religious status of Islam had to be proven to the court of Rutherford County, Tennessee. Some in the media compared the case proceedings to the 1925 Scopes Monkey Trial that effectively put evolution on trial. Brandon put Islam on trial.

To help end the circus, on October 18 the US Department of Justice filed a brief explaining that the United States has always recognized Islam as a religion: "The plaintiffs' claim that Islam is not recognized by the United States is false and no authority sustains such an idea. Freedom of assembly and religion is literally the foundation of this country." The US attorney, Jerry Martin, commented at a press conference that "all three branches of government have repeatedly recognized Islam as a religion. Presidents, as far back as Lincoln and Jefferson and as recent as President George W. Bush, have, indeed, publicly recognized Islam as one of the world's largest religions."

Corlew not only permitted baseless stereotypes to enter the courtroom, but also on May 29, 2012, he published a memo halting the mosque construction. He said the mosque had violated the Tennessee Open Meetings Act, under which the government has to issue a public announcement of its planned meetings—which the planning commission, in this case, had done. But according to Corlew, the mosque's approval required a "higher degree" of care because it was "a subject of very great importance for the citizens." In other words, the mosque required more scrutiny and had to face a higher burden than did projects not associated with Islam and Muslims.

The Department of Justice and the Becket Fund for Religious Liberty filed a separate lawsuit in federal court challenging Corlew's decision. On July 18, the federal judge, Todd Campbell, issued an opinion stating that the unequal treatment of Muslims violated religious liberty.

The legal battle may have been won, but the mosque continued to feel the effects of the controversy in ways that limited its religious liberty. Contractors began refusing to work on the project, fearing backlash from their religious leaders or community members. As one contractor told the mosque, "I don't want to get on bad terms with my preacher." The mosque ended up having to pay significantly more than it would have otherwise paid for the construction, including hiring a security guard to protect the construction site and installing a security system. The mosque was completed in August 2012.

The threat to religious liberty still lurks in Middle Tennessee and increasingly across the country. The arson attack on the mosque construction site remains unsolved. In July 2017, vandals draped bacon on the handles of the mosque's main entrance doors and graffitied the mosque with a neon green: "F—k Allah." In 2016, Tennessee state representative, Susan Lynn, distributed to her colleagues a DVD titled, "America's Mosques Exposed!"; the film summary says Muslims are treasonous and mosques are "war factories." Lynn herself said the film's central theme is to expose Islam as a "political philosophy and not a religion." In 2015, the sheriff of Sevier County, Tennessee, admitted to contacting the US Department of Homeland Security to monitor Muslims in his town. Current anti-Muslim politics, supported from the top echelons of American political power, are emboldening voices that were once relegated to the peripheries. Where once there were years of cohabitation and community, there is now anger, distrust, and even violence. The false idea that "Islam is not a religion" is gaining ground.

|||||||||||||||||||||||||||||||||||||||||||||||||||||||||||||||||||||||||||||||||||||||||||||||||||||||||||||||||||||||||||||||||||||||

"RELIGIOUS LIBERTY IS AMERICA'S FIRST FREEDOM"
Pastor Rick Warren, *Washington Post*

|||||||||||||||||||||||||||||||||||||||||||||||||||||||||||||||||||||||||||||||||||||||||||||||||||||||||||||||||||||||||||||||||||||||

I am an American Muslim lawyer who has spent the past decade defending religious liberty for Americans of every religion, and for people of diverse faiths outside our borders, too. In the Murfreesboro case, I was part of the legal team defending the mosque's right to exist. I was incredulous when the Department of Justice had to file a brief explaining that the United States considers Islam a religion. Were the religious credentials of a worldwide faith boasting 1.8 billion followers seriously being questioned? While courts sometimes struggle to define religion when it comes to new, possibly fabricated, belief systems, Islam fits any legal definition easily.

Before I pondered the legalities, though, I processed the necessity for the brief emotionally. Were my fellow citizens actually questioning my human dignity? After all, religious liberty is what the drafters of international law would call a dignity-based right. That means it is inherent to human beings and cannot be negotiated away, nor is it something one has to earn or contract for. Under American law, it stands as the "first freedom"—it's covered in the first part of the first sentence of the First Amendment, privileged even above freedom of speech, press, and assembly: "Congress shall make no law respecting an establishment of religion, or prohibiting the free exercise thereof; or abridging the freedom of speech, or of the press; or the right of the people peaceably to assemble, and to petition the Government for a redress of grievances." As the well-known

American evangelical Christian pastor, Rick Warren, explained in the *Washington Post*, religious liberty is the first freedom "because if you don't have the freedom to live and practice what you believe, the other freedoms are irrelevant."

My religion advocates similarly. The Qur'an says in chapter 49, verse 13: "O mankind, indeed We have created you from male and female and made you peoples and tribes that you may know one another." There's also verse 2:256, "There shall be no compulsion in the religion." But more than the obvious statement of freedom, it is the Qur'anic celebration of diversity as a tool for education and deeper understanding that I have found most profound.

In a world where many people in my local and global community see me as the Other, the importance of this Qur'anic reminder has always been front and center. The verse teaches me that people will always be different from each other in important ways, because that is how God created them. My job, and the job of all of us living among other human beings, is to appreciate that difference. We don't fight diversity or resent one another because of it; instead, difference is an inherent and indispensable part of humanity. To reach out across divides and "know one another" is to fulfill God's plan.

Given the faith framework from which I operate, it is perhaps inevitable that the difference I have always been keen on knowing most about is religious difference. How do other people experience the Divine? And how is that spiritual experience reflected in their everyday lives? Even as a child, I wondered about these questions, lugging around religion scholar Karen Armstrong's *A History of God* in middle school as I tried to generate interfaith conversations among my peers.

The trajectory of my life has been to first get to know others, particularly their relationship with God, and second, to help protect that relationship, particularly from government intrusion. After all, God in the Qur'an tells me that it is my duty to celebrate and protect

diversity, and just as I am compelled to fulfill my obligation, I understand that other religious believers are, too. It's a version of the Golden
Rule, which is laid out more explicitly in the traditions of the Prophet
Muhammad, "None of you have faith until you love for your neighbor
what you love for yourself."

It's also a cardinal principle of religious liberty and human rights
generally—you cannot apply the rights selectively; all humans are
deserving of them. I know that believers of other faiths are, like
me, duty bound to follow what their conscience demands—within
the limits of the law, of course. For Americans, the bounds created
by the religion clauses of the First Amendment define the scope of
our religious liberty. The US Constitution protects the right of every
American to live their faith out fully and authentically except in the
narrowest of circumstances.

I also know that despite my best efforts, and others', to "get to know
one another," we might not always understand each other's practice or
belief. But we can still appreciate the religious impulse behind it. I do
not have to believe that it is sinful to shave or cut one's hair in order
to defend Sikhs who want to serve in the US Army but face army uniform policies that prohibit turbans and require shaving. I do not have
to believe that eagles are sacred to help protect a Native American's
ceremonial use of eagle feathers.

Today, however, many Americans refuse to extend that acceptance to Muslims. Unlike other people or other Americans, Muslims
have to earn their human rights; they aren't accorded those rights
simply by virtue of being human. American Muslims are dehumanized and denationalized, stripped of their national identity and legal
rights and treated not like other religious believers, but like American Nazis during World War II. And in our current reactionary environment, the argument for denationalization is gaining ground in
politics, media, and the law and policies they affect.

This line of advocacy will continue to gain ground as religious freedom in the US goes from being a largely uncontested human right to a highly politicized concept. Many commentators on anti-Muslim sentiment have reflected on the ways that Muslims are dehumanized: detained by law enforcement, turned away at the borders, stripped of their citizenship. But the stripping of religious liberty is far more fundamental a deprivation—it is, after all, the first freedom. As it turns out, because forcing one religious group to earn its human rights ultimately opens the door to diluting human rights for everyone, our current anti-Muslim politics pose dire consequences for all Americans.

A law professor at the University of Virginia, Richard Schragger, predicted this shift in religious liberty law not too long ago. The "war on terror" that followed the September 11, 2001, terrorist attacks changed the way American culture and politics view Islam and Muslims. Writing in 2010, Schragger said he did not see the effects yet on how the religion clauses of the First Amendment were being interpreted and applied, but "it is a looming presence on the Court and—of course—off it." This book demonstrates the many ways anti-Muslim politics have translated into concrete effects on religious liberty.

Part and parcel of the phenomenon are the general politics of free exercise—the regular push by religious individuals or groups asking the government to not apply a certain law to them because doing so would force them to violate their religious freedom. In religious liberty law, these are called exemptions, meaning the religious group is exempt from a law that everyone else has to follow. Many Catholic groups, for example, brought suit against the part of the Affordable Care Act that required them to cover contraceptives in their employee health insurance. This requirement, the groups argued, violated a basic tenet of Catholicism, which strictly forbade the use of contraception or playing any role to help someone else use contraception. The lawsuit inevitably became embroiled in the larger abortion culture wars.

These ongoing politics of the religious culture war are now tangled up with the uptick in anti-Muslim sentiment post-9/11. Some people who demand religious exemptions from various government laws also argue that Muslims don't deserve the same rights to exemptions. These people who want to selectively apply religious freedom face a dilemma: "How could they square their love of religious freedom with their desire to clamp down on one particular religion?" Their solution, at least in part, is to argue that Islam is not a religion.

Murfreesboro reflects this phenomenon perfectly: the mosque opponents were not challenging the special protections afforded religious institutions, like churches, in county and federal zoning law (more about these special protections in chapter 4). They just did not want Muslims to benefit from those protections. Unfortunately, this moral inconsistency, if implemented into law, will destroy the core constitutional right to religious liberty.

|||||||||||||||||||||||||||||||||||||||||||||||||||||||||||||||||||||||||||||||||||||||||||||||||||||||||||||||||||||||||

"AMERICAN MUSLIMS ARE A DIVERSE GROUP WITH CHANGING VIEWS"
Dhrumil Mehta, FiveThirtyEight

|||||||||||||||||||||||||||||||||||||||||||||||||||||||||||||||||||||||||||||||||||||||||||||||||||||||||||||||||||||||||

In December 2015, a poll by the Associated Press-NORC Center for Public Affairs Research found that Americans favor protecting religious liberty for Christians over other faith groups, ranking Muslims as the least deserving of this right. Eighty-two percent voted in favor of protecting religious liberty for Christians, while only 61 percent said the same for Muslims. An August 2017 poll by the Annenberg Public Policy Center of the University of Pennsylvania found that almost one in five Americans believes that, under the US Constitution, American Muslims do not have the same rights as other American citizens.

The general climate of anti-Muslim bias correlates with a sharp rise in hate crimes, defined as "a criminal offense motivated by either race, ethnicity, religion, disability, sexual orientation, gender or gender identity." According to FBI data, between 2001 and 2015, there were 2,545 hate crimes "targeting 3,052 Muslims." Over the course of 2015, anti-Muslim hate crimes were up 78 percent, apparently due to terrorist attacks in the US and abroad and to contentious language on the campaign trail. In 2016, the number of crimes "surged 67%, reaching a level of violence not seen since the aftermath of the 9/11 attack." The 2016 data were collected from approximately 15,000 law enforcement agencies that participate voluntarily—which, according to experts, means that the actual number of hate crimes is probably much higher. In 2017, hate crimes across the board—against Muslims and other groups—rose by 17 percent: 1,054 more incidents than the year before. In addition to these hate crimes, more than 42 percent of Muslim children in grades K–12 have experienced some type of bullying because of their faith. Many times, it's the teacher who's bullying the student.

One of the underlying forces of these hate incidents is a deep-seated fear that Islam is an evil ideology that fosters values and morals fundamentally antithetical to Christianity or Americanness. A 2016 survey by the Pew Research Center found that almost half of all US adults believe that some American Muslims are anti-American. A 2017 poll found that half of US adults believe that Islam does not have a place in "mainstream American society," and almost half (44 percent) think there is a "natural conflict between Islam and democracy."

There are multiple reasons why this distrust of Muslims is misplaced. For starters, painting all Muslims with a broad brush conceals tremendous diversity, just as it would be inaccurate to see all Christians as the same. Muslims in the United States are the second most diverse religious groups in America. They come from more than seventy different countries and a range of Islamic traditions. The Pew Research Center estimated that in 2017 nearly 3.45 million Muslims were living in the US, making Muslims 1.1 percent of the US population. A little over half (55 percent) of American Muslims are Sunni, 16 percent identify as Shi'a, and 4 percent identify with other traditions, like Ahmadiyya and Nation of Islam.

Beliefs across sects overlap in many respects, but there are also important differences. The two largest denominations of Islam are Sunnis and Shi'as. Because of events in Islamic history, the split between Sunnis and Shi'as has led to distinct worldviews. Shi'a identity is rooted in religious sacrifice in the fight for truth. Sunni Muslims generally value "God's power in the material world," which can sometimes include the public realm.

Ahmadis are distinct from Sunnis and Shias because of their belief that Prophet Muhammad was not the last prophet, and that God will (and does) send prophets subordinate to Muhammad to revive Islam. Sufism refers to the tradition of Islamic mysticism that exists across sects. Oxford Islamic Studies Online describes Sufis as striving to "constantly be aware of God's presence, stressing contemplation over action, spiritual development over legalism, and cultivation of the soul over social interaction." And the US specifically has inspired the Nation of Islam, which combines aspects of Islam with black nationalist ideas.

Across these sects, 64 percent of American Muslims "say there is more than one true way to interpret the teachings of Islam" while 31 percent think there's only one true interpretation. "About half say traditional understandings of the faith need to be reinterpreted to address current issues." The breakdown is similar to American Christians: "60% say there is more than one true way to interpret the teachings of Christianity, while 34% say there is just one true way to interpret their faith."

Despite this and so much more internal diversity than I could discuss here, in post-9/11 politics, all Muslims are the same, and all arouse suspicions in those inclined or incited to distrust them. It does not matter to opponents whether a particular Muslim espouses the types of beliefs that opponents consider "dangerous," because each Muslim has the possibility of doing so. It also does not matter what Muslims say publicly, as they are always suspected of harboring secret, more sinister plans. Even a US president cannot be trusted.

A 2010 national survey by the Pew Research Center found that the proportion of Americans who believed that Barack Obama was a Muslim had increased. In 2009, 48 percent of American adults believed Obama is Christian, but the next year only 34 percent still believed it. Forty-three percent claimed that they had no idea what his religion is. Conservative Republicans were more likely to doubt Obama's Christianity (34 percent said he is Muslim), but Democrats had some doubts, too; in 2010, fewer Democrats believed Obama to be Christian than in 2009 (55 percent compared to 46 percent). One of Obama's former spiritual advisers, Reverend Kirbyjon Caldwell, summed up the phenomenon well: "Never in the history of modern-day presidential politics has a president confessed his faith in the Lord, and folks basically call him a liar."

||||||||||||||||||||||||||||||||||||||||||||||||||||||||||||||||||||||||||||||||||||||||||||||||||||||||||||||||||||||||

"WHY DO SO MANY AMERICANS BELIEVE THAT ISLAM IS
A POLITICAL IDEOLOGY, NOT A RELIGION?"
Michael Schulson, *Washington Post*

||||||||||||||||||||||||||||||||||||||||||||||||||||||||||||||||||||||||||||||||||||||||||||||||||||||||||||||||||||||||

In 2017, conservative columnist David French wrote in the *National Review*:

> There are a remarkable number of Americans—including
> influential commentators, pastors, and religious leaders—
> who simply refuse to believe that Islam is a religion. Or,
> if they believe it's a religion, they believe the sincere

practice of it is antithetical to other American constitutional values. In other words, they believe that Islam and
the Constitution simply don't mix. It's a belief that's been
circulating in conservative and Christian circles for some
time, and now . . . it's bursting into the open.

French breaks down the argument. First, none of the Islam detractors
would stand for someone outside the community sifting through their
body of beliefs and determining which constituted "true" Christianity
and which did not. Second, "news flash: Both religious and political
activities are protected by the First Amendment. Calling Islam 'political' is no more an argument against the First Amendment protections
enjoyed by Muslims than calling a church a 'club' or a 'civic organization' would be an argument against the First Amendment protections
enjoyed by Christians."

Islam detractors might object to others sifting through their beliefs,
but they have no qualms about doing it with Islam. For some truly
dedicated to the cause, it's the inspiration of tremendous "research."
The Center for the Study of Political Islam (CSPI) claims to use "statistical methods" to prove that Islam is an ideology. The "statistical
analysis" states that Islamic sources encouraging good behavior are
mere covers for the true aim of Islamic doctrine: "dislike, hatred and
conquest of unbelievers." Another key "piece of evidence" of Islam's
political core is the rapid growth of the Muslim community, a process unimaginable for religion but wholly possible for politics: "politics was almost a thousand times more effective than religion." The
center uses statistics to break down the full corpus of three of Islam's
foundational texts—the Qur'an, Sira (the biography of the Prophet
Muhammad), and Hadith (the traditions of the Prophet). CSPI
researchers count the number of words devoted to particular themes,
on the "assumption . . . that the more content that is devoted to a
subject, the greater the importance of the subject is." Their "research"

leads them to conclude that Islam, a 1,400-year-old religion that was once widely practiced in Spain, Portugal, Southern Italy, and parts of China, "is not constructed on the same civilization principles as the rest of the world."

CSPI's "statistical analysis" may be the foundation for claims like "only 16 percent of Islam is a religion—the rest is a combination of military, judicial, economic, and political system. Christianity, by comparison, isn't a judicial or economic code—but a faith." This statement was made in 2016 by Tony Perkins of the Family Research Council. Perkins was appointed to the US Commission on International Religious Freedom in 2018 despite his claims that Islam is "not a religion in the context of the First Amendment."

CSPI was founded by Bill French (known under his pseudonym, Bill Warner), one of the most vocal opponents of the Murfreesboro mosque. Warner would show up to the demonstrations outside the court, wrapped in the American flag, and explain to whomever would listen that Islamic law posed an imminent threat to America's very foundations. His "statistical analysis" was a type of self-confirming claim that parodied the research and expertise of non-partisan think tanks like the Pew Research Center, Gallup, Institute for Social Policy and Understanding, and others that present a very different picture of Islam and Muslims. Anti-Muslim discourse, like a lot of other populist discourse, rejects social science research but also tries to mimic it. And by asserting particular claims, such as the notion that Islam is inherently violent or more political than religious, it compels scholars and specialists to respond. In this way, groups like CSPI frame the debate according to their own lines of inquiry.

And what have Pew, Gallup and others learned about Muslims? CSPI's research attempts to prove that Islam at its core is about violence and that violent Muslims are the "true Muslims." Peaceful Muslims are, in the words of CSPI and other groups like it, merely putting on a mask or, at best, not really following their faith at all.

But Gallup found directly the opposite. Gallup explained that since 9/11, some analysts have argued that the only way to defeat violent extremism is through "a wholesale revision of Muslim theology." But "empirical evidence paints a different picture." In the "largest global study of its kind, covering 131 countries," Gallup compiled empirical evidence showing "that one's religious identity and level of devotion have little to do with one's views about targeting civilians." According to the study, "it is human development and governance—not piety or culture—that are the strongest factors in explaining differences in how the public perceives this type of violence."

As Dalia Mogahed, the former director of the Gallup Center for Muslim Studies, told me, "Gallup found that those who condemn violence explain their position by citing religion. Those who condone it use politics to explain their position." Another expert explained, "most of the perpetrators of terrorist attacks in Europe have been petty criminals who were known to drink alcohol and take drugs. Their radicalization has little to do with theology . . . What they all have in common is a belief that the Muslim world and the West are locked in an irreconcilable clash of civilizations."

The Institute for Social Policy and Understanding also gathered empirical evidence refuting connections between Muslim religiosity and propensity toward violence. It found zero correlation between "Muslim religious identity, the importance of religion or frequency of mosque attendance and Muslim attitudes toward violence." It also found that American Muslims "who regularly attend mosques are more likely" to be civically engaged. Regular mosque-goers are more likely than others to "work with their neighbors to solve community problems (49 vs. 30 percent), to be registered to vote (74 vs. 49 percent), and are more likely to plan to vote (92 vs. 81 percent)."

Mogahed noted that if Warner and other anti-Muslim propagandists were to be believed, "we would expect Muslims as a group to be more likely than the general public to condone violence in the name of a cause." But that's simply not the case. The Pew Research Center has found consistently that Muslims are more likely than the general public to condemn violence. In its 2017 study, it reported: "Although both Muslim Americans and the U.S. public as a whole overwhelmingly reject violence against civilians, Muslims are more likely to say such actions can *never* be justified. Three-quarters of U.S. Muslims (76%) say this, compared with 59% of the general public."

As for extreme outliers like the so-called Islamic State in Iraq and Syria (ISIS): they may present their violent politics in theological terms, but the fact is we'd be struggling with these groups even if Islam didn't exist. Again, Mogahed elucidated this for me: "ISIS is not the product of the Quran. It's the product of a failed state in Iraq and a genocidal dictator in Syria and a lot of weapons from Western capitals. They would exist without Islam if all else were held constant—so Islam is their context, not their cause."

"The key is to reverse the arrow of cause and effect. Brutality drives interpretations" not vice versa. "How do I know? Because the same behavior exists anytime the same geopolitical conditions exist and takes the flavor of its local social currency." By "local social currency," Mogahed means "the symbols, language and narrative" of a particular society at a particular time in history.

The "local social currency" is "sometimes Christianity . . . sometimes Judaism . . . sometimes Buddhism. And it is sometimes secular ideologies." For example in the 1950s, when Arab nationalism, not Islam, was the "prevailing social currency" in the Middle East, "the secular, left-wing *fedayeen* committed attacks on Israel in the name of Arab nationalism." History also shows that "from Peru to Northern Ireland to Japan," terrorism has "emerge[d] again and again from societies with no Islamic traditions to speak of." Mogahed says the same of the Ku Klux Klan, when it emerged after the American Civil War "as a group of vigilante terrorists meant to restore the honor of the humiliated South through violence and intimidation." The

Nazis came about from "similar origins of circumstance," but for the Nazis, the prevailing social currency was German nationalism, whereas for the KKK it was Christianity.

In addition to Mogahed's examples, consider the Ugandan Lord's Resistance Army, a self-described Christian terrorist group that has tortured and displaced over 100,000 people in its attempt to establish a Christian state; Christian militias in the Central African Republic (CAR) that have destroyed every mosque in CAR and are ethnically cleansing Muslims, including cannibalizing them; India's National Liberation Front of Tripura, a paramilitary Christianist movement that since 1989 has attempted to "establish a Christian fundamentalist government in northeastern India" by killing, kidnapping, and torturing Hindus resistant to conversion; the Concerned Christians "doomsday cult" in Israel that seeks to convert all Jews to Christianity and violently force all Muslims out of Israel; the Christian Sebrenica Army that killed 9,000 Bosnian Muslims and raped an untold number of Muslim women; the three Christian "Crusaders" in Kansas convicted in 2018 for their terrorist plot to mass slaughter Muslims; the Phineas Priesthood that bombs abortion clinics; and finally, the Christian white supremacists that have, according to the FBI, "carried out more violent attacks than any other domestic extremist group over the past 16 years."

"So," Mogahed says, "a world without Islam would still have a group like ISIS—they would just be called something else that may be less catchy." Indeed, "where the conditions don't exist, Muslims do not interpret the Quran this way and the entire scholarly class of Muslim leaders has condemned [ISIS's] interpretations on Islamic terms."

That the entire Muslim scholarly class rejects ISIS does not deter Islam detractors from broadly smearing all Muslims. Nor does the extensive empirical proof by numerous think tanks that Americans' "harsh perception" about Muslims "is not one based on truth and does not correspond with reality." Pseudo-scientists and, even more bizarrely, real scientists engaging in pseudoscience, continue to press their claims. Warner is a former physics professor from Tennessee State University. And folks like Jordan Peterson, a former Harvard University professor and currently a clinical psychologist and professor at University of Toronto, feel comfortable making sweeping declarations about a religion that, by their own admission, they do not fully understand. Peterson persists in declaring, "Islam is not a religion of peace," and so, he says, it is not a religion at all—it is a political ideology.

A few prominent commentators on the Left have also argued, in some form or another, that Islam is not a religion. Author Sam Harris and talk show host Bill Maher have each argued that Islam is "not a religion of peace." In their view, Islam is more akin to a mafia than a religion. Maher, for example, has stated, "the Muslim world has too much in common with ISIS [Islamic State]" and "Islam is the only religion that acts like the mafia, that will kill you if you say the wrong thing." Maher and Harris take a reality—extremist actors who misuse Islam—and call it "Islam" instead of "some Muslims." But they fail to explain why then, since "Islam has been around for 14 centuries," we haven't "seen 14 centuries of this behavior." More fundamentally, by describing the political actions of some Muslims as inherent to Islam, they suggest that "Islam is more civilization than religion, and Muslims a homogeneous bloc whose free exercise of religion is a threat."

Democrats and progressive advocacy groups are usually very protective of Muslims, but in the service of progressive goals, they are willing to tap into anti-Muslim tropes. This shows up most prominently when progressives seek to counter religious freedom legislation they fear will protect Christians who want to discriminate against people whose views or lifestyles they dislike. For example, a few years ago, the Arizona legislature was contemplating a bill that would protect religious business owners who wanted to run their businesses in line with their religious beliefs. Opponents, concerned mostly about conservative Christians using the protection to refuse services for a gay wedding, seized on what they knew was a latent fear of Muslims and warned that such a law would enable Muslim employers to force their employees to wear face veils. Other claims put forth by these groups: "The proposed law is so poorly crafted it could allow a Muslim taxi driver to refuse service to a woman traveling alone," and "This would mean that a Muslim landlord could forcibly evict single women or a convert to Christianity, since either action would be covered by Sharia law." The state legislature nevertheless passed the bill, but the Republican governor vetoed it.

Scientists, social commentators and laymen aside, where this discourse really has an impact is in the legal arena, where it erodes constitutional protections for American Muslims. Chapter 3 will explore the effects on federal judges who are deciding cases where Muslims and Islam are involved. In addition to judges, lawmakers, too, are showing signs of buying into the argument.

Tim Schultz of the First Amendment Partnership develops coalitions in state legislatures to help pass religious freedom protection laws. In other words, he spends a lot of time talking about religious liberty with state lawmakers. And he's baffled by the frequency with which these lawmakers fret about any such law protecting Islam:

> When I first began going to state legislatures to discuss religious freedom in the spring of 2012, our immediate organizational priority was the formation of bipartisan religious freedom caucuses in statehouses . . .

> In my initial meetings with lawmakers, I would try to explain briefly the general threats facing religious freedom in the United States, and why it would be prudent for lawmakers to begin to think strategically and collectively about these issues. Of course, I never viewed "more Muslims" or "Sharia Law" as among those threats.

But on a surprising number of occasions, lawmakers raised with me their concerns about Islam. Some (I would say numbering between 7 and 10) raised with me the issue of whether we should be seeking to pass legislation banning Sharia law . . .

I also had an equal number of lawmakers raise with me the question of whether Islam is even a religion deserving First Amendment Protection. This was never strongly asserted . . . it was more like these legislators had a tentative-to-medium strong opinion and wanted to get my opinion. Of course, I explained that this was a terrible idea for a lot of reasons, beginning with its falsehood, etc.

This is not exactly scientific, but since 12–15 lawmakers total (out of maybe 200–250 I spoke with in that first year) raised this issue, and there have to be more that did not volunteer these concerns, then approximately 5–10% of state lawmakers hold to some version (perhaps a weak version) of the "Islam is not a religion" belief.

All of the lawmakers were Republicans. None were senior level members of legislative leadership, but none were known in advance to be "bomb throwers" who I generally avoided at that point anyway.

Public statements also support what Schultz gleaned from private conversations. Jody Hice, US representative from Georgia's Tenth District, once argued:

Most people think Islam is a religion, it's not. It's a totalitarian way of life with a religious component . . . But it's much larger. It's a geo-political system that has governmental, financial, military, legal and religious components. And it's a totalitarian system that encompasses every aspect of life and it should not be protected [under U.S. law] . . . This is not a tolerant, peaceful religion even though some Muslims are peaceful. Radical Muslims believe that Sharia is required by God and must be imposed worldwide . . . It's a movement to take over the world by force. A global caliphate is the objective. That's why Islam would not qualify for First Amendment protection since it's a geopolitical system . . . This is a huge thing to realize and I hope you do. This will impact our lives if we don't get a handle on it.

Hice also emphasized what he saw as a fundamental conflict between Islam and the US Constitution: "These things are in no way compatible with the U.S. Constitution . . . Islam and the Constitution are oceans apart . . . It's about controlling your behavior, when and where you can worship and legal issues. The number one threat is to our worldview and whether we chunk it for secularism or Islam."

So, Hice is not only falsifying the evidence—ignoring what actual Muslims say, as documented by Pew, Gallup, and others—but he's also using his fabrications to argue that Muslims should be stripped of their constitutional rights.

And others continue to echo him. In a January 2018 press release, state senator of South Dakota, Neal Tapio, a Republican running for a spot in the US House of Representatives, questioned whether the First Amendment applies to Muslims. In his words: "Does our Constitution offer protections and rights to a person who believes in the full implementation of Islamic Law, as practiced by 14 Islamic countries and up to 350 [million] self-described Muslims, who believe in the deadly political ideology that believes you should be killed for leaving Islam?"

John Bennett, a Republican lawmaker in the Oklahoma state leg-islature, said in 2014: "Islam is not even a religion; it is a political system that uses a deity to advance its agenda of global conquest." In response to Bennett's statement, the conservative UCLA law professor, Eugene Volokh, wrote in the *Washington Post* that the lawmaker uses "logic under which much of Christianity would have not even been a religion for much of its history."

> I'm delighted that modern Christianity prefers to advance its agenda of global conversion through peaceful means rather than through conquest. But it's pretty clear that many varieties of Christianity have been spread more forcefully than that at various times, and have been "social [and] political system[s]" as well as purely theological ones. This didn't make them "not even a religion" back then, and similar behavior on the part of some streams of Islam doesn't make Islam "not even a religion" today.

Volokh raises an important point. When Bennett, Tapio, and others like them think of Islam as "political," their reference point is, as Tapio made explicit, Muslim-majority states that have Islam as their official state religion. But many countries in Europe for a long time had Christianity as their official religion and some still do. The Holy Roman Empire, which encompassed vast swaths of Europe, had Roman Catholicism as its single official religion and the Holy Roman Emperor was always a Roman Catholic. After Emperor Theodosius issued the Edict of Thessalonica in 380 CE, making Nicene Christi-anity the official religion of the Roman Empire, most other Christian sects were stripped of their legal status and had their properties con-fiscated by the state.

France was regarded for a long time as the "eldest daughter" of the Roman Catholic Church. Charlemagne, or King of the Franks, was appointed Holy Roman Emperor in 800, and in the coming centuries, the church "became the largest landowner in France and oversaw hospitals, primary, and secondary education." In that time period, there was a "mutual dependency between Church and nobility, the exclusion and persecution of religious minorities, and the monopoly of the Church over various institutions." In 1838, the French king Louis XIII published a royal edict dedicating "our person, our state, our crown and our subjects" to the Virgin Mary. This was not unusual at that time; during the Renaissance, kings throughout Europe considered themselves appointed by God. In their view, it was their divine right to apply religious law to the land.

The Church of England was also aligned with the Roman Catholic Church until 1534, when Henry VIII declared himself the religious and spiritual head of the church within his kingdom so that he could annul his marriage to Catherine of Aragon. His son, Edward VI, adopted many of the Protestant views of his regents and councilors, initiating the divergence of the Church of England from Catholicism. For many years after, England's state religion flip-flopped with each succession, often with bloody consequences. Henry VIII's eldest daughter Queen Mary made England Catholic again and burned many Protestants at the stake; later, his other daughter Queen Elizabeth I turned England Protestant, executing Catholics primarily by having them hung, drawn, and quartered. Also in the early 16th century, during the Spanish Inquisition, three Spanish monarchies forcefully converted Muslims to Christianity.

Nowadays, several countries continue to have state churches or consider themselves Christian states, among them Vatican City, England, Denmark, Greece, Greenland, Iceland, Norway, and Monaco. In the United Kingdom, the reigning monarch has to be an Anglican and is both the head of the nation and the head of the church. And while many Christian states have now adopted laws separating church and state, religion continues to play a vital public and political role.

Christianity has a robust political theology that is evident even in the United States. A number of the US colonies had established churches: The Church of England was the official, state-supported religion of Virginia, New York, Maryland, North Carolina, and South Carolina; the Congregational Church was the official religion of Connecticut, New Hampshire, and Massachusetts. Today, constitutional limits on church-state relations notwithstanding, many Christian leaders "seek to enact policies they perceive to be embodiments of Christian values." In 2008, Gallup found that "forty-six percent of Americans say that the Bible should be 'a' source, and 9% believe it should be the 'only' source of legislation." Prominent conservative Christian groups like James Dobson's Focus on the Family teach that Christianity is a "worldview" that necessarily affects every aspect of one's life— personal, public, social, and *political*. And under President Trump's leadership, the Christian nationalist movement has become particularly emboldened "to bring the nation back to the Lord." Despite these trends, however, no one in the United States has argued seriously that Christianity's role in politics (actual or aspirational) makes it a political ideology and not a religion.

These obvious hypocrisies aside, it also makes no practical sense for Christians to advocate that a religion with political theology ceases to be a religion. Professor Chad Bauman has warned that legitimizing the idea that "Islam is not a religion" will only support efforts in other countries to criminalize Christian minorities. For example, authorities in several Indian states believe that "Christianity has never been a religion; it has always been a predatory imperialism par excellence"; this belief has since the 1950s motivated freedom of religion laws that ban efforts by Christian leaders to missionize. The laws purport to ban "forced" or "fraudulent" conversions but those terms are hard to define and have been enforced discriminatorily by Indian police to "regularly harass Christian evangelists, priests, pastors, and catechists even for doing things as innocuous as preaching in their own churches." Bauman concludes, "If the entanglement of a religion with politics disqualifies it from the assurances of religious freedom, then no religion anywhere could possibly qualify. Those who make such claims succeed only in making it easier for others to deny the religious rights of their co-religionists elsewhere." It might also be helpful to recall that early Christianity was considered "atheistic" and not a "true religion"—in that case, because it condemned the pagan gods.

These complexities notwithstanding, American authorities at the highest level of government are eager to keep advancing the anti-Islam argument. Allen West, a former US congressman from Florida, has said "Islam is a totalitarian theocratic political ideology; it is not a religion. It has not been a religion since 622 A.D." In 2015, former assistant US attorney, Andrew C. McCarthy wrote in the *National Review*, "When we discuss 'Islam,' it should be assumed that we are talking about both a religion and a political-social ideology. Clearly, one can accept the religious tenets and not the ideology . . . 'Islam' . . . should be understood as conveying a belief system that is not merely, or even primarily, religious." In 2016, retired Lieutenant General William "Jerry" Boykin was named an advisor to Ted Cruz's presidential campaign despite past statements that Islam "should not be protected under the First Amendment."

Also in 2016, former national security adviser, Michael Flynn, told an ACT! for America conference in Dallas, "Islam is a political ideology" that "hides behind the notion of it being a religion." In 2017, then–White House aide Sebastian Gorka could not unequivocally state that Islam is a religion; when asked by Steven Inskeep of NPR, "Does the president believe Islam is a religion?" Gorka failed to give a direct answer, instead opining, "This is not a theological seminary. This is the White House. We aren't going to get into theological debates."

Steve Bannon, the former White House chief strategist who helped design and implement President Trump's executive order banning entry into the US of citizens of seven Muslim-majority states, once mocked former President George W. Bush for stating that "Islam is a religion of peace." According to Bannon, "Islam is not a religion of peace. Islam is a religion of submission. Islam means submission."

If Bannon is trying to make a linguistic argument, he should know that "Islam" in Arabic is a verbal noun originating as almost all Arabic verbs or nouns do from a triliteral root, which in this case is S-L-M. A large class of words is formed using these roots—and those words all relate to concepts of safety, security, peace, submission, humility, sincerity, gentleness, and elegance. Islam means "submission," but it is linguistically related to "peace" (in Arabic, *salam*), thus denoting a type of peaceful submission. According to some scholars, S-L-M are also the root letters of Solomon—as in Prophet Solomon, whom the Qur'an celebrates as a king so just that he was given a kingship like no one else before or after him. And what made him just? His complete faithfulness, or peaceful submission, to God. Peaceful submission to the divine is a thoroughly religious act, just as Islam is thoroughly a religion.

|||||||||||||||||||||||||||||||||||||||||||||||||||||||||||||||||||||||||||||||||||||||||||||||||||||||||||||||||||||||||||||||||||||||||||

"CONSERVATIVES CALL FOR 'RELIGIOUS FREEDOM,' BUT FOR WHOM?"
Tom Gjelten, National Public Radio

|||||||||||||||||||||||||||||||||||||||||||||||||||||||||||||||||||||||||||||||||||||||||||||||||||||||||||||||||||||||||||||||||||||||||||

While some scholars and commentators, like Volokh and David French, see how preposterous the claims are against Islam, not many of the usual proponents of religious liberty see the absurdity or care to call it out publicly. This failure to speak up has caught the attention of a few journalists. In a 2015 piece titled, "When Muslims Are the Target, Prominent Religious Freedom Advocates Largely Go Quiet," the *Washington Post*'s Michelle Boorstein wrote about the relative silence from the religious liberty camp when Republican presidential candidates made shocking statement after statement denying Muslims their civil rights. Just that September, Ben Carson had declared that a Muslim "absolutely" could not be president. Two months later, Donald Trump one-upped Carson and promised to establish a database to track Muslims. Throughout the campaign, Trump suggested shutting down mosques, and Ted Cruz advocated for surveilling "Muslim neighborhoods." Rick Santorum made the overall theme of the debate clearer with his own proclamation that the US Constitution does not protect Muslims, because Islam "is different from Christianity."

These statements are all the more worrisome because these same candidates insisted they were the protectors of American religious liberty. Cruz called the 2016 election the "religious liberty election," explaining that "religious liberty has never been more threatened in America than right now" and that he would be the one to save it. Trump also promised protections for religious liberty. The obvious contradiction between these statements and their calls to violate the basic religious liberty of American Muslims only makes sense if the latter are thought to be outside the purview of the First Amendment. The politicians were aiming to please American evangelicals and other Christian conservatives. It was the ideal time for principled defenders of the right to decry the contradiction—but few spoke up.

The silence is particularly noteworthy at a time when several of America's biggest, most powerful religious groups have made religious liberty their top priority. In the past few years, conservative religious groups like the US Conference of Catholic Bishops (USCCB), the Southern Baptist Convention (SBC), and the Church of Jesus-Christ of Latter-day Saints (LDS) have all decried social changes like same-sex marriage and the wide availability of contraception and abortion, which, in their view, threaten traditional, religious mores. In time, these groups did stand up for American Muslims, and I am grateful for that. But the support was too slow coming when the US presidential candidates brazenly questioned Muslims' rights.

Only after Trump proposed in December 2015 to ban all Muslims from entering the United States did some of the leaders speak, foremost among them the SBC's Russell Moore, who challenged his fellow religious liberty warriors and all Americans to "denounce this reckless, demagogic rhetoric" if they care "an iota about religious liberty." Moore called the moment a "moment of clarity." "When one takes into account the context of a candidate who has at least raised the possibility of shutting down mosques and issuing ID badges based on what people believe to now openly say he would ban people based on religious beliefs—that's not a difficult question. One need not parse the statement to understand what he's trying to say," Moore said.

The LDS, too, issued a short press release urging Mormons to follow the commands of their faith's founder, Joseph Smith, to defend everyone's liberty, not just their own: "It is a love of liberty which inspires my soul—civil and religious liberty to the whole of the human race." Two years later, in 2017, the majority-Mormon state of Utah adopted the resolution, "Guarding the Civil Liberties and Freedoms for All American People," in which the governor and lawmakers committed to "protect the civil liberties, religious freedoms, [constitutional rights] and dignity of all Americans, legal immigrants, and refugees seeking protection against persecution." To the credit of the LDS Church, Utah and its Mormon politicians stood out among conservatives in their vocal support of Muslims. BuzzFeed News reported in April 2018 that Republican politicians and lawmakers in all states *except Utah* had issued strong anti-Muslim statements. In May 2018, I wrote about this unique phenomenon in my *New York Times* piece, "What Islamophobic Politicians Can Learn from Mormons."

I have worked with all of the groups that Boorstein mentions in her piece—the LDS, the SBC, the USCCB, and other Christian groups beyond these. I do not doubt the sincerity of many of these Christians in their concerns about religious liberty; they genuinely fear the effects of liberalizing social changes on their lives and, to the extent the changes are enforced by government regulations, the ability of their religious institutions to function in accordance with their religious convictions, free from state control. On several occasions, they have graciously reached out to me as a Muslim. But in the course of my advocacy, there have been many times when I couldn't help but feel betrayed—times when intellectual and moral integrity demanded a stronger defense of Muslims' rights from the defenders of religious liberty.

I shared this disappointment with Tom Gjelten of National Public Radio (NPR) when he interviewed me for a piece that aired in December 2015 called "Conservatives Call For 'Religious Freedom,' But for Whom?" In that piece, I recount the time I spoke at a "Stand Up for Religious Liberty" rally, one of many rallies taking place nationwide to drum up support for Catholic institutions' legal battle against the Affordable Care Act's mandate that all employers, including Catholic ones, cover contraception in their employee health plans. The rally I spoke at was in downtown Chicago. It was a hot, sunny day and as I sat on the speakers' platform waiting for the Jewish speaker before me to finish, I scanned the crowd in front of us. A sea of mostly white faces, families of all sizes, expressions alight with joy at being able to stand up for their deepest held beliefs. The crowd cheered loudly at every pronouncement of the importance of religious liberty. They waved their signs and beamed from cheek-to-cheek. But, as I told Tom, when "I went up to the podium and said, 'I'm here as a Muslim American supporting your religious freedom, but I fully expect that in return you support mine,'" the "response from the crowd . . . was hundreds of people just silent and looking at me."

In April 2017, Peter Beinart wrote about the phenomenon for *The Atlantic* in a piece called, "When Conservatives Oppose 'Religious Freedom.'" He talks about the vile backlash faced by public supporters of religious liberty for Muslims, among them the Becket law firm (where I myself learned the jurisprudence of religious liberty and the rooted-ness of the right in human dignity). Beinart catalogues the many times

Becket has been attacked by conservative groups for this moral consistency. *Crisis*, a conservative Catholic magazine, denounced Becket's support for the Islamic Center of Murfreesboro. Its denunciation was echoed by the Tennessee-based Christian group, Proclaiming Justice to the Nations, in whose view "Islam" and "sharia" are "absolutely antithetic [sic] to freedom of speech, freedom of religion or freedom of the press." And the conservative Thomas More Center has come out against Becket time and again. One of the center's staffers tweeted, "Believe Islam a religion, then support the Becket Fund. Believe it will destroy US, then supt thomasmore.org." In 2016, when Becket filed an amicus brief supporting the Islamic Center of Basking Ridge, New Jersey, to build a mosque, the Thomas More Center announced that it would defend the mosque's opposition.

Russell Moore, too, has faced fierce opposition for his strong statements in support of Muslims. His predecessor, Richard Land, also faced the same—in 2010, when Land was the president of the SBC, he participated in an interfaith coalition to defend the construction of mosques. Popular pressure soon forced him to withdraw. And in January 2017, the SBC's International Mission Board was also forced to back out of its support for mosques when several megachurches threatened to revoke their funding.

Robert George, a Becket board member and the McCormick Professor of Jurisprudence at Princeton University has also spoken out in favor of religious liberty for Muslims—in lectures, magazine publications, and social media. In 2014, he wrote a piece called "Muslims, Our Natural Allies," for the conservative Catholic publication, *First Things*. The negative reaction was immediate. Robert Spencer, co-founder of Stop Islamization of America, called George "naïve" and George's positive attitude toward Muslims as unfitting for anyone "genuinely committed to justice and moral values."

The incessant backlash is undoubtedly scaring other voices from speaking up for Muslims' rights. What defenders need is a compelling argument, rooted in the rights discourse, to push back against the acrimony. This book gives them that argument. It explores the impact of Americans' fear of Muslims on the "first freedom," the most essential freedom, of all Americans.

Woven throughout this story is my story. There are other lawyers devoted to protecting freedom of religion. And there are other American Muslims experiencing the deep injustices of our current political climate. I am entrenched in both: the experience of Islam as a religious truth, and the legal and philosophical appreciation of religious liberty as inherent to all human beings. From this vantage point, my goal is to provide a view of the terrain in America and chart a path forward so that people of all faiths—and agnostics and skeptics as well—can be allies in defending America's most vital and cherished freedom.

CHAPTER 2

"I THINK ISLAM HATES US."

"I think Islam hates us," proclaims Donald Trump. His voice is interrupted by a door slam as my six-year-old son, Eesa, rushes into the house and straight to the living room. I quickly grab the remote control and shut off the television. Eesa cannot hear the president of his country demonizing his faith. Not today.

I know that eventually, Eesa will hear the words—and much more. He will see the front doors of his or a friend's mosque covered in graffiti. He will see a politician on the news railing against sharia. He will receive a text from a loved one checking to see if he is okay after another anti-Muslim hate crime. To prepare him for the inevitable assault on his faith and innocence, I have to first nurture his already wondrous perspective on the world and God.

My son wonders aloud about ontology, "Where was I before God made me?" He imagines Heaven to be something like his Candyland game board: "The bushes will grow candy!" In his world, Islam offers answers to his deepest spiritual inquiries. Through the prism of Islam, Eesa sees a world that is wondrous and perfectly synchronous, even as it is complex. "Why is my skin darker than Zaynab and Mikael's?" he asks, comparing himself to his slightly paler siblings. "Because God designed you and he thinks your skin color is the most beautiful for you." I remind him of the peacocks that hang around my mother's home in Miami—the male ones brilliant blue and the females different shades of brown, with luminous green necks. "God gave only the boy peacocks the big feathers, but the girl peacocks are beautiful, too. They are all different but they are all beautiful." We pull up a YouTube video of peacocks in all different shades, and as he watches with attention and delight, I know he understands. He's part of a larger plan like everything else in God's creation, and it all makes sense.

Conversations with Zaynab, eleven-years-old, can be trickier. She's entering the part of her life when she has to carry Islam's ritual obligations, such as fasting from dawn-till-dusk for thirty days in Ramadan and praying five times daily. Sometimes she tries to negotiate the terms of the fast with me: "Can I have just one banana during the day? How about a tangerine? Or some Jell-O?" I try to explain that I'm not the one making the rules, that they come from a higher source; my job is simply to relay them to her and help her abide by them the best she can. In response, she nods silently, though not despondently. She's beginning to understand that whatever exists between her and God, it is something unlike any of her other relationships.

Zaynab, Eesa, and baby Mikael are all rapidly growing up. And I'm rushing to root them in faith so that they can repel hate and shore up their hearts for when they will be peppered with arrows. It's not easy to keep faith innocent in a world constantly wracked with terrorism and a politics of hate and fearmongering.

Even family vacations can raise awkward questions. As we packed the car with our luggage for a plane trip to Miami to visit my family, Zaynab grabbed a large drink bottle from the refrigerator to take with her. "You can't take that with you on the plane, Zaynab," I said, taking the bottle out of her hands and placing it back in the fridge. "They'll just take this away from you when we go through security."

"Why will they do that? What's the big deal about a drink?"

I sigh. We'd had this conversation a few times before, and because the rule doesn't make obvious sense, the kids tend to think I've simply made it up. On my smart phone, I pull up the TSA page with its rules about liquids and show it to Zaynab, who skims it and looks up at me, confused.

"Some very bad people have done bad things on planes with liquids, so now none of us can bring liquids with us," I try to explain.

"What type of bad things?" The question was inevitable, but on that day, and till this day, I avoid it.

The "bad things" are tragic. And the "bad people" profess the same religion as Zaynab. And for that, everyone in her religious community is demonized daily, with some pulled off airplanes because they wore a headscarf or used Arabic phrases like *inshallah* ("God-willing"). How do I even begin to explain this to her?

The ever-thoughtful Eesa has also made the hairs on the back of my neck stand on end. At six-years-old, he already has a deep fascination with religion, and he loves learning the Qur'anic stories of the prophets—Jesus, his namesake ("Eesa" is Arabic for "Jesus"), Joseph and his revelatory dreams, Moses floating in a basket on the river, and of course, Jonah living in the belly of the whale. The prophetic stories are where magic meets love and divine nurturing, and Eesa delights in them.

But when Eesa, in his open and gregarious manner, tries to share his wonder with his school classmates and reports it back to me, I gasp. "Eesa, don't talk about that in school!" All I can think of is the bullying epidemic sweeping America's schools. The Council on American-Islamic Relations reports that anti-Muslim harassment spiked by 91 percent in the first half of 2017, compared with the same period in 2016. And a 2017 poll by the Institute for Social Policy and Understanding (ISPU) found that 42 percent of Muslims with children in grades K–12 "report bullying of their children because of their faith, compared with 23% of Jews, 20% of Protestants, and 6% of Catholics." Accompanying this school-based bullying is the sharp rise in anti-Muslim hate crimes, as documented by the FBI, the Department of Justice, and other groups.

As any mother would, I want desperately to protect my children from that hurtful comment or hard shove or punch in the face. One Muslim mother I spoke to reported that her seven-year-old son had been bullied so badly that he told her he no longer wanted to live. One of her son's classmates challenged others to make him cry and another student took up the challenge and stabbed him with a pencil. I have to do everything in my power to make sure Eesa never experiences what that little boy experienced.

This perpetual sense of insecurity is something experts describe as a lack of "psychological citizenship." There are four general dimensions of citizenship: citizenship as legal status, rights, political activity, and identity. Citizenship as legal status means you are a member of an organized political community. Citizenship as rights points to the entitlements that come with that membership. Membership also means you get to engage in and be empowered by political activity in the political community. And citizenship as identity is the psychological dimension of citizenship, the part that makes you feel like you actually belong to the political community.

Much of this book argues that Muslims lack the rights, as they are realized through the legal process, that many other Americans have. But just as fundamentally, Muslims also lack the psychological security that many other Americans have. We sense that we are valued less by our government and by our fellow citizens.

In 2017, Pew conducted 1,001 interviews with Muslims and 75 percent of the respondents reported experiencing discrimination. Sixty percent of Muslims said media coverage of Muslims is unfair and 75 percent of respondents said President Trump is "unfriendly" to American Muslims. The hard evidence supports this perception. According to one study, on a "thermometer" rating towards religious groups, where 0 degrees indicates the coldest, most negative feelings and 100 indicates the warmest, Americans gave Muslims a rating of 48 degrees. Americans rated Muslims more negatively than Jews, Catholics, Protestants, Hindus, Mormons, and Buddhists (and slightly more negatively than atheists). No other religious group was ranked lower. A 2017 poll found that 50 percent of Americans say Islam is not part of "mainstream American society" and only 12 percent of

Americans attribute this divide to misunderstanding. And numerous medical studies have shown how Islamophobia heightens psychological distress and how this distress impacts physical health; one study, for example, found a correlation with neurological, digestive, blood, and respiratory disorders.

Feeling (and being) less valued, less protected—this is what I want desperately to stave off for my children. In this trepidation, I am drawn to the parents who don't just fear in anticipation, but fear because it is their lived reality. In this way, I can feel for parents like the ones at the US-Mexico border who were forcibly separated from their children in the summer of 2018, breastfeeding babies ripped from their mothers. I can feel what parents like the Muslim mother at Dallas–Fort Worth airport felt when her breastfeeding baby was taken from her while she was questioned for hours by authorities. I share the horror of the parents whose five-year-old boy was detained at Dulles International Airport after President Trump's first executive order banning entry of people from seven majority-Muslim countries. I experience the sadness of parents of immigrant children who cried almost every day during the 2016 presidential elections because they no longer knew their place or value in this country.

Aysha Khan, a journalist for the *Religion News Service*, traced this connectedness in her piece, "For American Muslims, Family Border Separations are Personal." She quotes one civic leader: "We view the family separation policy and the Muslim ban as connected and part of a broader agenda by the administration." Amr Al Azm, a history and anthropology professor whose family has been unable to reunite because of the travel ban, sees each family separation policy as successively worse. "Every time the pendulum swings, it becomes more extreme . . . "

||||||||||||||||||||||||||||||||||||||||||||||||||||||||||||||||||||||||||||||||||||||||||||||||||||||||||||||||||||||||||||||||||||||

"TRUMP WON'T TAKE BACK HIS
'MUSLIM BAN' CAMPAIGN PROMISE"
Ed Kilgor, *New York Magazine*

||||||||||||||||||||||||||||||||||||||||||||||||||||||||||||||||||||||||||||||||||||||||||||||||||||||||||||||||||||||||||||||||||||||

Khan wrote her piece just weeks after the US Supreme Court's decision upholding the president's third iteration of the travel ban. Until that ruling came down on June 26, 2018, total hopelessness about the state of the American republic was staved off by faith and trust in the US Constitution. It was a hope that had fueled the thousands of protestors who flooded airports in major US cities after the president issued Executive Order No. 13769, or, as it came to be known, Travel Ban 1.0. Protests continued for days as air passengers were detained or sent home. The ACLU raised more than $24 million over a single weekend from Americans demanding that constitutional rights be vindicated in court. That number grew to $79 million in the following three months.

Travel Ban 1.0 temporarily blocked individuals from seven majority-Muslim countries from entering the United States. Within hours after it was issued, several courts intervened to block its enforcement and, after the government lost in appellate courts, the government withdrew the ban instead of appealing to the US Supreme Court. Travel Ban 2.0 soon followed. This second version again temporarily blocked travelers, this time from six majority-Muslim countries. As with 1.0, courts across the nation halted the policy. This time, however, the government did take it up to the Supreme Court, and the court allowed most of 2.0 to go into effect. The court's main caveat was that the president could not bar travelers who had relatives in the United States.

Then came Travel Ban 3.0, which is not temporary, as the prior two were, and permanently blocks travelers from eight countries (Libya, Iran, Somalia, Syria, Yemen, Chad, North Korea, Venezuela), five of them majority-Muslim (Libya, Iran, Somalia, Syria, Yemen). The ban exempts lawful permanent residents, dual nationals, and visa-holders as of October 18, 2017, when the third ban went into effect. Unlike 1.0 and 2.0, Travel Ban 3.0 does not ban refugees.

The Trump administration justified 3.0 by saying that the eight targeted countries are either unable or unwilling to adequately manage and share information about their nationals, or do not cooperate on immigration issues, or are linked to terrorism. There are varying degrees of bans on each country. Venezuela got the least restrictive ban and of the majority-Muslim states, Syria is the only one subject to a total ban. Like 2.0, Travel Ban 3.0 permits government officials to grant discretionary waivers on a case-by-case basis, but the process for applying for a waiver is unclear. Generally, applicants have to prove that they are not a security threat and that being denied entry would cause them "undue hardship." In no case are waivers guaranteed.

Travel Ban 3.0 (or, Proclamation No. 9645) was challenged just like the previous two iterations, and again, the litigation made it up to the Supreme Court. Relying only on the Establishment Clause (instead of the Free Exercise Clause), the plaintiffs said that the travel ban was issued for the unconstitutional purpose of excluding Muslims from the United States. Advocates of minority and immigration rights fought the case with passion and sincerity, aghast at a policy so blatantly premised on hostility.

But the advocacy ultimately failed. The US Supreme Court upheld President Trump's travel ban, in its entirety, by a vote of five to four stating that Trump had the constitutional authority to ban or restrict travel and immigration. The decision split along political lines, with Justice Anthony Kennedy—the swing vote—siding with the conservatives. The court held that the copious evidence of the president's egregious, anti-Muslim prejudice did not matter. In delivering the court's opinion, Chief Justice John Roberts claimed, "This is an act that could have been taken by any other president."

As American Muslims receiving the opinion would later respond: "Are you f—ing kidding me?" And that, precisely, was the response of Justice Sonia Sotomayor who disagreed that President Trump was just like "any other president." As the courtroom fell silent, she began: "The United States of America is a Nation built upon the promise of religious liberty. Our Founders honored that core promise by embedding the principle of religious neutrality in the First Amendment. The court's decision today fails to safeguard that fundamental principle." As Sotomayor went on to explain, the policy was President Trump's way of delivering on his promise of a "total and complete shutdown of Muslims entering the United States." In upholding it, the court had basically signed off on prejudice packaged as a national security policy: "But this repackaging does little to cleanse Presidential Proclamation No. 9645 of the appearance of discrimination that the President's words have created."

This was the president who had tweeted as a layperson in 2011 that the Qur'an teaches "tremendous hatred," which "absolutely" creates a "Muslim problem." When he ran for president, he made the "Muslim problem" central to his campaign. In December 2015, he praised an author for acknowledging "Muslim problems." He later declared, "I think Islam hates us," and clarified during an official presidential debate that, "I mean a lot of them. I mean a lot of them." He also insisted time and again that Muslims in America celebrated the September 11 attacks. He backed up his statements with policy proposals, such as "a total and complete shutdown of Muslims entering the United States," warrantless surveillance of American Muslims, closing American mosques, and creating a registry of all Muslims in the US. To justify this systematic exclusion of Muslims, Trump cited Japanese-American internment camps during World War II, and even strongly suggested that he would favor internment camps for Muslims. Immediately after he was elected, Trump put his words into action. In preparing for the travel ban, he summoned his advisor, Rudolph

Giuliani, to "put a commission together" to "show me the right way to do it legally."

"Take a brief moment, and let the gravity of those statements sink in." Sotomayor sat grim faced, letting her audience absorb what the Court had just rubberstamped. "The majority ignor[es] the facts, misconstru[es] our legal precedent, and turn[s] a blind eye to the pain and suffering the Proclamation inflicts upon countless families and individuals, many of whom are United States citizens."

For most American Muslims, the pain and suffering had enveloped them for over a year and a half, ever since President Trump signed the first executive order. Since that day, history was forever redirected, as they or their loved ones or someone they knew had to rethink their next moves, divert their career or education or even delay their wedding. Flying abroad for research was no longer tenable. Family members outside the country could no longer join their American relatives for even their biggest life events. Even Muhammad Ali Jr., the son of boxing legend and "America's champion," Muhammad Ali, was detained and interrogated for almost two hours at the Fort Lauderdale Airport. "Where were you born?" "Are you a Muslim?" "Where did you get your name from?" he was asked.

For Said Hajouli from Syria, any hopes of seeing his wife—who had been living in Turkey since the couple fled Syria—were dashed. He had eagerly anticipated her arrival after being separated for two years, only to have her detained at the airport. For nine-year-old Ahmed Alhuthaifi, a Yemeni-American, the travel ban meant he wouldn't be able to see his mom, who was stuck in Saudi Arabia. She and Alhuthaifi's four siblings couldn't travel to be with him on his birthday. "He expected them to be here, all his brothers and sisters; he's depressed all the time," said Alhuthaifi's father, who loves America so much that he "named his youngest son McCain, after the Arizona Republican senator he admire[d]." For others, their relatives are trapped in war-torn countries, unable to travel to the US to reunite with their families.

And on June 26, 2018, that anguish became their status quo.

"We had to tell people that there is no hope," says Zahra Billoo, the executive director of the Council on American-Islamic Relations for the San Francisco Bay Area (CAIR-SFBA). She was at a leadership retreat the day the decision was announced. Her first response was to "do something!" She worked feverishly trying to understand, communicate, and organize around what she calls the "worst possible decision," so absorbed in her desperate attempt to fix the problem that she barely remembered to eat that day. The tasks temporarily blunted the emotions, but they inevitably set in the next day, Wednesday, when Zahra was overwhelmed with a headache and then a fever. A decade-long civil rights crusader, Zahra is no stranger to these highs and lows. But even she "took a few days to cry it out." The last week of June 2018 was forever marked in her memory as the week her resolve crumbled, even if momentarily.

Zahra has been a civil rights organizer since she graduated law school from University of California Hastings College of Law. As a young activist affected by the way her community was shaped by 9/11, she went to law school to help ease the suffering she saw plaguing her community. Her hard work, plus a twist of fate, led her to become the executive director of CAIR-SFBA at the age of twenty-five. She has been at the forefront of civil rights issues facing Muslims for a long time, but she says the present era is different. "Everyone is constantly on edge now . . . and that might be the hardest part." The cases are more frustrating, and "we are having to tell people that there is *no hope*." The best thing she can tell clients directly affected by the travel ban is that they can submit a waiver, but the likelihood of success is dismal.

For her clients, family separation happens not only at the border or at airports, but also in the most bureaucratic and mundane of government offices. She recalls a difficult conversation she had with a Yemeni father who was able to secure a visa for his eldest child.

His wife and two younger children were denied. He didn't want to risk losing the eldest child's visa, so he and his wife had no option but to parent separately. The father and oldest child are in the United States, and the mother and two younger children remain in war-torn Yemen. In describing this disturbing, yet not-so-unique case, Zahra takes a long pause. The break in the conversation mirrors the state-sanctioned schisms forced between familial bonds. "There is nothing that I can do . . ." she trails off. "I became a lawyer to help people, and I can't do that in the same way in this moment." When I asked her what's next for our country, she says, "I am worried that we are in this epic fight for our souls."

A few months later, her prediction came true. In the fall of 2018, the travel ban nearly prevented a mother from making it to her two-year-old son's deathbed. Abdullah Hassan had been born with a brain condition that caused weekly seizures. In October 2018, his father, Ali, brought him to the US from Cairo for medical treatment—they were US citizens, but the boy's mother was not. She was a Yemeni national and the travel ban blocked her entry into the US.

In the United States, the boy's condition only worsened, and in November, Abdullah was put on life support at Benioff Children's Hospital in Oakland, California. Doctors told Ali that patients with Abdullah's condition survive on life support for only a few weeks, at most a month. Abdullah was on it for over a month while his father moved frantically to get his wife, Shaima Swileh, into the country to be by her son in his final days. She was alone in Cairo, waiting for the US State Department to issue her waiver. As she waited, she cried constantly. It was bad enough that her toddler son was at his life's end; it was even worse that she couldn't be there with him in his final moments.

Ali's story was championed by his lawyers, who not only filed a lawsuit, but also mobilized over 20,000 emails to members of Congress and the US Embassy in Cairo, had three congressmen intervene to urge the State Department to expedite the waiver process, and facilitated wall-to-wall media coverage reaching millions of viewers. In the end, it worked; shortly after Ali appeared on CNN, the State Department approved Swileh's waiver on December 18 and permitted her to travel. On December 29, 2018, two-year-old Abdullah died.

The story is worth pondering: Because of the travel ban, it took extraordinary measures to get a mother to her son in time for his death.

||||||||||||||||||||||||||||||||||||||||||||||||||||||||||||||||||||||||||||||||||||||||||||||||||||||||||||||||||||||||||||||||||||||||||||

"DOES THE SUPREME COURT HAVE
A DOUBLE STANDARD ON RELIGION?"
Daniel Burke, CNN

||||||||||||||||||||||||||||||||||||||||||||||||||||||||||||||||||||||||||||||||||||||||||||||||||||||||||||||||||||||||||||||||||||||||||||

In a piece titled, "'What's Next?' Muslims Grapple with Supreme Court Ruling that They Believe Redefines Their Place in America," the *Washington Post*'s Abigail Hauslohner interviewed American Muslim citizens and permanent residents who had awaited the decision anxiously. The sense of betrayal was palpable. "The message to Muslims is that you're not welcome here, we don't want you here, we want to ban you from traveling to the U.S. and picking the U.S. as your future home . . . The message is that they cannot really count on the United States as their home, and they should probably seek other places to live."

Making this betrayal even more acute was the contrast between the travel ban ruling and the Supreme Court's language in another case, decided just three weeks earlier. On June 4, 2018, the court had ruled in *Masterpiece Cakeshop v. Colorado Civil Rights Commission*, a case that involved Jack Phillips, a Christian baker who refused on religious grounds to bake a wedding cake for a gay couple. Phillips was fine with the couple buying a cake off his shelf, but making a cake specifically for the occasion would implicate him in the celebration of the union. That, in Phillips's view, was out of the question because to celebrate a same-sex union would be to violate his religious beliefs about marriage being between one man and one woman.

The ruling was, like the travel ban decision, highly anticipated, as it posed a still-open and controversial question: Do religious believers engaged in for-profit businesses have to produce goods and services that violate their deeply held religious beliefs? (The popular framing of that question is, of course, far more contentious than my phrasing.) In its *Masterpiece* ruling, the court sidestepped the thornier questions altogether. The facts of the case gave the court the opening it needed to punt, leaving Americans either to resolve the question on their own or wait for the court to decide on another day. The court ruled seven to two in favor of the Christian baker, holding that the Colorado Civil Rights Commission, in reviewing the gay couple's complaint against the baker, had treated religion with overt hostility, at one point even comparing Phillips to Nazis. This, the court held, was unacceptable. Religion, under the US Constitution, cannot be treated with so much contempt. "The Commission's hostility was inconsistent with the First Amendment's guarantee that our laws be applied in a manner that is neutral toward religion," the court's opinion read.

And yet, just weeks later, the court's majority utterly failed to comprehend the gravity of the president's hostility against Muslims. It upheld the travel ban despite evidence of prejudice far more egregious than the evidence in *Masterpiece*; the great importance of national security pushed the court to defer to the president almost completely.

There are a number of reasons why the court ruled the way it did. Part of the reason the court did not even consider the religious liberty issue is because the plaintiff's lawyers used the wrong Religion Clause to argue their case. As Becket explained in its amicus brief, plaintiffs should have invoked the Free Exercise Clause, not the Establishment Clause. The "core" of plaintiff's theory is that the Proclamation is unconstitutional because it "'singl[es] out' members of one particular religion—Muslims—'for disfavored treatment.' . . . That claim sounds in free exercise, not establishment, both historically and today." (Plus, as Jeffrey Toobin has noted, the trend among the conservative justices is to "read . . . the establishment clause out of the Constitution, and turn . . . almost every issue into a free-exercise case," so the Free Exercise Clause is a more winning strategy.)

When the lawyers argued the case using the Establishment Clause, they failed to realize that all of the precedents they were using dealt with domestic policy only. But as the court explained, there's good reason to distinguish foreign policy issues from the mundane domestic issues where the Establishment Clause is typically applied—stuff like school prayers or nativity displays in the public square (where courts assess whether the prayers or displays "establish" religion generally or a particular religion). In the domestic context, the court had no problem looking behind a policy to figure out the intention motivating the policy. But there was no precedent that would justify the court looking for animus in order to "invalidate a national security directive regulating the entry of aliens abroad."

Then there's the "presidential avoidance canon," or the rule that because of the president's "unique role in the separation of powers, the law applies differently to the president than it does to anyone else." Who gets to enter and not enter the country is well within the realm of executive, or presidential, authority, and the court, or judicial branch of government, could not interfere with that or even comment extensively on it. While the president is not above the law, "domestic Establishment Clause precedents" definitely "cannot restrict the president's statutory and constitutional power to exclude."

This distinction is the reason why the majority of the court did not look at animus in the travel ban case but did look at it in the *Masterpiece* case—the former involved the president of the United States, with all of the special rules that apply to him, while the latter involved a "mere member of the Colorado Civil Rights Commission."

But Justices Sotomayor and Ginsburg had a different interpretation of the law. They argued in their dissent that both *Masterpiece* and the travel ban case involved "official expressions of hostility and the failure to disavow them," and the majority's failure to treat antireligious hatred the same way across both cases reflected a double standard.

Sotomayor and Ginsburg also held that extreme deference to the president is unwarranted where the prejudice is so strong. In their view, "national security" was a mere "window dressing" that, try as it might, just could not conceal the obvious fact that the ban was steeped in "impermissible discriminatory animus against Islam and its followers." Put another way, the dissent thought this particular president, with his blatant animosity toward Muslims, should not be treated just like any other president.

The *Washington Post* captured this issue perfectly in its headline, "In travel ban case, Supreme Court considers 'the president' vs. 'this president.'" While the majority of the court treated President Trump just like any other president, the dissent thought Trump was sufficiently *unlike* any other president that he should, in this case, be treated differently. He didn't deserve the deference that other presidents routinely get.

Outside the court, there was an uneven response to the case by religious liberty advocates. While the majority of the court felt limited by separation of powers in commenting on the president's animosity, civic groups were not similarly constrained—yet many of them also failed to comment. Michelle Boorstein of the *Washington Post* investigated the matter in her piece "Why Many Religious Liberty Groups are Silent about the Supreme Court's Decision on President Trump's Travel Ban." She took to task the religious liberty groups that celebrated Phillips's win in *Masterpiece* but failed to decry the travel ban decision or say anything at all. Even if they thought the court had sound legal bases for its ruling, why weren't more religious liberty advocates speaking out about the president's anti-Muslim animus?

Another *Washington Post* writer thought these groups were silent because "to take a stand against the 'Muslim ban' is also a stand against Trump, who remains popular among conservatives and white evangelicals, and for the rights of foreign Muslims, who are often vilified by conservative Christian activists." Boorstein, though, got to the heart of the matter: "The difference in response raises new questions about what precisely is meant by religious liberty in America today."

The very definition of religious liberty is the biggest question facing the First Amendment today. Does it apply to all Americans equally?

||||||||||||||||||||||||||||||||||||||||||||||||||||||||||||||||||||||||||||||||||||||||||||||||||||||||||||||||||||

"UNITED STATES OF ANTI-MUSLIM HATE"
Tanvi Misra, *CityLab*

||||||||||||||||||||||||||||||||||||||||||||||||||||||||||||||||||||||||||||||||||||||||||||||||||||||||||||||||||||

On February 10, 2015, three Muslim university students in Chapel Hill, North Carolina—Deah Barakat, his wife Yusor Abu-Salha, and Yusor's sister Razan—were gunned down in their home.

The initial accounts of what happened on February 10 were sparse. Some Muslim students on the University of North Carolina at Chapel Hill campus got texts in the early evening that someone had been shot and the shooter was still at large. Information on what had happened, who was shot, and whether danger was still imminent, were circulated by text message, and some students heard the news before others. One student, Nicole Fauster, recalls exactly where she was when she found out what happened. She was working feverishly with another student, Layla, on a project that was due the next day. The two had been working on the submission for the past couple of weeks and had met in Layla's dorm to finalize the documents. They were sitting in the common area of the dorm, which had large glass windows. It was getting late, and they were both glad they decided to meet before it got too dark; their phones had been lighting up with emergency alerts about a shooting nearby.

Nicole and Layla briefly speculated what could have happened but didn't pay too much attention since it was common to receive phone alerts about crimes that occurred off campus. Then the text messages started to hit closer to home. "Deah is dead." Layla showed Nicole the phone, who at first brushed off the text as a distasteful, immature joke. Deah, Yusor, Layla, and Nicole were all part of the same close-knit Muslim community of college-age youth in the Research Triangle of North Carolina. The news seemed too tragic to be true.

But they had to make sure. After scouring the Internet, the vague reports turned into unadulterated horror. Deah *was* dead. The girls, afraid to be by the bay windows in the common area, went to the adjoining dorm, Kenan, where the Muslim women from Chapel Hill's Muslim Students Association occupied half of the third floor. When the elevator doors parted, they knew that this was not a joke at all. Tears flowed throughout the hall. As everyone desperately grasped for information, one question hung over them. *Why?*

It was a surreal moment for the girls on the third floor of Kenan. They turned on the TV to catch the evening news, trying to make sense of the fragmented bits of information. When the story of the shooting came on, they recognized the faces on the evening news. The news camera panned to their friends who were sobbing on the curb on Summerwalk Circle, where Deah and Yusor lived.

The tears on that floor turned to catatonia, then to anger, then to confusion, and then to sobbing once more. The sobbing continued in Chapel Hill, grew louder in Raleigh, where Deah, Yusor, and Razàn grew up, and reverberated around the world for the three souls that were murdered that day.

Deah had been living in Finley Forest Condominiums for some time. He was a dental student at the University of North Carolina at Chapel Hill. He had been recently married, and his lovely new bride, Yusor, had moved in with him a few weeks earlier. She was going to begin dental school at UNC along with Deah that fall. Razan, who would often chaperone Deah and Yusor when they were still courting, was visiting that night. She had come over for the day, as she often would.

On the afternoon of February 10, a woman at Finley Forest called 911, reporting that she heard shots and "kids screaming." The police found Deah's body at the front door of his apartment and Yusor and Razan's bodies on the floor inside. They had been murdered in cold blood by their neighbor, Craig Hicks, who had banged on their door earlier that day. Deah opened it and Hicks shot him seven times in the chest. Hicks entered the house and shot Yusor at point-blank range, execution style. Then he found Razan, the last to be murdered, and did the same. Stated another way, a non-Muslim terrorist has to kill on average seven more people than a Muslim terrorist does to get the same media coverage.

Federal investigators looked into whether the murders were hate crimes but have not yet publicly disclosed the results of that investigation. Meanwhile, the media portrayed Hicks as an "irrational actor" who was not influenced by anti-Muslim policies and rhetoric. But law professor and critical race theorist, Khaled Beydoun, has challenged the narrow framing. He has a name for what he thinks is really going on: "dialectical Islamophobia." Dialectical Islamophobia is the process by which private actors are emboldened by state-sponsored policy, programming, or rhetoric to engage in violence against actual and perceived Muslims. When we understand anti-Muslim sentiment in a way that ties it to private actors only, we fail to acknowledge the effect of state policies that perpetuate misconceptions and stereotypes of Islam.

The media plays a role, too, by amplifying and disseminating hateful views. Headlines like "Muslims Must Do More against Terrorism" and "Why Aren't Muslims Condemning ISIS?" place the onus to prevent terrorism on Muslims, and no matter how much Muslims do to counteract violence, it's never enough. Implicit in this messaging is the idea that if Muslim leaders do not publicly denounce a terrorist attack, they approve of such actions, even though no similar onus is placed on Christian leaders after white supremacist terrorist attacks.

News outlets further cement the connection between terrorism and Muslims by giving terrorist attacks committed by Muslims much more coverage than violence committed by others. Controlling for other factors that could contribute to heightened media coverage, researchers Erin M. Kearns, Allison E. Betus, and Anthony F. Lemieux found that attacks by Muslims received 357 percent more coverage than attacks committed by others. Stated another way, a non-Muslim terrorist has to kill on average seven more people than a Muslim terrorist does to get the same media coverage.

The format of news programs also plays a role in equating terrorism and Muslims in the public mind. With news programs dependent on short segments to accommodate time for commercials, news commentators have "little incentive to ask whether or not Islam really explains 'Muslim terrorism,'" so instead they mention the religious backgrounds of terrorists over and over again without providing any context. To snag high ratings, the news also replays footage of violent attack. This repetitive footage, coupled with repetitive and simple commentaries about the perpetrators' Muslim backgrounds, creates a "looping effect that fuels Islamophobia . . . [through] the association of Islam with violence." With such a distorted message in the minds of many Americans, it is not surprising that some act on that belief and commit hate crimes.

According to neuroscientists, widely disseminated and hateful rhetoric, especially when it comes from authority figures, has neurological effects on potential violent actors. Princeton psychologist Dr. Susan Fiske and her colleagues have demonstrated "that distrust of an outgroup is linked to anger and impulses toward violence." The impulse to lash out is especially accentuated when one feels threatened in some way. In her words, "Both science and history suggest that people will nurture and act on their prejudices in the worst ways when these people are put under stress, pressured by peers, or receive approval from authority figures to do so." For a hate crime perpetrator, hateful, dehumanizing rhetoric not only strips the targeted people of human worth, but also robs them of their human rights. It puts them beyond the "beyond the reach of empathy, stripping them of moral protection and making it easier to harm them."

Whether it's dialectical Islamophobia, the media, or the neurological effects of hateful rhetoric, or all three, we can see why American Muslims today face hit-and-runs, shootings, stabbings, and violent murders.

In May 2015, white supremacists in Phoenix, Arizona, planned to protest at their local mosque on a Friday afternoon when Muslims congregate for special prayers. Protestors gathered with assault rifles outside of the mosque gates with the intention of intimidating and harassing the mosque-goers. In September 2015, Ahmad Mohamed, a fourteen-year-old high school freshman built and brought a clock to school to impress his teacher, only to trigger a panic that his contraption was a bomb. "I built a clock to impress my teacher but when I showed it to her, she thought it was a threat to her," he later explained to reporters. He was arrested for possession of a "hoax bomb" and detained at a juvenile facility.

Beth Van Duyne, the mayor of Mohamed's hometown of Irving, Texas, met his arrest with approval. She had stoked fears long before the incident about sharia "courts" in the United States threatening to supplant the US Constitution. Van Duyne, along with rest of the city council, had backed the Texas "anti-sharia bill," which the *Dallas Morning News* described as "a way to stop the influence of 'large populations of Middle-Easterners.'"

To close off 2015, in October there was another round of mosque protests, fiercer than the Arizona protests earlier that year. This time white supremacists planned and executed armed protests in twenty cities across the nation including Dallas, Atlanta, Detroit, Las Vegas, and Cincinnati.

And then there's the phenomenon of the "hijab grab" (the Muslim headscarf is called "hijab" in Arabic). In September 2016, a woman was charged with hate crimes after she punched, kicked, and tried to rip the hijab off two Muslim women who were pushing strollers in Brooklyn. "Get the f—k out of America, b-tches, you don't belong here!" the woman yelled, as she pushed aside the strollers with the children still sitting in them. The day before the attack, on social media, she had warned of her plans to attack Muslim women: "From this moment on, every woman that waers (sic) the jihab/hijab will go to hell!! I cant (sic) stand you f—ing hypocrites. You have been warned."

A day after President Trump was elected on a platform laden with anti-Muslim rhetoric, a man grabbed a San Jose State University student by her headscarf, pulling at it with such force that she could no longer breathe. She struggled to free herself from her attacker, who remained silent during the struggle. In 2017, a group of teenage girls punched and kicked a woman in hijab dining at a New York Panera Bread and called her a "f—ing terrorist." The NYPD is investigating the occurrence as a hate crime. On April 3, 2018, or "Punish a Muslim Day," a Houston Muslim woman wearing a headscarf was sideswiped and forced off the road by an SUV. When she got out of her car to assess the damage, the male driver of the SUV pulled up next to her, calling her a "n-gger," "desert monkey," and a "raghead." When the victim attempted to get back inside her car, the SUV driver waved a knife in her face, hitting her shoulder and arms with the knife handle before he stabbed her in the arm, severing an artery. Fortunately, she survived the attack. In May 2018, in Atlanta, Georgia, a man tried to strangle a female Muslim delivery driver with her headscarf when she delivered his order. In June 2018, in Manchester, New Hampshire, a man, without provocation, pulled a Muslim woman's headscarf as she sat in a restaurant.

The prevalence of the hijab grab led one millennial Muslim woman, Rana Abdelhamid, to start a women's empowerment initiative. A black belt in karate, Abdelhamid teaches women ages sixteen to twenty-one self-defense skills, including the hijab grab technique that involves "lowering your chin, turning towards the attacker, elbowing them with one arm and hitting them in the face with the palm of your other hand." "It's so messed up. Why should we even have to invent that?" Abdelhamid told the *New York Post* when it featured her work. Her vision for her program is that "every single Muslim woman can live a life free of violence with dignity and respect."

Muslim women in America today face a double whammy—harassment on behalf of their faith and their gender (a phenomenon the scholar Kimberlé Crenshaw termed "intersectional discrimination"). They aren't the first women of faith to face these obstacles. In November 2018, a man in Los Angeles attacked three Orthodox Jewish women by attempting to grab their wigs from their heads. Police, who say the perpetrator has been targeting Orthodox Jewish women in that area for months, are investigating the incident as a hate crime. In 2017, a Catholic nun in her habit was threatened by a man while she was praying in church. The man said he was going to kill her because "I don't believe in this because you don't help the poor."

The New America Foundation, a nonpartisan, nonprofit think tank, recently introduced its data visualization project. Its interactive map displays anti-Muslim activities by state, divided by type of activity (antisharia legislation, mosque controversies, hate crimes, etc.). The long list of hate incidents reported to the media in 2018 includes: In Kansas City, Missouri, a man broke into a Muslim family's home, "spray painted religious and racial slurs inside the home, and set the staircase on fire." In St. Augustine, Florida, "a man attacked Muslim students with a stun gun and knife . . . One of the officers reported that 'the statements made by the defendant to the victims showed that the assailant only committed the acts due to the victim's religion.'" In Livingston Paris, Louisiana, "a man rammed his pickup truck through a store because he thought its owners were Muslims." In Carmel, California, "a man was deliberately hit twice with a car while he was walking with his family. The family was recognizably Muslim because the women were wearing hijabs." In New York, "Muslim police officers with the NYPD . . . found their lockers vandalized by colleagues, who wrote anti-Muslim messages [including "F—k you, Muslims"] and spread feces on the lockers."

And the list goes on.

These crimes cannot be chalked off as the doings of uneducated, old, racist "bumpkins." They have occurred at educational institutions and in large metropolitan cities at the hands of people as young as twenty. Nor can these incidents be dismissed as "hoaxes," as for example Michelle Malkin insisted in the *National Review*. While not all reported crimes always turn out to be real and "fake news" does happen, we can't let the one-off hoax diminish our attention and concern for real hate crimes, of which there are undoubtedly many.

The fact is that something deeply insidious is at work. But what is it and where does it come from?

||||||||||||||||||||||||||||||||||||||||||||||||||||||||||||||||||||||||||||||||||||||||||||||||||||||||||||||||||||||||||||||||||||||||||||||||||

"FEAR, INCORPORATED: WHO'S PAYING FOR ALL THAT ISLAMOPHOBIC PARANOIA?"
Stephen M. Walt, *Foreign Policy*

||||||||||||||||||||||||||||||||||||||||||||||||||||||||||||||||||||||||||||||||||||||||||||||||||||||||||||||||||||||||||||||||||||||||||||||||||

I had just finished one of my talks on religious liberty in the United States, one of my favorite presentations. It covered issues as diverse as religious garb, prisoner rights, mosque cases, and the words "under God" in the Pledge of Allegiance. I had even talked about the spate of litigation over the US government requiring religious non-profits to provide their employees access to contraception. The issues were diverse, seemingly unrelated, but I tied it together coherently through reference to abiding principles of religious liberty.

I was so certain that this principle would shine through that I even included a discussion of so-called antisharia laws, or laws against Muslim religious arbitration. I acknowledged to my audience that the mere mention of sharia may be startling and even frightening to them, but that they could rest assured that the "sharia law of America" was nothing to worry about. Regardless of whether sharia posed a threat or not (I argued there—and later in this book—that it does not), the American legal system works quite well in protecting American public policy and constitutional rights from any external threats.

After I was done and the room had almost emptied, I was approached by a young man from the audience. He was interning then with a conservative Christian law firm specializing in religious liberty. He appreciated how I had tied the diverse topics together—including matters championed by his own firm. But he couldn't help but feel queasy about my remarks on sharia.

"You said the sharia law of America is nothing to worry about. But what about the people who come here from countries where sharia *is* something to worry about? Shouldn't we be worried about those people threatening our values? Making our women cover themselves in burqas? Bringing terrorism to America?" He was talking about sharia, but he was also talking about the travel ban and implicitly arguing that it was a good idea.

I nodded, as if to say, "I understand." But even as I went on to explain how our legal system protects against a foreign "takeover" (see chapter 5) and why the travel ban is likely overbroad in its scope, unnecessarily restricting rights when it needn't, inside, I was frustrated. His questions reflect a narrative that is common and constant. The underlying assumption every time a person asks these questions is that every Muslim is a spokesperson for Islam, every Muslim must pay for the actions of every other Muslim, and a deprivation of Muslims' rights is justified and reasonable because some Muslim was wreaking havoc somewhere else in the world. American

Muslims' rights are forever examined through the prism of national security.

What he doesn't realize is that I, as a fellow American—a fellow *human*—also worry about my security in an age of violence and uncertainty. I feel anxious as I follow the DC rush hour swarm into the subway, knowing that none of these hundreds of people has gone through security before boarding and any one of them could be armed. I am filled with trepidation every morning when I send my kids to school, afraid that that day, again, our national headlines would be ablaze with news of a school shooting. I also have fears that this young man who approached me does not have to confront: I am afraid of wearing a headscarf in busy, urban areas, because of a potential hijab grab. I am afraid that my son will be bullied for sharing stories of his faith and my daughter will be taunted because of her Muslim name. The omnipresence of fear afflicts us all, and for some of us, it is compounded.

What he also doesn't realize is that, aside from the real fear generated by terrorism and violence, there is a fear that is carefully manufactured, amplified, and propagated by a cottage industry of professional anti-Muslim fearmongers. He may be one of millions of Americans who has absorbed this messaging without even realizing that it's designed to stoke hatred and distrust of their Muslim neighbors.

These professional fear manufacturers are what South African sociologist Stanley Cohen would call "moral entrepreneurs." Cohen coined the phrase "moral panic" to describe phenomena similar to the widespread anxiety about Muslims that we see in America today. Moral panic spreads with the aid of "moral entrepreneurs," interest groups and political elites that direct public anger towards marginalized individuals. A panic is only successful if the public is receptive to arguments offered by moral entrepreneurs. In the US, the 9/11 attacks helped create this receptivity. Moral entrepreneurs build on this anxiety using three rhetorical methods, all of them reflected in talking points used by pundits, politicians, and even religious leaders. These methods include: (1) creating an "us" versus "them" dynamic; (2) emphasizing that any Muslim can be a culprit, regardless of what they do or say; and (3) expanding the scope of things to fear about Islam and Muslims.

First, moral entrepreneurs use melodramatic language that demonizes a particular group while glorifying society and creating pride in its fundamental goodness. President Trump does this very well. But he is neither alone nor the first to do this.

In April 2018, BuzzFeed News detailed strong anti-Muslim statements made by Republican politicians, at both the state and local level, in forty-nine states since 2015 (Utah was the sole exception). The public statements all reflected a deep fear and distrust of Muslims. In his 2016 State of the State address, Alabama governor Robert Bentley made false statements about "the threat of Muslim refugees," alleging, among other things, that a Syrian refugee was the perpetrator of the Paris terrorist attacks in November 2015. In 2017, a Texas lawmaker surveyed mosques and Muslim Students Associations on whether they supported protecting people who left Islam. The surveys, which the respondents rightly perceived as a "loyalty pledge," also asked whether they supported a ban on the transnational organization the Muslim Brotherhood.

Oklahoma congressman John Bennett called Islam "a cancer" and met with Muslim constituents only after they filled out questionnaires asking them questions that included whether they beat their wives. In 2015, a former state senator from Nebraska, Bill Kintner, proposed an even more novel loyalty test: coercing Muslim entrants to the US to eat pork as their ticket for admission. That same year, in an email to colleagues, Rhode Island state senator Elaine Morgan said Muslims are "murderous" and recommended "that Syrian refugees be housed in camps"; she later publicly stood by her comments.

Outside of government, highly active "misinformation experts" have influenced the national and international political conversation about Islam, its teachings, and its followers for the past decade perpetuating a phenomenon that some have termed Islamophobia. A report by the Center for American Progress, "Fear, Inc.: The Roots of the Islamophobia Network in America," examines these groups in detail, describing their extensive sources of funding (professional fearmongering is lucrative business!) and the media enablers who help amplify their message. The individuals highlighted in the report include, among others, Pamela Geller and Robert Spencer, the cofounders of the Stop Islamization of America organization, which is entirely devoted to stoking fears about a supposed Islamic conspiracy to take over America.

Geller and Spencer are well-known for their active fomenting of anti-Muslim fear. In May 2015, in response to the *Charlie Hebdo* massacre in France, Geller sponsored an "art contest" where participants drew the Prophet Muhammad. The event was intended to reinforce the stereotype that Muslims are irrational, hypersensitive, volatile, and violent when prodded. In mid-2017, Geller won a bid to place anti-Islam propaganda on New York City buses and transportation hubs. One of her posters read, "In any war between the civilized man and the savage, support the civilized man . . . defeat jihad." In a speech in Mission Viejo, Robert Spencer conflated Islam with ISIS: "[W]e see not only that [ISIS] embodies Islam . . . that's all in the Quran what they [ISIS] do, but also that they embody what may be, the foremost evil force that the world has ever seen."

Brigitte Gabriel's ACT! for America, a group with nearly 17,500 volunteers, seventeen staff members, and half a million "warriors" devoted to creating a "safer America," is another big player among anti-Muslim moral entrepreneurs. In ACT!'s view, a safer America is an America free of all Muslim influence. The group claims various victories in this effort, including twenty-two legislative wins at the state level "many of them laws that stiffen criminal penalties for terrorism, keep Islamic or foreign influence out of U.S. courts, or aim to protect free speech." It has also succeeded in removing from Texas school textbooks what it calls "errors"—or what it thinks are pro-Muslim, anti-Christian statements. The effort is part of its attempt across multiple states to change the way public schools teach Islam. ACT! issued a report in 2012 titled "Education or Indoctrination? The Treatment of Islam in 6th through 12th Grade American Textbooks," and has reviewed at least thirty-eight textbooks as part of its initiative. ACT! is also responsible for the questionnaire John Bennett, the Oklahoma congressmen, used to ask Muslim constituents whether they beat their wives.

The Center for Security Policy (CSP), run by Frank Gaffney, is funded by donors who have a keen understanding of how to influence US politics by promoting a particular narrative about Islam and Muslims. It is no surprise then that CSP is the source of the talking points used by right-wing politicians, pundits, and grassroots organizations that insist Islam is a threatening political force. And CSP's political influence is real. In May 2018, CSP's senior vice president for policy, Fred Fleitz, was named chief of staff for President Trump's National Security Council. Fleitz has claimed in the past that Muslim communities in America are susceptible to a "radical worldview that wants to destroy modern society, create a global caliphate and impose sharia law on everyone on Earth."

CSP's report, "Shariah: The Threat to America," fuels campaigns to restrict Muslim religious arbitration, an initiative that has translated into antisharia bills in more than forty-three states (twenty-three new bills were introduced in 2017 alone). And CSP's "Mosques in America: A Guide to Accountable Permit Hearings and Continuing Citizen Oversight" outlines tactics and talking points for Americans who want to stop Muslims from building or expanding houses of worship.

Prominent Christian leaders are also successful in stoking moral panic about Muslims. Franklin Graham, a Christian evangelist and close Trump supporter, publicly said Islam "is a very evil and wicked religion." In a CNN interview, Graham said Muslims are incompatible with life in American because "you can't beat your wife. You cannot murder your children if you think they've committed adultery or something like that, which they do practice in these other countries." (Graham was referring to the practice of "honor killings," which have never been sanctioned by any Islamic scholar, modern or medieval).

In addition to melodramatic us versus them language, moral entrepreneurs also "emphasize the randomness of the underlying incident, suggesting that anyone, anywhere might become the next victim." In this case, the underlying incident is the 9/11 attacks and the spate of terrorist attacks in the US and abroad that have followed. President Trump has done this well, on the one hand stating that America is at war with radical Islam rather than all Muslims, but then injecting uncertainty into his message: "It's very hard to define. It's very hard to separate. Because you don't know who's who."

Anti-Muslim agitators have made this uncertainty a major part of their moral entrepreneurship through their misappropriation of the concept of *taqiyya*. *Taqiyya* is the "action of covering, dissimulation," which in religious practice means you can let go of religious obligations in contexts where compliance would cause you harm. The *Oxford Dictionary of Islam* defines *taqiyya* as the "precautionary denial of religious belief in the face of potential persecution." In Islamic history, it was a concept largely relevant to intra-Muslim disputes, a doctrine Shi'as used to weather Sunni persecution.

But today, *taqiyya* is portrayed by moral entrepreneurs as a sinister doctrine of "lying and deception" that "allows Muslims to lie to non-believers in order to protect their reputation and the reputation of Islam as a whole." Pamela Geller's website tells readers: "Muslims are especially expected to do this in foreign lands in order to make non-believers think the Islamic invaders are actually peaceful neighbors. That is, until there are enough Muslims to overtake the native population." In other words, Americans are always at risk of an attack by a Muslim, even the ones who may appear friendly or nonviolent.

The third tactic used by moral entrepreneurs to stoke fears about American Muslims is domain expansion. Moral entrepreneurs expand the domain of things to be feared by tying terrorism to something that is entirely different. They argue not only that the two are connected but also that both intrinsically stem from Islamic theology. Daniel Filler, in his essay "Terrorism, Panic, and Pedophilia," talks about this expansion by looking at popular linkages between Muslims and pedophilia.

> A new sort of rhetoric has surfaced, creating less familiar links between Muslims, terrorism, and pedophilia. These are not necessarily intuitive connections. Why would Islam produce more pedophiles than Christianity, Judaism, or other religions practiced in America? And how can terrorism, a political action designed to produce long-term, society-wide repercussions, really be compared to pedophilia, a personal crime perpetrated on a single individual?

Despite the tenuous connection, the reference has popped up time and again. At the 2002 Pastors Conference of the Southern Baptist Convention, Reverend Jerry Vines delivered a talk against Islam, stating, "Some would have us believe that Islam is just as good as Christianity . . . Christianity was founded by the virgin-born son of God, Jesus Christ. Islam was founded by Muhammad, a demon-possessed pedophile who had 12 wives, the last one of which was a nine-year old girl." His remarks were reported by many of the major national newspapers, from *The New York Times* to the *Chicago Tribune* to the *Los Angeles Times*, and CNN even made the comments the topic of one of its *Crossfire* episodes.

On Frontpage.com, one of the magazine's columnists argued that Muslim culture promotes both terrorism and pedophilia. His argument was that Islam represses adult sexuality, which then expresses itself in sexual abuse of boys, who then grow up to be sociopaths who engage in terrorism. The rampantly anti-Muslim website, WikiIslam, connects Islam and pedophilia even more brazenly, "Pedophilia is permitted in the Qur'an, was practiced by Prophet Muhammad and his companions, and some Muslims today continue to commit the crime, following their prophet's example."

Controversial and denigrating portrayals of Muhammad also connect him to pedophilia. For example, the amateurish "Innocence of Muslims" short film that caused a massive international uproar in 2012 portrayed the Prophet as "a child of uncertain parentage, a buffoon, a womanizer, a homosexual, a child molester and a greedy, bloodthirsty thug." These portrayals in popular media go back decades. In 2005, the Danish newspaper *Jyllands-Posten* published a series of cartoons of the Prophet, including one portraying him as a pedophile. Another image depicted him standing outside of heaven saying, "Stop, Stop, we have run out of virgins!" These sex-obsessed, violent tropes of the religion are pervasive.

||||||||||||||||||||||||||||||||||||||||||||||||||||||||||||||||||||||||||||||||||||||||||||||||||||||||||||||||||||||||||

"100 YEARS AGO, AMERICANS TALKED ABOUT CATHOLICS
THE WAY THEY TALK ABOUT MUSLIMS TODAY"
German Lopez, *Vox*

||||||||||||||||||||||||||||||||||||||||||||||||||||||||||||||||||||||||||||||||||||||||||||||||||||||||||||||||||||||||||

The anti-Muslim fear industry didn't invent hatred of Islam, even if it diligently and strategically amplifies it. The origins of the hate are far deeper. It's partly due to a subconscious fear long-embedded in Western culture. As religion scholar Charles Kimball has explained, "Islam is the only religious tradition that has ever threatened the existence of Christianity. . . . That's deeply woven into our subconscious, into Western literature and culture, and so this image of an Islamic threat taps into a notion that's there already." The hate is also partly rooted in Orientalism. Edward Said, the founder of the academic field of postcolonial studies, was the first to articulate and define Orientalism as the "discourse that the West, and particularly the United States, was rightly locked in a cultural, civilizational, and military crusade against Islam." Orientalism has a racial component, too, as it conflates Muslim identity with Arab or Middle Eastern ethnicity. According to Khaled Beydoun, Islamophobia is not something new; it is merely the modern iteration of Orientalism.

The Haas Institute for a Fair and Inclusive Society explains the recent work of the anti-Muslim fear industry as an attempt to "utilize Muslims as scapegoats for political, economic, and social challenges facing the country. Most importantly, this was carried out vis-à-vis the convergence of Islamophobia and the birther movement to distract the public, and to attack President Obama's agenda." And, of course, the recent spate of terrorist attacks by individuals claiming to act in the name of Islam only exacerbates the situation and gives Islam critics more ammunition.

The roots and recent history of American anti-Muslim discourse are complex. For purposes of this book, however, the relevant point is that the extreme, melodramatic rhetoric results in "successfully nudging the default setting of public debate on Islam further and further to the right." Coupled with tremendous resources, moral entrepreneurs significantly influence public discourse and facilitate a climate where harmful words lead to harmful actions—ranging from hate crimes to problematic policies and, as Murfreesboro shows, impact in the legal arena, too.

The discourse is always consistent about one thing: Islam is a threat. The element of threat adds urgency to the conversation and focuses the solution on a complete deprivation of rights that would prevent the private and public exercise of Islam. In other words: If Islam is an ideology that is, furthermore, in conflict with American values, then Islam loses its religion status. And once Islam is cast as a threatening political ideology, rather than a religion, it becomes far easier to deny American Muslims all of the safeguards and protections that are part of religious freedom.

There are multiple threads to this phenomenon. A subtler form of the argument is that religious liberty is for "good Muslims" only. Prominent First Amendment scholars have held that Muslims do not deserve protection by virtue of their human dignity. Instead, Muslims have to earn their human rights by proving their conformity to Western "constitutional and cultural values."

This isn't the first time America has seen this line of argument. The idea that religious liberty is "merely a reward for good behavior" has been used in American history to deny religious liberty to other religious groups, most prominently Catholics, Jews, and Mormons. In nineteenth-century America, nativists resented the new influx of Catholic immigrants. The anti-Catholic animosity was so strong that, on more than one occasion, it resulted in mass violence. In 1844, after months of fearmongering by nativists that Catholics wanted to take the Bible out of public schools, riots broke out in Philadelphia. Known as the Bible Riots, the violence raged for three days, during which two Catholic churches were burned down and hundreds of people were wounded. In 1845, riots again broke out, this time in St. Louis, Missouri, where mobs ransacked Catholic homes, smashing windows and breaking furniture.

As with anti-Muslim claims today, American nativists claimed that the Catholic Church acted as a foreign entity with monarchical tendencies, portraying the Catholic Church as incompatible with American democracy, and calling into question the loyalty of Catholic citizens. Anti-Catholic sentiment culminated in the formation of a political party, the Know-Nothing Party, which sought a type of political purity and advocated for laws that banned public aid to parochial schools and prohibited public school teachers from wearing religious garb.

The antigarb statutes targeted Catholic nuns, and both sets of laws sought to limit Catholic influence over American public life.

A similar rationale motivates religious persecution against Catholics in American history and Muslims today. To the opponents of these religious communities, there is a conspiracy to be unraveled and a civilization to be saved. Moral entrepreneurs see themselves as saviors—even prophets—tasked with protecting America from an urgent, looming threat. In each case, former members of the religious community play a central role in justifying the crusade. At the height of anti-Catholic sensationalism in nineteenth-century America, Maria Monk's *Awful Disclosures of Maria Monk* provided that gruesome inside look. Monk's book claims that priests entered a convent through a secret tunnel and sexually abused the nuns living there. Nuns who resisted disappeared. If the sexual union resulted in children, the babies would be baptized, strangled, and discarded in a lime pit in the basement.

Awful Disclosures was published two years after the 1834 Ursuline Convent Riots near Boston, which were triggered when suspicions arose that nuns were being held at the convent against their will. A mob attacked the convent and burned it down. In 1835, another woman, Rebecca Reed, published a dramatic account of the abuse she suffered at the Ursuline Convent. Reed's book became a bestseller, and historians have suggested that Monk's publishers aimed to bank off the success of Reed's book. In 1964, historian Richard Hofstadter called Monk's book, which some scholars consider a hoax, "probably the most widely read contemporary book in the United States before *Uncle Tom's Cabin*."

Today, ex-Muslims are given a similar platform to share dramatic stories of abuse at the hands of Muslims. The message is that the abuse is inextricably linked to Islam, and the platform afforded such speakers is prominent. Ayaan Hirsi Ali, for example, was catapulted to public fame with her books *Infidel* and *Heretic*. These books detail stories of female genital mutilation, child marriage, forced marriage, and honor killings purportedly justified on the basis of Islam. One commentator describes *Heretic* as a "home-made intellectual bomb—a cobbling together of the most vicious examples from Muslim societies." Like Maria Monk to Catholicism, Hirsi Ali, as a former Muslim, provides the type of insider testimony that helps make the outsiders' claims about Islam believable.

The tactic of denying religious status to a disfavored religion has not been reserved for Islam. As recently as John F. Kennedy's run for the presidency in 1960, some of the nation's most prominent Protestant pastors said that the Vatican would exert nefarious political influence if a Catholic won the White House. In September of that year, a "group of 150 Protestant ministers met in Washington and declared that Kennedy could not remain independent of Church control unless he specifically repudiated its teachings." Only one Catholic before Kennedy, Governor Alfred E. Smith of New York, had ever been a presidential candidate for the Democratic or Republican parties, and his 1928 campaign was vexed with claims that "he would build a tunnel connecting the White House and the Vatican" and amend the Constitution to establish Catholicism in America.

A few decades before Kennedy's campaign, Henry Ford distributed the tract, "The Protocols of the Elders of Zion," an anti-Semitic fabrication that falsely claimed to detail meetings of Jewish elders seeking to control the press and the world economies. Many Americans don't realize how deep anti-Semitism runs in US history; according to historian Stephen Norwood, it's "much more deeply entrenched" than we realize. During the last years of World War II, the Christian Front, "a right-wing Irish group . . . inspired by the wildly popular radio preacher Charles Coughlin," regularly harassed Jews. From 1942 to 1944, members of the Christian Front engaged in what the *New York Post* called "an almost daily occurrence" of "physical intimidation, beatings and slashings" that, according to *Politico*, "probably warrant the name pogrom."

> Jews in [the Boston neighborhoods of] Dorchester, Rox-
> bury and Mattapan (and, to some extent, in Jewish neigh-
> borhoods of New York) were attacked and beaten on the
> streets, in parks, with some victims stabbed or disfigured,
> and some girls having had their clothes ripped off. Gangs
> robbed Jewish merchants, defiled synagogues and cem-
> eteries, and committed other acts of vandalism. Jewish
> Girl Scout troops and other clubs had to stop meeting.

And as the violence raged, "police officers and even elected officials looked the other way."

Mormons, or members of the Church of Jesus Christ of the Latter-day Saints, have also faced immense persecution in the United States. From 1831 to 1839, Mormons in Missouri were locked in a conflict with their neighbors. On October 27, 1838, two days after Missouri governor Lilburn W. Boggs had been informed that armed Mormons had clashed with state militia, Boggs issued an expulsion and extermination order directing Missourians to treat Mormons as "enemies" who "must be exterminated or driven from the State if necessary." Three days later, and as a result of the order, a militia unit attacked a Missouri settlement in Caldwell County, Missouri, firing 1,600 shots and killing eighteen boys and men in an attack that lasted under an hour.

In 1883, Mormons faced what many have called a precursor to President Trump's travel ban. That year, President Grover Cleveland asked Congress to find a way to "prevent the importation of Mormons into the country." Four years earlier, secretary of state William Evarts in President Hayes's administration had asked US diplomats to "seek help from European governments to keep Mormon converts from traveling to the U.S."

And in 1903, after the election of US Senator and Mormon apostle Reed Smoot, the US Senate subjected Smoot's faith to a "four-year Senate proceeding" that, according to scholar Kathleen Flake, "created a 3,500-page record of testimony by 100 witnesses on every peculiarity of Mormonism." The controversy, partly concerned with the Mormon practice of polygamy (which was officially abandoned in 1890), largely centered on the Mormon belief in revelation. According to his rivals, Smoot's role as an apostle in the Mormon Church made him "one of a self-perpetuating body of fifteen men who, constituting the ruling authorities of The Church of Jesus Christ of Latter-day Saints, or 'Mormon' Church, claim, . . . supreme authority, divinely sanctioned, to shape the belief and control the conduct of those under them in all matters whatsoever, civil and religious, temporal and spiritual." Among the allegations against Smoot was that he, as a Mormon, believed revelation trumped the laws of the land. The hearings, beginning in 1904, concluded in 1907 when the Senate vote fell short of the number needed to expel a member. Smoot kept his seat.

As with Catholics, Jews, and Mormons in US history, Muslims today are facing efforts to deny them religious liberty unless and until the majority finds them deserving of it. Another way news pundits argue that Muslims shouldn't have religious freedom is, as I discussed in the introduction, by blaming all American Muslims for the actions of authoritarian governments in majority-Muslim states. Exponents take a cursory look at the state of religious liberty in various authoritarian states and use that to justify the deprivation of rights for Muslims in America.

For example, NPR did a story in 2016 about conservative Christians struggling with religious freedom for American Muslims. Among others, NPR quoted Pastor John Wofford, who had stated at a national meeting of Southern Baptists:

> I would like to know how in the world someone within the Southern Baptist Convention can support the

defending of rights for Muslims to construct mosques in
the United States when these people threaten our very
way of existence as Christians and Americans? . . . They
are murdering Christians, beheading Christians, impris-
oning Christians all over the world.

A similar sentiment can be seen in the Trump administration's first
travel ban, which gave preferential treatment to Christian refugees
from the Middle East because "they were chopping off the heads of
everybody but more so the Christians."

Muslims are told they don't deserve human rights. Or they're told
they have to earn those rights through good behavior. Or, they're told:
what you're experiencing is not real. It helps to deny American Muslims their rights if the very existence of Islamophobia can be rejected.
ACT!, for example, describes Islamophobia as a "deceptive narrative"
that the mainstream media propagates.

During the 2016 US presidential election, several Republican candidates minimized anti-Muslim discrimination. Senator Marco Rubio
in particular lambasted President Obama's first US mosque visit for
sowing divisions: "Always pitting people against each other. Always!
Look at today: He gave a speech at a mosque. Oh, you know, implying
that America is discriminating against Muslims."

Critics were quick to point out that anti-Muslim discrimination is
real—so far in this book, I have already cited numerous studies on
anti-Muslim attitudes in the United States and the documented spike
in hate crimes. Philip Bump of the *Washington Post* also noted, "In
2014, 70 Catholics were targeted for hate crimes, of some 64 million
Americans. That same year, 184 of America's 3 million Muslims were
similarly targeted."

Rubio's dismissive attitude echoed two ideas espoused by prominent commenters, in some cases on both sides of the political aisle:
(1) that anti-Muslim hate crimes are largely hoaxes or "fake news";

and (2) that the very term Islamophobia is an attempt to shut down criticism of Islam as a "special offense associated with racism." Liberal talk show host, Bill Maher, and biologist and public intellectual, Richard Dawkins, regularly admonish other liberals for their treatment of Muslims as a "protected species." Maher has stated on his show: "If we talk about them at all, or criticize them at all, it's [as if we're] somehow hurting or humiliating Muslims. It's ridiculous." As Rubio summed it up, anti-Muslim rhetoric is as trivial as sports rivalries: "We can disagree on things, right? I'm a Dolphins fan, you're a Patriots fan."

Yes, we can disagree on things, and Islam is no exception. But when politicians and pundits dismiss anti-Muslim hate as merely "offended feelings," they are not, as they insist they are, defending free speech or protesting political correctness. They are instead intentionally turning a blind eye to the very concrete harm of hate crimes and the very real threat to the religious liberty of their fellow Americans.

My son, Eesa, hasn't yet heard our country's president tell him he hates Eesa's religion. If we can correct course now, he might never have to hear those words or face the animosity they inspire.

CHAPTER 3

"WHAT IS RELIGIOUS FREEDOM, ANYWAY?"

"*Eid Mubarak*," my father called with a smile from just beyond my bedroom door. It was 7:00 A.M. on a Saturday—May 6, 1995—and unlike anyone else in the house, Abu was ready to go (*Abu* is Arabic for "father").

Abu was accustomed to getting up bright and early, as he awoke at the break of dawn each day so that he could sit outside in the dewy air and recite the Qur'an. He had committed the entire Qur'an to memory when he was a ninth grader in Pakistan, and his daily morning ritual helped keep his memorization fresh.

Each of those morning recitations had a certain magical element. Abu would spread out his prayer mat on our outside patio, our swimming pool glistening as the subtle waves caught the early morning rays. Within minutes, Miami's thick humidity would drench his clothes, but he wouldn't mind, continuing ceaselessly with his melodic Arabic. The *alifs* and *bas* and *thas* at the tip of his tongue, the *khaas* and *gayns* emerging from his upper throat, the *haas* and *ayns* from his midthroat, and still other letters surfacing from someplace deeper. The letters would loop and sweep and interlace with one another as the sun crept higher and higher into the sky.

On many of those days, I sat in the kitchen, sipping my hot tea, catching the letters as they seeped in through the window. I've held onto those letters these past twelve years, ever since my father passed way. His recitation always resonated with a deep, spiritual certainty in the existence of God, the perfect order of the world, and the inevitability of everything God had ordained for each of us. My father exemplified this certainty then, in the glow of the rising sun, in the hours and days that stretched therefrom, and in those final days after he had been informed not just of his cancer diagnosis but also that he only had a few months to live.

On that May day in 1995, when Abu woke me up with his jubilant *"Eid Mubarak!"* he was celebrating the man who had modeled for him the complete spiritual certitude that Abu lived by. It was Eid al-Adha ("Feast of the Sacrifice"), the annual holiday commemorating Prophet Abraham's act of complete obedience and trust in God. Abraham had been instructed by God in a dream to sacrifice his son, Ishmael. A total devotee to God, Abraham knew that even if he did not understand the purpose of the act, God knew best. Ishmael went along readily, as unquestioning of God's will as his own father.

Readers of the Bible may be familiar with the story, with some notable differences. In the Bible, it was Isaac, not Ishmael, who was to be sacrificed. Unlike Ishmael in the Qur'an, Isaac in the Bible does not know he is about to be sacrificed. And the biblical accounts depict Abraham as struggling with God's command, whereas the Qur'anic version makes it clear that Abraham was completely trusting, completely certain. In both versions, though, Abraham ultimately complies and takes the chosen son to the place of sacrifice. As he brings the blade to his son's neck, God intervenes and replaces the son with a ram instead. The son lives. Abraham has passed the divine test. God's infinite mercy is, once again, made evident. Eid al-Adha is as much a celebration of Abraham's commitment to his faith as it is about God's mercy in releasing Abraham from his obligation.

Every Eid al-Adha, my father would take us to a local farm in Miami, where he would sacrifice a small farm animal. On our car ride over, we would softly repeat the same prayer: "God is Great, God is Great there is no one worthy of prayer but God, and God is Great; God is Great, all praise be to God, it is He Who guides." The journey and the prayers—it was a pattern mirrored by millions of Muslims across the United States and the world, who would, like us, take the meat of the sacrificed goat, cow, or sheep and distribute a third of it to the needy and another third to relatives and friends. On Eid, Muslims follow in Abraham's footsteps both physically and spiritually, and in its culminating act of charity, they are drawn closer to their families and to the destitute.

Charity, kinship, spiritual strength, and a story shared with the other two Abrahamic faiths—Christianity and Judaism—to boot. Indeed, the "centrality of the sacrifice story in Islam is a reminder of how Islam is a deeply and literally Abrahamic religion." Still, the holiday does not always occasion familiarity and trust among fellow Americans. Muslims on Eid al-Adha have faced resistance in North Texas, Northern Virginia, and other places. My father, when he was alive, had the opportunity to perform the ritual free from government interference. But a few years after his death, the commissioner of Sunrise, Florida—the city where my father now lies buried in the Sunrise Muslim cemetery—blocked Eid sacrifices. Commissioner Sheila Alu told reporters in 2011 that she was motivated by her love of animals rather than prejudice toward her Muslim neighbors. "Yes, I was trying to stop it. It's shut down. I'm trying to protect innocent animals." Many questioned her reasoning though; as the property caretaker, Derek Matherly, noted: "I find it appalling that people are so upset when they eat lambs and goats every day . . . I don't see the big story here. It's not like animals are being tortured."

The Muslims of Sunrise complied with Alu's demands and moved their ceremony elsewhere, despite the fact that Alu had no legal grounds to challenge the animal sacrifice—all thanks to a seminal religious liberty case that also arose from events in Miami-Dade County, in the city of Hialeah, Florida. Hialeah is a dense, urban landscape that is 96.3 percent Hispanic and known for its streets clogged with traffic and a cacophony of honking cars. The 1993 US Supreme Court case of *Church of the Lukumi-Babalu Aye v. Hialeah* addressed lawmakers who targeted the Santeria religion for its practice of animal sacrifice.

The court held that the local laws violated the Free Exercise Clause of the First Amendment because they were designed to oppress a religion or its practices. In other words, if lawmakers enact laws with the specific purpose of discriminating against a religion, those laws will be struck down as unconstitutional. With this ruling, *Lukumi* gave religious liberty law one of its most foundational principles.

The Santerian Church of the Lukumi-Babalu Aye had just announced its plans to build a house of worship, along with a school, cultural center, and museum in Hialeah. Their neighbors found the news distressing, prompting the city council to first hold an emergency public session, then enact ordinances and resolutions that prevented animal sacrifice—at least of the Santerian variety. The same law that forbade Santerian sacrifices made exceptions for a host of other types of similar animal killings, including among others, kosher slaughter.

The Santeria religion merges Yoruba beliefs with certain aspects of Roman Catholicism, such as saint worship. The saint-like figures in Santeria are called orishas. Followers cultivate a relationship with their orisha by sacrificing animals and offering the meat as food. Without the ritual, Santerian priests cannot be ordained, and followers cannot be initiated into the religious community.

When the *Lukumi* case made it up to the US Supreme Court, the court saw through the city's claims that its new laws meant to protect public welfare or ensure the humane treatment of animals. Writing for the court, Justice Kennedy pointed to the Free Exercise Clause of the First Amendment, which states that "Congress shall make no law respecting an establishment of religion or *prohibiting the free exercise thereof*." Kennedy explained that the Free Exercise Clause protects against both explicit and implicit governmental hostility: "Legislators may not devise mechanisms, overt or disguised to persecute or oppress a religion or its practice." If a law targets a particular religion or religious practice, the government has to show that the law serves a compelling government interest and is narrowly tailored to serve that interest—in other words, if there's a way to reach the same result without violating people's constitutional rights, the government won't be able to satisfy this stringent test.

Again, it's not that the government cannot protect public welfare or ensure the humane treatment of animals—it just has to do this in a way that doesn't limit religious liberty too broadly. As the court explained, "If the city has a real concern that [Santerian] methods are less humane [than kosher methods] . . . the subject of the regulation should be the method of slaughter itself," not a broad religious classification that has some vague, "general relation" to the things the government is trying to accomplish.

In the jurisprudence, these balancing principles make up the strict scrutiny test. The laws in *Lukumi*, clearly designed to target Santerian animal sacrifice and not the least bit narrowly tailored to achieve the government's stated interests, were struck down.

If the court's assessment of antireligious hostility sounds familiar, it may be because it formed the centerpiece of its decision in *Masterpiece Cakeshop*, the case I discussed in the last chapter. There, the court relied on *Lukumi* to hold that the Colorado Civil Rights Commission had violated the Free Exercise Clause because it was openly hostile to the religious believer, which in *Masterpiece* was the Christian baker who refused to create a wedding cake for a gay couple. During one of its meetings, for example, one commissioner said:

> Freedom of religion and religion has been used to justify all kinds of discrimination throughout history, whether it be slavery, whether it be the holocaust [sic], whether it be—I mean, we—we can list hundreds of situations where freedom of religion has been used to justify discrimination. And to me it is one of the most despicable pieces of rhetoric that people can use to—to use their religion to hurt others.

About this, the court said,

> To describe a man's faith as "one of the most despicable
> pieces of rhetoric that people can use" is to disparage
> his religion in at least two distinct ways: by describing
> it as despicable, and also by characterizing it as merely
> rhetorical—something insubstantial and even insincere
> . . . This sentiment is inappropriate for a Commission
> charged with the solemn responsibility of fair and neutral
> enforcement of Colorado's anti-discrimination law . . .

Animus was also at play in the travel ban decision. Three federal
appellate courts that halted the ban relied, in part, on *Lukumi*. The
renowned religious liberty scholar, Douglas Laycock, who had argued
the *Lukumi* case in front of the US Supreme Court, explained to the
Miami Herald, "In Hialeah in the 1990s, it was Santería. With Trump,
it's Muslims." But when the case made it to the Supreme Court, a
majority of the court chose to sidestep the proof of anti-Muslim hostility and uphold President Trump's policy.

This is where the dissent diverged from the majority. Justice Stephen
Breyer, joined by Justice Elena Kagan, cited *Lukumi* when he said, "If
[the travel ban's] promulgation or content was significantly affected by
religious animus against Muslims, it would violate the relevant statute
or the First Amendment itself." But the majority of the court felt that
it couldn't question the ban because the president required near complete deference on questions of foreign policy and national security. In
other words, despite copious evidence that national security may be a
pretext to achieve more sinister ends, the court refused to look beyond
the surface.

But what if the justices' avoidance of the evidence was itself an act
of animus?

II

"YOU'RE BIASED, I'M BIASED.
SO WHAT ARE WE JUDGES GOING TO DO ABOUT IT?"
Honorable James M. Redwine, Judges.org

IIIIIIIIIIIIIIIIIIIIIIIIIIIIIIIIIIIIIIIIIIIIIIIIIIIIIIIIIIIIIIIIIIIIIIIIIIIIIIIIIIIIIIIIIIIIIIIIIIIIIIIIII

In 1961, two Muslim prisoners in a federal prison in Lorton, Virginia, alleged that they, and all thirty-eight Muslim prisoners in that facility, had suffered gross deprivations merely because they were Muslim. They had not broken any rules or regulations but were still separated out from the rest of the prison population and put in isolation for ninety days, during which they were deprived of basic privileges, including medical care. During their isolation, these Muslims were allegedly given a mere teaspoon of food, to be eaten with a single slice of bread, three times a day. And despite the cold, concrete floors of their cell, they had access to a blanket only between the hours of 10 P.M. and 5 A.M.

They were also deprived of basic spiritual privileges. Unlike the other religious believers in the Lorton prison, the Muslim prisoners were not allowed "to wear medals symbolic of their faith," communicate with their religious advisers, pray, or even have access to religious literature. And when they brought a lawsuit to reclaim their constitutional rights—rights no one loses at the prison door—the federal district court said it had no jurisdiction to hear the case and dismissed it without holding a hearing or even asking the prison officials to respond to the allegations.

The two prisoners who brought the case, Theodore Sewell and Joseph Watson, appealed the court's dismissal and in time were able to find some recompense. But the deprivation and discrimination they alleged has been replicated in prisons across the country, and in courts across the country, too. In the early 2000s, the Department of Justice's inspector general, Glenn A. Fine, detailed the extensive abuse of Muslim prisoners by federal prison wardens and guards. In just one detention center in Brooklyn, Fine found taped evidence "that guards slammed [Muslim] detainees against walls, twisted their arms and conducted unnecessary strip searches." A news report four years after Fine reported this abuse found that the guards still had not been punished. In another case, a warden retaliated against an inmate for speaking to Fine's investigators by transferring the inmate to solitary confinement for over four months. The warden was not prosecuted.

More recently, in February 2019, Alabama executed Domineque Ray, a Muslim death row inmate, without accommodating his request to have an imam in the room with him. The clergy allowed in the execution chamber were limited to the ones on staff, but the prison employed Christian clergy only. Ray challenged the prison's denial on religious liberty grounds. His case made it to the U.S. Supreme Court, which ruled against him and permitted the execution to proceed without the imam. The decision shocked many Americans, leaving them wondering, in the words of The New York Times Editorial Board, "Is religious freedom for Christians only?"

For African American Muslims, racial discrimination can compound religious discrimination. Especially if they belong to the Nation of Islam (NOI) sect, black Muslims are perceived as gangsters or militants. In early cases brought by NOI inmates, "the gang label stripped the NOI of its religious dimension and projected an image based on insubordination, criminality, and violence—stereotypes attributed most closely to an African American male identity." The NOI's teachings about the superiority of the black race also fueled judicial backlash and undermined for judges "its legitimacy as a religion," which meant that black Muslim prisoners' could not have their religious needs met the way other religious prisoners could. They were not allowed to have the Qur'an or even an Arabic grammar book, they were denied a place of worship, and they couldn't pray in congregation because prison officials, and courts, thought their "collective worship would bring about a disruption of prison discipline."

In recent years, courts have treated these prisoners more fairly, thanks in part to a federal statute enacted in 2000 that made it much harder for prisons to violate basic religious rights. But entrenched stereotypes still create hurdles for Muslims, black and nonblack, seeking religious liberty in prison. And the bias isn't limited to prisoners— recent empirical studies looking at twenty years of religious liberty cases in federal courts found that Muslims more than any other religious group face judges who are predisposed to rule against them.

The evidence supports Professor Schragger's argument in 2010 that, in today's politicized climate, the outcome of a case could be different merely if one switches out a Christian plaintiff for a Muslim one, with Christians more likely to win. Judges would, of course, never admit to harboring anti-Muslim prejudices or that such prejudices affect their decision-making. It's a hard reality to swallow, because if there were ever a professional who needed to be neutral and objective, it would be a judge. Political preferences and religious affiliation should not affect a judge's decision-making—and neither should their preconceptions of a particular religion. But Islam appears to be testing the judiciary's commitment to impartiality.

At some level, the explanation is easy: judges are humans, not robots. Unless they are self-conscious or made aware of their deliberative process, humans may make automatic or quick decisions based more on emotion or subconscious prejudice rather than fairness or deference for human dignity. As humans, judges live in the real world, including the world that is wracked with fears and stereotypes. And they do not interpret legal doctrine in a vacuum; they interpret it based on their participation in American society, which in turn embeds in them certain interests and expectations.

Social psychology bears out this explanation. Consider first how intuition connects to reasoning. Social psychologist Jonathan Haidt details this process in his book, *The Righteous Mind: Why Good People Are Divided by Politics and Religion.* He describes the work of Howard Margolis, a public policy professor who was trying to figure out why people's beliefs about political matters were so disconnected to "objective facts." Margolis turned to cognitive science for the answer and found that a better way to think of higher cognitive processes, such as political thinking, was to look at "lower cognition, such as vision, which works largely by rapid unconscious pattern matching." He also looked at research on logic problems and found that regardless of whether people answered the problem correctly or incorrectly, they could devise an explanation for their answer and defend it with equal confidence. This, Margolis said, shows that people's rationales are only "ex post rationalizations."

Margolis thus proposed that "there are two very different kinds of cognitive processes at work when we make judgments and solve problems: 'seeing-that' and 'reasoning-why.'" Seeing-that is a simple process of matching patterns, so that even the simplest animals are wired to respond to particular patterns with particular behavioral reactions. Humans, with bigger and more complex brains, engage in a more sophisticated version of this process, but the basic psychology remains the same: pattern matching. "It's the sort of rapid, automatic, and effortless processing that drives our perceptions"; something we can think of as "intuition."

In contrast, reasoning-why is not automatic—it's the sometimes very laborious process by which we try to rationalize our or other people's judgments. The two processes, seeing-that and reasoning-why, are linked: "The intuition launched the reasoning, but the intuition did not depend on the success or failure of the reasoning."

In thinking about judicial biases, consider also the impact of group-think. Our membership in a particular group shapes our emotions and cognitive processes. When someone encounters another person who belongs to their group, they perceive that person's interests as similar to their own. In contrast, when people encounter out-group members, they fail to see an alignment of interests. There is a tendency to favor in-group members and disfavor out-group members.

This in-group, out-group phenomenon comes into play with religious affiliations, too. A person's religious identity shapes their values and perceptions. And if that person happens to be a judge in a religious liberty case, their religious identity influences their interpretation of the First Amendment. Studies show that among all group identities that affect judicial decision-making, a judge rules more often for claimants who share his or her religious identity.

This point is underscored by empirical research on how judges rule in religious liberty cases. A 1999 study of decisions by the United States Courts of Appeals under the Free Exercise Clause of the First Amendment and/or another law called the Religious Freedom Restoration Act found that religious believers generally lose (they won only 26.1 percent of their cases). The study's author, James Brent, said this was because legislatures already passed laws that protect majority, Christian beliefs, which means Christians generally do not experience violations as often as outgroup religious believers do. And when members of mainstream Protestant and Catholic sects did bring claims, Brent found they were more likely to win (38.9 percent versus 24.5 percent). A 2004 study by John Wybraniec and Roger Finke found similarly: "Protestants seldom appeared in the courts and their rate of favorable rulings towered over [that of] all other religious groups." Mainline Protestants brought approximately 4% of the cases and judges ruled in their favor 68.3% of the time. Muslims, who constitute only 1% of the U.S. population, brought 7% of the cases and received favorable rulings only a third (33%) of the time.

Gregory C. Sisk, Michael Heise, and Andrew P. Morriss also conducted an empirical study (known in the field simply as the "Sisk study") of religious freedom cases in federal district courts and federal appellate courts. For their study, they looked at claims under the Free

Exercise Clause of the First Amendment, the Free Speech Clause (for restrictions on religious speech), federal statutes that specifically protect religious actions and speech, and laws that protect against religious discrimination by the government, including government employers (they did not, however, look at Title VII cases of religious discrimination in private employment). Examining cases between 1986 and 1995, the Sisk study found that religion exerted the most prominent and consistent influence on a judge's decision-making, whether it was the judge's religion, the claimant's religion, or the religious demographics of the judge's community. A judge's religious background determined how he or she would rule. As for the claimant's religion—if he or she were a Muslim bringing a religious liberty claim, he or she was more likely to lose than a claimant of any other religion.

This particularly emphasized slant against Muslim claimants inspired Sisk and Heise to take a closer look at just how disadvantaged Muslims are in court. Their second study (Sisk Study II) looked at religious liberty cases (Muslim and otherwise) decided between 1996 and 2005 and found again that Muslim claimants faced a marked disadvantage. Compared to non-Muslims, Muslims are half as likely to win their religious liberty case in federal court. The number shrinks further when it's a Muslim prisoner bringing the case, with Muslim prisoners succeeding only a third as often as non-Muslim prisoners. This percentage is significant, since prisoner cases comprise three-fourths of all Muslim religious liberty claims. The only other group with significant losses consisted of black separatist sects.

What might account for the Muslim disadvantage? Sisk and Heise considered a number of theories. First, since most Muslim claims are brought by prisoners, and prisoners bring frivolous claims more often than others, one might assume their claims deserve to lose. But Sisk Study II was based only on written court opinions, which means the cases went well beyond the initial stages of litigation when judges throw out frivolous claims. So if there were a weak claim, it would have been weeded out long before it got to the stage where a judge would write an opinion.

Since most cases involve prisoners, one might also think a claim was treated differently for substantive reasons. For example, there may be an assumption that Muslim sects in prison are more dangerous or violence prone than other religious groups, thus posing legitimate security concerns and justifying a higher level of restrictions. Judges ruling against Muslim prisoners as a class may then be justified on a substantive basis rather than on stereotypes. Recent studies have increased awareness of extremist groups operating in prisons—groups like racial supremacists, radical environmentalists, and anti-government right-wingers. With these findings comes the fear that extremist Muslim groups tied to terrorism abroad are successfully recruiting prisoners to their ideology. But federal prison statistics show a different reality: 85 percent of Muslim prisoners belong to nonviolent, nonradicalized groups, and most prisoners are not even attracted to Wahhabism, a branch of Islam that is commonly considered linked to terrorism.

Sisk and Heise also examined whether the Muslim disadvantage could be credited to the "culture wars," in the same vein that traditional Christians clash with the secular state. But Muslims don't bring culture war claims to court—the majority of claims by Muslims involve prisoner treatment or employment discrimination. A fourth theory is that Islam fares badly simply because it is a non-Judeo-Christian, minority religion. But members of other minority religions, such as Jews, Sikhs, and Native Americans, are faring better than Muslims are, so that can't be the full explanation. Islam is now also the third largest religion in the United States (and is on track to become the second-largest by 2040), so it is less of a minority than many other religions in America.

Having considered then dismissed a number of explanations, Sisk and Heise settle on their final explanation: Muslims are "at a pronounced disadvantage . . . because they are Muslim." The cases Sisk

and Heise examined involve a religious believer challenging some decision by the government—a decision that a public officer defends as
necessary to American law and order. These types of cases trigger base
stereotypes about Muslims or Islam. After all, a religious liberty claim
by a Muslim puts Islam front and center. A judge may rule on the basis
of these assumptions without even realizing it. Wybraniec and Finke
came to a similar conclusion with their study; they noted that "those
religions in tension with society are significantly less likely to receive a
favorable decision" and "those in higher levels of tension have higher
odds of an unfavorable ruling."

The evidence shows that the wider phenomenon of moral panic
about Islam and Muslims as a threat to American values and safety
infects judges, too. Even if judges might try to avoid the constant
negative news stream, Islam poses a particular challenge. Few, if any,
individuals were untouched by the psychological trauma of the 9/11
terrorist attacks. Judges' tendency to associate Muslims with violence
also accounts for the particularly pronounced effect in prison contexts; "stereotypes about Muslims as security risks and Islam as a religion of violence are especially likely to be activated in contexts that
already breed negative stereotypes." And, as we've seen, with African
American Muslims, the stereotypes are even more sharpened.

Further exacerbating the mistreatment of Muslims in prison contexts is the high degree of deference courts give to prison officials.
Deference to prison officials makes sense in many cases, given the
"complex, challenging and hazardous" job of running prisons. But deference, mixed with a pervasive misunderstanding and fear of Muslim
beliefs, also makes it far likelier that prison officials, and courts, will
fail to protect religious liberty for Muslim prisoners.

This was the point the Sikh Coalition and Muslim Public Affairs
Council made in an amicus brief they filed in the 2015 US Supreme
Court case, *Holt v. Hobbs*. The case involved a Muslim prisoner's
right to grow a half-inch beard in accordance with his religious beliefs,

which the prison refused to let him grow because of so-called security concerns that the prison couldn't even back up with reasonable evidence. The amicus brief used the Sisk studies to show that base misunderstandings and fears of Muslim beliefs can lead prison officials, and the courts that defer to them, to "unfairly burden" Muslim religious practice.

The Supreme Court agreed. While the lower courts—starting with the magistrate judge, then the federal district court, then the federal appellate court—all deferred to the prison's alleged security concerns, the Supreme Court unanimously held that the prison had to do better. It wasn't enough to just say a half-inch beard posed security threats; you had to show evidence that it actually does.

The *Holt* case—in both the lower court rulings and the Supreme Court decision that reversed all those rulings—shows that while Muslim religious liberty has in many ways become a casualty of the social and cultural backlash against Muslims, change is possible. Rigorous application of our law is the path to that change.

Indeed, not only can judges overcome their biases, they can also be instrumental in helping end discrimination. Whatever their prejudices and political loyalties to their appointing coalitions, federal judges function within the bounds of the law and legal traditions. They are expected to be neutral and objective and they generally strive to meet those professional standards. Judges are also buffered from politics with life tenure. They have affected real change in other civil rights contexts, and with religious liberty, too, judges can push back against political and social discrimination by applying their First Amendment tools.

What are these tools? For this we turn to the Church of the Flying Spaghetti Monster.

||||||||||||||||||||||||||||||||||||||||||||||||||||||||||||||||||||||||||||||||||||||||||||||||||||||||||||||||||||||

"IS GOD A SPAGHETTI MONSTER?
THAT'S A SERIOUS LEGAL QUESTION"
Noah Feldman, *Bloomberg*

||||||||||||||||||||||||||||||||||||||||||||||||||||||||||||||||||||||||||||||||||||||||||||||||||||||||||||||||||||||

I was preparing breakfast one Saturday morning and my husband, Shabbir, was reading the news on his iPhone. "Hmm," he murmured, staring at his phone, his brow crinkled. "What do you think about Pastafarianism? Do you think it's a real religion?"

The Dutch Pastafarians—or members of the Church of the Flying Spaghetti Monster—had just lost their bid to wear pasta strainers on their heads for their government IDs.

"I honestly don't know what to think," I said as I watched a swirl of water envelop my soon-to-be poached egg, "On the one hand, it seems like a commentary on religion more than a religion in itself. But line-drawing can be tricky."

"Well, the Netherlands court said it wasn't a religion," Shabbir pointed out.

"Yeah, but New Zealand takes it seriously," I countered.

Pastafarians claim to wear the colanders as a sign of devotion, in true allegiance to the spaghetti monster. And the love of pasta does not stop with the deity. Pastafarian mass services typically offer noodles and beer instead of bread and wine. Pastover involves eating copious amounts of pasta with family members who are dressed as pirates. Ramendan requires that followers spend a few days of the month eating pasta only. At the culmination of Ramendan, Pastafarians are encouraged to give their extra Ramen to individuals who are more in need. Wherever a Pastafarian finds spiritual peace, there is pasta.

"They've actually won some big battles," I say. The ribbons of egg white in my pot are beginning to look like noodles.

Russia, Australia, and even the US, permits Pastafarians to pose for their driver's license photos with colanders on their head. And New Zealand recognizes "pastafari weddings" (where the couple avows, among other things, "till death do us pasta"), and has ruled that Pastafarianism constitutes "genuine philosophical convictions."

The origins of Pastafarianism start with the beginning of the world— or at least theories of how the world started. In 2005, the Kansas Board of Education voted to let public schools teach the creationist theory of intelligent design alongside lessons on evolution. Intelligent design, part of "creation science," posits that the world was created by a "master intellect" and that only the existence of an "intelligent being" can explain the world's complexity. Intelligent design does not specify what the master intellect is, just that it exists. The Board of Education permitted it because, among other reasons, one cannot prove that a master intellect had *not* created the world.

In response, Bobby Henderson—a physicist—wrote on his website that because intelligent design does not specify who the designer is, the designer could just as well be a Flying Spaghetti Monster. In his view, there is as little evidence of the creator being a Judeo-Christian deity as it is anything else. And so he issued an open letter demanding that if intelligent design was taught in schools, Pastafarianism be taught as well: "Let us remember that there are multiple theories of Intelligent Design. I and many others around the world are of the strong belief that the universe was created by a Flying Spaghetti Monster. It was He who created all that we see and all that we feel."

The Kansas Board of Education reversed itself two years later, but Pastafarianism is still going strong. Though it started as a movement against the teaching of creationism and intelligent design, its mission has expanded to testing the boundaries of church-state relations. Some scholars describe Pastafarianism as a "satirical religion"— meaning, a religion with a serious purpose: to "hold up a mirror to established religions—especially regarding the non-provability of their gods, the inconsistency of religious argumentation and the

special position they demand in society due to unchallenged beliefs."
Pastafarians are not antireligion though (and they say as much on
their website: "We are not anti-religion, we are anti-crazy nonsense
done in the name of religion"). Some of their activism is aimed at
broadening the range of religious accommodation. When American
Pastafarian, Sean Corbett, won the right in 2017 to wear a colander
in his driver's license photo, he described the victory as a victory for
all religions: "I think it really drives in the point that if you're going
to include one, you have to include all. You have to respect everybody's beliefs if you're going to respect one." He hoped his actions
would pave the way for people of other religions to wear what they
want in their license photos, like a hijab or a turban.

Still, for most courts, this activist bent is not enough to make it a
religion. In August 2018, the Netherlands' Council of State said that
Pastafarianism has none of the "seriousness and coherence" that religions are supposed to have. In the court's words, "It may be the case
that the colander is considered a holy object for Pastafarians, worn in
honor of the Flying Spaghetti Monster but there is no obligation to do
so." Germany, too, has prohibited the Pastafarians from putting up a
sign advertising "noodle mass" in the same manner Catholic, Evangelical, and Protestant groups in the country publicize their religious services. The court ruled that the Church of the Flying Spaghetti Monster
was not "a recognized religious community."

And while a US court said that Pastafarianism has both seriousness
and coherence, it, like the Dutch and German courts, found that Pastafarianism is not a religion. (The Arizona DMV permitted Corbett
to wear the colander only because it did not obstruct the state's facial
recognition technology—not because it considered Pastafarianism a
religion.) In *Cavanaugh v. Bartelt* (2016), a Pastafarian prisoner sued
prison officials because they refused to accommodate his religious
requests to dress up as a pirate (pirates being the "original Pastafarians") and celebrate communion by eating a large bowl of pasta. The

court dismissed the lawsuit, saying Pastafarianism was a not a real religion and therefore Pastafarians do not get the type of accommodations that religious believers get. It acknowledged that Pastafarianism "contains a serious argument" about "science, the evolution of life, and the place of religion in public education." But merely having a serious point to make doesn't confer religion status.

It was important for the court to engage in this inquiry because religious liberty protections only cover religious activity. The First Amendment specifically marks religion as a category that deserves special constitutional protection; before judges can decide whether a particular religious liberty law applies to the case before them, they have to confirm that they are dealing with religious and not cultural beliefs or "secular philosophies." Despite the importance of this question though, courts tend to want to avoid the inquiry. They recognize that any definition may be too broad or too narrow; even when contemplating the status of Pastafarianism, the *Cavanaugh* court said it was "well-aware of the risks of such an endeavor: it might be too restrictive, and unduly exclusive of new religions that do not fit the criteria derived from known religious beliefs." Not only do courts have to take into account social understandings of religion, they also have to come up with a test that is legally workable.

There are a few cases where judges have tried to draw perimeters around what exactly is or is not a religion. In America's early history, James Madison's "Memorial and Remonstrance," defined religion as "the duty we owe the Creator." The court used this theistic definition of religion until 1961, when, in *Torcaso v. Watkins*, it extended the definition of religion to include non-theistic belief systems, such as Buddhism, Taoism, and secular humanism. The court fleshed out this ruling a few years later when it looked at whether people who do not belong to a known religious sect could claim a conscientious objection to military service. In those cases, the court said that even though the statute exempting conscientious objectors from the draft required a belief in a

"Supreme Being," Congress really intended to cover all religions, even the non-theistic ones, as long as the belief "occupies a place in the life of its possessor parallel to that filled by the orthodox belief in God."

This functional definition of religion showed up in *US v. Meyers* (1995), where a lower court had to figure out whether the "Church of Marijuana" was a real religion. Mitchell Meyers had been convicted for possessing and distributing marijuana. In his defense, Meyers claimed that he was the reverend of the Church of Marijuana and that his religion required him "to use, possess, and distribute marijuana for the benefit of mankind and the planet earth." The court, however, said Meyers had to prove that his beliefs were religious, otherwise the law "could easily become the first refuge of scoundrels if defendants could justify illegal conduct simply by crying 'religion.'"

After a thoughtful review of past attempts by courts to define religion, the court articulated a range of factors that could be used to define whether a set of beliefs constituted religion or not. The list included things like whether the purported religion had "ultimate ideas" about "life, purpose, and death," metaphysical beliefs, a moral or ethical system, a "comprehensiveness of beliefs" ("an overarching array of beliefs that coalesce to provide the believer with answers to many" human concerns) and various accoutrements of religion, like a founder, important writings, a gathering place, ceremonies and rituals, holidays, a special diet, religious garb or grooming requirements, and so on. These factors combine the functional definition of religion (Does the belief system provide answers to a person's big life questions?) with an analogic approach (How does the belief system match up against other religions?).

Taking all of these factors into consideration, the *Meyers* court listed a range of beliefs that fit its definition of religion:

> Judaism, Christianity, Islam, Hinduism, Buddhism, Shintoism, Confucianism, and Taoism. Undoubtedly, the test

also would lead to the conclusion that the beliefs of the
following groups are "religious": Hare Krishnas, Bantus,
Mormons, Seventh Day Adventists, Christian Scientists,
Scientologists, Branch Davidians, Unification Church
Members, and Native American Church Members
(whether Shamanists or Ghost Dancers). More likely
than not, the test also includes obscure beliefs such as
Paganism, Zoroastrianism, Pantheism, Animism, Wicca,
Druidism, Satanism, and Santeria. And, casting a back-
ward glance over history, the test assuredly would have
included what we now call "mythology": Greek religion,
Norse religion, and Roman religion.

What did the court expressly exclude? "Purely personal, political, ideological, or secular beliefs" such as "nihilism, anarchism,
pacifism, utopianism, socialism, libertarianism, Marxism, vegetism,
and humanism." As for the Church of Marijuana—Meyers himself
conceded that it had no services, no real moral code, no teachings
on "ultimate ideas." Reviewing these responses against its multi-
factor test, the court said the Church of Marijuana was not a religion and that its beliefs were primarily "medical, therapeutic, and
social" rather than religious.

The *Cavanaugh* court relied on *Meyers* when it ruled that Pastafarianism is not a religion. It looks a lot like religion, the court said,
but only because it is designed to parody religion. At its core there are
no beliefs about "deep and imponderable matters"; it has no position
on matters of "ultimate concern": "the only position it takes is that
others' religious beliefs should not be presented as 'science.' Despite
touching upon religion, that is a secular argument."

Pastafarianism may have lost in the *Cavanaugh* court, but it succeeded in at least one aspect of its mission: to help define the contours
of church-state relations. *Cavanaugh* and *Meyers* are two of just a

few cases where a court tries to define religion. It is an important and necessary task, particularly in cases where people hijack religious liberty to get away with criminal behavior. Meyers wasn't the first to try circumventing drug laws—in 1968, Judith Kuch tried to get her seven-count indictment dismissed by claiming she bought and sold LSD for religious reasons. According to Kuch, she was the ordained minister of the Neo-American Church, a church head up by the Chief Boo Hoo, who "guides members on psychedelic trips." The church's "Catechism and Handbook" states: "we have the right to practice our religion, even if we are a bunch of filthy, drunken bums." The church symbol is a three-eyed toad, the church key is a bottle opener, and its official songs are "Puff, the Magic Dragon" and "Row, Row, Row Your Boat."

These are the easier cases: marijuana, psychedelic trips, and flying spaghetti monsters. But when claims of religion aren't an obvious ruse (and even when they are), line-drawing can be incredibly complex. The task is further complicated by the various limitations that religious liberty places on what a court can and cannot do.

First, judges cannot inquire into the truth of religious beliefs or determine whether a belief is "acceptable, logical, consistent, or comprehensible to others in order to merit First Amendment protection." As the former Supreme Court justice, William O. Douglas, explained in US v. Ballard, "Religious experiences which are as real as life to some may be incomprehensible to others . . . If one could be sent to jail because a jury in a hostile environment found those teachings false, little indeed would be left of religious freedom." In Ballard, the defendant claimed that he was a divine messenger who received revelation directly from Jesus.

Even though courts, even though courts cannot say whether a belief is true or false, one thing they *can* do is determine whether the individual's belief is "sincerely held." Like, if a person claims that it is against her religion to eat meat from an animal that has not been ritually sacrificed but has on several occasions been known to eat such meat, then the court is allowed to ask whether she actually believes that she cannot eat non-ritually sacrificed meat.

A second big restriction is that a court cannot limit religious freedom to beliefs that it thinks are important or central to a person's religion. Religious freedom extends to even the most tertiary element of your religion. After all, in every religion, what may be an important part of the faith for one may be of secondary importance to another.

Third, courts cannot act as a religious authority and interpret scripture. For example, in one case, the Serbian Eastern Orthodox Diocese removed one of its bishops, but the bishop refused to recognize his suspension and continued to control church property and assets. He sued the church, claiming it had interpreted its own penal code and constitution incorrectly. The Illinois Supreme Court agreed with him and said that the church's decision should be set aside as "arbitrary." But the US Supreme Court said that was completely the wrong approach. Judges should never "substitute [their] own inquiry into church polity and resolutions" of internal church disputes.

The best way to steer clear of all these restrictions is for a judge to defer to the individual's interpretation of her religion. To understand the importance of this deference, consider what is happening with Islam in America. First is the crazy fact that Islam's religion status is being questioned at all; whereas the jurisprudence to date tries to define religion largely in cases involving illicit drugs and spaghetti monsters, opponents of the Muslim community are trying to extend this parsing to a world religion with almost two billion followers.

Second, these provocateurs who, for the most part, know nothing about Islam and are by no means qualified experts on the religion, are determining which parts of Islam qualify as a religion and which do not. They are sifting through a complex belief system with endlessly diverse interpretations and picking out the parts American law should protect and the parts American law should not protect. Even qualified experts on Islam cannot make this judgment—because one person's Islam is very different from another person's Islam. Religious experience is inherently multifaceted and often deeply subjective.

If judges started parsing Islamic beliefs to protect only those they deemed acceptable, they would violate the most basic tenets of religious freedom. Basic principles of religious liberty law protect against this violation—but they aren't foolproof. Many judges are still influenced by anti-Muslim biases in their decision-making. And with constant and strategic messaging questioning Islam's religious status, the incursion into the legal space is foreseeable.

"WHY I DEFEND GOAT SACRIFICE"

Eric Rassbach, *Wall Street Journal*

In August 2017, I traveled home from Washington, DC, to South Florida to address the eighth World Congress of the International Religious Liberty Association. The conference was organized by the Seventh-day Adventist Church and drew the top scholars and activists in the religious liberty world, with attendees hailing from China to Nigeria to Jamaica. As the sole Muslim speaker among an extensive speaker lineup, it was my job to do as I always do in these spaces: speak up about the dire constitutional threats facing American Muslims.

The audience responded with thoughtful enthusiasm. As Seventh-day Adventists, religious liberty is a central tenet of their faith and a top priority for the church. The international conference itself was an impressive reflection of the church's prioritization of religious liberty and its dedication to upholding that right for all Americans.

Those contributions have come at multiple levels, not the least of which is through the spiritual dedication of one of its members: Adell Sherbert. When Sherbert stood by her convictions in the landmark Supreme Court case *Sherbert v. Verner* (1963), she ended up giving American religious liberty law its biggest asset: the strict scrutiny test (or as it used to be known, the Sherbert Test).

As a Seventh-day Adventist, Sherbert believed that Saturday was a required day of rest (Saturday is the seventh day, or the Sabbath). For five days a week, Sherbert worked at a textile mill—until her boss told her she would have to work Saturdays, too, and then fired her because she refused on religious grounds. In her search for alternative employment, she faced the same request time and again: to work on her Sabbath. Sherbert had no choice but to decline.

Unable to find employment, Sherbert applied for unemployment compensation but the state denied her the benefits. The state permitted individuals to refuse employment for "good cause" but refusing to work on Saturdays for religious reasons did not make the cut. The government refused to help Sherbert merely because she chose to live out her faith.

Facing defeat after defeat in the lower courts, in 1963, her case finally made it to the US Supreme Court. Her claim was heard under the Free Exercise Clause of the First Amendment: "Congress shall make no law respecting an establishment of religion, or *prohibiting the free exercise thereof.*" In *Sherbert v. Verner*, the court ruled that disqualifying Sherbert from unemployment compensation because she refused work on religious grounds violated her rights under the Free Exercise Clause.

To reach its conclusion, the court used the strict scrutiny test, which asks the following series of questions: Did the state impose a "substantial burden" on Sherbert's free exercise of religion? The court said yes. The state's eligibility rules forced her to choose between following her religion and giving up her unemployment benefits, on the one hand, or abandoning her religious belief so that she could accept work, on the other hand. When the government forces religious believers to make these kinds of choices, it categorically places a burden on their free exercise. Think about it from a free speech perspective: If the government denies certain benefits to people because they engage in a particular form of speech, it's essentially penalizing them for engaging in that speech.

Having satisfied this first inquiry, the Court then asked, did the government have a really, really important (or "compelling") interest that required it to impose this choice on Sherbert? The Court answered in the negative. The state claimed that it was worried about people "feigning religious objections to Saturday work" that would not only deplete the unemployment compensation fund but also deprive employers of Saturday workers. But the state failed to offer evidence that its concerns were warranted. It's one thing to claim there is a compelling concern something will happen and wholly another thing to show that your concern is based on facts.

The court also said, assuming the state had offered such evidence, the state would then have to prove that there was no better way to protect its interests. This part of the strict scrutiny test is called the least restrictive means. The Court said if there's a way to do what the government needs to do without violating people's constitutional rights, that's the route the government has to take. And, the Court made clear that protecting freedom in this way does not "establish" the Seventh-day Adventist religion—it doesn't somehow make the church the official religion of the state or favor it above other religions. It simply reflects the government's decision to be neutral "in the face of religious differences."

The requirements of the strict scrutiny test are obviously rigid. There's even a myth that it is "strict in theory but fatal in fact"— that is, that it is near impossible for the government to satisfy the standard. That fact is, though, that it functions less as a deadly force and more as a context-specific tool that requires evidence and not just empty assertions, precision and not sloppiness. It's a tough test, but our freedom requires it.

Importantly, this context-specific analysis means that a court's ruling applies only to the specific fact scenario before it. In *Sherbert*, the Supreme Court made clear that its ruling does not "declare the existence of a constitutional right to unemployment benefits on the part of all persons whose religious convictions are the cause of their unemployment." Its ruling was simply that South Carolina, where Sherbert lived, "may not constitutionally apply the eligibility provisions" of its unemployment benefits program, "so as to constrain a worker to abandon his religious convictions respecting the day of rest."

Strict scrutiny was the law of the land until 1990, when, ironically, Justice Antonin Scalia, known as a conservative stalwart of the court, stripped Free Exercise Clause protections and reduced the standard from strict to something far less rigorous. In the 1990 case, *Employment Division v. Smith*, two members of the Native American Church, Alfred Smith and Galen Black, ingested peyote during their religious rituals. Peyote, however, was an illegal substance under Oregon law. For this, Smith and Black were fired from their positions as counselors at a drug rehabilitation center and were barred from receiving unemployment benefits because of their workplace "misconduct."

Interestingly, the center had hired Smith precisely because he had expertise in Native American spiritual traditions and was able to offer culturally relevant care to the center's Native clients. While Smith had no interest in bringing ceremonial peyote use to his clients (he and Black used peyote outside of work as part of their religious observance), medical studies do show that "ceremonial use of peyote . . . is a powerful boost to the chances a Native patient will recover from addiction."

The Supreme Court reviewed the case and determined that the religious freedom of the men did not immunize them from the consequences of criminal law. Since the law against peyote use applied to everyone equally, the court said there was nothing unconstitutional about the statute limiting Smith and Black's religious expression.

What happened to the Sherbert Test? The court in a six to three decision said it was too broad. When it comes to laws that are religiously neutral (they do not discriminate against religion generally or a religion in particular) and are generally applicable (they apply in the same way to all people), then the government did not have to satisfy the strict scrutiny standard. (For laws that do discriminate—such as the law in *Lukumi*, or laws that might appear neutral but are applied so as to discriminate against religion—strict scrutiny still applies.) In cases with neutral, generally applicable laws, the government has to meet a far more diluted standard called rational basis.

Under this standard, the government gets a lot more deference. Courts will uphold a law as long as the government has a rational reason for it—the government doesn't have to show a compelling justification, simply a legitimate one. In *Smith*, the government had a rational basis for outlawing peyote use, so the Supreme Court held that the Free Exercise Clause does not carve out an exception for the Native Americans who used it for religious reasons.

Most people who follow religious liberty law thought the court's decision was a mistake. Without strict scrutiny, advocates feared that religious believers, especially minority believers, would be crushed. The concern was wholly bipartisan; religious and public policy groups across the political spectrum were aghast at the ruling. A flurry of lobbying culminated in the 1993 Religious Freedom Restoration Act (RFRA), introduced at the federal level by New York congressman, Chuck Schumer. The purpose of the bill was to reassert the power of the First Amendment's Free Exercise Clause after *Smith* watered it down. RFRA was Congress's way of bringing back the legal standard of strict scrutiny.

The federal RFRA and the RFRAs or RFRA-like protections that states have enacted over the years have been paramount in protecting religious minorities. Some states without RFRAs read the strict scrutiny standard into their state constitutional protections for religious liberty. To understand the significance of RFRA, consider this: If there's a law that burdens a person's religious practice, that person might ask that the law make an exception for his or her practice. Without RFRA, religious believers cannot go to the courts for this protection. Instead, they have to rely on their legislature to carve out an accommodation in a new law. Dominant religious groups with lots of political capital will win in that process—but small, minority religious groups with little or no political capital are bound to lose. When Scalia watered down the strict scrutiny standard in *Smith*, he understood the risk, calling it an "unavoidable consequence of democratic government." The alternative, in his view, was "a system in which each conscience is a law unto itself or in which judges weigh the social importance of . . . laws against . . . religious beliefs." This, Scalia said, was tantamount to "courting anarchy."

But RFRA has not resulted in anarchy. Instead it has fostered a context-specific inquiry and protected diverse religious practices that a majority-white, majority-Christian legislature would have a hard time even understanding. How would animal sacrifice fair under a RFRA-free regime? Or a Native American schoolboy who violated the school dress code when he grew his hair for religious reasons? Or a Jehovah's Witness who refused to pledge allegiance to the US Constitution because her faith said allegiance belongs to God alone? And what would America be without these diverse minorities free and able to live out their faith? RFRA protected all of these religious believers—and I'll show you how below.

The practices of religious minorities can seem foreign, and at times can be uncomfortable for many Americans. Without the law to protect them, religious believers would be subject to the whims of the majority culture; religious practices that conform to this culture would be protected more often than practices that don't. Anything different or strange would be discarded. Perhaps nothing encapsulates this better than the Santerian animal sacrifice ritual.

Imagine the following scene: A group of men and women, their hats, shirts, skirts, bandannas, socks and shoes all white, carry a small, black-and-white goat into a dimly lit room and place it on a white tiled floor. One of the women steps out from the group to present the goat to the priest-initiate, Virginia Rosario-Nevarez, who is wearing a yellow satin robe over her long skirt, a crown adorning her shaved and painted head. Nevarez leans toward the goat, cupping its head in her hands as she whispers into its ear. After she is done imparting her message, the goat is swiftly picked up and handed to a broad-shouldered man standing at the periphery of the shrine. He holds the goat firmly as the high priest, the Babalawo, takes a sharp knife, pinches the skin on the goat's neck and starts to cut—first through its fur, then as the priest begins to sing a Yoruban song, he inserts the knife into the goat's neck.

Beneath the goat is a group of orishas, or spirits that represent Olodumare, the supreme deity. Their presence is marked with little axes and spears and small pots holding shells. As the Babalawo cuts into the goat's neck, the blood drips down his blade into the containers below to feed the orishas. The men and women dressed in white begin to sing as the orishas are fed. Soon, the Babalawo rests the goat on the floor, swiftly severing its head and shaking its body over the orishas. With the goat sacrifice complete, the high priest moves on to repeat the ceremony with another thirty-nine animals, including roosters, pigeons, and another goat.

This is the Santerian priest initiation ceremony that, on September 4, 2004, Jose Merced was holding in his home shrine. A neighbor called the police, who arrived at Merced's house in the middle of the ceremony to stop Merced from proceeding. The police officers informed Merced that if he planned on killing any animals on the premises, he had to obtain a permit. But when Merced later went to the Euless, Texas, permits office, he was told that no permit existed for animal sacrifices; the practice was strictly prohibited, even if Merced complied with disposal and health standards, which he was more than willing to do. Merced stopped performing the sacrifices. Having to forego animal sacrifice meant, however, that he would no longer be able to initiate aspiring priests.

In December 2006, Merced filed a complaint against the city of Euless alleging a violation of his religious liberty. But the court couldn't see how Euless was burdening Merced's religious exercise. As Merced's lawyer explained to the *Dallas Observer*, the judge could not rule in favor of a religion that was so unlike his own religion: "I think what happened in Euless is that we have people who don't understand what the Santeros are up to . . . It's not that they're against dogma; it's just that this is the wrong dogma."

Fortunately, when Merced appealed his case, the appellate court sided unanimously with Merced. The court said that because Euless' ordinances prevented Merced from performing ceremonies critical to his faith, the law put a substantial burden on his religious exercise. And even though the government argued it had two compelling reasons for prohibiting the ceremony (public health and animal treatment), the court noted that Merced had conducted the ceremony for 16 years without causing any of the problems the government was worried about. The government, in other words, did not show that its concerns were rooted in evidence. (There was no evidence the animals were kept in unsanitary conditions, treated badly, disposed of in an illegal manner, or caused any harm greater than is normal in every other, legal animal slaughter.) And finally, the government also failed to show that there weren't other ways to serve its purported concerns about public health and animal treatment without restricting Merced's religious practice.

This was the strict scrutiny standard in action, made possible by the Texas RFRA. It enabled the court to protect precisely the type of religious practice that is most in need of protection: the type against which the social majority is more likely to discriminate.

It did the same for a five-year-old Native American boy who was told by his public-school district that school policy forbade boys from having long hair. The boy could not cut his hair in violation of his religious beliefs, but the school district refused to make any exceptions to its policy, even though girls were allowed to have long hair. The school district told the court that the boy had to violate his religious beliefs because he had "twice been mistaken for a girl while at school." It was obvious to the court that the school had no good reason for violating the boy's religious exercise, and the Texas RFRA gave the court the tools it needed to protect him.

RFRA also protected a Jehovah's Witness from having to pledge allegiance to the US Constitution in violation of her belief that she should only pledge allegiance to God. In 1992, Tenella Bridges, a Jehovah's Witness, applied to be a bookstore cashier at the State Center Community College District. The employment application form required her to affirm that she would be willing to pledge allegiance to the US Constitution. When she challenged the requirement, the court applied RFRA retroactively to prevent the employer from requiring prospective employees to pledge allegiance to the US Constitution.

The law also came to the rescue for two Sikh children who were not allowed to wear their *kirpans* to school. *The kirpan*, a three- to nine-inch dagger with a curved edge, is one of five Sikh Articles of Faith. It obligates a Sikh to generosity and service to humanity, serving as a constant reminder to its bearer of his or her obligation to protect and serve the weak. In *Cheema v. Thompson*, the Sikh children were religiously required to wear their *kirpan* at all times, but the California Penal Code prohibited carrying knives longer than two-and-a-half inches on school grounds. The school forced the students to choose between school expulsion and criminal prosecution and the violation of their religious convictions. While the school's concern was, of course, understandable, the court said RFRA required the school to be more careful in its prohibition and to find a solution that protects religious exercise. A wholesale ban on weapons did not strike the right balance, especially since there was no evidence that the school district had even considered other ways to protect both safety and the Sikh students' religious liberty. With some accommodations for the school's concerns, such as requiring that the blade be dulled, no more than three and a half inches, sewn tightly to the sheath, and worn underneath their clothing, the court was able to strike the right balance.

RFRA was also used in 2006 to help União do Vegetal (UDV), the New Mexican branch of a Brazilian religious group that uses hoasca, a hallucinogenic tea, in its religious rituals. Hoasca is a Schedule I substance prohibited by the Controlled Substances Act. When UDV had drums of the tea shipped to the United States, it was seized upon arrival. In *Gonzales v. O Centro Espírita Beneficente União do Vegetal*, the US Supreme Court used the federal RFRA to hold that there was no compelling government interest in stopping members of the UDV from using hoasca for the limited purpose of their religious ritual. The government definitely had a compelling interest in stopping hoasca use in other contexts, just not in this particular one, the court said.

This focus on the person bringing the claim was a new development. The court interpreted RFRA more robustly than it had ever been interpreted before. It said that RFRA requires the government to prove it had a compelling interest in stopping the particular religious claimant before it from violating its law. Or, in the court's language, the government must show that its interest is compelling when its law is applied "to the person." This context-specific analysis of religious claims shores up RFRA's protection of religious practices that may be strange, unfamiliar, and even objectionable to the average American.

Sisk and Heise, writing in 2012, six years after the *O Centro* decision, thought that *O Centro* could be a solution to anti-Muslim bias in judicial decision-making. The case emphasizes the need to look more closely at each individual religious liberty claim and determine whether strict scrutiny really justifies the government's actions in the very specific context of that claim. This social-psychological process of "individuation," Sisk and Heise argue, "loosen[s] the grip of stereotypes." The government can no longer describe its interest in broad terms—the war on drugs, or national security and safety—without the court stepping in to parse the rationale. And when the judge engages in that parsing process, he or she "is encouraged to abandon stereotypical generalizations and engage in a differentiated and individualized analysis of each claim."

And beyond the individual claim is the individual herself. *O Centro* says judges have to look at that person as an individual, which means the claimant is less likely to be cast off as just "one of them"—just another scary or threatening Muslim. This gives judges the opening they need to get to know the claimant a bit better than the stereotype: "the judge should learn about each claimant's faith perspective, objectively and rigorously but also sympathetically, thereby substituting new information and understanding for implicit beliefs."

This was Sisk and Heise's hypothesis and their hope for fairer treatment of Muslim litigants. In the seven years since their writing, *O Centro* has borne some fruit—the Court in *Holt v. Hobbs* relied on *O Centro* to hold in favor of the Muslim prisoner. More research is needed to understand the fuller effect of *O Centro*, but one thing is for sure: judges have potent tools to set things right.

What are those tools? To recap: In cases where the government has placed a substantial burden on someone's religious exercise, RFRA requires judges to apply strict scrutiny. In a narrower set of cases, judges use strict scrutiny under the Free Exercise Clause—for example, cases where the government targets religion for disfavored treatment or applies its otherwise-neutral-seeming laws selectively to disfavor religious people. As for the Establishment Clause, for this book the most relevant point is that it prohibits the government from favoring or disfavoring one particular religion over others or preferring one religious interpretation over another—chapter 6 looks at how the government does that with different interpretations of Islam.

The next chapter examines one other potent tool, the Religious Land Use and Institutionalized Persons Act (RLUIPA). Unfortunately, the growing anti-Muslim opposition is agitating to take away precisely these protections for American Muslims.

CHAPTER 4

"YOU HAVE TO DEAL WITH THE MOSQUES."

It was a typically breezy Miami spring day in 2004. A crowd gathered around my father, Tasnim Uddin, the president and co-founder of the Islamic center and mosque in Kendall, Florida (located fourteen miles outside of Miami proper). Smiling widely, he lifted a shovel and, after a pause for dramatic effect, plunged it into the ground. The crowd cheered joyfully. "Yay!" squealed a little girl standing to my left. Her father smiled in response and swooped her up onto his shoulders. This was the groundbreaking for the new mosque these people had been fundraising for and planning for years. Many of them immigrants to the US, they saw again in that moment the fulfillment of America's vow to protect them and give them a place to worship freely.

After the cheers died down, the men, women, and children gathered in a semicircle around my father as he led them in prayer. Like my father, some wore hard hats, others wore headscarves, and still others wore hard hats on top of their headscarves. Each of them had their palms open and facing upward as they recited in unison, "In the name of God, the Most Beneficent, the Most Merciful."

It was a diverse bunch, ranging from Arab-Americans like Bilal Karakira and his wife Susan, longtime teachers at the Sunday school, to South Asian Americans like my father, and African Americans like the inimitable Linda Raheem, always a strong presence on the Islamic center's board of directors. Standing alongside the city and county officials who had come for the celebration, were Dr. Mohammad Farouk, Mohammad Ibrahimuddin, and Nour Abdullah. These handful of individuals were the founders of the Islamic center. They had cultivated this community of Muslims in South Florida for over a decade. The mosque component of the center started out in a rented apartment, then, as the congregation grew, in a small section of a strip mall. The school component started with Sunday school in rented classrooms— first at South Miami Middle School, and then at Florida International University. When these spaces inevitably proved too small, the Islamic center moved to purchase land of its own, with separate facilities for the school and for the mosque.

I was a child throughout much of this period, but it's clearly marked in my memories because of my father's excitement as he worked on all of the different puzzle pieces. In many ways, the story of Miami's Muslim community reflects the story of who my father (*Abu*) was. Every Sunday morning, he would be moving about in a flurry, getting his books together, and leaving extra early to prepare his classroom before his students arrived. A religiously learned man, he was one of the Islamic center's most respected teachers and sharing his knowledge with others was his life's joy.

But teacher was just one of many of his titles. Mirsad Krijestorac, a professor of public affairs at Florida International University, calls my father one of the "early Muslim pioneers" of the South Florida Muslim community. It was in Abu's apartment where the first-ever South Florida *tarawih* (night time congregational prayers during Ramadan) took place, made possible by the fact that both my father and his roommate at the time had the entire Qur'an committed to memory (ideally, during the thirty days of Ramadan, the prayer leader should complete a full recitation of the Qur'an from memory). It also helped that my father had an open-door policy, creating in his tiny home a communal space for others to meet and socialize.

At that time in the 1970s, my father had recently graduated from Carnegie-Mellon University with a civil engineering degree. He chose Miami as the place to settle not just because of its verdancy and abun- dant sunshine, but also because it was relatively undeveloped at the time. In the decades that followed, my father's insignia would become etched into Miami's most important structures. He would structurally remodel public schools, design the seaport where the cruise ships dock, and work on affordable housing. His biggest project, though, was the Miami International Airport: Terminal H with its white tiles specked with tiny, shimmering dots and images of shells, meant to evoke Miami's famous beaches. The helipad that you can gaze at from the American Airlines terminal. The rainbow glass-paneled walkway filtering the Miami sunshine in a multitude of colors. In the days before 9/11, we'd be able to saunter through the security with a simple flash of his badge when he took me to tour the airport. This was his home; Miami was *his* city.

In constructing Miami, he wanted so badly to add to its religious landscape, too. The Islamic center bears those indelible signs of his passion. Not just the wide-open prayer space or the dome or the fine construction—all designed and managed carefully by my father—but, quite simply, in the very fact of its existence. Abu was the one who mastered the herculean task, as his colleagues called it, of gathering all of the permits and county approvals. He was the one who pushed his team at the Islamic center to fundraise with passion—and then, when he was satisfied with their efforts, cover what remained to reach their fundraising goal. Hundreds of thousands of dollars and not once did he take credit or seek the limelight. "I have never seen a more humble person than your father," Dr. Farouk told me. "He never bragged about his wealth or knowledge or skills, connections, or contributions. He insisted on working behind the scenes." Miamians weren't the only beneficiaries of his friendship. Every Islamic center in South Florida came to him for help. "They were a little envious of us that we had Tasnim," Dr. Farouk chuckled as he remembered.

But what I loved most about my father's contributions was that it wasn't just about the buildings. It was about the people. Abu reflected his gratitude for everything God had given him by helping dozens of others make Miami their home. He gave interest-free loans to friends and acquaintances who wanted to buy homes but couldn't afford a mortgage. He helped new and prospective arrivals in Miami fill out their immigration paperwork, pay for college, get jobs, and find places to live. He contributed to local, state, and federal political campaigns and hosted fundraising events for the candidates. And he didn't limit his support to people of a particular religion or ethnicity.

Abu did this because of his unshakeable belief in God and in Islamic principles of charity. In the Qur'an, God asks, "Who is it that would loan God a goodly loan so He may multiply it for him many times over?" (2:245) What made my father's contributions to his city and his community a "goodly loan" is because it contributed to a good cause: the cultivation of the next generation. My father's charity was his investment in the promise of America.

He didn't live to witness that promise coming undone.

In 2009, the Islamic center was sprayed with fifty-one bullets. The bullets shattered the windows and shot "the mosque's golden dome . . . to pieces." Six months later, two teens attacked the building in the middle of the night, smashing two windows with an iron rod and slashing the tires of a vehicle parked in the mosque parking lot. One of the teens told police that "he'd been planning the vandalism for months" and that "he believes all Muslims are terrorists."

The members of the Islamic center were frightened by these attacks, but their first inclination was to build bridges. Because the teens lived in the nearby neighborhood, the mosque-goers decided to canvass the neighborhood. They knocked on doors, introduced themselves, extended a hand of friendship.

And their efforts, at least in this case, paid off. The teens paid for their crimes by completing community service hours, and one of them chose to do his hours at the mosque. Naveed Anjum, now the president of the center, recalls how the young man became humbled throughout the process. On the day students graduated from the Islamic school, the teen joined in the celebration and his mother even took the mike to express her sincere gratitude for the mosque's attitude of forgiveness and reconciliation. "It was a beautiful moment," Anjum reminisced, "A new chapter."

But the peace didn't last long, and Eid became a special target. The mosque-goers learned to become accustomed to local youth blasting music during the annual Eid prayers. Two days before the Eid al-Adha holiday in September 2015, things started to get much more serious.

Two worshippers arrived that day for the early morning prayers and found a book bag sitting by the front gate. Thinking the bag belonged to one of the students of the Islamic school, they fetched it and brought it into the school. When the school principal opened the bag to find it filled with a chisel, hammer, batteries, wire cutters, and books on the terrorist group, ISIS, he immediately informed Anjum, who in turn called the police.

The police dispatched the bomb squad, who assessed the bag's contents. Confident the bag did not contain a bomb, they scoured the property and found other puzzling totems scattered throughout. The large Islamic center sign in front of the building was defaced with graffiti, and perched on top of the sign was a small skull. Nestled at the foot of the sign were baby bottles. The gate at a second entrance to the property was also defaced, with a cluster of wire cutters and chisels carefully placed by nearby.

Anjum recalls his confusion at this seemingly absurd makeup of items, but the police quickly had a theory of what the perpetrator was trying to communicate: "The books on ISIS are his way of calling you all terrorists," the police told Anjum, "He's also saying that he's watching you. And the milk bottles indicate that he knows children come to this property." The police's theory was that the perpetrator was targeting the children; he wanted to hurt them in order to exact revenge for what ISIS was doing overseas.

One of the teen members of the mosque deciphered the message similarly. Thirteen-year-old Iyad Sheikh, who first found the items, told reporters, "I got really scared cause skulls like death and milk is like for kids, babies, so they're threatening the youth of this community." The Islamic center's leadership put on a confident front, but the threat to their children frightened them. "It doesn't scare me, but we have children here. We have children, a full-time school," said Bilal Karakira.

Two days later, during the Eid al-Adha prayer service, the worshippers discovered more items planted in various spots on the property. "A hammer, chisel, a book signed by Hillary Clinton and bouquets of flowers" were "stacked on a sign outside the suburban mosque. A vandal had also sprayed green paint and splashed Ensure, a nutritional supplement, on a gate." And inside the mosque they found "a wooden cross, a laptop, a navy blue sport coat emblazoned with stars and sunglasses depicting the American flag." The next day, they again found signs of tampering—a sign outside the Islamic center had been pulled down.

And then came the most disturbing event in the string of incidents. On the first Sunday when Sunday school was back in session, parents were dropping their children off at the school when a car came careening into the parking lot, maneuvering erratically at what Anjum estimated was fifty miles an hour, and almost ran over one of the kids. Some of the mosque-goers followed the driver off the property, only to see him pull down his pants and expose his buttocks. The man was eventually arrested but never faced prison time because he was deemed mentally ill.

The Islamic center's experience is frightening, but it is not unique among Muslim institutions in the United States. In the broad contours of its story—and the story of my father and the burgeoning community he so carefully nurtured—I see reflections of what so many other Muslim communities in America have faced and continue to face. In each case, I see hopeful beginnings. Tiny groups of Muslims hoping to live out the American dream and, in turn, contribute positively to their new home. I see that group start to gradually grow as families get bigger and more Muslims move to town. I see them facing the inevitable need to find larger and larger spaces for communal worship, and to eventually build a place of their own. And I see what happens next.

In Florida alone, mosques and mosque leaders have faced bomb threats, death threats, arson, and vandalism. In 2018, a mosque in Pembroke Pines received bomb threats. In 2017, authorities in Jacksonville arrested a man they said was planning on shooting people at a local mosque; the man was charged with possession of an unregistered silencer. That same year, a man intentionally crashed his truck into the gate of the Islamic Society of Tampa, and another man in Pompano Beach called the local mosque to threaten them. "Your mosque is going to be blown the (expletive) up tonight. We are going to kill all of you and ISIS in America."

In July 2016, worshippers at the Islamic Center of Fort Pierce were physically harassed; one attacker even beat up and attempted to rob one of the worshippers. Two months later, the center was set on fire by arsonists. In June 2016, a woman entered the mosque in Sunrise, Florida, with a cell phone, exposed battery, and an unknown object wrapped in a brown paper bag and warned the worshippers that they were going to die. In 2010, the Islamic Center of Northeast Florida in Jacksonville was firebombed.

This is just a snapshot of hate incidents in Florida. Elsewhere in America, arson has become a common intimidation tactic. In 2011, a mosque in Wichita, Kansas, suffered more than $100,000 in damages because of an arson attack. In 2012, portions of mosques in Joplin, Wisconsin, and Toledo, Ohio, were set on fire. In 2016 the same Joplin mosque had its roof burned down, and then a month later, the entire mosque was burned down. In 2017, fires raged at five mosques, burning down properties in places like Ypsilanti, Michigan; Victoria, Texas; and Bellevue, Washington.

Again, this is merely a snapshot. The full list of hate incidents is long and growing; the phenomenon constitutes nothing less than a nationwide movement against mosques. It's a movement that commenced in full force just a few years after my father's death, in the aftermath of the Park 51 debacle in New York City.

"PARK51 AND THE SHAME OF AMERICAN SKITTISHNESS"
W.W., *The Economist*

"It's Official: Ground Zero Mosque Defeated!" read Pamela Geller's gleeful headline in the conservative online magazine, *Breitbart*, when news sources started reporting that the developer behind the Park 51 project, Sharif El-Gamal, had scrapped his initial plans and replaced them with a luxury condominium proposal. Geller proclaimed, "The infamous Ground Zero Mosque project is officially dead. We won. We the People." The "People" had succeeded in their effort to "halt and roll back the advance of Islamic law and Islamic supremacism in America." Geller gloated: "My organization, the American Freedom Defense Initiative (AFDI) hosted rallies . . . in lower Manhattan against the mosque. Both were attended by tens of thousands of people and featured speeches" by prominent anti-Muslim activists, journalists, and talk show hosts. Even former ambassador John Bolton, who currently serves as President Trump's national security advisor, attended Geller's rallies.

But Park 51's mission was nothing like what Geller claimed. It was going to be a sixteen-story interfaith community center, a type of "Muslim YMCA" with a swimming pool, basketball court, library, auditorium, restaurant, catering school, and childcare facilities. It would have been open to people of all faiths, as would have the area designated as prayer space. The wider ecumenical purpose of its mission would be evident from its proposed design, which did not reflect

Muslim religious elements and did not include a "minaret, or room for ablutions, or other essential features of a mosque." Altogether, it was a genuine attempt to communicate "a bold statement that Islam was constructive, not destructive." Through Park 51, "Muslims would mount a proactive response to the destructive agendas of hatred and terror."

But the project's location proved to be its undoing. The developers planned to use an abandoned Burlington Coat Factory building in Lower Manhattan, located two blocks north of the site where the World Trade Center towers fell on September 11, 2001. The proximity to the site of the 9/11 attacks gave Geller the opening she needed to distort the project into something sinister. She quickly labeled it the "Ground Zero mosque," concocted a theory that it represented the threat of Muslim domination, and organized an extensive and enduring campaign against it. In the end, her campaign worked.

Americans didn't always see it her way. The media coverage at the start was, by any account, pleasant. On December 8, 2009, the *New York Times* published a lengthy article on the project and its ambitious goals. In the article, the mosque leader, Imam Feisal Abdul Rauf, described the project as a counter to everything 9/11 stood for: "We want to push back against the extremists." Diverse religious leaders and city officials who had previously worked with Rauf pointed to his lifelong career of "preaching tolerance and interfaith understanding." He was the man for the job, they said, and they supported him in this "delicate project."

Laura Ingraham on Fox News also found the project admirable. She hosted Daisy Khan, Rauf's wife and project partner, on her show and told her she liked "what you're trying to do." After Ingraham's interview, no other media source reported on Park 51 for almost six months.

Then, on May 6, 2010, the New York City community board committee approved the project twenty-nine to one, with ten abstentions.

The Associated Press reported on the approval and interviewed relatives of 9/11 victims, who expressed a range of opinions on the project. But it was the *New York Post*'s article that gave Geller her opening; the *Post* called Park 51 the "'WTC' Mosque." On the same day, Geller published a blog post on her site, "Monster Mosque Pushes Ahead in Shadow of World Trade Center Islamic Death and Destruction," and laid out her theory that Park 51 was an attempt by Muslims to takeover America.

In the days that followed, Geller's other group, Stop the Islamization of America (SIOA), launched its campaign, "Campaign Offensive: Stop the 911 Mosque!" Geller encouraged her readers to submit complaints about the project and indeed, the community board later reported receiving "hundreds and hundreds" of calls and e-mails.

On May 13, *New York Post* columnist, Andrea Peyser, wrote a piece, "Mosque Madness at Ground Zero," making the *Post* the first newspaper to use Geller's negative framing of Park 51. Given the *Post*'s wide readership among conservative thought leaders, it wasn't long before mainstream conservative media started pushing the same theory. Sean Hannity interviewed Geller on his talk show, Fox News made it a regular topic, the *Post* took things further by dedicating numerous reporters to around-the-clock coverage of Park 51. The *Washington Examiner* and *Business Daily* also jumped on the bandwagon, depicting Park 51 as an affront to the 9/11 victims. Outside conservative media, other news channels featured diverse views of the Park 51 project and whether or not it was insulting or inappropriate.

And with the media coverage came the political attention. In the weeks following Peyser's initial column, former New York City Mayor Rudy Giuliani, Alaska Governor Sarah Palin, Congressman Peter King, former Speaker of the House Newt Gingrich, and Minnesota Governor Tim Pawlenty all described Park 51 as a celebration of the 9/11 perpetrators. In Gingrich's words: "Nazis don't have the right to put up a sign next to the Holocaust Museum in Washington.

We would never accept the Japanese putting up a site next to Pearl Harbor. There's no reason for us to accept a mosque next to the World Trade Center."

Geller used this nationwide attention to organize her first anti-Park 51 protest on June 7, 2010. By August 22, the mosque hysteria was out of control as supporters and opponents physically clashed with each other. On September 11, the ninth anniversary of the 9/11 attacks, mosque opponents burned copies of the Qur'an on the streets of New York City.

Through it all, the small, well-meaning team behind Park 51 faced an onslaught of media attention and personal attacks. Oz Sultan, the project's social media brain and head of public relations, recounted for me the way he was suddenly and involuntarily thrust into the national media spotlight and made to represent all Muslims in America. "If anything happened at any other mosque in the country, the media required me and my team to comment on it." And they were, at all times, under a powerful microscope with the media ready to exploit any weakness or putative fault. "We had to deal with what no one else had to deal with."

Throughout the ten-month ordeal, Sultan had three police chiefs on speed dial and would often need a SWAT team to clear the mobs of protestors crowding the Park 51 premises. "This was Charlottesville on a daily basis," he said, referring to the 2017 riots that took place around the Unite the Right white supremacist rally in Charlottesville, Virginia. "On the weekdays, we faced anywhere between 5–50 protestors. On the weekends, we saw people bussed in from all over the country to make *sure* we knew that Park 51 was not wanted."

He recalled carrying a knife with him for protection, and the police escorts who would accompany him on many days. He credits them for saving his life. "Do you understand?! This was like a regular thing for like months," he said with a chuckle because of how absurd the whole ordeal became. "For God's sake, there was a protestor who would

ride around the building on a decommissioned ICBM (an interconti-
nental ballistic missile) yelling into a megaphone, 'Go back to Islam!'"

Even with his life in peril, though, Sultan was most troubled by the
way Park 51 was consistently depicted as a foreign institution. In his
view, Park 51 was imbued by America through and through. We are
"a people who are thrust upon one another in this new nation, formed
from all of us . . . from all these different places," he told me. There
could be nothing more American than this project, this envisioned
space where people of every faith would come to swim and play basketball and even worship together. It encapsulated all of the freedom
Sultan thought of when he thought of America.

But the fierce opposition he faced reflects just how fragile freedom
can be.

||||||||||||||||||||||||||||||||||||||||||||||||||||||||||||||||||||||||||||||||||||||||||||||||||||||||||||||||||||||||||||||||||||

"DOES A RELIGIOUS COMMUNITY
NEED ITS OWN BUILDING TO FLOURISH?"
Michelle Boorstein, *Washington Post*

||||||||||||||||||||||||||||||||||||||||||||||||||||||||||||||||||||||||||||||||||||||||||||||||||||||||||||||||||||||||||||||||||||

The Park 51 saga unleashed years of vicious attacks on mosques that
continue to this day. At the core of these disputes is one of the most central aspects of religious liberty, the right of religious believers to build,
expand, or own a building in which to engage in communal gathering.

In most religions, believers gather together to worship and share
their love for something or someone beyond. Many religions even give
specific instructions on where to worship such as the top of a mountain (Moses and other prophets), in forests (druids and Shinto), or
even facing a certain direction (Islam and early Christianity). Simply
worshiping on one's own isn't enough. People need to gather together
and follow specific rules to create unity—to feel that they belong to

something more than themselves—and they need a physical place for their gatherings.

But even though communal worship is clearly a part of religious exercise, government officials aren't always very good about protecting it. The decision-makers involved in zoning processes usually care little for the First Amendment rights at stake. There are multiple reasons for this hostility. One is, of course, overt religious discrimination. The Park 51 saga exemplifies this hostility. Another reason is "NIMBY resistance—the classic land-use demand to build somewhere else, but Not In My Back Yard." Nearby residents will raise concerns about traffic, property value, aesthetics, and the effect on the environment. And a third reason is that houses of worship are tax-exempt and local officials do not want to lose tax revenue by permitting one in their jurisdiction. These factors, combined, make religious land use a particularly disfavored land use.

To make matters worse, the zoning approval process gives decision-makers wide discretion to make choices based on their own preferences. For example, they get to decide whether a church or mosque will be "consistent with the character of the neighborhood," or "consistent with the health, safety, and welfare of the community." Given these vague standards, local officials can easily disguise their religious hostility; instead of describing their objections in discriminatory terms, they can reject permits based on concerns about property values, traffic, parking, and noise.

To help address this problem, in 2000, Congress unanimously passed a statute, the Religious Land Use and Institutionalized Persons Act (RLUIPA). RLUIPA is meant to stop city officials from ruling against religious organizations simply because they don't want them around or don't value them the same way they do secular establishments. The act's Senate sponsors wrote that, "the right to assemble for worship is at the very core of the free exercise of religion. Churches and synagogues cannot function without a physical space adequate to their needs and consistent with their theological requirements." The statute was backed by a wide coalition of religious and civil groups representing tremendous religious and ideological diversity. Congressman Jerrold Nadler stated on the House floor, "Every religious group that I am aware of supports this bill. I am aware of no opposition from any religious or civil rights or civil liberties group." When President Bill Clinton signed RLUIPA into law on September 22, 2000, he said, "Religious liberty is a constitutional value of the highest order, and the Framers of the Constitution included protection for the free exercise of religion in the very first Amendment. This Act recognizes the importance the free exercise of religion plays in our democratic society."

RLUIPA was part of the same process that produced RFRA—Congress passed both in order to buttress religious liberty after the US Supreme Court weakened the protection in the *Smith* case. RLUIPA takes the stringent strict scrutiny standard of RFRA and applies it to religious land use (for example, constructing or expanding houses of worship or religious community centers) and religious exercise by prisoners and people in mental institutions ("institutionalized persons"). It takes constitutional principles based on the Free Exercise, Free Speech, and Equal Protection Clauses and translates them into a statute that can help enforce those principles.

There are five sections on land use protections. Section 2(a) has the strict scrutiny standard which, again, states that where a government regulation substantially burdens religious exercise, the government has to justify the law by showing that it had a compelling interest in limiting religious exercise and that there was no way for the government to serve that interest without violating rights. That is, the government absolutely had to limit religious exercise to get its job done.

Another section says that religious assemblies and institutions have to be treated the same way that secular assemblies and institutions are. The Free Exercise, Free Speech, and Equal Protection Clauses stand for the principle that the government cannot favor non-religion over religion and vice versa. RLUIPA's nondiscrimination section implements that principle. A subpart of that section emphasizes that the government also cannot discriminate between religions or religious denominations—for example, churches cannot be favored over mosques.

Consider, for example, the case of Rocky Mountain Christian Church, a nondenominational church and school that set out to expand its facilities in 2004. The church, based in Niwot, Colorado, applied for the necessary permits, but the Boulder County commissioners rejected its application even though they had permitted a secular school just a mile away to expand its facilities. Because the church had been treated unequally, it sued the county using RLUIPA and won.

Two other sections address scenarios where the government would want to unreasonably limit or completely exclude religious institutions from a particular area. For example, a case in Leon Valley, Texas, involved a city ordinance that created a new retail corridor designed to boost the city's tax revenues. The ordinance said non-religious assemblies like private clubs and movie theaters could locate in that retail corridor, but houses of worship were not permitted. The Elijah Group, a small Christian congregation, bought a former church building that wasn't suited for most other purposes but was located in the retail corridor. When the church applied for the necessary permits to move its operations to the new location, the city let the church move its daycare and administrative offices but said the congregation could not worship there. The Elijah Group used RLUIPA to sue the city and won.

RLUIPA's broad provisions, taken together, provide comprehensive protection for religious land use projects. In passing the statute, Congress reviewed a wide array of evidence on state and local violations of religious land use laws, including statistical and anecdotal evidence, and detected a strong pattern of discrimination. The discrimination, both overt and subtle, for the most part involved "new, small, or unfamiliar churches." A House report stated, "the motive is not always easily discernible, but the result is a consistent, widespread pattern of political and governmental resistance to a core feature of religious exercise: the ability to assemble for worship." Again, what made this discrimination possible were the vague and inconsistent standards of zoning processes, leading to highly subjective decision-making. Land use regulators had complete discretion to reject or approve land use permits and otherwise implement zoning laws to their liking.

RLUIPA was passed less than a year before the 9/11 attacks. So when Congress was reviewing all of the evidence, Islam wasn't really on their radar. Even the anecdotal evidence considered only two mosque cases. But 9/11 changed all that. In RLUIPA's first ten years, 14 percent of RLUIPA investigations conducted by the Department of Justice (DOJ) involved Muslim institutions.

Far more significant than 9/11 was the Park 51 controversy. In the period between 2010 and 2016, 38 percent of all DOJ RLUIPA investigations involved a mosque—an especially startling statistic if one considers that Muslims make up only an estimated 1.1 percent of the American population. Park 51 catapulted mosque construction to national and international headlines. Suddenly, the indisputable right to religious land use—a right around which Americans of different political and religious affiliations once united—became deeply politicized. One law professor noted: "Would RLUIPA be adopted in the current political environment and specifically in light of the Manhattan mosque controversy? I do not think so."

The national discourse on Park 51 was centered on the idea that, while Muslims may have the right to build a house of worship, it is not right for them to do so near the "hallowed ground" of the 9/11 attacks because the terrorists were motivated by a virulent strain of Islam. To build a Muslim center there would be an insult to the victims of that horrific day.

Then-president Obama echoed the sentiment. At the 2010 White House *iftar*, or fast-breaking dinner, during the Muslim holy month of Ramadan, Obama delivered a statement in support of Park 51, only to partially retract it the next morning: "I was not commenting, and I will not comment, on the wisdom of making the decision to put a mosque there." The implied lack of "wisdom" connected all Muslims to the 9/11 attacks and sent the message that while American Muslims might technically have legal status as citizens, they were not entitled to exercise their rights in the same away as other Americans. Then-New York mayor Michael Bloomberg was one of the few who defended Muslims' legal rights unconditionally.

It also quickly became apparent that, for many Americans, the dispute wasn't just about "wisdom." As one commentator noted, "the argument that [Park 51] is offensively provocative [was] to a significant extent cover for less noble sentiments." An August 2010 poll by *The Economist* found that "more than half of those identifying themselves as Republican" thought Muslims didn't even have the *legal* right to build near Ground Zero. In September 2010, former Harvard professor Martin Peretz opined in the *New Republic*: "Frankly, Muslim life is cheap . . . there is hardly one who has raised a fuss about the routine and random bloodshed that defines their brotherhood. So, yes, I wonder whether I need honor these people and pretend that they are worthy of the privileges of the First Amendment which I have in my gut the sense that they will abuse."

In the months and years following the Park 51 controversy, Peretz's resistance to Muslims laying claim to religious liberty was echoed in cities across the United States.

||||||||||||||||||||||||||||||||||||||||||||||||||||||||||||||||||||||||||||||||||||||||||||||||||||||||||||||||||||

"THE FIGHT FOR THE RIGHT TO BE A MUSLIM IN AMERICA"
Andrew Rice, *The Guardian*

||||||||||||||||||||||||||||||||||||||||||||||||||||||||||||||||||||||||||||||||||||||||||||||||||||||||||||||||||||

"There's a special gift about America—you become part of the family. No one can say 'I am more American than you,' because we come from everywhere. America is always eager to increase its society, enrich its people. I love this idea about America.

"I've always believed there is something fundamentally right about America's Constitution. It stands for something that's right—for freedom and liberty."

These are Imam Ossama Bahloul's words, a man who saw his life's work burned, his mission protested and mocked in court, and his name nationally shamed. He was the imam of the Islamic Center of Murfreesboro in 2010. When the Park 51 fire stretched outside New York City, his was the first mosque to burn. You may recall from chapter 1 the charred construction site, the gasoline-doused equipment, the smell of burning oil and singed grass and the Muslims of Murfreesboro who were confused and frightened by the fire and by the sound of distant gunshots. The Rutherford County Sheriff's Office ruled the August 2018 incident arson.

Those flames revealed the frightening, violent underbelly of this all-American town. Driving into Murfreesboro the first week of July 2010, you would think you had driven into a Fourth of July episode of the *Andy Griffith Show*. The sights were predictably charming: local ice cream shops overflowing with children, American flags lining window boxes, townsfolk waving across streets as the crowds gathered for festivities in the historic town square. Many church signs also posted greetings, including one banner on a vacant lot just outside of town. "Welcome to the Town of Murfreesboro—the Future Home of the Islamic Center," it read.

Murfreesboro, like many towns in Tennessee and the south, was home to a friendly and religious people. Farmers' markets, sporting events, and school functions were well-attended by a populace eager to form a cohesive community. The town boasted more than one hundred churches and one mosque. Even after September 11, the predominantly Christian community embraced their Muslim members. There were stories of Muslims who were stopped on the street, to be assured of the town's support. "We are the same," one townsman told his neighbor. "We are going to treat you in the same way."

Because of this sense of community, Imam Bahloul and his family chose to live in Murfreesboro. He had found this welcoming nature typical of most Americans, and in fact, it was the reason he had decided to stay in the United States after having traveled to Texas years before on a one-year visa. Imam Bahloul had been studying at a theology school in Cairo, after his father convinced him a career as an imam was a beautiful service because he could "help people and be an advocate for what is good." Once in Texas, Imam Bahloul was surprised by the kindness and generosity of Americans. They loved diversity as much as he and his faith did. This, besides meeting a woman he would later marry, convinced the imam to accept an offer to permanently live with the Muslim community in Corpus Christi.

Eventually, he and his family were invited to Murfreesboro, to a community seeking religious leadership. Weighing the decision to move, the Imam and his wife considered the most important factors to be their children's education and their need for an active religious community. Murfreesboro offered it all, with respectable schools, dynamic and kind inhabitants, and even opportunities to pursue their family hobbies, including horseback riding and fishing. The Muslim community itself was small but thriving. In 2008, Imam Bahloul transplanted his family, restarting his backyard garden and a new life as a leader in the community of Murfreesboro.

At the time, the Muslims met for prayer in the room of a residential home, donated for the purpose by a local therapist. But as their population in town doubled between 2000 and 2008, they moved into a slightly larger office building. Members eventually filled the room, the sidewalks, and the parking lot—and had to kneel on rough pavement during prayer. Concerned mosque leaders began searching for a new home for their congregation. They prayed to find land near the middle of the city, for accessibility and also to benefit the entire town with the view of a beautiful new building.

In 2009, the search team located a fifteen-acre vacant lot just outside the town, but the Muslim community wondered how they could afford it. Imam Bahloul led a well-organized fundraiser, raising enough money to move plans forward on a 10,000 square foot mosque with a school, gym, swimming pool, and cemetery for the congregation's estimated 250 families. Some of their neighbors congratulated the community; everyone was thrilled. Imam Bahloul submitted the application for a building application permit, which was granted.

Then the town erupted. First, there was repeated vandalism. Then came the arson. And then the death threats and obscene messages. Muslim children were bullied in school. One man who challenged the bias of the local newspaper, *The Rutherford Reader*, had his home address published both in the paper and online, causing him to fear for his life.

The community was "completely blindsided." Murfreesboro had never been a place of animosity or conflict. Despite many neighbors assuring the Muslim community of their continued love and support, the town's deep trust and respect seemed to have gone up in the flames of the construction site. While fear in the Muslim community grew gradually, the construction stopped abruptly.

Meanwhile, in the county courthouse in Rutherford County, attorney Joe Brandon Jr. had put Islam on trial. Over the course of the six days of the proceedings, Brandon would pace back and forth in the courtroom, peppering witnesses with incendiary questions. "Isn't it true that in the Qur'an, Mohammad had a six-year-old wife that he had sex with . . . Is that your idea of what a religion is?" Brandon asked a county commissioner on the stand. "Sharia law includes instruction on how to beat your wife . . . How is Sharia law going to affect our society, our jobs and our freedoms?" Brandon asked County Mayor Ernest Burgess. "Do you believe in having sex with children?" he asked Commissioner Gary Farley. Judge Corlew stood by as Brandon continued, "How can something be called a religion that promotes the abuse of women?"

The trial became an airing of grandiose theories—accusations that the mosque was simply to "provide a foothold for radical Muslims," a Trojan horse for terrorists to plant themselves in American suburbs. Yet, of the twenty-three witnesses called to testify, not one was a member of the mosque. Amid the proceedings, Brandon was very open about his goal: to prove that Islam was at odds with the US Constitution and that Muslims were not protected by that Constitution.

Brandon wasn't alone in defining the battle lines. Mosque projects across the US have come to serve "as proxies for a number of more complex struggles commonly reduced to simple dichotomies: Islam versus the West, Islam versus Judeo-Christian culture, and the culture wars between 'red' and 'blue' America." Those battles to some extent raged before 2010, but they became more frequent and fiercer in the years since Park 51.

As Park 51 became distant in America's memory, there was a lull in the conflict, which spiked again with Donald Trump's campaign and presidency. Throughout both, President Trump embraced Geller's and others' sinister theories about Muslims and even installed in numerous high-level positions individuals who publicly engaged in Geller-type fearmongering. The result: Fourteen mosque disputes were documented in 2016 alone. One expert sees them as local iterations of President Trump's travel ban: "When you have the person occupying the highest office in the United States . . . calling for Muslims to be banned from the country, or compelled to carry special identification cards, that heightens the fear and concern that people at the local level have."

Today, mosques face long approval processes, with public hearings dominated by hours of statements by local residents expressing concerns about terrorism and "the role of mosques in terrorist training."

They repeat Brandon's imagery of mosques as Trojan horses for terrorists. Neighborhood associations echo Pamela Geller when they assert that a mosque will "subvert the Constitution of the United States." All of these conspiracies have at their center the assertion that Islam is not a religion. It is a political ideology or cult that is against everything Americans stand for. Outside public sessions, where mosque organizers can respond to the opposition, objectors take to the street in loud and fiery protest. In many cases, the fury of the debate is highly disproportionate to the size of the Muslim community at issue.

More sophisticated opponents know to hide their fears behind concerns about traffic, parking, and congestion. But even in those cases, discourse on social media and elsewhere makes clear that behind the seemingly neutral concerns lies deep anti-Muslim hostility. That is the story of the Islamic Society of Basking Ridge in New Jersey. When local Muslims outgrew their makeshift prayer space and decided to build a place of their own, they had to endure "five years, 39 public hearings, and two lawsuits" before they could finally move ahead with construction. At public hearings, those opposing the mosque would use the language of land use—criticisms about drainage, parking, landscaping, the size of the facility and the number of people expected to attend services. The people raising these concerns insisted that the conflict "was always about land use" and that the mosque leaders had "made it about religion." But even as the mosque submitted revised plan after revised plan addressing each subsequent set of land use concerns, opponents found more things to complain about. They even got the town government to adopt a new ordinance increasing the minimum plot size needed to build houses of worship.

The tactics come straight out of the playbook. Frank Gaffney of the Center for Security Policy (CSP) is a leading moral entrepreneur stoking and perpetuating fear of Muslims. According to CSP's "Mosques in America: A Guide to Accountable Permit Hearings and Continuing Citizen Oversight," "concerned citizens must learn to express questions and reservations in a manner appropriate to the relevant civic forum's purpose." The guide discourages readers from "expressing alarm as hysteria" as that could be "used to characterize the entire oversight effort as racially biased and ignorant." In other words, cloak your intentions well.

But it's near impossible for many of these adversaries to hide their true intentions. The New Jersey mosque was founded by Mohammad Ali Chaudhry, who served first as deputy mayor in 2003 then mayor in 2004 of Bernards Township in Basking Ridge. He was also elected to the township committee in 2001 and again in 2005, each time for a three-year term. Despite his unquestionable dedication to the well-being of Basking Ridge—a community *The Guardian* describes as "wealthy and well-educated"—when he began the process of building the mosque in 2011, he quickly became the subject of suspicion and disparagement. In the course of the mosque's resulting lawsuit against the town, "lawyers uncovered racially charged emails among officials opposed to [Chaudhry's] plan." On a national level, activists smeared him as a "terrorist sympathizer." Some residents of Basking Ridge even received an anonymous letter titled "Meet Your Neighbor" that alleged Chaudhry's "serene, grinning" demeanor was mere *taqiyya*; as you'll recall from Chapter 2, moral entrepreneurs use *taqiyya* or an "action of covering, dissimulation" to explain away any act of goodwill by a Muslim.

Chaudhry's story, like Bahloul's story, like my father's story, is repeated across the US. In Temecula, California, when the Muslim community grew to 150 families and could no longer fit in the warehouse where they used to pray, they decided to build out a 25,000-square-foot facility with classrooms and a playground. They inevitably faced protests. In Sheboygan, Wisconsin, a small group of Christian ministers led the "noisy fight" against a Muslim group that wanted to convert a health food store into a mosque. In Bensalem, Pennsylvania, the Muslim community faced a long and arduous approval process that no other religious group had ever been asked to undertake.

In each of these and many other mosque cases, the opposition is clear about its target. "Their problem is Islam itself." They wield *taqiyya* to "argue that even the most Americanized Muslim secretly wants to replace the Constitution with Islamic Shariah law." As the *New York Times* stated as far back as 2010:

> These local skirmishes make clear that there is now wide-spread debate about whether the best way to uphold America's democratic values is to allow Muslims the same religious freedom enjoyed by other Americans, or to pull away the welcome mat from a faith seen as a singular threat.

American Muslims working on building mosques and other facilities for the Muslim community have learned not to expect a welcome mat. The obstacles are apparent. They know that even the broad RLUIPA protections are not enough, that the opposition will far surpass anything any other house of worship has to face. So, Muslim communities concede to restrictions and other demands even if those restrictions place significant burdens on the right of congregants to exercise their religion. They are forced to compromise more than any mainstream faith community would find acceptable for itself.

While RLUIPA may have attempted to enforce equality across faith groups, the reality on the ground is that some groups are freer than others to practice their faith. In this climate, RLUIPA fully protects only those religious groups who think they have enough political capital to demand protection under those laws.

And sometimes Muslims forego their rights simply because they fear for their lives.

"SPATE OF MOSQUE FIRES
STRETCHES ACROSS THE COUNTRY"
Holly Yan and Mayra Cuevas, CNN

Imagine you are in your house of worship—church, synagogue, temple, mosque—absorbed in your prayers. It's been a difficult week with a new project at work, after school activities, an argument with your partner. So many things seem to be going wrong. Will you have enough money for next month's bills?

Tears of frustration sting your eyes as you look around the building. Familiar objects greet you and the tightness in your throat eases. You love coming here. The cool, tranquil interior is so distant from your hectic life. Perhaps you gaze up at a statue or painting of the one you came to with your troubles. The face smiles down at you, an old friend.

Your swirling thoughts settle as you remember all the things that have gone right in your life. You are alive. You have a home and food (which created some of the bills you are so worried about). You have people who love you (enough to argue with you). Silently, you offer a prayer of gratitude for all the things you do have. Your heart warms until you feel yourself smiling with the images around you.

Once more you gaze up at that beatific smile, basking in the serenity you now feel. The silence is broken by a crack, as the face you were looking at shatters. Fragments shoot across the room. You throw yourself to the ground, covering your head with your arms. The structure rumbles ominously. Quickly, you jump to your feet and dash for the exit.

There are no graven images in mosques, but the other elements of this scenario are familiar to mosque-goers in America and abroad. In March 2019, the world was roiled by the worst such case in the cultural West—a gunman ambushed two mosques in Christchurch, New Zealand, killing 50 worshippers and wounding 50. He captured 17 minutes of the carnage on his helmet camera; in the video, he remarks as he begins shooting: "There wasn't even time to aim, there was so many targets."

In years past, the attacks took place right here at home. On the morning of August 5, 2017, at a mosque in Bloomington, Minnesota, worshippers were in the midst of morning prayers when an explosion went off. The perpetrators later said their intention was to bomb the mosque to "scare" Muslims "out of the country" and to signal that they were "not welcome here." Elsewhere in America, three men conspired to bomb an apartment complex in Garden City, Kansas, that serves as a mosque to Somali refugees. Two men threw an acid bomb at mosque officials standing near their mosque in Glendale, Arizona. Two pipe bombs detonated outside of a mosque in Cincinnati.

Then there's the arson. In 2017, five mosques were burned in the span of ten weeks. On January 7, the Islamic Center of Lake Travis in Austin, Texas, was burned to the ground. Seven days later, the interior of the Islamic Center of Eastside in Bellevue, Washington was destroyed. Two weeks after that, and only hours after President Trump signed his first executive order banning immigrants from seven majority-Muslim countries, the Islamic Center of Victoria in Texas was consumed in flames. On February 24, a small fire broke out at the entrance to a mosque in Tampa. On March 15, the Islamic Center of Ypsilanti in Michigan went up in smoke. And then in 2018, a year after the Bellevue mosque's interior was destroyed, its façade was set on fire.

If you're a Muslim in America, you genuinely fear for your life. You're not alone in this fear, even if the risk is particularly accentuated for you. Worshippers in American churches, synagogues, and temples have lost or nearly lost their lives in murderous shootings.

On October 27, 2018, Robert Bowers stormed the Tree of Life synagogue in Pittsburgh, shouting anti-Semitic slurs and opening fire on the congregants, killing eleven of them in a furious, hate-filled, twenty-minute-attack. Bowers had a habit of posting anti-Semitic rants on social media, including one right before the shooting, where he accused the Hebrew Immigrant Aid Society "of bringing 'invaders in that kill our people.'"

On November 5, 2017, Devin Patrick Kelley killed twenty-six people and wounded twenty at the First Baptist Church in Sutherland Springs, Texas. He was clad in all black, a ballistic vest strapped to his chest and an AR-15 style semi-automatic rifle in his hand. Victims included children and the elderly and everyone in between, including a pregnant woman and the pastor's teenage daughter. Investigators said the attack was related to a domestic dispute Kelley was having with his mother-in-law, a congregant at the church.

On June 17, 2015, Dylann Roof shot nine African Americans during religious services at the Emanuel African American Methodist Episcopal Church in Charleston, South Carolina. The church was one of the oldest black churches in the United States, and the site of ongoing community organizing for civil rights. Roof admitted to police that he murdered the worshippers in the hope of starting a race war.

On August 5, 2012, Wade Michael Page entered a Sikh temple in Oak Creek, Wisconsin, and shot six people and wounded four others. After police shot him in the hip, Page turned his gun on himself. Investigators called the shooting a "domestic terrorism incident" and uncovered evidence of Page's ties to white supremacism.

The ongoing violence can leave religious leaders wondering what to do. After the second burning of the Bellevue mosque, Omer Lone, a mosque elder and board member, mused: "If we build, is this (a fire) something we will see again?" Sometimes, congregations are just unable to recover.

That's what happened with the Islamic Center of Columbia, Tennessee, located just fifty miles from Murfreesboro. The trajectory should be a familiar one by now: the local Muslim community first gathered in a small, rented space at the mall. As the congregation grew, they moved to an auto garage that had no carpets and no heating. "It was a cold Ramadan," recounted Daoud Abudiab, one of the prayer leaders. Realizing they needed a bigger space—with heating—they began looking for a building to purchase. In 2000, just a few months shy of the 9/11 attacks, they purchased a modest, one-story property on Main Street.

When 9/11 happened, the Muslim community received mixed responses from its Christian neighbors. A few local churches asked Abudiab to give lectures on Islam to help educate their congregants. But other churches offered classes of their own; one called its class, "Islam—the Evil Religion." The proliferation of antagonistic, anti-Muslim messages, especially because they came from trusted religious leaders, soon began to show its effects. Suddenly, the Muslims of Columbia began to feel different in a way they knew their neighbors did not welcome. Friends of the Abudiabs stopped coming by, explaining simply, "Our children can't play with your children. My husband learned in Sunday School that Muslims want to convert you or kill you."

Muslims went from feeling alienated to fearing for their physical safety. First came the death threats. Then came the firebombing.

In the early morning hours of February 9, 2008, Abudiab received a phone call from the fire department. "Robin, I am going to the mosque!" he called out to his wife as he and his daughter sped out the door. Well before he even turned onto Main Street, he saw the column of smoke in the sky. He pulled up in front of the mosque slowly, stunned as he surveyed the collapsed roof and flames roaring through the empty windows. Through the smoke, a giant black swastika was just visible on the side of the building. Soon others arrived to witness.

It took hours to extinguish the fire. The police and fire departments searched through the charred ruins to discover the cause. A smashed window on the back door pointed to arson. One fireman brought Abudiab what was left of a Qur'an. It was Abudiab's Qur'an, one with large print that his parents had given him and that he had lent to the mosque for Ramadan. Now it was nearly half gone, the pages crumbling in his hands. "It was like they were delivering your dead child," Abudiab's voice still catches as he remembers. "I hope you never find out what that's like, but it was such a personal loss."

In the years since the firebombing, Abudiab has attempted to reconvene the congregation in a new building, a former church. But he hasn't managed to build up the numbers—and he thinks the reason is that many of the local Muslims are afraid of backlash from fellow Tennesseans. In many places in the United States, building a house of worship now means risking your safety and the safety of your family and community. There is a genuine struggle to practice our faith.

In some parts of the country, that struggle follows us to our graves.

‖‖

"TEXAS TOWN TO MUSLIMS: 'WE WON'T BURY YOU'"
Rod Dreher, *The American Conservative*

‖‖

Although we know death is inevitable, it is still devastating. One moment you're talking with your father, and the next he's silent forever; your friend said she'd meet you at eight, then she's hit crossing the street. At times like this, we look for ways to remember family and friends, either in a photograph, a letter, or even a tombstone. Cemeteries aren't just for the deceased but also for comforting those left behind. Coping with the death of our beloved is a shared experience of poignancy and pain that any human can relate to. So it's almost unfathomable how vandals can destroy cemeteries.

Cemetery destruction has become common. In 2017, 105 separate incidents were reported to the local press. In 2016, 184 incidents were reported. From 2016 to 2017, the total number of headstones and markers affected by vandalism (stolen, toppled or graffitied) increased from 1,811 to 2,353, and the repair costs increased from $488,000 to $1,766,000.

There's something particularly sad about the vandalism when it happens to religious cemeteries, maybe because they're imbued more obviously with the sacred. The vandalism also seems to carry a different, more ominous message. For example, three Jewish cemeteries were desecrated in the span of a few weeks in 2017. On February 20, 120 headstones in St. Louis's Chesed Shel Emeth cemetery were knocked over and cracked, causing $30,000 in damage. A few days later, 275 headstones were toppled and destroyed in Philadelphia's Mount Carmel cemetery. And then a few days after that, the Waad (Vaad) Hakolel Cemetery in Rochester, New York, was vandalized. The cemetery vandalism came in the midst of more than a 120 Jewish community centers facing bomb threats. While the motives of many of the vandals were unclear, the broader context suggested that hate was at least part of the equation.

When it comes to Muslim cemeteries in the US, the resistance goes to an even more fundamental matter: the right to have a religious cemetery at all. In 2016, the Associated Press reported that Muslim communities in four US cities were facing fierce opposition. Muslims in Farmervsille, Texas; Walpole, Massachusetts; Carlisle, Pennsylvania; and Farmington, Minnesota, set out to build cemeteries, thinking that laying their dead to rest would be a fairly uncontroversial task. It was anything but. "We were absolutely flabbergasted, to be honest, to see that kind of opposition," Ismail Fenni from Walpole told the Associated Press. "All we're trying to establish is a . . . final resting place for the loved ones of the Muslim community members."

The complaints ranged from the typical, not-in-my-backyard type, to environmental and public health concerns that because Muslims don't embalm their dead or bury them in coffins, the water supply would become contaminated (a hydrogeologist debunked this claim and even explained that "not embalming is better for local groundwater in most cases"). Pro-mosque activists found many of these complaints mere cover for anti-Muslim hostility, which came out in explicit form, too. One resident said he didn't want to deal with "crazy music," which is how he referred to the Muslim call to prayer.

In Farmersville, the Islamic Association of Collin County, Texas searched extensively before settling on a 34-acre site just outside of Farmersville. The land was in keeping with state requirements, and even overlooked a lake—a tranquil view for family visiting their departed grandparents, brothers, sisters, and children. The rural area promised peace, and comfort for the mourning.

But, for some Farmersville residents, the plans for a Muslim cemetery dredged up memories of the deadly shooting that had occurred just a few months prior and only 20 miles away in Garland, Texas. Two men had opened fire on the controversial "Draw the Prophet Mohammed cartoon contest" that was organized and attended by Pamela Geller and her group, the American Freedom Defense Initiative. Alarmed by this recent terrorist attack, some Farmersville citizens, led by Baptist pastor David Meeks, said that the proposed cemetery site was actually for a mosque or even possibly a terrorist training center. Islamic extremists were coming to Texas! According to Meeks, Islam was a "quasi-pseudo religion" and that "the danger is so real that I must do everything I can to try to stop it." Other residents sent death threats to the city council and planning members.

Fear about terrorism is no doubt reasonable—even warranted—but why was it extended to the entire Muslim community, and to their cemeteries in particular? The Muslim community was stunned. Were they to be denied a source of comfort in their grief? Recent years have already plagued Muslim religious life with so many obstacles, but they couldn't imagine that the trouble would follow their beloved to the grave. As Rod Dreher, a columnist at *The American Conservative* wrote,

> Denying people a place to bury their dead? Who does that? Seriously, what kind of person do you have to be to protest people trying to buy ground to have a place to commit their deceased loved ones to the earth in an honorable way? For shame.

The Farmersville Muslims were saddened but they understood that the core of the chaos was propaganda. As Khalil Abdur-Rashid, a spokesman for the Islamic association, said, "This is about misinformation, and fear and hate. And until we confront that, in open honesty, it will continue to persist."

In September 2018, after the Department of Justice intervened in the matter, the Farmersville city council approved a settlement with the Islamic association. For the Muslims of Farmersville, their human dignity and that of their deceased had been insulted, but they could finally move on.

|||||||||||||||||||||||||||||||||||||||||||||||||||||||||||||||||||||||||||||||||||||||||||||||||||||||||||||||||||||||||||||||||||||||||||||||||||

"MOSQUE BACKED BY BAPTISTS WINS IN LAWSUIT SETTLEMENT"

Bob Allen, *Baptist News Global*

|||||||||||||||||||||||||||||||||||||||||||||||||||||||||||||||||||||||||||||||||||||||||||||||||||||||||||||||||||||||||||||||||||||||||||||||||||

The stories I've shared in this chapter follow a pattern. Communities start, grow, build new spaces for worship or spiritual communion—and then face hostility to an oftentimes frightening degree. But there's another common feature that runs throughout these stories: the kind neighbors and members of other faith communities who have stood up for their Muslim friends and colleagues. When some Americans try to pull the welcome mat away, other Americans tug it back into place. And Muslims, for their part, have created new public service initiatives and worked diligently and sincerely to support other faith communities facing hate.

During the Islamic Society of Basking Ridge's fight to build a new mosque, I filed a brief in its support. A multitude of diverse religious groups signed onto that brief. The American Association of Jewish Lawyers and Jurists, the Baptist Joint Committee for Religious Liberty, the Ethics and Religious Liberty Commission of the Southern Baptist Convention, the International Mission Board of the Southern Baptist Convention, the International Society for Krishna Consciousness, the National Asian Pacific American Bar Association, the National Association of Evangelicals, the Queens Federation of Churches, the Sikh American Legal Defense and Education Fund, the Sikh Coalition, the South Asian Bar Association of New Jersey, the South Asian Bar Association of New York, and the Unitarian Universalist Legislative Ministry of New Jersey.

A few of these groups received pushback from their members for their stand in support of American Muslims. The negative reaction to the International Mission Board's involvement was so strong that one of its trustees was forced to resign. Russell Moore, president of the Ethics and Religious Liberty Commission (ERLC), the public-policy arm of the Southern Baptist Convention (SBC), also faced criticism for the ERLC's involvement in the case. Some in the SBC even called for his removal and the removal of any other church official who supported Muslims.

Messenger John Wofford of Armorel Baptist Church of Armorel, Arkansas, requested a motion . . . calling for the firing of SBC officials who support the building of mosques. "I move that all Southern Baptist officials or officers who support the rights of Muslims to build Islamic mosques in the United States be immediately removed from their position within the Southern Baptist Convention."

Moore's predecessor, Richard Land, also faced fiery protest in 2010 when the ERLC joined a multifaith coalition to protect Muslims' right to build houses of worship. Land was forced to withdraw mere months after ERLC joined the coalition. In his words, "While many Southern Baptists share my deep commitment to religious freedom and the right of Muslims to have places of worship, they also feel that a Southern Baptist denominational leader filing suit to allow individual mosques to be built is 'a bridge too far.'"

Despite this resistance, many faith leaders persist in supporting religious freedom for all. Moore has adamantly held onto his position. Other local leaders have also stepped up. In the midst of the Farmersville cemetery controversy, Bart Barber, a Southern Baptist pastor, told his congregation to stand up for Muslims' rights because protecting religious liberty requires consistency.

> We are telling the government that we think they ought to choose between religions they like and religions they don't like and then use city government to make life impossible for the religions they don't like. And this is a particularly foolish time for us to be articulating that point of view so persuasively . . . Tell me, please, how do you expect us to argue at the national level with a straight face that we believe in religious liberty for all people while at the local level we're running the Moslems out of town on a rail?

When protests raged in Murfreesboro, supporters from the broader Murfreesboro community showed up to counter the mosque opponents. In 2017, years after those rocky early days, when the mosque was again vandalized, community members showed up in the hundreds. Many of them came with signs reading, "Love thy neighbor," "Everyone be cool to each other," and "I stand with my Muslim neighbor." Some of the visitors handed out long-stemmed roses.

Shortly after the firebombing of the Islamic Center of Columbia, the neighboring Muslim communities held a vigil where the mosque had stood. Many non-Muslims attended as well. Among them was Reverend Bill Williamson from First Presbyterian Church, who went out of his way to ease his neighbors' suffering. He had collected money during a service at his church and presented it to them during the vigil, along with a set of keys to a room he had set aside for Muslim meeting and prayer use.

Strengthened by this kindness, Daoud Abudiab took action so that other families could be safe, and other parents wouldn't have to fear for their sons and daughters. Engaging the larger Muslim community in Nashville, he created the Faith and Cultural Center, whose principal project is Our Muslim Neighbor. The initiative fosters direct, personal relationships between Muslims and non-Muslims in Middle Tennessee. "Those who know us are not afraid of us," Abudiab says. "It is those who don't know Muslims who are afraid of Muslims." These friendships have challenged him to grow. "There is nothing to fear or compromise in such a friendship and everything to gain. Let us all honor the best of our traditions."

The conversations Abudiab hosts are frank, and sometimes hard. But he persists. Imam Ossama Bahloul has also persevered. He started an initiative called Islamin500.org, "an intellectual electronic tolerance hub" that prevents stereotypes by raising awareness and educating Americans about Islam in a "simple" but "comprehensive" way. The project aims to educate in order to "build an inclusive society."

Oz Sultan, too, hasn't given up. He grew up hearing tales of his father's forced migration from Andhra Pradesh, India and how he had to dodge "British snipers, who thought killing Muslims was sport." Sultan's father eventually made it to Europe where he managed to finish his studies and bring his wife to live with him. From there, they migrated to Canada and then to the United States. Struggle is part of Sultan's family history, and with Park 51, struggle became part of his present, too. He couldn't let it bring him down and he wouldn't give up.

And so, even though Park 51 never came to fruition as an interfaith community space, Sultan picked up valuable lessons from his experience and has created a new, separate initiative called Our House. The interfaith spirit is still present in his praxis. Our House's space for Muslim congregational prayer also serves as a synagogue and church. "The goal is to get the conversation going between faiths," he said. He wants to make Our House "an Americana-based reality, a project whose richness comes from the ethnic, racial, and religious diversity of its participants."

And Muslims know that dialogue is not enough. When Jewish cemeteries in St. Louis and Philadelphia were vandalized in 2017, the Muslim community raised hundreds of thousands of dollars to help them rebuild. It again sprang into action when the Tree of Life synagogue shooting happened in October 2018, raising close to a quarter of a million dollars. In the days after the shooting at the Emanuel African Methodist Episcopal Church in Charleston, and the series of fires at black churches in the South, Muslims raised over $100,000 to help rebuild those churches. The Muslim-run crowd-funding site, LaunchGood.com, is entirely dedicated to raising money quickly for people and organizations in need.

Muslim groups have also worked in solidarity with Jewish, Sikh, Christian, Hindu, and other religious communities on projects of mutual importance. After the Oak Creek Sikh temple shooting, a diverse coalition of faith-based groups came together to push for accountability; they succeeded in getting a senate hearing and press conference on the shooting. In February 2019, an interfaith group numbering in the hundreds helped clean and repaint the Swaminarayan Temple in Louisville, Kentucky, days after the Hindu temple was broken into and vandalized. As one Muslim leader explained, undergirding all of these solidarity efforts is the simple fact that, "putting our religious differences or even your political differences aside, the core of all of us is that we have a shared humanity."

These stories of service, of giving back, remind me of my own father's legacy. Community service was in his blood, and it's what animates me, too. This book with these narratives is just another way of my giving back, so that we may learn and grow.

CHAPTER 5

"WHAT IS SHARIA AND WHY DOES IT MATTER?"

"Water as God's blessing. Water as miracle. Water creating oases. Water as reward. Water as the instrument of ritual cleansings. Water as the condition of happiness. Water as heaven." If you're a devout Muslim, you need to get to the water, and there's a path that will take you there. Sharia, literally "a straight, smooth path that leads to water," is the road to redemption.

As with many other religions, water is an important symbol in Islam, Garry Wills explains in *What the Qur'an Meant: And Why It Matters*. "In the Old Testament, the righteous flourish like trees along the water's edge. Yahweh, when displeased, withholds rain . . . Pleased, he sends it. With it, he answers Elijah's prayer." In the New Testament, water again plays a prominent role. "Jesus promises to give believers an endless inner spring of 'living water' . . . He works a miracle through the waters in the pool of Siloam . . . He is baptized in it, and others become his followers by being baptized in it."

The Old and New Testaments give water a prominent role—but in the Qur'an, it's not just important, it's central. The Qur'an, as Wills explains, is "haunted" by the Arabian Desert. "It is always there, always in the background." And with the desert omnipresent, the yearning for water is everywhere, too. Water is the preeminent "symbol of God's blessing." It is "more precious than gold" because it is "vital in every way"—physically, "symbolically, even theologically." The Qur'an says it is the first material substance created and the "medium through which other things are individuated and kept alive."

Water is also one of God's important signs. There's a common urging throughout the Qur'an for the reader to ponder his or her surroundings, especially the patterns and processes found in nature, and arrive at truth not through blind obedience but through contemplation. According to the Qur'an, the evidence of God's existence and wisdom is all there, if you just take a moment to see and interpret it. In one verse, God says (referring to himself with the royal "we"): "We will show them Our signs in the horizons and within themselves until it becomes clear to them that it is the truth." (41:53) In another verse, God points to the birds: "Do they not see the birds controlled in the atmosphere of the sky? None holds them up except God. Indeed in that are signs for a people who believe." (16:79)

Elsewhere, God tells us to take a moment to ponder how the day slides into night, and the night into day. "Indeed, in the creation of the heavens and the earth and the alternation of the night and the day are signs for those of understanding. Who remember God while standing or sitting or [lying] on their sides and give thought to the creation of the heavens and the earth, [saying], 'Our Lord, You did not create this aimlessly.'" (3:190–191) Mountains, rivers, and fruits contain helpful hints, too: "And it is He who spread the earth and placed therein firmly set mountains and rivers; and from all of the fruits He made therein two mates; He causes the night to cover the day. Indeed in that are signs for a people who give thought." (13:3)

Like these other signs in nature, water, too, represents something bigger. In the form of rain, water is the Qur'an's favorite way to illustrate a part of the divine message many in Prophet Muhammad's time staunchly resisted: the resurrection of the body. In the Qur'an, Muhammad is asked to recount many times the "desert miracle, the rebirth of plants and flowers."

> And of His signs is that you see the earth stilled, but when We send down upon it rain, it quivers and grows. Indeed, He who has given it life is the Giver of Life to the dead. Indeed, He is over all things competent. (41:39)

He brings the living out of the dead and brings the dead out of the living and brings to life the earth after its lifelessness. And thus will you be brought out. And of His signs is that He created you from dust; then, suddenly you were human beings dispersing [throughout the earth]. (30:19–20)

And of His signs is [that] He shows you lightning, for fear and longing (of Him), and that He has been sending down from the heaven water; so He gives life to the earth after its death. Surely in that are indeed signs for a people who consider. (30:24)

Water is the source of our revival, of our resurrection, and God, in His infinite mercy, has shown us the way. "Now We have set you [Muhammad] on a clear religious path, so follow it. Do not follow the desires of those who lack [true] knowledge." (45:18)

In Arabic, the language of the Qur'an, the word used in this verse for "clear path" is sharia. Even though the word "sharia" is used only once in the Qur'an, it eventually came to be used to refer to Islamic Law. In the life of a believer, then, sharia—the fine details of the law that structures a Muslim's life and the overarching spirituality that infuses those actions with meaning—paves the way to salvation. It's not just a technical set of rules or a list of do's and don'ts. Instead, sharia offers us guidance and comfort when we are most in need of that guidance.

I know, because it has done this for me.

|||||||||||||||||||||||||||||||||||||||||||||||||||||||||||||||||||||||||||||||||||||||||||||||||||||||||||||||||||||||||||||||||

"AMERICA'S NEXT GENERATION OF MUSLIMS
INSISTS ON CRAFTING ITS OWN STORY"
Leila Fadel, NPR

|||||||||||||||||||||||||||||||||||||||||||||||||||||||||||||||||||||||||||||||||||||||||||||||||||||||||||||||||||||||||||||||||

It's not easy growing up in America as a Muslim kid of immigrants. Because your own parents didn't grow up in this country, they can't offer you a blueprint to follow. Mine grew up in Pakistan, where they were just like everyone else. They didn't look or speak or dress differently, and they shared a faith with the vast majority of the citizenry. When, in their adulthood, my parents arrived in the US and another Muslim told them about difficulties finding *halal* meat, they weren't sure what to make of it. Grocery stores actually sold meat that wasn't *halal*? It was a tiny reflection of just how far they'd traveled from home: Islam was no longer the de facto dominant religion. They'd have to deliberate and articulate their religious needs in a way they never had to before.

It's one thing to face these questions when you're an adult, but an entirely different task growing up with that challenge. My religious identity made me stick out from the crowd even when I desperately wanted to meld in. I was the one with the unusual name. I was the one who had to wear jogging pants during gym class when everyone else wore shorts, because I was the only one with religious modesty requirements. I was the one who didn't stay late at drunken parties. (More frequently, I avoided them altogether.) I was the one who never tried—and still hasn't tried—illicit drugs or even a drop of alcohol.

Growing up in the 1980s, 1990s, and early 2000s, I didn't see myself or my community represented in popular culture. The family dynamics in *Full House* or on Disney Channel sitcoms where the parents seemed all too eager to acquiesce to their children's demands, were foreign to me. My parents never reacted that way to my childish insolence. And why did no one in American music, television, and fashion look like me? Why wasn't the modest, flowing style of my preferred dress celebrated on runways and in fashion magazines?

Some of my questions were even more foundational. Like, what is the proper way to navigate interactions with the opposite sex? Or how do I deal with the apparent clash between American feminism and Muslim gender norms—the first centered on the individual, the second on family and community? Islam requires Muslim women to be educated (in the US, they are second only to Jewish women in educational achievements), but marriage and motherhood are also of abiding importance. And what about my peers' derisiveness toward their parents when my own religion required obedience and gratitude—especially when it came to my mom, for as the Prophet Muhammad said when he mandated that children be respectful to their mothers: "Paradise lies under the feet of mothers"?

In answering these questions, I had to sketch out my own template, find my own path. In time, I found the guidance of several preeminent Muslim scholars who showed me that "clear path" (sharia). I studied with Dr. Umar Faruq Abd-Allah, whose work on "Islam and the Cultural Imperative" was groundbreaking for me. I learned that the history of my religion was one of "sustained cultural relevance to distinct peoples, diverse places, and different times." Wherever Muslims went, Islam "became not only functional and familiar at the local level but dynamically engaging, fostering stable indigenous Muslim identities and allowing Muslims to put down deep roots and make lasting contributions." He urged me and all of his students to find a unique American Islam that drew from its American environment. Don't sit back and let culture be dictated to you; create culture. Because Islamic law demands it.

One of the five universal maxims of sharia is: "Cultural usage shall have the weight of law"—that is, Muslims cannot "reject sound custom and usage." If a particular local custom didn't violate some clear Islamic precept, Muslims should embrace it and make it their own. "Another well-known principle of Islamic jurisprudence" emphasized that "cultural usage is second nature." In other words, "it is as difficult for people to go against their established customs as it is for them to defy their instinctive natures." So, Dr. Abd-Allah said, Islamic law (or sharia) requires that Muslims, wherever they live, accommodate local norms whenever possible.

Islam isn't about contesting your local culture—it's about becoming part of it and in the process elevating it through your faith-inspired contributions. "The Islamic legal tradition must not be seen as a program of detailed prohibitions and inhibitions." It has to be "made relevant to the day-to-day imperatives of our lives with an eye to fostering positive identity and dynamic integration into American society. We cannot remain true to the sacred law, if we are unable to see the forest for the trees."

In recent years, many American Muslims have taken this task to heart. Muslim comedian, Hasan Minhaj, hosts *Patriot Act*, a political comedy show on Netflix. Muslim fashion designer, Lisa Vogl, created a modest clothing line sold in Macy's stores across the US. G. Willow Wilson and Sana Amanat, both Muslim women, cocreated *Ms. Marvel*, a comic about a Muslim female superhero for Marvel Comics. Wilson is also the newest writer for *Wonder Woman* at DC Comics. Zareen Jaffery runs a children's book imprint, Salaam Reads, at Simon & Schuster. Aisha Saeed wrote a bestselling middle grade novel with Muslim characters. Hena Khan introduced Ramadan to Curious George. I produced an Emmy- and Peabody-nominated docuseries on American Muslims, *The Secret Life of Muslims*.

In his Netflix shows, Minhaj teaches his audience to pronounce his name correctly ("Ha-sun Min-haaj"). He fluidly uses terms and concepts from his immigrant, Muslim life in his standup routine—for example, *lota* (the watering can Muslims use in the cleansing process at the toilet) and *tel* (the coconut oil Minhaj, like many Indians, uses to slick up his hair). He also explicitly stated on air that he abstains from alcohol, as many religious Muslims do. Minhaj is "a person who relishes and catalogs the cultural specificity of his life—who sees, too, that the latter can secure, not hinder, mainstream success," *The Atlantic* said. This aspect of Minhaj's work is, as I interpret it, the cultural imperative in action. The celebration of our "cultural specificity" and the melding of this specificity into the cultural mainstream.

Dr. Abd-Allah taught me about the importance of culture. Shaykh Abdullah Adhami taught me about myself (*Shaykh* here refers to a religious scholar). Religious traditions often teach what seem like antiquated gender roles, but Shaykh Adhami transformed those teachings, pulling from religious texts and Arabic linguistics to unearth something truly wondrous, the elevated status of women and femininity in Islam. Women are carriers of divine beauty and men are required to protect and nurture that divine element through kindness and service to them, he said.

Islamic rules of marriage reflect that careful protection. Shaykhs Hamza Yusuf and Nuh Ha Mim Keller, both scholars of traditional Islam, taught me about rights and responsibilities in marriage. A wife (and husband) can stipulate any number of things in their marriage contract. Because marriage in Islam is at its most basic level a contractual relationship, you can be as detailed as you want, and then hold your spouse to those requirements. For women especially, this is a boon—our religion requires us to know our rights and urges us to exercise those rights. We can demand a dowry to cover our expenses in the case of divorce or our husband's death (we could also negotiate an annuity or a fixed monthly stipend). A woman can stipulate that her prospective husband give her or her nominated agent the right to divorce herself at any time without having to specify a reason. We can even ask that our husbands seek our permission before they do certain things, like travel.

A husband is also tasked with providing his wife with basic necessities, like food, clothing, and comfortable housing, but if a woman by virtue of her culture or socioeconomic status is used to luxuries, the husband must ensure she has those, too. The clothing, food, and house the husband pays for must be up to par with her usual standards and tastes. A wife is not required to cook and clean, the husband must inform her of this privilege, and if the wife decides not to cook and clean for her husband "as an act of charity," he's required to *pay her wages* for doing this work. If the wife prefers to hire someone to keep house, the husband has to provide her with a paid employee, if he can afford it. A wife is also free to have her own career, and Islamic law does not require her to share her earnings with her husband or use them to pay for household expenses.

Of course, while a woman is not required to share her earnings, she is free to do so—and in many cases today where families need dual incomes, Muslim women do share their earnings. These baseline rules are there to help clarify expectations and resolve likely disputes up front. None of these guidelines is meant to detract from the core purpose of marriage, which is to foster love and companionship.

As the Qur'an says, a husband and wife are like "garments" to each other (2:187), which refers back to the story of Adam and Eve in Paradise. Adam had no needs in Paradise except that "he yearned for human company" and God gave him Eve as his company. (Importantly, though, unlike biblical teachings on Eve, Qur'anic speech does not suggest that Eve's purpose was to be Adam's helper; Eve's purpose, like the purpose of all humankind, is to worship God (Qur'an 51:56)). Later, when Adam and Eve transgressed God's rules and ate from the forbidden tree, "divine Grace left them and they became acutely aware of their nakedness. It is then that both Adam and [Eve] felt a second need, the need to cover themselves up." As one religious scholar goes on to explain, "The need for company and the need for clothes were two of the first needs that Adam . . . experienced in paradise, it then comes as no surprise that [God] refers to the relationship between a husband and wife using the metaphor of clothes and garments."

The metaphor of clothing also reflects the equality God establishes between spouses and each partner's reciprocal role in the relationship. Clothing is something that is close to us; it keeps us warm, protects us, makes us comfortable, and hides our faults. In a healthy marriage, spouses do all of these things for each other.

So many Muslim women living in patriarchal cultures around the world have no idea that Islamic law provides such extensive protections, and I had no idea either until I set out to mine my religion for answers. When it came time to get married, I approached with my rights front and center. I had previously been engaged to a man who made me feel unseen and taken for granted. Coming out of that experience, I found that sharia offered me a template for articulating my needs in marriage.

I wanted love, romance, electricity, butterflies—but even more, I yearned for a relationship fundamentally rooted in the mundane. I wanted a career and a professional life, and I also wanted children. That meant, for me, that I needed a husband who could support both of those desires and recognize that I could not possibly provide all or even most of the household or childcare labor alone. I also wanted to be financially secure in the event of a divorce or my husband's untimely death; reserving at least part of my earnings for myself gave me that security.

Marriage is a series of micro- and macrotransactions—emotional, spiritual, sexual, logistical, financial—and in Islamic law, I found the tools to negotiate the terms of those deals. Lawyer, wife, Muslim, feminist: my multiple identities intersect in my prenuptial agreement, which carefully details the rules of my marriage. My husband cannot travel without first informing me; he owes me a cash payment of a certain amount if we ever divorce; as long as he can afford it, he needs to pay for housekeeping and childcare. And my earnings are for me (it's entirely up to me whether I want to share).

I negotiated because my religion told me not only that I could negotiate, but that I *should* negotiate. As clichéd as this may sound, my
religion empowered me.

||||||||||||||||||||||||||||||||||||||||||||||||||||||||||||||||||||||||||||||||||||||||||||||||||||||||||||||||||||||||||||||

"A WORLD OF WAYS TO SAY 'ISLAMIC LAW'"
David Rohde, *New York Times*

||||||||||||||||||||||||||||||||||||||||||||||||||||||||||||||||||||||||||||||||||||||||||||||||||||||||||||||||||||||||||||||

My experience of sharia probably does not square with your idea of
sharia.

I get it. Sharia can be a hard concept to grasp, and the gruesome
headlines (and intentional fearmongering) don't help with their images
and stories about public beheadings in Saudi Arabia and issuance of a
fatwa, or Islamic legal opinion, that authors or artists should be executed because of their irreverent depiction of the Prophet Muhammad.
We recoil in horror at the life sentences handed out in Pakistan to
anyone accused of blaspheming Islam, and we are shocked that anyone
would defend female genital mutilation on religious grounds.

But sharia cannot be viewed only through the lens of shocking
headlines, just as "Catholic Priests Abused 1,000 Children in Pennsylvania" and "Alabama Official: Bible Justifies Roy Moore's Sex Abuse
of Teen Girls" don't represent the views of other religious communities. In fact, sharia is so complex and diverse that Muslims across
the globe have a wide range of views on what sharia actually means
in practice. Pew reports that most Muslims in Afghanistan, Iraq, and
Pakistan want sharia to inform their country's law, but Muslims in
other Muslim-majority states are less interested: 12 percent in Turkey,
10 percent in Kazakhstan, and 8 percent in Azerbaijan. But even in
states where Muslims want a sharia-based legal code, what they are
asking for is not beheadings and amputations, but justice and fairness.

How is it that the Western conception of sharia "as the most unap-
pealing and premodern aspect of Islam is, to many Muslims, the
vibrant, attractive core of a global movement of Islamic revival?"
As Harvard law professor, Noah Feldman, points out, it can't be
that "Muslims want to use Shariah to reverse feminism and control
women." After all, large numbers of women support the overarching
ideal of what sharia represents. One reason the Western and Muslim
views of sharia diverge is because "we are not all using the word to
mean the same thing." It's common to use "sharia" and "Islamic law"
interchangeably, but this equation of the two fails to capture the full
breadth of what sharia means to a believer.

As Feldman explains, "properly speaking, Shariah refers to God's
blueprint for human life," or as we've seen, the clear path to water or
salvation. "It is divine and unchanging, reflecting God's unity and per-
fection. It can be found in God's revealed word in the Quran and in the
divinely guided actions of the Prophet Muhammad." But that divine
blueprint is distinct from the rules that we derive from it. The interpretation and application of religious texts is referred to in Arabic by a
different term—*fiqh*.

Unlike God's perfect word ("sharia"), "fiqh is Islamic law as practiced by people." Importantly, "because it's a product of human reasoning used to understand God's word, Islamic law is subject to debate
and imperfection." Whereas "almost all faithful Muslims would say
that they believe there is a single, truthful answer that lies in Shariah"
they also "all agree that humans are imperfect interpreters of God's
will." Sharia is infallible, *fiqh* is not. And in deriving legal rules, or
fiqh, from sharia, all Muslims realize that they can never be "absolutely sure as humans" if what they've arrived at is the truth.

What this means is, if you're opposed to a particular implementation or articulation of Islamic scripture, what you're really opposed
to is *fiqh*, not sharia. And probably some Muslim jurist somewhere
agrees with your dissent, no matter what it is, not just because dissent

is natural, but because Islamic law specifically encourages scholarly debate. As one legal scholar explains, the fallibility of *fiqh* is "hard-wired into the foundations of Islamic jurisprudence," resulting in great legal diversity. There are multiple schools of jurisprudence (each considered equally orthodox), and plenty of debate and dissension within each of those schools. (Interestingly, during the classical period of Islam when these schools of law emerged, Muslim jurists developed legal institutions that later influenced Western law. For example, the *waqf*, or unincorporated and inalienable charitable trust, was developed in the first three centuries of Islam [from the seventh to the ninth century C.E.] and are very similar in form to trusts in English trust law, which emerged in the early thirteenth century during "a period of increased contacts between Europe and the Muslim world." The *aval* in medieval French law is derived from Islamic law's *hawala*, or informal system of transferring debt. There are many other examples, too. So, if you oppose sharia, you also technically oppose a system of legal institutions and methodologies that are built into Western law.)

Some of these *fiqh* rulings match up pretty well with American law—for example, they require that all parties agree to a contract before it's applicable to them, that defendants be afforded a presumption of innocence, and that people have rights to personal property. Other *fiqh* rulings are pretty progressive when you compare them to contemporary Western law—women have a right to wages for housework, and a right to participate in "front-line military combat." Some *fiqh* rulings, like the ones prescribing particular physical punishments, are quite at odds with American law. In all of these areas—the good, the bad, and the neutral—*fiqh* remains subject to scholarly reinterpretation.

Anthropologists and legal scholars also note that law is inseparable from culture; when legal officials make decisions, cultural assumptions play a key role. Lawrence Rosen, an anthropologist of Islamic law, says that "law is so deeply embedded in the particularities of each culture that carving it out as a separate domain and only later making note of its cultural connections distorts the nature of both law and culture."

In the US context, *fiqh* is relevant in varying degrees. Many American Muslims prefer to implement these rulings only in their private, ritual worship, like how to wash properly before praying, which supplications to use while praying, and how often to pray during the day. *Fiqh* rulings also tell us which foods to eat and not eat; for example, many devout Muslims don't just abstain from pork and alcohol, but often any foods derived from them: they may avoid foods with gelatin because the gelatin may be derived from pork and beer-battered fish or bourbon pecan pie because they contain remnants of alcohol.

Other American Muslims see *fiqh* as more broadly relevant to their lives; they want to utilize *fiqh* rulings to order their marriage, divorce, inheritance, business transactions, and property matters. This is where *fiqh* becomes relevant to US law: the point at which religion steps out of the private realm and emerges in the public arena, where our relationships and transactions have legal implications. My discussion below will explain that it's important to religious liberty to give religious Americans some leeway in how they order their personal lives. I also make clear that the right is carefully constrained so that it can never threaten American law. Importantly, when the US legal system constrains *fiqh*, it brings it into conversation with secular law, thus opening the possibility that "Islamic communities will improve from these interactions with secular law, and secular law will advance as well."

But before we dive into how *fiqh* actually works in the US, let's look at how it's flagrantly distorted by America's foremost moral entrepreneurs.

III

"THE 'MARCH AGAINST SHARIA' PROTESTS
ARE REALLY MARCHES AGAINST MUSLIMS"
Christopher Mathias, *Huffington Post*

IIIIIIIIIIIIIIIIIIIIIIIIIIIIIIIIIIIIIIIIIIIIIIIIIIIIIIIIIIIIIIIIIIIIIIIIIIIIIIIIIIIIIIIIIIIIIIIIIIIIIIIIIIIIIIIIIIIII

There are people in America who want to rid the country of "sharia," though what they really mean is *fiqh* and the fact that they don't articulate the difference tells you that their proposed solutions are simplistic and superficial. Still, in recent years, they've gained traction in forty-three states across the US and show no signs of slowing down. At the core of this movement is the idea that Islam, and thus Islamic law, is not a religion.

By this point you've seen some repeat players engaging in anti-Muslim fearmongering across the board. The Center for American Progress, in its "Fear, Inc." report calls them "misinformation experts." The people generating "false facts and materials" include Pamela Geller, Brigitte Gabriel, Frank Gaffney, Daniel Pipes at the Middle East Forum, Robert Spencer of Jihad Watch, Steven Emerson of the Investigative Project on Terrorism, David Horowitz at the Freedom Center, and David Yerushalmi of the Society of Americans for National Existence.

This last player is the one that stands out most. The *New York Times* calls Yerushalmi the "man behind the anti-shariah movement." He's the one who developed a model statute called American Laws for American Courts, or ALAC, which was the "spark that ignited a wave of anti-Muslim laws and proposed legislation" and gave rise to the antisharia movement.

In January 2006, Yerushalmi started a nonprofit called the Society of Americans for National Existence, which he dedicated entirely to the cause of fighting sharia. It was on the group's website that he first proposed a law that would make observance of Islamic law (which he likened to sedition) "a felony punishable by 20 years in prison." But it wasn't until 2009 and the emergence of Tea Party that "Yerushalmi saw an opening." With the help of Frank Gaffney, he began writing the model ALAC statute that would stop "state judges from considering foreign laws or rulings that violate" American constitutional rights.

But the statutes weren't his primary goal: "If this thing passed in every state without any friction, it would have not served its purpose . . . the purpose was heuristic—to get people asking this question, 'What is Shariah?'" Or as the Haas Institute explains, "the purpose of the bills [i]s to spread fear about Muslims living in America and to portray them as untrustworthy and out of step with American values. 'Even if these bills do not become law they help to subject Muslims to surveillance and other forms of exclusion and discrimination.'"

The "exclusion and discrimination" includes deprivation of religious liberty. Yerushalmi and the other misinformation experts have pushed the idea that Islam is not a religion, and that sharia specifically is a "legal-political-military doctrine" committed to annihilating Western civilization as we know it today. The antisharia movement thrives on the idea of "creeping sharia"—that is, the United States and all of our fundamental rights are at risk every time we let any Muslim engage in even the most minute aspect of sharia. As the argument goes, in order for America to protect itself, Muslim religious exercise must be prohibited.

Consider, for example, statements by the Family Research Council's Tony Perkins, who currently sits on the US Commission on International Religious Freedom and should, given his credentials, understand how religious freedom works. First, he uses the infamous "statistical analysis" of Islam I discussed in chapter 1 to advocate that religious protections be extended only to "16 percent" of Muslim religious practice. According to Perkins, the other 84 percent is sharia, which is "not a religion in the context of the First Amendment," and must be stopped at all costs because it will otherwise "tear and destroy the fabric of a democracy. So we have to be very clear about our laws and restrain those things that would harm the whole."

Recall that very similar language was used to foment hatred of Catholics in the nineteenth century, and more recently, to oppose the presidency of John F. Kennedy. In both cases, Catholics were painted as agents for a foreign entity (the Vatican); the idea was that their Catholicism required allegiance to a law other than American law. In a similar manner, a mutated concept of sharia is used to paint Muslims in America as loyal to a foreign law, as if there's some central religious authority (there isn't one in Islam) or grand puppeteer pulling the strings from afar.

These talking points are repeated by many other false alarmists who have spurred state lawmakers to take action. To date, Yerushalmi's model statute has been virtually cut and pasted into bills considered in forty-three states. A total of 217 bills have been introduced, of which twenty have been enacted.

There are three categories of anti-sharia laws. In the first category are bills that single out sharia specifically from all other legal traditions and describe it as anti-American and treasonous. For example, a proposed bill in Alabama said that a court cannot look at the law of other countries or cultures in deciding cases, and then specifically singled out international law and sharia as prohibited sources. The second category of bills mentions sharia explicitly but lists it as one of several religious legal traditions that are prohibited. An Arizona bill said courts cannot consider "religious sectarian law," and then defined the term to include sharia, canon law, halacha (Jewish law) and, strangely, karma. Finally, the third and most common type of bill flat-out denies courts any consideration of foreign law. Sharia is not mentioned specifically, and foreign law is defined to include any law, rule, or legal code, or system other than the state and federal constitutions, state and federal statutes, and the ratified treaties of the US.

A particularly broad version was introduced in 2011 by Tennessee Republican state senator Bill Ketron. The bill gave the state Attorney General authority to designate "Sharia organizations," defined as "two (2) or more persons conspiring to support, or acting in concert in support of, sharia or in furtherance of the imposition of sharia within any state or territory of the United States." If the origins of the bill were in question, the text clarified it—the bill repeated the misinformation experts verbatim when it defined sharia as "a legal-political-military doctrinal system combined with certain religious beliefs." Its proposed punishment was also reminiscent of the language Yerushalmi posted on his website back in 2006: the Tennessee bill said that anyone who provided material support to a designated sharia organization could be charged with a felony and face up to fifteen years in jail. Altogether, the bill sounded like a statute about material support for terrorism but instead of naming terrorism, the drafters of the statute described it as "sharia." All of Muslim religious law was deemed de facto felonious. More foundationally, sharia was painted as political rather than religious.

The antisharia movement has been going strong ever since Yerushalmi gave it a kickstart a decade ago. Some scholars think presidential rhetoric has given the movement a boost. In 2017 alone, twenty-one new bills were introduced, and Idaho introduced one in 2018. On June 10, 2017, ACT! for America held "March Against Sharia" rallies in twenty-one states and twenty-nine cities. Brigitte Gabriel was present, in her pretty pastel yellow dress and flower décolletage, inciting the protestors to action. They had *to do* something to stop Muslims from destroying American values.

But there was no need to remind the marchers of that. Just a few days prior, on May 26, 2017, Jeremy Joseph Christian had taken action. He first verbally then physically attacked two women, one of them wearing a headscarf, who were commuting by subway in Portland, Oregon. He hurled epithets: "'Get the f—k out,' 'Pay taxes,' 'Go home, we need American here!' 'I don't care if you are ISIS,' 'F—k

Saudi Arabia!' 'Free speech or die!'" When three men intervened to protect the women, Christian stabbed them. One, Micah Fletcher, suffered wounds—the other two, Myrddin Namkai-Meche, twenty-three, and Rick Best, fifty-three, died.

"THE TRUE STORY OF SHARIA IN AMERICAN COURTS"
Abed Awad, *The Nation*

Antisharia agitators talk a big game about trying to save America from an existential threat, but they don't actually stop a scary, sharia swamp creature from eating us all alive. (They don't stop the *fiqh* monster, either. Because the movement uses "Islamic law" or "sharia," I'll use those terms in the remainder of the discussion.) Sharia is applicable only in a narrow set of circumstances and in no case can it be used to contravene American law. The legal effect of antisharia laws is to intervene in the rather humdrum matter of whether American Muslims can figure out their family matters (marriage, divorce, inheritance), business disputes, and internal community matters according to their own religious tradition.

As Professor Volokh explains, "people sometimes write contracts or wills motivated by their desire to follow or accommodate their felt obligations under Islamic law. A union and a business might, for instance, negotiate a contract that gives a day off for a Muslim holiday. A lender and a borrower may structure a financial transaction in a way that complies with Islamic law related to financing and insurance, but still gives the lender the economic payoff it seeks." These contracts are then "enforced by secular, American courts."

When people write these contracts, they may include a provision that requires disputes to be arbitrated under Islamic law. The US

Constitution, and religious liberty specifically, protects various forms of religious arbitration. It's limited to civil law matters and does not extend to criminal law issues. Faith-based arbitrators also cannot "impose physical punishments, violate people's rights or overstep the bounds of the authority granted to them by the law and the parties regardless of what their religions may teach." So, no cutting off hands of thieves, stoning of adulterers, or other punishments that Americans may popularly associate with sharia (but that were, in fact, common across several cultures in the premodern era).* Even in certain civil matters—for example, when children are involved—the state tends to exercise a bigger role; some states even flat-out prohibit divorced parents from arbitrating disputes over child arrangements.

Muslims aren't the only religious Americans who make use of arbitration (and sharia arbitration is pretty rare compared to other types of arbitration in the US). Many Christian and Jewish Americans consider religious arbitration indispensable to a faithful life. Jews use the Beth Din of America, a court of Jewish law that, as its website describes, helps believers arbitrate "disputes through the din torah process, obtain Jewish divorces, and confirm . . . Jewish personal status issues." Prominent Christian groups like Promise Keepers have long required Christian arbitration clauses in their contracts with vendors, even when those vendors do not share their religious beliefs. Parties to the contract agree to submit disputes to an arbitral panel called Christian Conciliation and abide by the panel's final decision.

Some Christian denominations require that if church leaders have a religious dispute, that they resolve it within the denomination. Even threatening to sue the church in secular court can get you fired—that's

---

* "To many, the word 'Shariah' conjures horrors of hands cut off, adulterers stoned and women oppressed. By contrast, who today remembers that the much-loved English common law called for execution as punishment for hundreds of crimes, including theft of any object worth five shillings or more? How many know that until the 18th century, the laws of most European countries authorized torture as an official component of the criminal-justice system?" Feldman, Noah. "Why Shariah?" *New York Times*, March 16, 2008.

what happened to Cheryl Perich, a commissioned minister who was fired for threatening to sue the church, and then actually did sue the church. Her case was heard by the US Supreme Court. In 2012, the court ruled against her, holding unanimously that her church has the right to hire and fire church ministers as it sees fit, including for their failure to abide by church teachings on dispute resolution.

Religious organizations have broad religious autonomy. Religious individuals have broad freedom of contract. "Jews and Christians may enter into contracts providing for religious arbitration of their disputes (including in situations where there is a good deal of community pressure to enter into such contracts). Jews and Christians may negotiate with employers to get days off on their religious holidays, such as Rosh Hashanah or Good Friday. Jews and Christians may organize their investments in ways influenced by their religions, for instance investing in funds that promise not to participate in projects that the religion views as sinful." The fact is that American law gives wide latitude to contracting parties, religious and irreligious, to use any agreed-upon set of rules to arbitrate their disputes. Muslims are entitled to freedom of contract just like any other American.

But just because Jews, Christians, Muslims, and Americans of every other religion, or no religion, are permitted to write contracts using their own special set of rules, that doesn't mean secular American courts have to accept the contract. Similarly, these groups can arbitrate disputes using the set of rules the parties agreed on, but it doesn't mean a secular court will enforce the arbitrator's decision in every case.

This is because before the civil court signs off on an arbitral decision, it checks to make sure the decision is fair in every way. It asks questions like, did the parties submit themselves to arbitration voluntarily, or were they coerced into it? Does the decision unfairly discriminate against one party? Does the decision comply with US public policy? Does it violate US law in any way? Religious arbitrators have to follow "a set of published, standardized and reasonable procedural limitations, such as allowing lawyers to be present, treating all parties and witnesses equally regardless of sex and avoiding even the hint of corruption or bias." Only after a court reviews the arbitration process and reward for all of these things does the court move forward with enforcement. Importantly, this review process brings Islamic law into conversation with secular law, which helps Muslims who use sharia integrate and "indigenize."

In the process of this review, courts are limited in how they deal with religious law. You might recall from chapter 3 that there are existing principles of religious freedom that shape what courts can and cannot do. Courts are not allowed to decide questions of religious doctrine or force people to conform to religious law.

To illustrate this rule, consider a case dealing with New York's kosher food laws. A judge in 2000 struck down the laws as unconstitutional because they required state inspectors to ensure merchants were keeping kosher in line with how one particular school of Judaism required it. State inspectors would visit supermarkets to check whether kosher meat and dairy products were being mingled or whether vegetable dips contained dairy products. They "would even stick their hands into the water used to defeather chickens in poultry plants to determine whether it was too hot to permit the birds' blood to drain fully." If the inspectors found that the merchants were breaking the rules of this one particular Jewish school of thought, they'd fine the merchants and in certain cases, the merchants could even face criminal charges.

The federal judge in that case said this was completely wrong. The First Amendment of the US Constitution does not permit this sort of "excessive entanglement" between religion and state. Government officials cannot be this involved in religious matters.

But the state does have a legitimate interest in regulating kosher fraud. In 2004, New York passed a new kosher statute, and this time the court upheld it. The 2004 law let kosher food merchants decide which kosher practices they wanted to follow—the state did not impose a particular set of Jewish rules on them. The merchants just have to disclose to the consumer which kosher methods they're using. The consumer can decide for him or herself whether those methods are satisfactory. That agreement between the kosher merchant and the consumer is a civil contract, and if courts ever had to review it, they could do so without getting into religious issues.

Unlike the previous version of the kosher law, the new one was also constitutional because it didn't require the government to monitor religious practices. State inspectors didn't have to keep an eye on kosher kitchens to see if dairy and meat were being kept separate, and they didn't have to fine people for not following religious law. The same rules apply in the sharia context, too. The state cannot decide questions of Islamic law and it cannot force people to comply with Islamic law.

Because we already have rules that regulate the way courts interact with religious doctrine, antisharia laws add no value. As many legal scholars will tell you, antisharia laws are a "solution in search of a problem." One law professor wrote in *Jurist*, "At their best, they do what the law already allows and requires. At their worst, they reveal an ugly underside of law and politics that seems calculated only to alienate and disempower certain disfavored peoples and to condemn certain disfavored faiths."

While they don't solve any existing problems, antisharia laws do create new ones. Antisharia laws don't stop people from writing their religious contracts or from using religious arbitration. But if the parties bring their case to a secular court for enforcement, antisharia laws prevent civil courts from stepping in. For example, let's say an employer agrees in an employment contract that his or her Muslim employee is permitted to take time off for the hajj pilgrimage or to work a different schedule during Ramadan, when Muslims go without food or water from dawn till dusk. The contract is about Muslim religious obligations based on sharia, but a court can enforce it without deciding religious questions. Normally, the law would permit the court to get involved because the contract merely requires the judge to look at the terms the parties agreed to. Similarly, if a person offered to pay for your travel expenses for hajj and then reneged on that agreement, a court can review the contract without deciding religious questions and would be able to step in. But in both of these cases, if the court were in a state with an antisharia law, judges wouldn't be able to enforce the contracts, merely because they involved religious acts like fasting during Ramadan and performing hajj.

More egregious examples of the impact of antisharia laws come from a women's rights context. Antisharia proponents portray themselves as advocates for women and the vulnerable, but as my own example and the example of other Muslim women in the US shows, when Muslim women turn to sharia, they turn to it because it offers them protections far superior to those found in secular law. Antisharia laws get in the way of women exercising these rights.

Consider the case of Elham Soleimani, who in 2012 filed for divorce from her physically abusive husband. Court records told a story of domestic violence, spousal abuse, rape, assault and battery. By the time she filed her case, Soleimani was living alone and destitute in a domestic abuse shelter. Her husband, who had lured her over the Internet to move from Iran to the US to marry him, had failed to deliver on any of his fairy-tale promises. He turned out instead to be domineering and abusive, intent on keeping Soleimani in servitude.

Under their Islamic marriage contract, Soleimani was owed 1,354 gold coins (worth $677,000) in the event of divorce. But just two months before she filed for divorce, Kansas had enacted its antisharia law, Senate Bill 79. When Soleimani turned to the Johnson County, Kansas, court for relief from the harrowing ordeal that her marriage had become, the court refused to enforce the marriage contract—because the Kansas antisharia law said it couldn't.

The irony is so thick. Antisharia laws purportedly protect America from an archaic draconian law. But it was the "draconian law" that gave a divorcée rights and an American court that took them away.

||||||||||||||||||||||||||||||||||||||||||||||||||||||||||||||||||||||||||||||||||||||||||||||||||||||||||||||||||||||||||||||||

"CALIPHATE ON THE RANGE?"
Asma Uddin, *Huffington Post*

||||||||||||||||||||||||||||||||||||||||||||||||||||||||||||||||||||||||||||||||||||||||||||||||||||||||||||||||||||||||||||||||

NEWSCASTER: The idea of Muslim law taking over in a place like Oklahoma where the wind comes sweeping down the plain may seem pretty remote, but still some state lawmakers there have decided it's time to make sure it never happens. They're hoping to get a question on the November ballot that would ask voters whether it should be illegal for state courts to consider anything but US federal and state law when it comes to deciding cases. Republican Rex Duncan is one of the lawmakers backing the vote on the amendment that some call "Save Our State."

(*Duncan's friendly face appears on the screen, a small smile tugging at the edges of his lips.*)

NEWSCASTER: What do you want to save your state from?

DUNCAN: Well, we want to save it from an attack on its survival, its future. Contessa, you know, Oklahomans recognize that America was founded on Judeo-Christian principles and we are unapologetically grateful that God has blessed America and blessed Oklahoma. And State Question 755, the Save Our State Amendment, is just a simple effort to ensure that our courts are not used to undermine those founding principles and turn Oklahoma into something that our founding fathers and our great-grandparents wouldn't recognize.

NEWSCASTER: Do you believe that there is imminent danger of judges considering sharia law when deciding cases?

DUNCAN: It's not just a danger. It's a reality. Every day, liberals and . . . um . . . just . . .

NEWSCASTER: *(Incredulity seeping into her voice despite her best efforts)* "Reality?" Wait, has that happened in your state of Oklahoma?

DUNCAN: It has not. This is a preemptive strike to make sure that liberal judges don't take the bench in an effort to use their position to undermine those founding principles and to consider international law or sharia law. The other part of the state question is to prohibit all state courts from considering international law or sharia law when deciding cases, even cases of first impression.

NEWSCASTER: I'm sorry, Mr. Duncan. But less than 1 percent of your population is Muslim, so where would that threat come from?

DUNCAN: It's a growing threat, frankly. And this again is a preemptive strike. They understand that this is a war for the survival of America. It's a cultural war. It's a social war. It's a war for the survival of our country. And other states while they've looked away too long, looked the other way, and kowtowed to political correctness, have lost an opportunity perhaps to save their state. I believe Oklahoma voters at a margin greater than 90 percent will approve this state amendment, and when we do, other red states and maybe even some lesser blue states will decide whether their states are worth saving, too.

NEWSCASTER: Are you worried about other kinds of religious fundamentalism creeping into the decisions judges make when it should really be based on secular law?

DUNCAN: It oughta be based on state law and federal law and any effort by any source to do anything else . . . frankly it's the face of the enemy, it's the face of the enemy. We need to call it what it is. And Oklahomans are going to do that, and they are going to show other states what it looks like to take a leadership role in saving their own future and sanctity of their state court system.

Muneer Awad couldn't believe the exchange. He was at his home in Atlanta, his television turned to MSNBC when Duncan made his plea to save Oklahoma and save America. "A war for the survival of America"? "Preemptive strike"? Awad recognized the terms immediately as part of the narrative of the war on terror. And now they were being used in reference to his entire faith tradition and faith community.

"After I saw that on TV, I started googling organizations to see if anyone was doing anything about it." His google searches brought up the Oklahoma chapter of the Council on American-Islamic Relations (CAIR), which also happened to be hiring a new executive director. It was serendipity. Awad had been looking to get involved in civil rights work, and here was his opening. Before he knew it, he'd been hired, so he packed up and moved to Oklahoma and brought the only lawsuit to date against an antisharia law.

It wasn't easy, though. He arrived in Oklahoma just one week before the midterm elections. Volatile emotions swirled around the Save Our State Amendment. "It was crazy . . . I would have never wanted it, but I had to have the FBI monitoring me because they thought people had my address, and they thought people were going to do something to my wife and kid." The FBI had good cause for concern; as Awad explained to me, "the building I worked in was being vandalized, the people who threatened to kill me had access to the building I worked in."

State Question 755, the Save Our State Amendment, appeared on the Oklahoma ballot in November 2, 2010 and was passed by 70 percent of Oklahoma voters. Just as Duncan had described it on TV, the bill required courts to only look to federal and state laws to decide cases, explicitly prohibiting the use of international law and sharia.

The Save Our State Amendment read:

STATE QUESTION NO. 755

LEGISLATIVE REFERENDUM NO. 355

This measure amends the State Constitution. It changes a section that deals with the courts of this state. It would amend Article 7, Section 1. It makes courts rely on federal and state law when deciding cases. It forbids courts from considering or using international law. It forbids courts from considering or using Sharia Law.

International law is also known as the law of nations. It deals with the conduct of international organizations and independent nations, such as countries, states and tribes. It deals with their relationship with each other. It also deals with some of their relationships with persons.

The law of nations is formed by the general assent of civilized nations. Sources of international law also include international agreements, as well as treaties.

Sharia Law is Islamic law. It is based on two principal sources, the Koran and the teaching of Mohammed.

SHALL THE PROPOSAL BE APPROVED?

FOR THE PROPOSAL—YES

AGAINST THE PROPOSAL—NO

Supported by CAIR and the ACLU, Awad filed suit against members of the State Board of Elections to prevent them from certifying the election results for that question. He argued that the amendment labeled him a political and social outsider because of his Islamic practice and belief—it did, after all, portray his religious beliefs as an existential threat to Oklahoma (Oklahomans needed to "save their state" by repudiating sharia). The message was "unmistakable": Awad's Muslim "faith is officially disfavored by the State generally, and the judicial system, in particular." The amendment also made his last will and testament unenforceable because those documents incorporated religious provisions.

The lower court ruled in his favor, and when Oklahoma appealed, the appellate court ruled in his favor, too. On the face of it, Awad appeared successful. But he knew the victory was a mirage. Awad recalled for me "the bittersweet moment" when he realized that his lawsuit paved the way for opponents to fix their mistakes and become savvier. "Unfortunately, because of this lawsuit, because of the court's opinion, they saw exactly how to do it [legally] in other states." The court's opinion said, for example, that it was obviously wrong for Oklahoma to single out "sharia" for special treatment compared to any other religious law. In response, Oklahoma enacted a new sharia law in 2013, this time replacing "sharia" with an all-encompassing reference to "foreign law." Oklahoma judges today cannot consider "foreign law" when deciding cases.

What antiforeign law proponents might not have realized, though, is that these broader laws impact not just Muslims but all religious believers who want to use religious arbitration, like the Promise Keepers and the Jewish rabbinical courts. Laws specifically limited to banning sharia are patently unconstitutional, because you can't single out a specific religious community for disfavor. But if you try to fix the problem by casting a wider net, you're going to implicate more than just Muslims.

Jewish groups understood this from the outset. As the Jewish Telegraph Agency reported in 2011, "If the state legislative initiatives targeting sharia are successful, they would gut a central tenet of American Jewish religious communal life: The ability under U.S. law to resolve differences according to halachah, or Jewish religious law."

The Greater Birmingham Ministries also understood the implications when Alabama was considering its antiforeign law bill. The Ministries' executive director, Scott Douglas, told Birmingham News: "This could simply incite religious intolerance and would interpose courts between faithful people [and] their God . . . Besides, they say they want to protect against 'foreign law'? I think, if they check back, Christianity was not founded in Alabama."

Antiforeign law bills also interfere with non-religious contracts that involve foreign transactions. These were among the concerns raised by Randy Brinson, president of the Christian Coalition of Alabama. In Alabama, it was Brinson who led the resistance against the antiforeign law bill. He was concerned it "would communicate to other countries that Alabama doesn't respect their laws," and that it would impose unnecessary obstacles to foreign adoptions, marriages abroad, and business deals with parties outside the US.

In the end, Alabama did pass its antiforeign law bill. But why pass a law that solves nothing and creates unnecessary problems? In Brinson's view, the law had little to do with actual progress and everything to do with "scor[ing] political points with the Christian community." And he was right. After Awad won his case in Oklahoma, Pamela Geller was quick to dismiss his victory as unimportant. She admitted that the Oklahoma amendment was "poorly written and poorly executed. It would never work." What mattered, she explained, "was that 70% of the people voted for it. That shows you the sentiment, because in America you can never get 70% of the people to agree on anything."

Oklahoma representative Rex Duncan had predicted on MSNBC that "Oklahoma voters at a margin greater than 90% will approve this state amendment." He didn't get to 90 percent, but 70 percent is, for all intents and purposes, pretty close. Generating unity had required time and money: months of lobbying, TV advertisements, and robocalls. ACT! for America alone paid for over 600,000 telephone calls to voters, featuring the voice of a former CIA director endorsing the amendment. In the end, it all paid off.

||||||||||||||||||||||||||||||||||||||||||||||||||||||||||||||||||||||||||||||||||||||||||||||||||||||||||||||||||||||||||||||||||||||||||||||||||||||

"'SHARIAH LAW DOES NOT APPLY'—BUT AMERICAN LAW DOES"

Eugene Volokh, *Reason*

||||||||||||||||||||||||||||||||||||||||||||||||||||||||||||||||||||||||||||||||||||||||||||||||||||||||||||||||||||||||||||||||||||||||||||||||||||||

When I look back at Duncan's televised defense of the Save Our State Amendment, what I find most striking is the way he melded concerns about "liberal judges" and "political correctness" with fears about Muslims and sharia. In his view, liberal judges (and presumably liberals generally) are trying to undermine America's founding principles, which he describes as "Judeo-Christian." And apparently, Muslims are their partners in crime.

Duncan's theory is not uncommon among Americans on the political right. Former *Breitbart* editor Ben Shapiro has argued that liberals use Islamophobia as a political tool. In "Why the Left Protects Islam," Shapiro argues: "the Left believes that the quickest way to destroy Western civilization is no longer class warfare but multicultural warfare: Simply ally with groups that hate the prevailing system and work with them to take it down. Then, the Left will build on the ashes of the old system."

After the November 2018 midterm elections, Republican leaders in Texas's Tarrant County wanted to remove the party vice chairman, Shahid Shafi, from his position simply because he was Muslim. They were moved to do this after a Democrat running for federal office (Beto O'Rourke) won Tarrant County for the first time in history. The Republican leaders were alarmed by O'Rourke's win, lamenting that they had become "lax," and then took it out on their one Muslim party member who they feared was "loyal" to Islamic law, without any evidence. *The American Conservative* summed up the county's argument: "no Muslim should ever be a GOP leader, because sharia. That's un-American." In the end, Shafi survived the ouster after Texas Land Commissioner George P. Bush, Texas Governor Greg Abbott, and even Senator Ted Cruz spoke out. In a rare (for him) defense of religious liberty for Muslims, Cruz tweeted: "Discrimination against Dr. Shafi b/c he's Muslim is wrong. The Constitution prohibits any religious test for public office & the First Amendment protects religious liberty for every faith. The Party of Lincoln should welcome everybody & celebrate Liberty." The fact remains, though, that Shafi's position was on the line (and forty-nine party members voted to oust him) simply because of his religion.

These are just snippets of the manifold ways Muslims figure into the ongoing tension between conservatives and liberals. In chapter 8, I discuss these politics in more detail. What's relevant here is how these politics ultimately weaken American law and generate distrust of the American legal system. While the targets may be liberals and Muslims, the results adversely affect all Americans.

Legal scholars have tried to depoliticize the debate. The prominent UCLA law professor, Eugene Volokh, has demonstrated that conservative values do not require measures like antisharia and antiforeign law statutes. In fact, he says, these types of laws create costs that "could be grave." They don't contribute anything new to American law, but they do get in the way of "routine matters applying existing American legal rules related to family law, contract law, tort law, evidence law, and the like."

In "Religious Law (Especially Islamic Law) in American Courts," Volokh states explicitly: "I myself am generally a political conservative, and one who shares some of the concerns about the use of Islamic law in certain contexts . . . Nonetheless, I think many other complaints about incidents of alleged 'creeping Sharia' in American law are misguided, partly because the complaints miss the way those incidents simply reflect well-settled (and sound) American law."

And again, in his piece "Foreign Law in American Courts": "I'm particularly interested in discussing the question because the initiatives that restrict the use of foreign law have mostly come from the political right, and I generally come from there, too . . . But I also think the criticism of the use of foreign law in the American legal system misses some important matters, and the proposed solutions to a real but relatively minor problem may cause much more serious problems instead."

For example, Volokh discusses a 2008 case involving a couple, the Ghassemis, who wed in Iran then came to the US and settled in Louisiana. When the Ghassemis later decided to divorce and petitioned the Louisiana court, the court first had to figure out if the husband and wife were validly married. It turned out that they were first cousins, and under Louisiana law, first cousins are not allowed to get married.

But the Ghassemis had wed in Iran, not Louisiana, and in cases like theirs, Louisiana law said that the court must look to wherever the couple was married. If their marriage was valid in that place, the court could enforce it—unless enforcing it violated strong public policy. The court confirmed that Iranian law permits first cousin marriages and moved forward with the divorce proceedings. As Volokh explains, by looking to Iranian law, the court didn't sidestep Louisiana law; instead, it did just as Louisiana law instructed.

Now, the Louisiana statute did say that the court doesn't have to recognize the marriage if the marriage violates "strong public policy." What does that mean exactly? As the Ghassemi court explained, even though Louisiana law prohibits first cousin marriages, such marriages are not "so 'odious' as to violate strong public policy of the state." The court looked not just at Iranian law but also the laws of Europe,

Canada, and Mexico, and found that first cousin marriages "are widely permitted within the western world" and are legal in many countries even outside of Europe, Canada and Mexico. The US, in fact, is unique in its prohibition against first cousin marriages.

So, "strong public policy" requires something more outside the norm. Volokh says polygamous marriages would fit the bill. And given that the case was decided in 2008, years before the US Supreme Court affirmed the constitutional right to same-sex marriage, if the Ghassemis were of the same sex, the Louisiana court could have considered their marriage against "strong public policy."

But where would the Ghassemis be if Louisiana had enacted a statute that categorically prohibited the court from looking at foreign law? Their marriage would be invalid, and their divorce proceedings moot—a series of unfortunate events with no apparent benefit to the state. After all, the Louisiana law already gave the court flexibility to measure up the marriage against US public policy. There was no need to ban foreign law altogether.

Conservatives might worry that liberals will hijack American courts to subvert America's foundational principles. And they might fear that sharia is the tool liberals will use to do this. But their proposed solution isn't working (and has the added disadvantage of maligning an entire religious community in America). The only thing that antisharia and antiforeign law statutes actually accomplish is the unnecessary weakening of American law. They also lead Americans to falsely believe that their legal system is unsuited to cultural and religious complexity. The fear and anxiety, completely avoidable, harm us all.

"SHARIA IS NOTHING TO FEAR"
Arsalan Iftikhar, *TIME*

Remember the well-meaning but fearful intern from chapter 2 who asked me:

> You said the sharia law of America is nothing to worry about. But what about the people who come here from countries where sharia *is* something to worry about? Shouldn't we be worried about those people threatening our values? Making our women cover themselves in burqas? Bringing terrorism to America?

I hope this chapter has answered his question. To recap: our law distinguishes between belief and action, giving the government ample room to step in and regulate acts that it finds contrary to US law or public policy. The law places limits: sharia arbitration does not extend to criminal law matters, and nobody can force anyone—Muslim or non-Muslim—to submit to sharia arbitration. The courts, in fact, check for exactly these: voluntariness, fairness, and nondiscrimination. With all of these safeguards in place, American values are not at risk. Or as conservative commentator David French put it, "Our system of laws can handle jihadist Muslims. Our Constitution is robust enough to repel any call for Sharia law."

If you're worried about the courts getting it right, it's likely because the current fearmongering has eroded your trust in our judicial system. We have to rebuild that trust. And if you still think we need a statute or some other "fix" to address unknown and farfetched possibilities, then at minimum, the solution needs to make our legal system stronger, not weaker, as antisharia and antiforeign law statutes do.

I hope this chapter has also shown that sharia is not the craziest aspects of Saudi or Iranian law. It is diverse in interpretation and application. It can (and does) mean different things to different Muslims. We have to keep that diversity and complexity of Islamic law in mind when we grapple with Muslim religious exercise in the United States. We can't just label all of sharia as evil and heinous and then ban it with broadly written, superfluous legislation in a frantic attempt to "save" America. Our freedom, our Constitution, requires more.

PART II

|||||||||||||||||||||||||||||||||||||||||||||||||||||||||||||||||||||||||||||||||||||||||||||||||||||||||||||||||||

"Good" versus "Bad" Muslims

*

"Congress shall make no law respecting
an establishment of religion . . . "

Establishment Clause of the First Amendment,
US Constitution

CHAPTER 6

"IF YOU HATE TERROR, STAY HERE."

Every Fourth of July, my family and I take a picnic out to a spot on the lush banks of the Potomac River. We get there an hour before sunset so that we have time to eat before the fireworks begin. And when they do begin, we can't help but hold our breaths.

From where we sit, the Lincoln Memorial is the focal point. The fireworks spark over the center of the memorial and expand outward from there like protea flowers blossoming in front of our eyes. The pistil of the blossom is red, expanding into white, then circled on its outer edge with luminous blue petals. Each successive wave of fireworks explodes with a thunderous clap, and we shudder slightly at every one. The light illuminates the kayaks scattered in front of us on the river, some of them strategically positioned to create the perfect silhouette. Unlike these kayakers in the limelight, we are anonymous in the dark, where we sit, perfectly still, as the specks of light sprinkle downwards, fading against the velvety black backdrop of the sky until they are consumed by it.

But before the show begins, we have to pray. Sunset is, after all, the time for the fourth obligatory Muslim prayer, *maghrib*. Devout Muslims pray at dawn, noon, afternoon, sunset, and at night. And the Prophet Muhammad taught us that "all the world is a mosque"—we should pray wherever we are when it is prayer time. On the Fourth of July, that means praying on the lawn by the Potomac River, in front of the hundreds of people gathered there for the same spectacle we came for.

It's not a particularly discreet prayer, as it does involve physical movements. Standing, then bowing, then prostrating. There are multiple cycles of these movements in every prayer. For the morning prayer, it's two sets of two cycles, for the afternoon prayer, it's a set of four cycles, and so on. But the movements are always the same: standing, bowing, and prostrating. In a Sufi book I once read, the movements were described as mimicking the letters *alif* (A), *daal* (D), and *miim* (M) in Arabic—the triliteral root for "Adam." *Alif* is a vertical line, *daal* is curved, like a *c* flipped around, and *miim* is like an elongated *o*, with a tail hanging downward vertically. Standing *alif*, bowing *daal*, prostrating *miim*. In the very movements of my prayer, I am connected to the first-ever human, the father of mankind—and to my own primordial existence.

The triliteral roots, A-D-M, also give rise to a whole host of words in Arabic, words for "surface," "soil," "earth," "red," and "ruddy." The act of prostration, with your forehead pressed to the ground, connects you to the earth and reminds you where you came from (the Qur'an says Adam was made from soil) and where you will return (when you are buried in the earth at death). It's a remembrance made particularly profound when you are praying on actual grassy earth, the way I do on the Fourth of July.

But the spirituality can be a little hard to muster when you're in the midst of a crowd. I do try for some privacy. There's one willow tree in particular that I have used to envelope me on this annual occasion. Its elongated leaves drape around me almost like curtains, but not completely so. There I stand, reciting softly, "In the Name of God, the Most Merciful, the Most Beneficent."

My voice is tinged with nervousness. I experience the same nervousness every time I pray in the willow's embrace, standing, bowing, and prostrating as required by the *fiqh* of Muslim prayer. Others can see me, and I know how they might react.

These same movements of prostration and bowing have prompted security alerts in the US. Two Muslims praying on a Massachusetts railway platform prompted a heavily armed response by police. Onlookers had called the police and reported that two people who "appeared to be Middle Eastern" were behaving "suspiciously."

Airports and airplanes are an even scarier place to be Muslim. A Muslim prayer simply proclaimed—an *inshallah* ("God willing")—is enough to have you kicked off a plane. It's easy to work *inshallah* into just about any statement, including ones directed at your family or friends who are on the plane with you or on the phone bidding you a safe flight: "*Inshallah*, our trip will go smoothly." "I look forward to seeing you soon, *inshallah*!"

Or, "I gotta go, but I'll call you again when I land, *inshallah*." That's what Khairuldeen Makhzoomi, a college student, was saying after he settled into his seat on a Southwest Airlines flight on April 17, 2016. He was on the phone telling his uncle, in Arabic, about the exciting event he had just attended with United Nations Secretary General Ban Ki-moon, when he noticed his fellow passenger staring, her neck craned in his direction. He cut his conversation short and told his uncle he'd call when he landed, "*inshallah*." That last word triggered the reaction—the woman who had been staring him down sprung out of her chair and headed to the airplane door.

"That is when I thought, 'Oh, I hope she is not reporting me,' because it was so weird," Makhzoomi later told the *New York Times*. But the woman did report him, saying he appeared to be making "potentially threatening comments." Makhzoomi was promptly escorted off the plane and brought into the terminal, where he was searched. Half a dozen law enforcement and a search dog surrounded him, and beyond them onlookers gawked. Though the police found no cause for concern, Makhzoomi was not allowed to reboard the plane.

Just two weeks prior, on April 2, 2016, a Muslim family was deplaned in Chicago's O'Hare International Airport. They were trying to secure their young daughter in her booster seat and asked a flight attendant if she had, as the airline advertised on its website, an extra strap for the booster seat. The attendant rebuffed them and walked away; moments later, a different attendant approached the family and told them they couldn't have the booster seat. The family gave up the booster seat but then came the request from the pilot to disembark. The mother, who wore a headscarf, wondered aloud whether they were being discriminated against, but she and her husband didn't want to frighten their children further or bother the other passengers. The family left the plane quietly.

A month later, on May 14, 2016, a man on a Southwest Airlines flight ripped off a Muslim woman's headscarf, telling her "Take it off. This is America." A couple months after that, two Muslim women were removed from an American Airlines flight after a passenger said they made her feel "unsafe." The airline blamed the Muslim women for "noncompliant behavior," just as it did a Sikh turbaned man and his three Muslim friends when all four were removed from another flight. "There were inconsistencies of their behavior traveling as a group," the airline said. But as the Sikh man, Shan Anand, pointed out, his traveling buddies also included two Latinos, but the only ones from his group taken off the plane were the Arabs and South Asians. These four men were told they made "the crew fe[el] unsafe."

A few more examples: A flight attendant announced on the loudspeaker, "Mohamed Ahmed, Seat 25-A: I will be watching you." She made no announcements about any other passenger. When Ahmed asked why she said that, he was taken off the plane for making the stewardess feel "uncomfortable" (American Airlines, December 2015). Hakime Abdulle, a Muslim woman wearing a headscarf, was taken off a flight after she asked the man sitting next to her if she could switch seats with him. He agreed, but a flight attendant approached Abdulle and said she wasn't allowed to swap seats, despite the airline's policy of not assigning seating. When Abdulle asked why not, she was removed from the plane. The flight attendant told police at the gate that there was no reason for removing Abdulle except that the attendant did "not feel comfortable" with her. (Southwest Airlines, April 2016). Nazia Ali, another Muslim woman in a headscarf, along with her husband, Faisal, were forced to disembark because the flight crew said Faisal was sweating and saying the word "Allah" and that made the flight crew feel "uneasy" (Delta Airlines, July 2016).

"Unsafe," "uncomfortable," "uneasy"—in a post-9/11 world where airlines are trying to make passengers feel safe, these are the code words to get Muslims (or "Muslim-looking" people) off of planes. In 2016, a dozen other cases were reported where Muslim passengers describe being scrutinized and asked to disembark.

Scholar Zareena Grewal sums it up in her book *Islam Is a Foreign Country*:

> The signs that make a person appear threatening . . .
> has grown long and unpredictable: Muslim names, Sikh
> turbans and ceremonial knives, silk veils, a pile of Arabic
> three-by-five flash cards, lingering too long on one page
> while reading (Heidegger), a T-shirt with Arabic writing
> across the chest, the smell of spicy food . . . "I have to
> go!" whispered so low and quickly into a cell phone . . .
> a phrase that, in the explanation of th[e] flight attendant,
> sounded too close to "It's a go!" to be worth the risk.

The religious profiling is now so routinized that it has moved from narrow-mindedness to a "full-blown social organizing principle." It's even got a name: "Flying while Muslim" (much like racial profiling and "Driving while Black").

The fear of Muslims on planes is, in a sense, understandable. We live in a world wracked by terrorism, both global and local, and memories of the 9/11 attacks, when planes were used as missiles, are seared into our subconscious. The Muslim perpetrators of the attacks described their motivations partly in religious terms, and so anyone identified (even mistakenly) as a Muslim puts some people on edge. But while the fear may be understandable, forcing innocent others to pay the price is not only unacceptable, it also doesn't make us more secure.

The indignities Muslims face on airplanes are just a drop in the bucket when it comes to criminalizing Muslims' religious exercise in the name of national security. This chapter will look at just how far the government is willing to go, and what the loss of liberty means for the security of our country.

||||||||||||||||||||||||||||||||||||||||||||||||||||||||||||||||||||||||||||||||||||||||||||||||||||||||||||||||||||||||||||||||||

"AMERICA: CHOOSING SECURITY
OVER LIBERTY SINCE 1798"
Hayes Brown, *Foreign Policy*

||||||||||||||||||||||||||||||||||||||||||||||||||||||||||||||||||||||||||||||||||||||||||||||||||||||||||||||||||||||||||||||||||

We have a tendency to think that security and freedom are in tension with one another, and that security is generally the more important of the two. The Pew Research Center has on several occasions asked Americans whether they were more worried antiterrorism policies will go too far in restricting our rights or not go far enough to protect our security. In 2013, reviewing their surveys from 2001 and 2011, Pew concluded: "The balance of opinion has consistently favored protection." That is, Americans are less concerned about civil liberties and more worried about the government not going far enough to protect security.

This attitude is reflected in our government's approach to security and rights, today and since its inception. Going back to the founding era, President John Adams enacted the Sedition Act of 1798 when he faced the Quasi-War against France. The act allowed the government to disregard the recently penned First Amendment and restrict citizens from giving speeches or publishing anything that could be interpreted as anti-government. During World War I, Congress passed the Espionage Act of 1917, criminalizing any interference with military operations, and the 1918 Sedition Act, expanding the 1798 version to restrict any speech casting the war in a negative light.

During World War II, shortly after Pearl Harbor, the First War Powers Act set up the Office of Censorship, giving it complete discretion to censor communications in the US. The Act gave the US Postal Service the right to open and investigate all mail passing through its hands and do follow-up investigation of anything deemed suspicious. In the 1950s, when the US faced a Soviet threat, the House Un-American Activities Committee and the Senate's Permanent Subcommittee on Investigation conducted numerous hearings, all probing for possible communist threats to the United States. Actors and writers in Hollywood were subject to high-profile investigations as were the many people in government that Senator Joseph McCarthy infamously accused of being communists. In the sixties and seventies, the FBI harassed civilians taking part in the activities of the civil rights movement. The Reverend Martin Luther King Jr. was himself the target of an FBI investigation, while the FBI's counterintelligence program COINTELPRO probed the activities of Americans across ideologies, from the Black Panthers to the Ku Klux Klan.

In the immediate wake of 9/11, American citizens learned they were being wiretapped without a warrant by the National Security Agency. The National Security Entry and Exit Registration System (NSEERS), an immigrant registry, was enacted and unequally targeted Muslims. The PATRIOT Act also targeted American Muslims in its surveillance of telephone and email communications, all justified under a vague definition of "terrorism."

So, this is our country's long-held tradition, aptly described in Hayes Brown's headline in *Foreign Policy*: "America: Choosing Security Over Liberty Since 1798." Today, despite FBI data that in the last sixteen years, white supremacists killed more Americans than "any other domestic extremist movement" and "are likely to carry out more attacks over the next year," American Muslims continue to bear the brunt of the burden. American Muslims' religious exercise and political activism are seen as security threats; both the government and many private citizens associate Muslims with terrorism and ignore (or are ignorant of) stories and evidences to the contrary.

First, Muslims worldwide are the most likely victims of terrorism. The National Consortium for the Study of Terrorism and Responses to Terrorism (START) keeps a database of attacks going back to 1970. Looking at attacks in the Middle East, Africa, the US, and Europe, it found "that Muslims are most frequently targeted." The National Counterterrorism Center has found similarly; in its review of terrorist attacks between 2006 and 2011, it learned that where the religious affiliation of victims could be determined, 82–97 percent of those killed were Muslim.

Second, American Muslims contribute to the security of America in a multitude of ways, including through military service. Two of the earliest recorded evidence of Muslims serving in the US army date back to 1775 and 1783, when Bampett Muhammad served under George Washington. Muslims served in the Union army during the American Civil War; 15,000 Arab Americans served in World War II, and more than 3,500 Muslims served in Afghanistan and Iraq.

At the 2016 Democratic National Convention, Khizr Khan took the mic, his wife Ghazala beside him. In a short but deeply passionate speech that captivated the nation, Khan celebrated the US Constitution and its protections of liberty and equal protection of the law—values his son died defending. US army captain, Humayun Khan, was killed by a suicide bomber in Iraq in 2004.

Captain Khan was born in Pakistan but immigrated with his parents to the US two years later, where his family settled in Silver Spring, Maryland. He was always deeply patriotic, and he was particularly fascinated by Thomas Jefferson. In college, he joined the Reserve Officers' Training Corps (ROTC) to prepare for service in the US military, telling his father that he joined because he "wanted to give back." After graduating, Captain Khan joined the army and during his four years there, he rose to the rank of captain. He was at that point ready to leave the army for law school but changed his mind when 9/11 happened. In 2004, he went to Iraq to assist with postwar efforts; when his mother, fearing for his safety, urged him to return, he assured her he would—just as soon as he fulfilled the "responsibility" he felt toward his fellow soldiers. "I cannot leave them unprotected."

A month after that call, Captain Khan died. The "soldier's officer" was inspecting soldiers entering the Baqubah base when a taxi sped toward his line of troops. Captain Khan instructed the troops to hit the ground while he walked toward the car, his arms outstretched in a halt gesture. Just before the car reached Captain Khan, it detonated a suicide bomb.

He didn't have to be out there, beyond the gates of his fortified compound, checking on lower-ranking soldiers, but he "was a hands-on supervisor who wanted to know what was going on with the men and women under his command." He cared for his troops to the point of putting his life in danger.

Captain Khan's story stands out for its sterling patriotism and heroism. He exemplified that there was nothing inherently at odds between his Muslim faith and his service to America. Thousands of other Muslim service members prove the same point every day.

Outside the military, American Muslims have been vital partners in the US government's fight against terrorism. A 2013 report by Duke University and the University of North Carolina at Chapel Hill found that "since 9/11, 54 Muslim-American terrorism suspects and perpetrators were brought to the attention of law enforcement by members of the Muslim-American community." In its review of terrorism cases from 2001 through the present, the New America Foundation reported that 24 percent of jihadists were "implicated by a tip from family members or the community."

Muslims in government also contribute to the fight. The Department of Homeland Security (DHS) honored Haroon Azar for his outstanding work managing national security matters related to the Middle East, Africa, and South Asia. Azar now directs a university program on security and religious freedom. Shaarik Zafar put in a decade of work on counterterrorism in the White House, DHS, and then the Office of the Director of National Intelligence. He was later appointed by then–Secretary of State John Kerry to serve as a special ambassador to Muslims worldwide. Samar Ali worked closely in 2010 with then–DHS Secretary Janet Napolitano. As the White House Fellows Foundation and Association explained when it honored her in 2018, Ali today works on local, national, and global projects to "strengthen democratic institutions" and "de-stigmatize and de-politicize the Muslim identity in America." Azar, Zafar, and Ali are just a few of the many Muslims working every day for American security.

|||||||||||||||||||||||||||||||||||||||||||||||||||||||||||||||||||||||||||||||||||||||||||||||||||||||||||||||||||||||||||||||||||||

"IT'S NOT THE RELIGION
THAT CREATES TERRORISTS, IT'S THE POLITICS"
Giles Fraser, *The Guardian*

|||||||||||||||||||||||||||||||||||||||||||||||||||||||||||||||||||||||||||||||||||||||||||||||||||||||||||||||||||||||||||||||||||||

Anticipation rippled through the crowd at the 2016 Democratic National Convention as former president Bill Clinton stepped up to the microphone. He beamed over the crowd as he told them how he had met his wife Hillary. He elaborated on her achievements and what she could do for America. He called out to African Americans and Mexican Americans and other minorities, telling them to go vote for his wife.

Then Bill addressed American Muslims. "If you are a Muslim and you love America and freedom and you hate terror, stay here and help us win and make the future together," he said. "We want you."

Hasan Minhaj was in the audience that night. Everyone around him was cheering but Hasan was incredulous. Seriously? Did the former president just tell Muslims that their only value to America was to help it find terrorists?

"Bill, I hate to tell you this, I don't know any terrorists. I'm not Terrorist the Bounty Hunter."

Bill's speech that night sowed the seeds for Hasan's epic rejoinder. Hasan was done being minimized, and so was his community. "Look, I'm not going to get my humanity from Bill f—ing Clinton. He's just not gonna get it. I'm an alien as far as he is—he will never understand where I'm coming from, my POV, the things my community has had to go through. We have to claim that s— on our terms.

"I'm going to show my perspective of what it's like to be an American."

Two years later, in October 2018, Hasan's show *Patriot Act* premiered on Netflix.

While many American Muslims contribute in concrete ways to American security, that doesn't mean that every Muslim does—or should. It's a cherished American tradition to criticize, even condemn, the government's actions and policies. Like every other American, American Muslims shouldn't be expected to put aside their qualms and play the role of the undiscerning patriot in order to be considered fully American. Our political discourse often elides this point; it wasn't a mistake that it was Khizr and Ghazala Khan, the parents of Captain Humayun Khan, who represented Muslims on the DNC stage. Or that Bill Clinton's address to Muslims was carefully moderated. In her recent memoir, Hillary Clinton comments on Trump's inauguration speech, "Americans across a broad spectrum felt alienated . . . Dreamers and patriotic Muslim citizens who were made to feel like intruders in their own land."

Why is there a patriotism qualifier every time Muslims are championed? The political discourse reflects what many experts have identified as a tacit favoring by the government of "good" Muslims over "bad" ones. Unlike the view that all of Islam is hopelessly flawed, the good versus bad Muslim dichotomy presupposes that there is an acceptable version of Islam. Scholar Arun Kundnani calls the first view "culturalism," the second "reformism." Culturalism posits a clash between Islam and Western civilization, reformism a clash between an "apolitical Islam that is compatible with Western values and a totalitarian appropriation of Islam's meaning that has transformed it into a violent political ideology." Reformism got its name because it seeks to reform both culturalism's stereotypes about Islam and, more fundamentally, Islamic culture itself.

So far in this book, I've mapped out the culturalist assault on Islam, the view that all of Islam is not a religion. Among the cadre of culturalists are: Pamela Geller, Frank Gaffney, Brigitte Gabriel, and other "misinformation experts" who portray all Muslim religious exercise —building houses of worship and cemeteries, arbitrating private disputes according to religious law, wearing religious dress—as political and dangerous. For culturalists, the only acceptable Muslim is the one who leaves Islam behind, converting out of the religion.

The focus in this chapter is on the reformist view; the view that *some* versions of Islam are not a religion and must be controlled has been the driving narrative of the global war on terrorism since 2007 (though it's worth noting that President Trump has selected many prominent culturalists to lead his national security policy). For culturalists, terrorism could be explained as easily as pointing to Islam writ large. While this strategy prevailed in the immediate aftermath of 9/11, governments soon realized that killing and capturing wasn't going to be the full solution. They needed a new discourse to guide their counterterror efforts, and thus emerged the reformist theory of radicalization.

Walter Laqueur, the founder of terrorism studies, in 2004 articulated the founding question of radicalization discourse: "How to explain that out of 100 militants believing with equal intensity in the justice of their cause, only a very few will actually engage in terrorist actions?" In other words, how do some people become radicalized and not others? In the years to come, the government would develop its policies based on theories of radicalization that downplayed nontheological factors, like politics and economics, and insisted that certain theological interpretations drive terrorism. These policies violate the most basic religious liberty principles, such as restrictions on government meddling in religious doctrine. The Establishment Clause of the First Amendment ("Congress shall make no law respecting an establishment of religion") prohibits the government from favoring one religion over another and one interpretation of a religion over another. And as we'll see, government policies based on flawed radicalization studies dissuade Muslims from engaging in religious exercise, in clear violation of the Free Exercise Clause.

Let's start, for example, with Daveed Gartenstein-Ross and Laura Grossman's 2009 case study of "the central role of theology in radicalization." The study reviews statements by terrorists, as documented in interviews, trial transcripts, and newspaper reports, to conclude that there are "clusters of indicators" that "suggest a shared trajectory of radicalization." It focuses on six manifestations of the radicalization process: adopting a legalistic interpretation of Islam, trusting only a few "ideologically rigid" religious authorities, viewing the West and Islam as inherently in conflict, exhibiting low tolerance for "perceived religious deviance," and expressing "radical political views." The study concludes that the first five of these behavioral changes show up enough times in their pool of jihadists to conclude that the terrorists' "theological understanding" is a "relatively strong" indicator of radicalization.

Kundnani notes, however, that the study is riddled with methodological and conceptual flaws. There is no control group of nonterrorists to test whether the same religious factors are present in nonterrorists. There's no reasoned basis for choosing the six behavioral changes listed above, as opposed to other behaviors. Plus, how much insight into ideology can really be gleaned simply from breaking down a person's beliefs into six discrete categories? The study also focuses on jihadists only instead of a wide range of terrorists and is based on the unexplained assumption that this form of violence is driven by a unique set of causes not applicable to other forms of violence. As Kundnani points out, the study actually found that the sixth manifestation of radicalization, the expression of radical political views (specifically, that the West is conspiring against Islam and that military action is the solution) was the only manifestation that showed up in every single case the study reviewed. "But the study seeks to evade the implications of its own data . . . Within the study's own framework, a more natural interpretation of the data would be that . . . political radicalization is the key factor in becoming a terrorist."

The study's eagerness to minimize political factors in terrorism can be explained in part by looking at who published and funded the study; it was published by a think tank set up in the wake of 9/11 to shore up support for the war in Iraq, and it was funded by several private foundations that also poured millions of dollars into funding Islamophobia propaganda groups like those led by Geller, Gaffney, and others. Plus, by focusing on theology and not politics, these studies help keep the focus off of state accountability.

But the main reason for Gartenstein-Ross and Grossman's skewed analysis is that it translates more easily into law enforcement policy: "Breaking down religious extremism into different manifestations that can be scientifically associated with terrorism is knowledge that law enforcement and intelligence agencies can easily utilize; on the other hand, painting a more reflexive picture, in which state agencies and terrorists are caught in a dynamic political conflict, is much harder to sell."

Other highly influential studies complicate the picture, even as they continue to downplay the role of politics and economics. For example, former CIA operations officer, Marc Sageman, developed a model that went beyond a purely theological explanation to considering how theological beliefs interact with people's "social psychological journeys." His view, dubbed the "bunch of guys" theory, is that the "most striking feature of the jihadist profile is that 'joining the global Islamist terrorism social movement was based to a great degree on friendship and kinship.'" Sageman says that there are two paths to radicalization: a bunch of guys collectively joining a terrorist organization, or an individual joining a longtime, trusted friend who is already part of such an organization. Social bonds, in Sageman's view, come before ideological commitment, but both elements are needed: radicalization emerges when theological radicalism is embedded in an intense group dynamic.

Again, Kundnani elucidates the obvious weaknesses: "Claiming social bonds to be the root cause of terrorism is inadequate. Even if we accept the implication that terrorism spreads like a virus from a person already infected to his associates, all we have done is explain that process of infection; we have said nothing of why the virus exists in the first place." Even more problematically, Sageman's work like other radicalization studies fails to separate radical beliefs from violent action; Sageman claims that his study is about why terrorists respond the way they do to their situations, but in the end, he has nothing to say about what leads people with radical ideas to engage in violence instead of using other means to advance their cause. He postulates a simple formula: a person with a literalist interpretation of Islam is predisposed to violence—simply add a friendship dynamic to the mix to activate violence. As with other radicalization models, theology remains a key factor and there's no substantive account of politics or economics.

In 2005, Quintan Wiktorowicz developed a still more complex model of radicalization. Like Sageman, he combines theology and social psychology but also introduces the idea of a "cognitive opening"—either a psychological crisis (death in the family, political repression, experiences of discrimination) or "consciousness raising" by persuasive activists shakes up one's previous beliefs and makes one more receptive to new perspectives. The cognitive opening may lead to "religious seeking," and if you happen to also be exposed to radical groups, you can be socialized into joining and accepting the religious authority of the movement's leaders. But in developing this theory, Wiktorowicz interviews only radical activists, not terrorists. His work, like Sageman's, makes "the question of what causes radical religious beliefs . . . a proxy for the question of what causes violence."

Wiktorowicz admits at the end of his study that he found nothing "all that different" in the social psychology of people who become active in violent Muslim groups as compared to nonviolent Muslim groups or non-Islamic social movements. His study, for these various reasons, cannot explain "why violence occurs." And because he, like other terror experts, does not account for the role of politics, he has no idea "what kinds of political circumstances, combined with what kinds of political narratives (even if expressed in religious terms), are necessary for particular kinds of violence to be seen as legitimate within a given movement."

Taken together, the Sageman-Wiktorowicz view is that radicalization results from a "theological-psychological process" in which "dangerous religious beliefs" are activated by either friendship dynamics or a cognitive opening to turn people into terrorists. Theology is always the core. This model of radicalization has strongly influenced American law enforcement agencies. Sageman was an adviser to the New York Police Department and in 2008 was named its scholar-in-residence. In 2011, Wiktorowicz was appointed to the National Security Council under Obama and was credited with developing that administration's counter-radicalization policy.

One example of the Sageman-Wiktorowicz model in action is the NYPD's broad surveillance of Muslims within a 250-mile radius of New York City. The NYPD report, "Radicalization in the West: The Homegrown Threat" identifies "jihadist theology" as the key motivator of radicalization and lists four stages a person goes through on the path to becoming a "likely" terrorist: (1) preradicalization, before the person is exposed to extremist interpretations of Islam; (2) a cognitive opening that leads to a sense of self-identification and association with like-minded others; (3) indoctrination, or the progressive intensification of one's beliefs through group socialization; and (4) jihadization, the acceptance of one's duty to engage in violent action.

The report says that each stage has a separate set of indicators; for example, stage two, indoctrination, is marked by the person becoming alienated from his or her former life; joining a group of like-minded individuals to draw closer to one's extreme theological interpretations; giving up smoking, dancing, and gambling; wearing Muslim religious garb and growing a beard; and engaging in social activism. Religious acts are indicia of radicalization because Islam is recast as a political movement, not a religion. Growing a beard and praying five times a day are no longer acts in the service of God and the purification of one's soul; instead, they are political proclamations, indications that you might be willing to take up arms against your country or engage in other political violence. In the eyes of the government, if you're praying more or studying the Qur'an more regularly than before, you may be moving through the stages of radicalization.

When the NYPD implemented this theory on the ground, it targeted some Muslims over others (the "bad" Muslims as opposed to the "good" ones), defined overtly religious Muslims as potential extremists, and in the process, dissuaded many Muslims from practicing their religion. The less Muslim you appear, the more likely the government won't target you as a security threat.

When a government penalizes your religious exercise, it gets to control what you wear, how you pray, who you associate with, which political views you voice. The incursions on Muslims' most essential freedoms should worry everyone.

|||||||||||||||||||||||||||||||||||||||||||||||||||||||||||||||||||||||||||||||||||||||||||||||||||||||||||||||||||||||||||||||||||||||||||||||||

"THE HORRIFYING EFFECTS OF NYPD ETHNIC PROFILING ON INNOCENT MUSLIM AMERICANS"

Conor Friedersdorf, *The Atlantic*

|||||||||||||||||||||||||||||||||||||||||||||||||||||||||||||||||||||||||||||||||||||||||||||||||||||||||||||||||||||||||||||||||||||||||||||||||

"Thank you so much for carrying that. I wish I could still lift bags like that." The elderly lady beams at you as you finish loading her purchases into her car. You smile and wave as you head back into the church.

Your youth group is holding a fundraiser to buy toys for the children's hospital. It feels good to do something with everyone again. You might suggest more activities especially after the whitewater rafting trip last month was such a success. The leaders had set it all up—reserving the bus and rafts, printing itineraries that allowed for Bible study and prayer time.

"Hey! Have you seen the pastor?" says your friend Talia, grabbing your arm. "Do you remember that friend Eric brought on the rafting trip? The funny girl who said she was trying to reconnect with God? Well, he just found out she was an undercover cop sent to keep an eye on us!"

"What? Why?"

Talia pulls you to the side. "We're a Christian youth group. All the recent school shootings were done by Christians—"

"So, the police were watching us to see if we were planning any school shootings?" You try not to let your voice get too loud. Who knows about this? Did Eric know his friend was a cop? No. Talia had said he had just found out. Poor Eric.

You look around the busy fundraiser. Talia catches your eye and you know she's thinking the same thing. If there was

*an undercover cop on your rafting trip, could there be one
here now? What kind of notes did someone take on a youth
group? Names and ages obviously. Wait! The police have
your name and information. They probably put it on a list
of suspects along with everyone else in your youth group,
too! Sarah had gotten a little carried away with the alcohol
at a recent party and made the mistake of getting behind
the wheel. Did the police know about her DUI? What
if they offered to waive it in return for information on their
group activities? Could Sarah now be spying on them for
the police?*

"It makes you wonder, doesn't it?" says Talia.

*You jump slightly at her voice. "I'm sure the police have
their reasons for watching us," you say, more to convince
yourself. "It's their job to keep everyone safe."*

*"Because a group of young adults is going to plan a school
shooting on a rafting trip," says Talia, rolling her eyes.*

*Your stomach drops and the room tilts slightly. "The spy
took notes on everything, including who we talked to and
how often we prayed."*

The police did not, in fact, spy on a Christian youth group in an effort
to thwart the next school shooter. But an undercover police informant
did accompany a Muslim student group on its white-water rafting
trip. The officer onboard the raft noted the names of the student club's
officers and throughout the trip, he kept tabs on how many of the five
daily prayers the group completed. "In addition to the regularly sched-
uled events (Rafting), the group prayed at least four times a day, and
much of the conversation was spent discussing Islam and was religious
in nature," his report says.

He was taking notes for the New York Police Department. In 2002,
the NYPD, with help from the CIA, began a decade-long program of

covert surveillance that monitored a wide range of Muslims without any probable cause or reasonable suspicion of illegal activity. Leaked NYPD reports plus a series of Pulitzer Prize–winning articles published in 2011 by the Associated Press, revealed how it all worked: the NYPD used census information and government databases to map ethnic neighborhoods in New York, New Jersey, Connecticut, and Pennsylvania. Even if the maps included groups other than Muslims, for example, Syrian Jews, Egyptian Christians, and Catholic or Orthodox Christian Albanians, the NYPD surveilled only the Muslims in that neighborhood. Undercover officers visited local businesses, schools, mosques, and nightclubs and engaged casually with the business owners to get a sense of their religious and political views and report them back to the NYPD. Using a secret unit called the Demographic Unit, the NYPD mounted surveillance cameras on light poles aimed at mosques, which police officers controlled remotely from their computers in order to collect the congregants' license plate numbers and generate footage of everyone entering and leaving the mosque. Over the course of the program, the NYPD surveilled "at least 20 mosques, 14 restaurants, 11 retail stores, two grade schools and two Muslim student organizations."

The invasion didn't stop there. Undercover officers inside the mosque recorded the imam's sermons and statements by mosque congregants. The NYPD also wanted to entrap Muslims in criminal activities and sought to place informants inside every mosque within a 250-mile radius of New York City. Crawlers, or confidential informants, infiltrated mosques, businesses, and schools and used a tactic called "create and capture" to start conversations about jihad or terrorism in order to "bait" people into making inflammatory statements. The informants would record the response for the NYPD and assiduously document each and every conversation. None of the information collected revealed any signs of criminal activity.

The informants included teenagers. Nineteen-year-old Shamiur Rahman was arrested by the NYPD on a marijuana possession offense.

While sitting in a Queens jail, he was approached by an NYPD plain-clothes officer, "Do you want to turn your life around?" he asked Rahman, offering him the opportunity to be an informant. Feeling trapped, Rahman agreed, and soon found himself spying on his community. "We need you to pretend to be one of them," the police told him. "It's street theater." Rahman was paid up to a $1,000 a month for his work.

Asad Dandia, one of Rahman's friends at the City College of New York (CCNY), recalls his shock when Rahman ultimately revealed himself on Facebook as a police informant. "He had told me he wanted to become a better person and to strengthen his faith. So, I took him in, introduced him to all of my friends, got him involved in our extracurricular activities. I would wake him up for prayer every morning. He even slept over at my house, and I let him in even though he smelled of marijuana but I tried to look past it because I knew he was new to Islam." When Rahman finally revealed his undercover role, Dandia not only found himself reeling ("When I was texted the news . . . the shock caused me to drop my phone. It took me 24 hours to get myself together"), but also instantly ostracized by other Muslim students at CCNY, who now all suspected Dandia of being an informant, too. Traumatized, Dandia severed his relationship with the mosque for a year and even after returning kept his distance from other congregants. He left promptly after he was done praying, "believing that anything more might put him at risk."

Dandia's feelings of shock and betrayal echoed throughout the targeted Muslim community when the workings of the NYPD program were first revealed. Before the revelation, Muslim congregants had observed unmarked cars and video cameras outside of mosques. At the time, they thought those cars and cameras were NYPD patrols and surveillance ensuring their safety. But when the AP articles and confidential NYPD documents came out and the Muslim community discovered that it was the target and not the beneficiary of the surveillance, many Muslims' first reaction was to limit their public religious exercise. The NYPD's message was heard loud and clear; as nineteen-year-old Brooklyn College student Sari said, "It's as if the law says: the more Muslim you are, the more trouble you can be, so decrease your Islam."

Many Muslims changed their outward appearance to appear "less Muslim." Debbie Almontaser, a Muslim community organizer and educator, observed the change: "I've seen this emerging again: the number of young women who are not wearing hijab, young men shaving their beard, people changing their names. These decisions are made in part based on [the] psychological trauma that these people are experiencing." One young woman in charge of youth activities at her mosque worried whether she had to change the Sunday school curriculum: "It's very difficult, it's very hard, you don't know what to say, I have to think twice about the sentences I say just in case someone can come up with a different meaning to what I'm saying." In the words of another community leader, the NYPD "created psychological warfare in our community . . . it completely messed with the psyche of the community."

The NYPD had, after all, infiltrated mosques and Muslim businesses and schools with police informants. There was no way of knowing if the person you chatted with at the café was an innocent passerby or an informant trying to lure you down a sinister path. The pervasive uncertainty generated so much paranoia that even prospective converts and others who came to the mosque wanting to learn more were treated with suspicion. As Faisal Hashmi, an activist in Queens, summed up: "I don't want any new friends. If I don't know you and your family, or know that you have a family that I can check you back to, I don't want to know you."

The sacredness of the mosque, too, was violated. Just as the relationship between Christians and their pastor, and Jews and their rabbi, is one of trust and confidentiality, so too is the relationship between

Muslims and their imam. The laws of many states, including New York, even protect all communications between a religious minister and a congregant from disclosure in court (the so-called priest-penitent privilege). But with spies and crawlers now lurking in mosques, documenting conversations and baiting Muslims into saying things that would place them under government suspicion, multiple imams no longer felt comfortable providing one-on-one guidance to congregants. They "could never be sure that a question posed by a congregant is a sincere one, or whether it is an attempt by an informant to elicit opinions that he or she will then pass on to their handlers." The NYPD had made the mosque a trap, a place of anxiety and insecurity instead of safety and spirituality.

The chilling effect extended to political organizing, civic engagement, and activism, particularly because a "radical" Muslim was defined in part by his or her criticism of US policy. (In the "good" versus "bad" Muslim dichotomy, overtly patriotic Muslims are the good ones.) Muslims reported being afraid to discuss any political issue—even ones unrelated to foreign policy and Muslim-majority states—because it may attract police scrutiny. As one Sunday school teacher explained, "I don't talk about the NYPD on Facebook. We'll put articles up, but we will never comment on them, put our own words. Maximum we'll say, 'It's sad that this is happening.' But we will never show our anger, that we're really, really angry. Some people aren't afraid, but I am."

Parents told their kids not to participate in political protests or speak out against policies they opposed, because political activism could make them a target of police action. One young man explained, "I come from a family of activists. My parents, when I first told them the Associated Press story is about to break, my dad told me don't do anything about it. That was the first time my dad ever told me anything like that. This was the first time in my own family where safety trumped what was the right thing to do." With informants hiding at universities and on student field trips, parents also did not want their kids joining the university Muslim Association. Students were even afraid to come to the prayer room: "They felt they couldn't meet in their own space. The idea of being surveilled—for a 19- or 20-year-old—is a terrifying thing."

And as Muslims were afraid to speak with other Muslims, non-Muslims also became hesitant. The NYPD program communicated to non-Muslims that the targeted communities must be connected in some way to terrorism—why else would the NYPD surveil them so heavily? All Muslims were portrayed as disloyal and needing to be monitored, which in turn strained relationships between the targeted Muslims and their non-Muslim neighbors, friends, and employers. In some cases, it results in more than strained relationships; the government's selective focus on Muslims as potential terror threats means Muslims are viewed as a "suspect fifth column . . . deserving discrimination."

Ten years of gross violations of religious liberty, free speech, freedom of association, and other fundamental rights. And in the end, nothing to show for it. The NYPD admitted that the decade-long surveillance did not result in a single terrorism lead. "I could tell you that I have never made a lead from rhetoric that came from a Demographics report," said Thomas P. Galati, the commanding officer of the police intelligence division. What the program did succeed in doing was destroying Muslims' trust in law enforcement, which meant Muslims were less likely to help the police much less call on them for help. The program "discourage[d] community members from reporting hate crimes, domestic abuse, and other crimes or from seeking assistance in emergency situations." Many Muslims no longer felt comfortable asking the police to investigate routine criminal matters; they were scared to report discrimination or even ask for directions because they feared that any interactions with the police could subject them to scrutiny.

They also no longer wanted to assist with national security matters and report suspicious activity. When the NYPD violated the priest-penitent privilege, it also compromised Muslim religious leaders' ability to serve as effective partners in fighting extremism. "After all, how can a leader give guidance in matters that he or she is hesitant to discuss in any way, for fear of covert monitoring or entrapment?" More generally, when the NYPD poured extensive resources into monitoring legal activity, it necessarily diverted time, money, and attention from action that was actually unlawful. In the end, then, the NYPD program made New York and surrounding areas less safe, not more.

And it all took place in a deep-blue state presided over by then-mayor Bloomberg, who somehow remained highly popular among the press and New Yorkers even after the surveillance program was exposed. As Conor Friedersdorf of *The Atlantic* noted, "If Catholics or Jews were targeted by a municipal police department in this way, utterly changing the dynamic of their faith communities for years on end, Americans would be outraged, doubly so if the surveillance produced zero leads and no evidence of averting any serious crime." But Muslims' rights are expendable.

|||||||||||||||||||||||||||||||||||||||||||||||||||||||||||||||||||||||||||||||||||||||||||||||||||||||||||||||||||||||

"THE FBI WANTS SCHOOLS
TO SPY ON THEIR STUDENTS' THOUGHTS"
Danielle Jefferis, *Just Security*

|||||||||||||||||||||||||||||||||||||||||||||||||||||||||||||||||||||||||||||||||||||||||||||||||||||||||||||||||||||||

The NYPD program did not go unchallenged. The Center for Constitutional Rights and the law firm Gibbons P.C. teamed up with the Muslim advocacy firm, Muslim Advocates, to sue the City of New York in federal court. The plaintiff was Syed Farhaj Hassan and other Muslim targets of the NYPD's program. In *Hassan v. City of New York*, the plaintiffs claimed that the NYPD violated their religious liberty when it used their Muslim identity as a "permissible proxy for criminality" and surveilled them without any evidence of wrong-doing.

The case presented cut-and-dry violations of constitutional rights but the court still somehow found a way to dismiss the case, saying the program probably didn't intend to discriminate and was likely just trying "to locate budding terrorist conspiracies." When the plaintiffs appealed the decision to the Third Circuit Court of Appeals, Judge Thomas Ambro called out the lower court for its outrageous decision: "That we might be able to conjure up some non-discriminatory motive to explain the City's alleged conduct is not a valid basis for dismissal." In a careful dissection of intent versus motive, Ambro explained that it wasn't enough for the city to say it instituted the program in a laudable attempt to curb terrorism. The city engaged in counter-terrorism by intentionally singling out Muslims and Muslims only. "Thus, even if NYPD officers were subjectively motivated by a legitimate law-enforcement purpose (no matter how sincere), they've intentionally discriminated if they wouldn't have surveilled Plaintiffs had they not been Muslim."

For procedural reasons, the court couldn't get into whether the city violated the religion clauses of the Constitution, but it did emphasize the key issues at hand. "Lurking beneath the surface . . . are questions about equality, religious liberty, the role of courts in safeguarding our Constitution, and the protection of our civil liberties and rights equally during wartime and in peace." Judge Ambro underscored the importance of courts enforcing the Constitution whenever "there is a fear of a few who cannot be sorted out easily from the many."

> Even when we narrow the many to a class or group, that narrowing—here to those affiliated with a major world-wide religion—is not near enough under our Constitution. "[T]o infer that examples of individual disloyalty prove group disloyalty and justify discriminatory action

against the entire group is to deny that under our system of law individual guilt is the sole basis for deprivation of rights." [. . .]

What occurs here in one guise is not new. We have been down similar roads before. Jewish-Americans during the Red Scare, African-Americans during the Civil Rights Movement, and Japanese-Americans during World War II are examples that readily spring to mind. We are left to wonder why we cannot see with foresight what we see so clearly with hindsight—that "loyalty is a matter of the heart and mind[,] not race, creed, or color."

Ambro's reference to history is particularly apt when it comes to the NYPD, which has long used controversial tactics. The intelligence unit was instituted in 1904 as the "Italian Squad" to surveil suspected anarchists. During the Cold War, the NYPD's "Red Squad targeted communists, trade unionists, civil rights organizations, and black radicals." It later shifted its focus to Vietnam War protestors, students and civil rights groups. "By 1970 it had collected dossiers on over 1.2 million New Yorkers," which it shared with investigators and prospective employers. A 1971 class-action lawsuit contested the NYPD's harassment, resulting fourteen years later in the Handschu Guidelines, which restricted NYPD investigations into non-violent political activity. But in the aftermath of 9/11, the NYPD petitioned the court to relax the guidelines and won the right to revive the old Red Squads, this time to target the local Muslim population. (The judge who granted the leeway later regretted his decision and pushed the NYPD to do more to protect against "potential violations of the constitutional rights of those law-abiding Muslims and believers in Islam who live, move and have their being in this city.")

As Kundnani points out, "once these tactics have become common-place in relation to Muslims, they can easily be extended to others." And in fact, they have been. The NYPD monitors nonviolent activism by pro-Palestinian groups and African American groups protesting police racism. The *New York Review of Books* also found compelling evidence that the NYPD's Intelligence Division spied on and harassed the organizers of Occupy Wall Street.

The NYPD program is now defunct. In 2014, the police department abandoned the program and switched its approach to direct engagement with community leaders. As its chief spokesman explained, "Understanding certain local demographics can be a useful factor when assessing the threat information that comes into New York City virtually on a daily basis . . . In the future, we will gather that information, if necessary, through direct contact between the police precincts and the representatives of the communities they serve." In 2018, the City of New York settled with the plaintiffs in *Hassan*, agreeing as part of the settlement to reform its practices and no longer engage in "suspicionless surveillance on the basis of religion or ethnicity" and give plaintiffs the opportunity to provide feedback on the NYPD's "first-ever Policy Guide, which will govern the Intelligence Bureau's activities, and to publish the Guide to the public." The NYPD now also has a Muslim Officers Society, which has increased police recruitment among Muslims from a handful in 2001 to more than 1,000 today.

Even with the NYPD program gone, other national security policies targeting Muslims continue to have a devastating impact on Muslims throughout the United States. The extensive Countering Violent Extremism (CVE) program instituted in 2014 under the Obama administration, and continued (in even more alarming ways) under President Trump, "aims to deter U.S. residents from joining 'violent extremist' groups by bringing community and religious leaders together with law enforcement, health professionals, teachers and social service employees." Even with the NYPD program gone, other national security policies targeting Muslims continue to have a devastating impact on Muslims throughout the United States. The extensive Countering Violent Extremism (CVE) program instituted in 2014 under the Obama administration, and continued (in even more alarming ways) under President Trump, "aims to deter US residents from joining 'violent extremist' groups by bringing community and religious leaders together with law enforcement, health professionals, teachers, and social service employees." Many of the efforts are framed as "community-building" initiatives, but what this often (though not always) means in practice is the institution of "soft surveillance." According to the Muslim Justice League, under CVE, the US government gives out hundreds of thousands of dollars as incentives to non–law enforcement professionals like doctors in community clinics, counselors, teachers, and religious leaders to, in effect, encourage them to monitor their patients, students, and congregants. If the patient, student, or congregant appears "vulnerable to extremism," the CVE "soft spies" can report them and refer them to deprograming interventions.

What are these soft spies looking for? In 2014, the assistant to the president for Homeland Security and Counterterrorism, Lisa O. Monaco, listed "sudden personality changes in . . . children . . . becoming confrontational. Religious leaders might notice unexpected clashes over ideological differences. Teachers might hear a student expressing an interest in traveling to a conflict zone overseas." Other signs of "extremism" in youth: "Questioning authority, experimenting with new identities, forming independent political views . . . and showing solidarity with oppressed communities."

Unsurprisingly, because of these tactics, many Muslims are afraid to share and receive information, voice dissent, or engage in public religious expression. In a letter to the National Security Subcommittee in the US House of Representatives, the Muslim Justice League explained that some Muslims even avoid seeking mental health services for fear they'll be spied on and reported by their healthcare provider.

Guided by the Sageman-Wiktorowicz theory of radicalization, parts of the CVE program downplay political and economic factors and focus on theology. They hold that beliefs—not actual violent actions—require interventions, even if the person holding such beliefs has never committed violence and has no plans to do so. CVE can thus serve as a type of thought police; as the League explains, "While promoted as a national security strategy, CVE operates as a social engineering campaign by suggesting that certain dissent, religious practices, or information seeking are 'pre-criminal.'" In this way, CVE creates a simplistic, discriminatory dichotomy between "moderate" and "radical" (or "good" versus "bad") Muslims, defined in large part by outward signs of religiosity.

||||||||||||||||||||||||||||||||||||||||||||||||||||||||||||||||||||||||||||||||||||||||||||||||||||||||||||||||||||||||

"15 YEARS AFTER 9/11, SIKHS STILL VICTIMS OF ANTI-MUSLIM HATE CRIMES"
Moni Basu, CNN

||||||||||||||||||||||||||||||||||||||||||||||||||||||||||||||||||||||||||||||||||||||||||||||||||||||||||||||||||||||||

Balbir Singh Sodhi set his newly purchased plants on the pavement outside the store. He looked into his wallet for some cash, smiling gently at the young woman taking donation for the 9/11 victims and their families. He only had seventy-five dollars after purchasing his plants. As a devout Sikh he must always help those in need.

Balbir loaded his plants into his car and drove back to his gas station. Owning his own business had been but a dream when he first arrived from India ten years ago. He smiled with pride as he looked around the neat little station. His brother would be over soon with some American flags to hang in remembrance for the victims. They should put them in the windows.

He placed the new plants on either side of the door, adjusting them slightly. He would plant them after he helped his landscaper Luis with the flowers near the road. A car rumbled past Balbir and Luis working. A truck pulled in and stopped, engine still running. Balbir looked up to see the driver pointing a gun at him. Five shots split the air in rapid succession and the truck roared off down the road.

On September 15, 2001, just four days after 9/11, Frank Roque shot and killed Balbir Singh Sodhi. Roque told friends that he wanted to "go out and shoot some towel heads" as revenge for the actions of Osama bin Laden.

Almost exactly twelve years later, Dr. Prabhjot Singh was walking home, as he usually did, after work at Columbia University, where he taught international and public affairs. He liked to stroll past Central Park to enjoy a bit of nature after being in the classroom all day. The dense New York air always seemed fresher under the trees.

He smiled up at the dim branches. It was a little after eight at night. Good thing he had already had dinner because he didn't feel like cooking when he got home.

"Terrorist! Osama! Get him!" A group of boys on bikes burst out of one of the many park paths, making straight for Dr. Singh. "Terrorist!" they yelled again. The closest boy leaned over his handlebars and yanked Dr. Singh's beard. The professor scrambled to get out of the way of the oncoming bikes, but a few broke away to cut off his retreat. A kick to his chest sent him to the pavement.

Some of the boys jumped off their bikes so they could punch him harder. The others contented themselves with kicking and continuing their jeering. "Osama! Terrorist!" A savage kick to Dr. Singh's jaw made his eyes tear up. He could barely breathe from the repeated blows to his chest and side. Faintly, he heard other pedestrians yelling at the boys to stop. Were they going to listen? Would he get out of this alive or would he be beaten to death on the streets of New York?

Suddenly, the gang took off back into the park. Dr. Singh recognized the voice of the nurse who lived near him calling for an ambulance. He said a quick prayer of thankfulness. He was alive.

Just a year prior, Paramjit Kaur hadn't been as lucky.

Paramjit dusted off her hands and gazed around the gurdwara. The Sikh temple was clean and ready for everyone to come pray. She glanced at her watch. Fifteen minutes until the rest of the congregation would start to arrive. She bustled into the kitchen to see how the cooking was going.

The other women laughed and chattered as they prepared for their meal that afternoon. Paramjit loved *langar*, when she served a meal to all of the temple visitors. It gave her the chance to see how everyone was doing, who needed help and what she could do for them. However, no one seemed to need her help here, so she walked back into the main hall. There was still plenty of time to pray.

She closed her eyes to focus better. There was so much to be thankful for—her two sons, the chance to come to America and make a good life for them, their chance at a good education. Everyone at the gurdwara was so kind.

What was that noise?

A hand urgently tapped her shoulder. It was her sister. "Get up! We have to go," she said. "Someone is shooting everyone in the building!"

Now she could hear the gunshots and the screaming. Had someone told the children in the classrooms? What about the other women? She took a deep breath and smiled. "Let me finish my prayers," she said. "You go ahead."

She closed her eyes again and turned her thoughts to everyone in the temple. Please, keep them safe. Please, help them and the person doing this. She stayed a moment longer. The door burst open behind her and a gun fired.

It was August 2012, and Wade Page had just entered the gurdwara in the Milwaukee suburb of Oak Creek, Wisconsin. The children were doing their Sunday school together while the women chatted and cooked. Minutes before the rest of the congregation was to arrive, Page did. He fired rapidly on the unsuspecting kitchen, murdering six of the congregants.

Balbir, Dr. Singh, and Paramjit were all attacked because the per-petrators mistook them as Muslims; their brown skin and the men's turbans fit the targeted phenotype. You can "look" Muslim without even being Muslim. And among actual Muslims, there are distinctions. "Muslim" in many Americans' minds means brown; South Asian and Middle Eastern fit the look but Southeast Asians don't (even though Indonesia has the largest Muslim population in the world—approx-imately 225 million Muslims). Even "mainstream media representa-tion—from news stories featuring 'Muslim experts' to TV and cinematic portrayals—have been generally limited to the 'Brown Muslim For-eign Other.'" This, despite African American Muslims constituting the largest group of Muslims in the US, a full third of American Muslims.

Several scholars argue that this construct of the "Muslim-looking" person racializes Muslim identity, that is, it makes Muslimness an immutable characteristic—more like race than a religion. And when the government, media, and private citizens conflate Islam and terrorism and view all Muslims as actual or potential terrorists, terrorism (or a pro-clivity to violence) also becomes an immutable aspect of Muslimness. As one writer notes, Muslims and Muslim-looking people are "projected as the fictionalized 'terrorist enemy' . . . whose violence, danger and disloy-alty is innate such that it transcends citizenship . . . they are neither citizen nor alien, but rather belong to this inherently evil world called 'Islam.'"

Chapter 7 will explore some of the "performance strategies" many Muslims employ to assimilate into the mainstream and escape this enemy classification. But a racialized Muslim identity means that you can carry the burden of Muslimness even if you stop wearing a headscarf, shave your beard, and never utter a prayer in public. Even changing your name is not enough. Indeed, the NYPD gave special scrutiny to those Muslims who changed their names.

This treatment of Muslimness as akin to race, and not religion, is another way the false claim that "Islam is not a religion" degrades Muslims' rights in America.

II

"LIBERTY IS SECURITY"

Karen J. Greenberg, *The American Conservative*

IIIIIIIIIIIIIIIIIIIIIIIIIIIIIIIIIIIIIIIIIIIIIIIIIIIIIIIIIIIIIIIIIIIIIIIIIIIIIIIIIIIIIIIIIIIIIIIIIIIIIIIIIIIIIIIIIIIIIIIIIIIIIIII

How does the government get away with such wide-ranging restrictions on religious liberty? At various points in this book so far, I have explained that in many cases, the legal standard governing religious liberty is strict scrutiny. For example, under the federal RFRA, state RFRAs, and sometimes under the Free Exercise Clause, if the government restricts religious exercise, it has to show that that restriction serves a compelling government interest and that there is no less restrictive means of serving that interest. The standard is utilized by judges to decide many religious liberty cases, so if the government is trying to figure out whether its policies are going to hold up in court, it should assess how they'd fare under strict scrutiny.

When it comes to national security, though, the government gets extra deference. In the travel ban case, for example, the Supreme Court did not even apply strict scrutiny, holding that at least when it comes to national security matters in immigration and foreign policy contexts, a much lower standard is appropriate (something called rational basis review under which the government generally wins). This sort of judicial deference is not uncommon; even though "national security" is "ill-defined and elastic," courts think of these policies as demanding "an additional degree of deference" and "triggering a distinct set of considerations for judicial review." In other words, the government in these cases can get away with a lot more than it usually would be able to. To take the travel ban example again, the Court deferred to President Trump despite former national security officials demonstrating in an amicus brief that the ban deviated in crucial ways from standard protocol. The ban "did not emerge from the sort of careful interagency legal and policy review that would compel judicial deference." But the court still chose to defer.

Special deference also gave us Supreme Court decisions that upheld the internment of Japanese-Americans during World War II and the severe curtailment of civil liberties during World War I and the early Cold War. Ceding such vast ground to the government empowered it to enact the Chinese Exclusion Act in 1888 and exclude many Jewish refugees fleeing the Nazis in the 1930s.

The willingness of judges to give the executive branch so much leeway reflects in many ways the broader American attitude toward national security and civil rights. As I noted earlier, many Americans tend to think that security and freedom are in tension with one another, and that security is generally the more important of the two. Purported threats to security evoke fears and uncertainties among the citizenry, giving governments an excess of discretion to abuse that power. Our history as a country reflects this approach; every time we face a national security threat, we allow wide incursions on liberty.

The United States is not unique in this regard. Across the world, it has become all too common for governments to use security as an excuse to violate human rights, including religious freedom, in the most blatant and egregious ways. These governments insist that more security requires less religious liberty. In my work with the Organization for Security and Cooperation in Europe (OSCE), where I serve as an expert advisor, I have noted numerous instances of this in the regions the OSCE covers (North America, Europe, and Central Asia). Many of these countries have poorly conceived laws, security policies and practices that are drafted too broadly or applied arbitrarily. Such measures are often enacted in the name of "national" or "state" or "public" security or in the interests of preserving "peaceful coexistence," "social stability," or "social harmony." The laws cover everything from "extremist" language in religious literature to religious dress—for example, numerous cities in France banned the modest swimsuit known as the "burkini" because they considered it a security threat. In many Central Asian states, the government limits the number of mosques in each neighborhood, restricts access to those mosques (Tajikistan, for example, prohibits anyone under eighteen from participating in public religious activities), and even monitors in-home religious study and discussion.

Underlying these human rights violations is the false belief that more security requires less freedom, when in fact the evidence points the other way. According to a global study by the Pew Forum on Religion and Public Life, the more the government restricts our rights, the more society loses cohesion—the rise in "social hostilities" includes more "mob or sectarian violence, crimes motivated by religious bias, physical conflict over conversions, harassment over attire for religious reasons, and other religion-related intimidation and violence, including terrorism and war." So, if the government wants to cultivate security and an orderly, peaceful society, it needs to protect, not violate, its citizens' rights.

Nilay Saiya, in his 2018 book *Weapon of Peace: How Religious Liberty Combats Terrorism*, also argues that "when governments violate the religious freedom of their citizens, they foment religious terrorism." Saiya's statistical analysis of 151 countries from 2001–2013 shows both that repression breeds violence, and that liberty helps religious communities further the common good. His 2014 study, "Explaining Religious Terrorism: A Data-mined Analysis," similarly looked at "the characteristics that contribute to a country experiencing religiously motivated terrorism. The analysis finds that religious terrorism is indeed a product of a dearth of religious liberty." Sam Brownback, the current ambassador-at-large for International Religious Freedom, has also emphasized the importance of religious freedom to American national security.

Scholars specializing in American counterterrorism policy have said the same: when we violate liberty, we make ourselves less secure. First, gross violations of liberty simply don't work in preventing security threats. For example, the National Security Agency (NSA) with its more than $10 billion annual budget was never able to thwart a single terror attack through its massive surveillance of phone records. Both the president's Review Group on Intelligence and Communications Technologies and the Privacy and Civil Liberties Oversight Board found that the surveillance program was completely ineffective: "We have not identified a single instance involving a threat to the United States in which the program made a concrete difference in the outcome of a counterterrorism investigation."

Similarly, the CIA torture program, in which the CIA brutally tortured terrorism detainees overseas, proved completely ineffective. And we saw the same admission from the NYPD's commanding officer of police intelligence about the NYPD's vast surveillance program: the demographics report yielded not a single lead.

Second, human rights violations weaken security. Sahar Aziz, a law professor and former civil rights attorney at the US Department of Homeland Security, has counseled US counterterrorism officials about the benefits of protecting liberty, and the risks of violating it. In "Protecting Rights as a Counterterrorism Tool: The Case of American Muslims," Aziz notes that "violent extremism is a tool employed in furtherance of a political agenda often based on perceptions or realities of subjugation, oppression, and marginalization." If the US government violates free speech and religious freedom, it provides an opening for "terrorist recruiters to provide an alternative means for vulnerable recruits to seek justice." Similarly, if the government fails to address inequalities in education, public services, and employment opportunities, it helps create a group of people who have "little to lose" and become receptive to "extremist recruiters' claims that hard work and patriotism are self-defeating. Coupled with severe mental health problems or desperate financial straits, the result can be predictably volatile."

Third, protecting liberty makes us more secure. If the state both refrains from human rights violations and vigorously defends Muslims' rights, allowing for free and open religious exercise and political dissent, the government will hinder extremist recruiting.

And it's not just the government's human rights violations that affect our country's security; discrimination by private individuals does, too. University of Chicago law professor Aziz Huq has empirical proof that "private discrimination against American Muslims increases the nation's vulnerability to terrorism." His research shows that when people experience private animus, they are less likely to cooperate with police because they believe the police hold those same discriminatory views. This reality, applied to Muslims, has ramifications for our national security; as Huq points out, compared to the general public, cooperation by American Muslims is plausibly more valuable to law enforcement. In the end, we have "a negative feedback loop between private discrimination and public security: terrorism provokes discrimination, which in turn increases vulnerability to terrorism."

How do we disrupt this negative feedback loop? If the discrimination takes a legal or official form, the solution lies in the religion clauses of the First Amendment. American courts can restore nondiscrimination by protecting Muslims' rights under the law. In this way, our constitution has the "tools to vindicate both core rights and security values." Stated another way, in order for us to be more secure, we need to protect liberty and equality under the law.

The American Conservative summed it up in its piece, "Liberty Is Security":

> It's a curious fact that what's actually lawful and mindful of liberty has turned out to be what also makes us more secure against our enemies . . . Put in a nutshell: the liberties designed almost a quarter-millennium ago by the Founding Fathers still turn out to be curiously well-aligned with the security of this country and the safety of Americans.

CHAPTER 7

"WHY HIJAB?"

I've broken down in tears at least 4 times in the past month alone. The struggle is too real . . . It's the little things that really break me. I can deal with racist comments and even fight off physical attacks. But it's the side-eyes, the tension, the tip-toeing of people around me that break me.

It's having such an unbelievably hard time making friends. It's constantly thinking, "Is the problem in me? What am I doing wrong?" How when I walk into a room, people tense up. Could've sworn I heard them cracking jokes and laughing before I walked in, but now you could hear a pin drop.

It's being treated so differently—like I'm this odd, for-eign, boxed-out creature. It's walking out of a job inter-view and wondering "when they said I'm unprofessional —were they talking about me . . . or my hijab?" It's trying to pretend like I don't notice those strangers pointing at me as I pass by because I am too tired to deal with this today. It's walking into a room with hundreds of people and not seeing ONE other hijabi—and feeling so, so alone.

It's how these things are so low-key I have to keep asking myself, "Am I crazy? Is it all in my head?" . . . I get it. I'm opening up about this because hijab isn't easy for ANY of us—not even the ones who are extremely proud of who we are and what we stand for (I love

my hijab). The fact is that hijab is so . . . hard. But the
reward is so worth it. Just taking this pain and absolutely
owning it. Normalizing hijab. Telling myself I'm going to
do EVERYTHING in my power so no little Muslim girl
has to face this. And above all, facing my Creator on the
Day of Judgement and telling Him ALL about it.

Above is a 2018 Facebook post by Essma Bengabsia, a young American Muslim woman. It reflects the multilayered plight that Muslim women in America have faced for years, and most acutely since 9/11. You might think of the layers of discrimination as being like the layers of the thick skin that Muslim women need to survive in today's politicized climate. The outermost layer, or epidermis, includes the incidents that impede a woman's ability to exist in public without fearing for her safety, or even being in social spaces without being ostracized in myriad ways. Beneath this layer is the dermis—the bias in the workplace and job application phase, which affects a woman's right to livelihood. Deeper still is the hypodermis—the imposed alienation and isolation that threatens to impede a woman's spiritual connection with her headscarf and the One for whom she wears it. In this chapter, I will look at each of these layers in turn.

I will also introduce another version of the statement "Islam is not a religion" that is cropping up in American politics and public discourse—in addition to right-wing pundits who are making this false claim explicitly, some Muslims are viewing Islam as taking on a secular character. In this context, I will explore how the hijab is being reimagined as a political symbol. In the next chapter, I will broaden the discussion to address the role of a secularized Islam in today's major debates about religious liberty and sexual freedom.

||||||||||||||||||||||||||||||||||||||||||||||||||||||||||||||||||||||||||||||||||||||||||||||||||||||||||||||||||||||||||

"CHOOSING BETWEEN A HEADSCARF AND A JOB"
Michelle Chen, *The Nation*

||||||||||||||||||||||||||||||||||||||||||||||||||||||||||||||||||||||||||||||||||||||||||||||||||||||||||||||||||||||||||

The recent #MeToo movement has shown just how big a problem the US has with sexual harassment and assault. And as we saw in chapter 2, certain subgroups of women—such as women of faith—experience their own unique version of this aggressive violation. For Muslim women, the assault (often in the form of the hijab grab) happens on the streets, in parking lots, and in restaurants. In diverse Brooklyn, two Muslim mothers were punched and kicked in front of their small children whom they were pushing in strollers. Fifty-one-year-old Souad Kirama was punched in a Panera Bread and called a "terrorist," Sonya King was strangled with her headscarf while trying to deliver a food order; the perpetrator allegedly said, "Oh, and by the way, I'm Jesus," before he grabbed her scarf and used it to try to choke her. One Muslim woman was sideswiped off the road by an SUV driver and then stabbed by that same driver, and another woman's hijab was grabbed while she dined in a New Hampshire restaurant.

For Yusor and Razan Abu-Salha, the violence followed them into their home. Each was killed execution-style by a neighbor who came to their door. Muslim women in airplanes are treated like terrorist suspects because of their headscarves, and they and their families are forced to deplane in order to appease other passengers. Muslim women as mothers in some cases forego the headscarf for fear that their children will suffer the consequences. If their kid can "pass" as non-Muslim, the last thing some Muslim mothers want is to show up at their school wearing a scarf and marking their kid for the faith-specific bullying that now plagues 42 percent of Muslims with children in grades K–12.

The harassment women face is not always explicit. As Bengabsia notes in her Facebook post, the hate manifests itself through hostile stares and dismissive statements that make her feel like an "odd, foreign, boxed-out creature." It also interferes with her ability to earn a livelihood and cultivate a career: "when they said I'm unprofessional —were they talking about me . . . or my hijab?"

Bengabsia's not alone in this struggle. The ACLU found that "69% of women who wore hijab reported at least one incident of discrimination compared to 29% of women who did not wear hijab." The Equal Employment Opportunity Commission said that in the initial months after 9/11, there was a 250 percent increase in incidents of workplace discrimination against Muslims. In more recent years, those numbers have stayed high. In 2015, out of 3,502 total charges filed for religious discrimination, 708 or 20.2 percent of them were Muslim cases—even though Muslims constitute only 1.1 percent of the US population. In 2016, Muslim cases made up 28 percent of the total, and in 2017, 23.3 percent.

The discrimination starts in the job application phase, simply by submitting a resumé with a Muslim name on it. For example, Shahida Muhammad applied to multiple jobs after she graduated from college but failed to receive even a response. At some point along the way, she realized it was her quintessentially Muslim name—Muhammad— that might be resulting in the hesitation, so she decided to put "Stacy Jackson" on her resumé instead. She used the resumé to reapply to jobs that had previously rejected her, partly to test her hunch that she had been religiously profiled. The results were staggering. She writes, "After a morning of applying, I had at least three email responses and two phone calls."

Showing up to a job interview wearing a headscarf can also hurt your job prospects. In 2013, researchers Sonia Ghumman and Ann Marie Ryan sent out students (ages nineteen to twenty-two) with and without the hijab to seek employment at mall retail stores and restaurants in middle-income, Midwestern cities. The study consisted of 112 trials and was designed to measure formal discrimination, such as outright refusal; subtle discrimination in the form of verbal and nonverbal behaviors; and the students' expectations about job offers. It looked at the various parts of the job application process, such as "the permission to complete job applications, job availability, job call backs, interaction time, and perceived negativity and lack of interest by the employer." Altogether, the study found that across these aspects of the hiring process, wearing hijab hindered job prospects. It also found that women in headscarves had lower job expectations and that they were more likely to be hired by employers with an existing diverse workforce.

A 2018 study interviewed thirty-five Muslim women who wore headscarves in the workplace. Sixty-three percent of the respondents reported small acts of intentional aggression. Samira, a chemist, said a coworker would "leave pork sandwiches on my desk, in an attempt to see how I will react." Nora, a receptionist, was asked by her employer to "Americanize"; he feared his customers would see her scarf and question her patriotism, so he asked her to wear an American flag pin on her collar. Sarah, a college professor, tried distinguishing terrorists from the majority of Muslims only to be told by a work colleague, "I think deep down inside you guys are all taught not to show us that." Reema, a dental hygienist, was told by several patients that she wasn't allowed to touch them because she wore a headscarf.

A few cases have made headlines. In 2008, twenty-eight-year-old Imane Boudlal, a US citizen born in Morocco, began working as a hostess at a Disneyland Park in Anaheim, California. Her job required her to greet customers and escort them to their tables. At the time, she didn't wear hijab at work, but still faced harsh comments from fellow staff, who called her a "terrorist," "camel," and other demeaning epithets. In 2009, Boudlal started wearing the hijab in all public settings outside her workplace. In 2010, she decided to be true to her beliefs and wear the scarf at work, too.

But when Boudlal asked permission to wear the headscarf, Disney refused, saying it violated the company's "look policy" (a list of guidelines a company gives its employees about what's required for their physical appearance). According to Disney, the headscarf would "negatively affect patrons' experiences at the café." Boudlal's managers proposed a compromise: she could wear the headscarf if she worked in the rear of the restaurant, out of the customers' view, or she could wear a large fedora hat over her headscarf to hide it. When Boudlal refused, she was fired. "Disneyland calls itself the happiest place on earth, but I faced harassment as soon as I started working there," Boudlal later said, "It only got worse when I decided to wear a *hijab*. My journey towards wearing it couldn't have been more American; it began at my naturalization ceremony. I realized that I had the freedom to be who I want and freely practice my religion. Neither Disney nor anyone else can take that from me."

Abercrombie & Fitch stores also have a look policy, and multiple women in headscarves have been told they don't fit the look—even as religious believers of other faiths have been accommodated, including a Jewish man in a yarmulke. In 2008, a seventeen-year-old Muslim woman named Samantha Elauf applied for a job at an Abercrombie & Fitch Kids store in Tulsa, Oklahoma. The hiring manager thought she was a "very good candidate," but the district manager rejected Elauf because of her headscarf. Wouldn't that constitute religious discrimination? The hiring manager had seen Elauf wearing the scarf regularly and also knew that Elauf was close friends with another Abercrombie employee whom the hiring manager knew was Muslim. But the district manager waved it all away; according to him, "Someone can come in and paint themselves green and say they were doing it for religious reasons, and we can't hire them." The hijab, a critical aspect of Elauf's religious practice and the religious practice of millions of women across the world, was easily dismissed.

In 2009, twenty-year-old Hani Khan was hired by Abercrombie to work in the stockroom of one of its Hollister Co. stores in San Mateo, California. But a few months into the job, Khan was told she had to stop wearing the hijab to keep her job. "When I was asked to remove my scarf after being hired with it on, I was demoralized and felt unwanted," Khan said.

In 2010, eighteen-year-old Halla Banafa was turned away from a job at Abercrombie; her interviewer allegedly told her that the head-scarf didn't fit the image they were interested in projecting. Banafa was crushed and said, "I never imagined anyone in the Bay Area would reject me because of my headscarf." Fearing continued repercussions from other, prospective employers, she stopped wearing the hijab.

All four of these women challenged the discriminatory look policies in court. Samantha Elauf took her case all the way to the US Supreme Court. Abercrombie in that case argued that Elauf never told the company explicitly that she wore her scarf for religious reasons—never mind that the hiring and district managers had figured it out on their own. Elauf's case was decided by the Supreme Court in 2015 and, in the years since her claim first arose in 2008, the company fired Hani Khan and refused to hire Halla Banafa, knowing full well that they wore their headscarves for religious reasons. Yet, in Elauf's case, the company continued to insist it had no idea the scarf had religious significance. And before the case made it to the highest court in the land, the lower courts continued to accept Abercrombie's far-fetched argument and give cover to the company's blatant discrimination. The Supreme Court saw right through it, and in June 2015, it ruled in favor of Elauf.

The experiences of Muslim women in the workplace have not been widely studied, but several researchers have already found that work-place discrimination and "chronic daily hassles" related to wearing hijab cause Muslim women to suffer from acute and chronic stress. This stress results in "increased blood pressure, anxiety, depression, and symptoms of PTSD." Feeling constantly judged, Muslim women "are three times more reluctant than males to leave their homes."

The economic, physical, and psychological stakes are high—as one writer said in the *Washington Post*, "Today, in a country where Islamophobia is so rampant, the choice to continue [wearing the scarf] has felt masochistic at times." It's no wonder then that many Muslim women are foregoing this important aspect of their religious practice.

||||||||||||||||||||||||||||||||||||||||||||||||||||||||||||||||||||||||||||||||||||||||||||||||||||||||||||||||||||||||||

"I'VE WORN A HIJAB FOR DECADES.
HERE'S WHY I TOOK IT OFF."
Saba Ali, *Washington Post*

||||||||||||||||||||||||||||||||||||||||||||||||||||||||||||||||||||||||||||||||||||||||||||||||||||||||||||||||||||||||||

In 2009, I founded altmuslimah.com, a web magazine that covers a wide range of issues pertinent to gender and the lived experience of Islam. When we first launched the magazine, "dehijabization" was a hot topic of discussion. It refers to when Muslim women who wear headscarves decide to stop wearing them—a phenomenon that many of my writers saw in their communities. They set out to investigate the reasons for dehijabization and found that while internal community expectations were part of the equation, broader societal bias led many women to take off the headscarf. As one writer explained, many women had grown "exhausted of the 'out-of-place' feeling" they experienced in a context where "the hijab was viewed as dehumanizing."

Two years after the discussion on altmuslimah.com, NPR decided to take an in-depth look at dehijabization. In "Lifting the Veil: Muslim Women Explain Their Choice," reporter Asma Khalid interviewed a wide array of women. Several respondents said that, in the post-9/11 landscape, wearing the headscarf ostracized them—strangers and colleagues alike treated them suspiciously. One woman told Khalid, "I'm the kind of person who likes to walk into a room and be unnoticed . . . When you wear hijab and you walk into a room, everyone notices you; everyone stares at you; everyone makes assumptions about you." This isolation was often coupled with the burden of diplomacy. "When you put the scarf on, you have to understand that you are representing a community . . . And that is huge. That's a huge responsibility. And I don't know if it's for everyone."

The burden has grown markedly heavier in the Trump era. Several assaults occurred just hours after President Trump's win, prompting pieces like Alaa Basatneh's, "It's Not Safe to Wear My Hijab Now That Trump Will Be President." At first, Basatneh was determined to overcome her fear. "I wore a blue flower-patterned hijab to my doctor's appointment at a Miami hospital. As soon as I sat down in the waiting room, an older white man one seat away began staring at me. His penetrating eyes made me uncomfortable, but I continued to sit in silence. Five minutes later, the man took out a pocket knife, opened it, and set it down on the empty seat between us. Terrified, I froze in place, just waiting to be stabbed . . . Eventually, the man grabbed the knife and put it back in his pocket. 'Deport them all,' he said as he walked away and found another seat far away from me." Shaken by the incident, Basatneh decided to stop wearing the scarf—at least for now.

Two days after the election, nineteen-year-old Fariha Nizam was accosted on the bus in Queens, New York. "About 10 minutes into the ride, a white couple, somewhere between the range of middle-aged and elderly, got on the bus and came towards the middle section where I was. The two of them started yelling at me, shouting to me to take off my hijab, yelling that it is not allowed anymore." It was enough to scare her father, who pled with Nizam to cover her hair in a less conspicuous way, such as with a hat or hoodie. His plea was echoed by other parents of young Muslim women: "My mom literally just texted me 'don't wear the Hijab please' and she's the most religious person in our family," one woman tweeted on November 9, 2016.

I understand these women's journeys. In the years after 9/11, I also chose to stop wearing a headscarf after wearing it for a long time. My reasons were all rooted in the sense that hijab, with all of its attendant complexities, was hindering my spiritual journey. I understand that hardships largely strengthen faith; they give us resilience and remind us of our total dependence on God. But, sometimes, for some people and in some cases, struggles can take away from spiritual fortitude instead of adding to it. This was my experience with the headscarf.

For years, my public existence was marked with a headscarf. I wore it all through my schooling, which went through 9/11, and at my first job at a white-shoe law firm—where, naturally, my headscarf declared (whether I wanted it to or not): "I am independent, educated, and strong—and I'm Muslim, too!" Such a simple point, an obvious rebuttal to a tired, old stereotype about Muslim women as oppressed and submissive. But the conversation beneath the headscarf, in my head and my heart, was far more complex.

The twenty-four-hour news coverage in a post-9/11 world about the latest atrocities committed against Muslim women—invariably represented with headscarves on (a prominent image at the time was the Pakistani and Afghan Taliban flogging veiled women)—hopelessly politicized the headscarf, not just in how others viewed it but also in how I felt when wearing it. The politicization eroded my spirituality because it tied me indelibly to the world and how it saw me. And I could never put away the political spokesmanship; with the hijab on me in public, I was always "on the job." Every time I stepped into public, even for a quick run to the grocery store, I felt like I was a diplomat for all 1.8 billion Muslims worldwide.

It's hard enough to battle the presuppositions of people outside your religious community. But I was also deeply concerned with internal community politics in which many Muslims believed that a woman had to wear the scarf regardless of the realities she had to face wherever she lived. Even worse, many in my community held that *only* a woman in a headscarf represented a truly devout, authentic Muslim; that you can't have devotion without hijab, and that somehow all women in hijab were de facto devout.

As in every religion, there are external politics, and there are internal politics. And then there's the even more raw experience of the social cold shoulder and the constantly lurking threat to physical safety. Try as I might, the headscarf stopped facilitating my relationship with God and instead put barriers in my way.

After years of reflection and prayer, I finally consulted with Dr. Umar Abd-Allah, whom you met in chapter 5 when I shared his work on the cultural imperative. His religious knowledge and keen insight into the complexities of lived religion are revered by traditional Muslims worldwide. When I was struggling with my headscarf, he explained to me in private, and later in an interview for altmuslimah.com, that rules about hijab cannot be applied in a vacuum. "Any jurist, any legist, who takes rulings right out of the book without looking at the social reality, the psychological reality, the personal reality of our society and just says, 'This is the rule,' they turn this religion into a procrustean bed . . . They make Islam completely unworkable." And so, with this aspect of Islamic law on my side, I decided to stop wearing the scarf.

I still wear it in private—in the mosque or at home during prayer when I wrap myself in a scarf that is so long that it covers not just my head but envelops me fully, down to my toes. Sofia Ali-Khan, a writer on altmuslimah.com, captured my experience (and hers) precisely: "Now, the prayer scarf is more of a step out of the mundane and into the sacred, a chivalrous cloak spread over the muddy puddle of the daily grind. It draws a special circle around me, now mother to . . . young children, marking me as child of God. It has become a celebration, a sanctuary, a sensory experience of God as *ar-Rahman* and *ar-Raheem*, the womb of mercy and of compassion."

I cherish this private communion with God. But I'm also fully cognizant of how insidious politics and the threat of physical violence have relegated this aspect of my religious expression to the private space. In a country with a professed commitment to religious freedom, my religious expression shouldn't have to be sequestered in this way—it should have a place in the public realm.

Given the diversity of *fiqh*, many Muslim women who wear head-scarves view the hijab as unequivocally obligatory. Even as he pointed out the possible exceptions to the rule, Dr. Abd-Allah made clear that all four major Sunni schools of thought hold that women are required to wear the headscarf in the public space: "A woman's covering and the scarf are highly regarded in Islam and it is obligatory for a woman to cover her hair and wear the scarf according to the four [schools of thought]."

And for many women who wear the hijab, it is not just a wardrobe accessory, or even a religious symbol; the very act of wearing it is a form of worship. How could this very basic form of religious practice be so difficult in a country whose Constitution provides broad latitudes for religious freedom? Not just broad protection—but the *broadest* in the entire world? The US is home to diverse religious believers, each with their unique forms of religious expression—Orthodox Jewish, Amish, and Mennonite women cover their heads for religious reasons, as do some Catholic nuns. There was a time when Americans viewed nuns with suspicion and even enacted antireligious dress statutes that pro-hibited nuns in habits from teaching in public schools (all states except Pennsylvania have since repealed these laws). But today, while many Americans may consider these women's dress choices quaint or peculiar, almost no one questions their right to choose religious dress. Few, if any, Americans make political assumptions about other women's modest dress, but many Americans stereotype Muslim women in headscarves.

Wearing hijab in America is complicated because the headscarf has been reconstituted from a religious act to a political one. According to political discourse, which grows more feverish by the day, the head-scarf is not religious because "Islam is not a religion." The hijab in particular "frames the female body as an icon of the 'clash of civiliza-tions'" and the very act of wearing a headscarf is perceived as an act of resistance.

With this definitional shift, actions that Americans would normally classify as religious discrimination are accepted as legitimate national security measures. "Recasting thus serves as the basis for calls to deny Muslims rights otherwise protected under the law." By this logic, "mundane religious accommodation cases" like the ability to wear a headscarf in the workplace "become evidence of stealth, imperial-istic designs" because the headscarf is seen as a "visible 'marker' of [a woman's] membership in a suspect group."

Pamela Geller enunciated this phenomenon when she argued in a 2016 *Breitbart* piece that Muslim women seeking workplace accom-modations are part of a "Muslim effort to impose Islam on the secular marketplace." That same year, a policy paper by the Air Force Research Laboratory called the headscarf a form of "passive terrorism": "'hijab contribute[s] to the idea of passive terrorism' and represents an implicit refusal to 'speak against or actively resist terrorism.'" Also in 2016, shortly after Minnesota elected its first headscarf-wearing legislator, Ilhan Omar, she found herself accosted by her cab driver: "The cab driver called me ISIS and threatened to remove my hijab, I wasn't really sure how this encounter would end as I attempted to rush out of his cab and retrieve my [belongings]." Two years later, when Omar was elected to the US Congress and asked Congress to reconsider its ban on headwear, she was immediately met with claims about a Muslim takeover: "Don't try to change our country into some sort of Islamic republic or try to base our country on Sharia law." (Omar succeeded in getting the rule changed in January 2018, fittingly the 233rd anniversary of the Virginia General Assembly's adoption of Thomas Jefferson's Virginia Statute for Religious Freedom.)

The argument is ludicrous on its face, but downright confusing when probed. Even as Muslim women in headscarves are portrayed as aggressors, spreading extremism by the mere act of covering their heads, they are also talked about as oppressed and subjugated. For many Americans and non-Muslims worldwide, the hijab stands for patriarchy. Outsiders cannot fathom why a woman would want to wear a headscarf out of her own free choice; it's seen as drab and movement-limiting, and thus could only be a sign that a woman is forced by her family members (usually the stereotypical domineering Muslim male) to wear it. As for the woman who insists she wears it out of free choice—she's considered brainwashed, as no woman could rationally choose this for herself. It is inconceivable to many people that a woman could choose to wear clothing that defies social expectations, that she could dress for herself and not for popular approval or the male gaze. As Ali-Khan wrote, "It baffles me, the politics of hijab today: the designation of it as anti-feminist, as regressive . . . Because what is the legacy of feminism if not the conviction that this body and this spirit are mine to steward?"

A Muslim woman in a headscarf is oppressed and submissive—but in a post-9/11 world she is also an aggressor. The argument is internally contradictory, but many pundits continue to push it, violent actors continue to act on it, and it is threatening women's legal rights, too. Already in Europe, the highest court of human rights has explicitly adopted this contradictory rationale to uphold bans on headscarves and face veils, and in America, Muslim women in the workplace and elsewhere are facing discrimination fueled by the same biases.

When Islam is stripped of its religious bona fides and positioned instead as an enemy of the state, Muslim women pay the price. In a land committed, at least on paper, to robust religious freedom, Muslim women in headscarves are forced to choose between their religion and their safety and livelihood.

"CONFESSIONS OF A SECRET MUSLIM"

Sarah Harvard, *Salon*

The pressure to conform to a non-Muslim norm has engendered various forms of "performance strategies." Many of these can be adopted by any Muslim but here I will look at how these strategies are used by Muslim women specifically. Two legal scholars, Sahar Aziz and Khaled Beydoun, have each come up with different, but largely overlapping, schema to explain the phenomenon. For example, Aziz sets out three main ways Muslim women perform their Muslim identities—converting, passing, and covering. Beydoun adds a few subcategories and also adds "conforming" to the list of strategies.

"Converting" involves changing your identity completely—leaving Islam and becoming Christian in order to be part of America's dominant religion. A Muslim woman who goes this route not only erases her spiritual ties to Islam but also scrubs clean any external signs of her Muslim past: changing her name, changing her wardrobe, marrying a white, Christian man, and raising Christian kids with Anglo-Saxon names who socialize only with other white Christians. Ultimately, the converted Muslim woman detaches herself from any remnants of her Muslim identity and switches entirely to a new Christian, white identity. She thinks of herself and is thought of by others as a member of America's dominant group.

"Passing" is when a Muslim woman stays Muslim but tries to hide any overt associations with that identity so that she can be mistaken for, or "pass," as a white Christian (Beydoun calls this "concealing Islam," or the trading in of one's Muslim identity for a non-Muslim one in certain settings or in public generally.) The Muslim woman who tries to pass socializes with "dominant group members"; she dances, drinks, and has American boyfriends—"all of which are at odds with the Islam practiced by her in-group." Her clothes bear no signs of her ethnic or religious roots, and she marries a man who also seeks to and can "pass" as a white man. In sum, this Muslim woman privatizes her Muslim identity and removes from public detection any indications of her Muslim identity. This particular form of passing is open only to those Muslims who phenotypically "look white."

For those who can't pass as white, Beydoun observes, there are two other forms of passing: passing as ethnic and passing as black. As an example of the first, consider the case of Sarah Hamdaoui, who was born to Moroccan and Japanese Muslim parents and grew up struggling to fit into the mostly white, middle-income town of Schaumburg, Illinois. After 9/11, the struggle became acutely worse and Sarah began the process of "passing."

"My identity crumbled when the Twin Towers fell . . . 'You're a terrorist!' said my best friend in the hallways of our elementary school, pointing at me, his innocent eyes turned menacing. I couldn't believe it. But this was the start of a new life for me." That year, her family changed its surname from Hamdaoui to "Harvard." Coupled with her "trans-religious" first name, Sarah Harvard was able to at least partly conceal her Muslim identity and "solidif[y] her American bona fides."

But matters at school got worse. "In sixth grade, a teaching assistant gathered all the students around the classroom for the last lesson of the day. 'Islam is an evil religion. Muslims all around the world kill innocent, non-Muslim people,' she said. 'In their holy book, they said that all good Muslim children must kill kids like you.'" Sarah was shocked; she wanted to speak out but felt powerless: "I was a child, a Muslim one, and she was an adult with authority. What voice did I have?"

Following the incident, Sarah's parents moved her to a new school an hour away from Schaumburg. Sarah saw the move as her chance to start over; she decided "to pretend to be somebody I was not. I completely disregarded my faith publicly as a Muslim—and my real life undercover began."

Living as a fraud is exhausting. It's exhausting to your mind, body and soul. It seemed like people asked me most about my faith when I kept it a secret. My father taught me how to reply:

"What do you say when someone asks what is your religion?" asked my dad.

"That there is no god but God," I replied.

"Nooooo," with his elongated gasp of disapproval, "you say that you are seeking the truth."

During those tumultuous years of her youth, Sarah was "thankful for [her] multi-ethnic background and Japanese-like physical appearance": "No one would assume I was a Muslim. It allowed me to 'pass.' And it kept me shielded from frightened stares and airport security checkpoint probes." In Beydoun's terms, Sarah chose to pass as "ethnic." Black Muslims can in similar ways choose to diminish public signs of their Muslim identity and pass as black.

"Covering" is when a Muslim woman stays Muslim but adopts behaviors and an appearance that allays others' discomfort or fear of her. It's different from "passing" or "concealing Islam" because it conceals only specific Muslim identity traits and not all of them. The woman who covers her religious identity distances herself from her Muslim connections so that she's seen as the "exception to negative stereotypes." (The "good" Muslim and not the "bad" one.) She doesn't want to be perceived as "too Muslim," and assures her coworkers that she won't one day decide to wear hijab or pray in her workplace or use Arabic terminology that would make them uncomfortable. She wears clothes that are distinctively Western and not so conservative that they link her to Islam. She gives her kids trans-religious names like Sarah, Adam, and

Zack so that they can also cover their Muslim identities if they choose. When she makes herself "acceptable," she also unwittingly makes herself a token—she is the one her employer will show off as an example of workplace diversity or to counter any claims of anti-Muslim bias.

Sometimes the "covering" is more subtle—Muslim women may decide to keep their hair covered but with a hijab styled in less traditional ways, like a turban, or to use a hat instead of a scarf. As one woman, a schoolteacher, explained: "After September 11 . . . I went to work and got unfriendly looks. I felt excluded. I started to dress like them, but in an Islamic way. I started to wear pants and shirts. I would wear a turtleneck and a hijab tied back, at the nape of my neck, so I can fit in. Not one hundred percent, but enough so that I would not get the bad looks."

The woman who covers is also proudly patriotic. She doesn't protest American foreign policy (even if she disagrees with it) and she doesn't challenge her colleagues and friends when they joke about or insult Islam and Muslims (even if she feels offended). Beydoun would call this political performance an aspect of "conforming" Islam to the mainstream: "Waving the American flag is the quintessential demonstration of patriotism and belonging. After 9/11, Muslim Americans prominently featured American flags on their cars, homes and businesses to stave off backlash, and perform the 'good Muslim' act to an impassioned public." The Muslim woman who conforms engages in these behaviors regardless of whether she really wants to or not, because her "individuality is subsumed in the negative stereotypes" about Muslims.

Of course, not all Muslim women respond to their current political climate in this way. Some in fact are strengthened by adversity to fight back, and in the process hew closer to their Muslim identity, and to Islam as their religion. Aziz calls this a "refusal to perform coercive assimilation"; Beydoun calls it "confirming" one's Islam, an affirmation and even amplification of one's religious identity. Muslim women who refuse to assimilate think of their struggles as a "badge of distinction." They find that the best solution to negative stereotypes is not to give into it, but to take control and redefine the narrative to better reflect what it actually means to be a Muslim woman.

Aziz and Beydoun's analyses appear to take for granted that a Muslim woman who confirms her Islam necessarily also wears the hijab in public; I'd contest that using my own example and the example of many other Muslim women I know, who publicly confirm their Islam sans hijab. You can wear your religion on your sleeve with or without overt religious dress. Women who confirm their Islam, with their dress and/or every day actions, seek to exemplify the positive impact Islam has on their lives. To their fellow Americans, they say: Our religion is deeply consonant with freedom and liberty.

This proclamation was on full view in the 2017 Women's March on Washington, DC. Among the sea of signs and banners waved at the protest, one image stood out time and again: A Muslim woman wearing the American flag as her headscarf. Under the photo: "We the people are greater than fear" proclaimed loud and clear. Muslim women can be distinctly Muslim, the sign announced, and also be fully American.

In America today, this "confirmation" of Islam has led to some pretty fabulous media and fashion collaborations—and some startling, unexpected effects, too.

||||||||||||||||||||||||||||||||||||||||||||||||||||||||||||||||||||||||||||||||||||||||||||||||||||||||||||||||||||||||||||||||||||||

"MUSLIM AMERICANS SHOULD REJECT THE POLITICS OF NORMALCY"

Nafisa Eltahir, *The Atlantic*

||||||||||||||||||||||||||||||||||||||||||||||||||||||||||||||||||||||||||||||||||||||||||||||||||||||||||||||||||||||||||||||||||||||

"USA! USA!" The crowd roared from the stands as thirty-year-old Ibtihaj Muhammad ran onto the strip and stood poised to take on her challenger.

It was the 2016 Olympics in Rio de Janeiro, and Muhammad was representing the country that she loved deeply, in spite of all of its challenges. Wrapped tightly under her fencing saber mask was her headscarf. She was the first Muslim American woman in hijab to compete for Team USA at the Olympics.

The USA women's saber team won a bronze medal that year, launching the already-popular Muhammad to massive fame. *TIME* magazine named her one of the "100 Most Influential People for 2016." Hillary Clinton tweeted about Muhammad during the 2016 presidential campaign. And in 2017, Mattel came out with a new Barbie doll modeled after Muhammad. "For the first time in Barbie's existence, there was a white head scarf tucked tightly around the doll's face, with not a wisp of fake hair in view." Barbie is an American icon, and in this iteration, she made Islam American, too.

Corporate America's embrace of Muhammad was a far cry from Disney and Abercrombie's treatment of women in headscarves. For Disney and Abercrombie, the hijab was not part of the "look" they wanted to be associated with. But in more recent years, the corporate trend has become exactly the opposite.

The trend is mostly inspired by the profit potential. According to the 2017–2018 Thomson Reuters' State of the Global Islamic Economy Report, Muslims globally spent nearly $254 billion on clothing in 2016 alone. That number is projected to go to $373 billion by 2022. In a December 2018 piece titled, "As Sex Ceases to Sell, Modesty Has Its Fashion Moment," *Bloomberg* reported that the "retail market for women who prefer to dress conservatively could be worth more than $350 billion in two years." It's no surprise, then, that in the last couple of years, Gap, H&M, and Target have all featured models in headscarves in their catalogues. Nike created a special headscarf for athletic Muslim women, which Ibtihaj Muhammad and other Muslim female athletes model on Nike's website. During the winter months, Gucci, Versace, and other high-end brands showcased models wearing "hijab-like headscarves." In 2016, New York Fashion Week included a runway show featuring models all in hijab. The same year, headscarf-wearing Nura Afia became CoverGirl's latest brand ambassador. In 2018, H&M and Macy's both launched a modest clothing line.

None of these fashion milestones has tempered the skyrocketing rate of anti-Muslim hate crimes. *The Intercept* notes, "Muslim women and Muslim fashion currently have unprecedented visibility in American consumer culture," but women in hijab are also "among the most visible targets for curtailed civil liberties, violence, and discrimination in the anti-Muslim climate intensified by Donald Trump's presidency." Representation does not always lead to justice and can make us feel that real change has happened when in fact it hasn't. Still, the visibility makes some Muslims feel safer and many Muslim women celebrate the attention.

For example, when the Italian fashion house Dolce & Gabbana released its line of headscarves and long, flowing cloaks (known as abayas) a few years ago, many Muslim women were excited that their traditional religious dress was becoming not only mainstream but also uncontestably cool and highly coveted. There was something undoubtedly fabulous about flowing black cloaks emblazoned with bright yellow daises, in D&G's signature loud and proud style.

Modest fashionistas on Instagram, YouTube, and other social media sites have seized the opportunity to showcase these styles to their legions of followers. In this, they are joined by women of other faiths. As I wrote in *Refinery29*, "there are a range of fashion stories celebrating modest designers (from Muslim, Jewish, and Christian backgrounds) whose headscarves, long skirts, and tunics are enthusiastically snatched up. Instagram buzzes with modest fashion galleries that feature every aesthetic from minimalist to frou-frou."

My *Refinery29* piece was published in November 2016, in the wake of France's ban on modest, Muslim swimsuits on French beaches and a day after President Trump was elected on a campaign full of anti-Muslim promises, including his travel ban. Both governments view Islam as oppressive (and Muslim women as brainwashed or victimized by their religion), but in fact, the rise of modest fashion has shown the opposite. Fashionistas on and off social media all proclaim one thing loud and clear: Personal style is about agency. Choice, and respect for different choices, is a key tenet of the modest fashion movement, and that includes fully accepting women who cover as well as those who don't or have stopped covering their hair, whether it is Muslim women who dehijabed or Jewish women who stopped wearing wigs to cover their hair.

The celebration in many cases is organic and authentic, even deeply spiritual, as it allows women to embrace their religion's teachings about modesty more completely. Fashion can help women understand the ways the headscarf amplifies, rather than covers, their femininity, and channels proud self-expression. It's not only okay to stand out from the crowd—it's practically required. The headscarf can be a woman's way to make a statement.

Sometimes, though, that bold statement, that focus on the external, can take primacy over religiosity. While this isn't the first time hijab has been politicized, its new political meaning stands poised, at any moment, to subsume its religious meaning. The title of an opinion piece in *TIME* magazine captured this perfectly: "American Hijab: Why My Scarf is a Sociopolitical Statement, Not a Symbol of My Religiosity." The author, Mariam Gomaa, writes:

> In spite of, or rather in response to, the negative portrayal of Muslims by those (Muslims and non-Muslims) who seek to define our narrative as one of barbaric killing and atrocity, women choose hijab—a piece of cloth that declares their identity as Muslims while simultaneously expressing their individual identity as smart, driven, successful, and independent. A simple yet powerful message.

A way in which Muslim women can reclaim their narrative. In choosing to wear the hijab, American Muslim
women reconstruct the narrative of Islam in America.

Gomaa is emboldened by this constant political spokesmanship, even
as others—me included—find it exhausting. I let go of my headscarf
because I felt the politicization weakening my spirituality. That threat
has only become more serious; compared to 2006, when I stopped
wearing the headscarf, the politics have only become more pronounced, more manipulative.

It starts with the "hijab fetish," as the *Guardian*'s Nesrine Malik
calls it. Commenting on corporate and political use of Muslim women
in headscarves, she notes, "How are you to know that a woman is
Muslim if she's not in hijab? How are you to package her? . . . Muslimness has today collapsed into an image of an over-filtered, hot,
bourgeois, fair-skinned hijabi woman, whose highlight is 'on fleek.'"
In one sense, the singular focus on hijab makes sense—to make their
point about diversity, corporations need a physical marker that makes
it clear to the viewer the person being featured is a Muslim. "It's easier
to check a box for diversity when your token Muslim representative
looks distinct. Muslim emoji? Put a hijab on it. Muslim in a movie?
Put a hijab on her. Worried about Mr. Trump's travel ban? Hit the
streets with a hijabi on a poster."

But this almost singular focus on Muslim women who wear the
headscarf erases the many Muslim women who don't wear it. Pew
found in 2017 that similar shares of American Muslim women always
wear the hijab and never wear the hijab in public. As a piece in the *Wall
Street Journal* noted, "Not only is the variety in dress ignored, but so
is the attitude of Muslims across the world toward the hijab. In Leb-
anon, a Muslim-majority country, nearly half of the population consider it appropriate for women not to wear headscarves in public . . .
About one-third of Turks agree, as does 15% of the Tunisian public."

So, first, the Muslim woman who is celebrated must wear a head-scarf: "You have to wear a headscarf, of course, because the media's lazy perception of Muslim women—and the only visual they're keen to perpetuate—is that all of them wear headscarves." But the hijab also has to be reshaped to make it acceptable: "You have to be fashion-forward. Like, you need to wear a headscarf and show that you're still different, but you need to make them forget that you're different by mixing it with the perfect combination of Western trends to remind everyone that you're also the same."

The fashionable hijab encapsulates an acceptable Muslimness (another "good" Muslim and not a "bad" one). "Fashionista" may yet be another performance strategy, a way to simultaneously "con-firm" and "cover" one's Islam. And when it's performed on prominent platforms, it can have implications for more than the individual per-former. (The very term "social media influencer" captures that broader implication; a social media influencer is someone with "access to a large audience" who "can persuade others by virtue of their authen-ticity and reach.")

For example, in 2013, a Muslim group that calls itself "Mipsterz" (a fusion of "Muslim" and "hipster") produced a video titled "Somewhere in America." Set to the uncensored lyrics of hip-hop artist Jay-Z's song "Somewhere in America," the video depicts a group of young, Muslim women in headscarves and "hipster swag" frolicking on streets and rooftops, skateboarding, posing, twirling, walking as if on a catwalk, their skirts and scarves swaying. For some of these women, participating in the video gave them a way to reclaim their hijab in a way they found empowering instead of marginalizing. As one woman wrote, she had a complicated relationship with her headscarf; it often magnified her inse-curities and "dysmorphic feelings" about not being "white enough, thin enough, or beautiful enough." By participating in this video in commu-nity with other women who wore their headscarf fashionably, she was able to step out of her body dysmorphia and embrace her hijab.

But as with so much else when it comes to Muslims in America, the video represented for many viewers not just the individual women in it but the Muslim community more generally. It also signaled to many Muslims the complexities and downsides of the increasingly prevalent "Islamofashionista culture" of which the hijab is a central fixture.

In the social media firestorm that followed the video's release, one Muslim woman tweeted, "Promoting 'palatable' and cool hijab to show we're not that diff screams insecurity & not progress." Another woman wrote: "I am not here to pass judgment on anyone, whether it is a woman who struts the streets with no clothes or a woman who walks in black from head to toe. But I am here to judge a trend that is pairing 'swag,' 'hijab,' and empowerment in a tightly wrapped bundle that conceals what hijab truly encompasses. The women in this video are strong and demand respect. The trend this video echoes are not."

Commentator Sana Saeed dissected it this way:

> Catwalk ready, catwalk strut, and catwalk 'tude seem so antithetical to what we know and expect, sometimes zealously, as Islamic modesty. This isn't about policing what we wear and how or about casting judgment, but about the sort of culture we're creating for Muslim women's dress that is no different than the images and lifestyles sans hijab we criticize . . .
>
> In the name of fighting stereotypes, it seems we're keen to adopt—especially for Muslim women who wear headscarves—tools and images that objectify us (either as sexualized or desexualized; as depoliticized or politicized) rather than support us where we need that support. We're so incredibly obsessed with appearing "normal" or "American" or "Western" by way of what

we do and what we wear that we undercut the actual
abnormality of our communities and push essentialist
definitions of "normal," "American" and "Western."
In that process of searching for the space of normalcy,
we *create* "normal" and through that a "good" Muslim.
And in all of this, we might just lose that which makes us
unique: our substance.

In 2016, I wrote in the same vein when Noor Tagouri, a Muslim
woman who wears a headscarf, was featured (fully clothed) in *Playboy*'s "Renegades" series. The series featured people who had worked
hard to accomplish big goals by "breaking the rules." In the interview, Tagouri, a journalist for Newsy, set out to "make a forceful case
for modesty," while talking about her quest to be the first anchor on
commercial US television to wear a Muslim headscarf (that milestone
has now been achieved by WHBF's Tahera Rahman). On her personal
Facebook page, Tagouri posted a video of her experience posing for
Playboy's photographers; she was giddy with excitement. The *Playboy*
opportunity was, in Tagouri's view, her chance to "eliminate stereotypes and break down barriers."

In a piece for the *Washington Post*, I reflected on what Tagouri's
high-profile presence in *Playboy* said about the direction my religious community was going in America. I situated her interview in
the broader context of what *The Atlantic* called the "politics of normalcy," a desperate need for Muslim women to "actively assert their
lack of oppression, rather than simply living it out in their daily lives."
The trend is not always harmful. It's uplifting to see Muslim women
of diverse professions celebrated for their skills and achievements. It's
incredible to see mainstream publications making space in their news
and opinion pages for Muslim women's voices. But hijab in *Playboy*
was a step too far—for me and many others. The *Playboy* interview
erupted into a controversy among American Muslims so big that it

caught the attention of numerous mainstream publications. What was it that was bothering us?

For one, I doubted *Playboy*'s intentions. *Playboy*'s founder, Hugh Hefner, had a clear position on religiously mandated modesty and sexual ethics: he saw them, and most any other limit on public sexual expression, as fundamentally antifreedom. What did it mean, then, when the magazine chose a woman in a headscarf to make, in its pages, a "forceful case for religious modesty"? When the interview first came out, two other Muslim women who wear headscarves wrote publicly that they had also been approached by *Playboy*. The magazine appeared to be adamant about including the hijab in its pages. In my view, it had something to do with more than just the media's general "hijab fetish"; it had to do with redefining the nature of the hijab.

I wrote: "Yes, *Playboy* has for a long time offered a range of hard-hitting political and social commentary unrelated to its pornography, but this topic in particular—religiously mandated modesty— does more than comment on a social phenomenon. Featured among overtly sexual content, a piece on Muslim modesty seems to mock and undermine those precise ideals. For many Muslim women, the hijab is about reclaiming ownership of their image—but the *Playboy* piece arguably takes away that agency and instead imposes its own frame, making the hijab sexy."

Playboy also made hijab one in a list of other costumes (nurse, secretary, etc.) that take feminine roles and representations and turn them into sexual fetishes (this is a burgeoning phenomenon; porn star Mia Khalifa used the headscarf to heighten her allure). I never said or suspected that Tagouri had any such intentions of sullying the hijab's religious import, and I respect her individual choice to interview with whomever she wants. But any public figure purporting to represent American Muslims (the interview was, after all, centered on Tagouri's goal of representing Muslim modesty on American television) bears some responsibility to represent the principles and values of that community more authentically. *Playboy*, to me, is clearly inimical to those values. Indeed, the "hijab as 'essentially a mode of living' that reflects the sanctity of privacy and private spaces," unambiguously repudiates the voyeurism that *Playboy* is all about.

In 2017, Tasneem Mandviwala, a doctoral student at the University of Chicago, looked more broadly at Muslim women's inclusion in American beauty and fashion industries. In an incisive analysis for altmuslimah.com, she wrote:

> First, by launching Muslim Americans into the mainstream through the beauty and fashion industries, the "Muslim woman" becomes yet another source of fodder for these mammoth businesses—businesses that bear the lion's share of the responsibility for skewed body image, depression, and feelings of worthlessness in our gender the world over. I fully appreciate the importance of little girls seeing women in magazines and on television who reflect their own Muslim identities; it helps these girls feel included and normal rather than marginalized and othered.
>
> However, I do not want to see these industries exploit Muslim women to reinforce the colonial-era cliché that beauty comes in one myopic form—slender, fair and slathered in makeup—all the while claiming to be champions of diversity because they featured Muslim models.
>
> Rather than expanding the scope of what it means to be a woman, the fashion and makeup machinery takes women and reshapes them to fit into the industry . . . And this is precisely why Muslim Americans trying to break into mainstream American culture via platforms that objectify women should give us all pause.

Mandviwala accepts and understands the need for American Muslims to become part of mainstream American society, but she doesn't want Muslims to lose sight of what makes their religion different. In her view, what makes it different is also what makes it better than the norms perpetuated by corporate America. She implores the reader to think more deeply: "Is this really how Muslim Americans want to merge into the mainstream?"

The fashion and entertainment industry's celebration of the hijab has not only secularized Muslim identity but also commodified it. Representation can be depicted in ads and entertainment to help subdue anger at systemic discrimination, but such pleasant-seeming depictions can—and are—used to generate more revenue for the very commercial empires that discriminated in the first place.

Other writers have also wrestled with the issue. In his book, *Out of Many Faiths*, scholar and interfaith activist Eboo Patel describes two groups of Muslims: "social Muslims" and "traditional Muslims." The first category includes Muslims who create "internal Muslim spaces" by "principally interpreting the contemporary Muslim social experience," whereas traditional Muslims interpret Islamic scripture, tradition, and philosophy. As Patel sees it, these groups derive authority from different sources. Traditional Muslims derive it from religious texts, whereas social Muslims derive their authority from their ability to publicly represent Muslims in a positive light. The first type is giving a sermon in the mosque, the second is being interviewed on CNN. (A few Muslims occupy both categories.)

"Social Muslims" as a category wouldn't exist but for Islamophobia. Islamophobia created a discourse, Americans wanted to hear the counterpoints, and major news and entertainment networks gave Muslims the platform to talk back: Netflix, *The New York Times*, CNN, Comedy Central, movies, docuseries, and the list goes on. "The *New Yorker* in the Trump era alone has run pieces on a Muslim poet, a Muslim cop, a Muslim lawyer, a Muslim comedian, and a Muslim tamale vendor." What's more interesting: all of these outlets are associated with "urban, multicultural, progressive" America and not white, conservative America, making Muslims a "totem" in today's culture wars. Each party in the culture wars "foist[s] on the category 'Muslim' its preferred set of characteristics."

In his review of Patel's book, Shadi Hamid of the Brookings Institution reflects on this phenomenon. The integration of Muslims is happening "within only one half of the country, the Democratic one." American conservatives are pushing Muslims away with their hateful rhetoric, whereas liberals are embracing Muslims—on specific terms. We see this phenomenon reflected in popular media. HBO's *Here and Now* features a "transgender, observant Muslim" and goes "out of its way to reflect a now dominant intersectional reality among Democrats."

But what are the effects of this "cultural mainstreaming" on the Muslim community itself? The cost is particularly high for religiously "conservative Muslims, who, like their evangelical Christian and Orthodox Jewish counterparts, have tended to view popular culture as corrupting." For example, the Muslim character in Amazon's *The Romanoffs* wears a headscarf—but "also finds herself in a steamy sexual entanglement with an older, non-Muslim man."

So, are Muslims "different, or are they the same—'just' one among many minority communities, each with their own secular grievances?" Religiously conservative Muslims, or in Patel's terms, "traditional Muslims," don't define Islam as an identity; they define Islam in terms of theology and religious practice. But as the Left embraces Muslims "as a group notable primarily for its marginalization," Islam in America may in time become secularized. The theological contributions of traditional Muslims to public life will become attenuated. Indeed, these Muslims are already under-represented, as the social Muslims have the biggest public platforms. The Right worries about "creeping sharia" in American Islam but what's truly emblematic of American Islam is, as one writer put it, "creeping liberalism."

At the core, Hamid, Patel, Mandviwala, Saeed, and I are all identifying the same trend: the mainstreaming of Islam in a way that might rob it of its distinctiveness. Of its religiousness, its spiritual character, maybe even its authenticity.

The secularization of Islam is both like and unlike the experiences of other American faith communities in the US. Jewish and Christian leaders, too, are bemoaning the "challenges of secularism." But with Islam, there's a distinct political refashioning that happens when it is secularized, a reconstruction of Islam from oppressive and "bad" to something those outside the religious community find liberating, acceptable, and "good."

I raise this issue with concern. I recognize that there will always be diverse members of every religious community, and that some Muslims will be deeply devout and others nominally. I know that religion can be experienced as cultural or political or spiritual. And I appreciate that the lived experienced of Islam is widely varied; my own spiritual journey reflects this plurality. But I worry about what will happen when Islam is not a religion.

*   *   *

The politicization and secularization of Islam, borne in part by the push and pull of American liberal-conservative politics, has the potential to change how American Muslims interpret and exercise their religion. It affects how they bring this faith to bear in the public arena, including in today's passionate debates about the scope of religious freedom. Many of those debates today center on the intersection of religious freedom and sexuality—abortion, contraception, and gay rights. I turn to those debates next.

CHAPTER 8

"WHO YOU GONNA CALL?

RELIGIOUS LIBERTY TASK FORCE!"

"One of the biggest threats to religious liberty for American Muslims is the growing salience of the argument that Islam is not a religion, and that therefore Muslims don't deserve religious liberty." I paused and looked out over the crowd.

Assembled in front of me in the Great Hall of the US Department of Justice, with its art deco light fixtures and terra cotta and marble floors, were distinguished lawyers and advocates from Christian, Hindu, Jewish, Muslim, and Sikh advocacy firms. These people had dedicated their entire lives to fighting for the rights of their religious communities. In that moment, all eyes were on me—some filled with anticipation, some with skepticism.

"Challenging the religious status of Islam, a world religion with almost two billion adherents, once seemed like a fringe argument, but it's gaining ground," I said, laying out my evidence, quoting state lawmakers, White House officials, and influential activists.

Then, with Lady Justice and Majesty of Justice standing on either side of me on stage, I went for the punch line: "We talk about religious liberty as a fundamental right rooted in human dignity, and then we hear all this talk about Muslims not deserving religious liberty—and it raises the question: Do we think Muslims aren't human enough for human rights?"

In the twenty-four hours that followed, every major national outlet and Stephen Colbert's *The Late Show* would cover the event, which the Department of Justice had titled, "Religious Liberty: Our First Freedom and Why It Matters." None of this coverage would mention my points about Muslims' religious liberty, or the Jewish and Sikh speakers' remarks about their communities. Instead, the news focused almost singularly on the talk by then-Attorney General Jeff Sessions, with most of the coverage centered on Sessions's culture-war rhetoric and his announcement of the department's new religious liberty task force.

Vox's Tara Burton, for example, pointed to what she saw as Sessions's "striking rhetoric and incendiary narrative of culture wars." Sessions, in his talk, warned of the dire threat posed by secularism, "A dangerous movement, undetected by many, is now challenging and eroding our great tradition of religious freedom." The department's job, in his view, was to defeat this movement. Sessions also lamented that "morality" can no longer "be a basis for law" and that religious groups cannot preach their traditional beliefs without being labeled "hate groups."

For Burton, these lamentations indicated the true direction and purpose of the proposed religious liberty task force: "treating the federal government as a necessary participant in the longevity of Christian America." By this she meant that the government would continue on the path of protecting conservative Christian objections to contraception, abortion, and gay rights. She also pointed to Sessions's use in June 2018 of Romans 13 from the Bible to justify the Trump administration's separation of families at the US-Mexico border and admonish Americans "to obey the laws of the government because God has ordained them for the purpose of order. Orderly and lawful processes are good in themselves and protect the weak and lawful."

Slate's Molly Omstead pointed out that, despite Sessions's brief mentions of religious freedom protections for Muslims, Jews, and Hindus, the culture-war rhetoric was the dominant theme. Sessions even referred twice to President Trump's protection of the right to say "Merry Christmas."

The *Washington Post, Salon, The Hill, Quartz*, NBC, NPR, CNN, the *Houston Chronicle,* and others also weighed in. Colbert's *The*

Late Show even made an animated film about it. Using footage of the Real Ghostbusters animated series from the 1980s, Colbert renamed the Ghostbusters the "Religious Liberty Task Force," and added a Sessions cartoon to the mix. In the film, Session appears in a Ghostbuster jumpsuit and proton pack, ready to battle not ghosts but emerging threats to religion. The Ghostbuster theme song is edited to "There's a gay cake in your neighborhood. Who you gonna call? Religious Liberty Task Force!" and "They speak Español or use birth control. Who you gonna call? Religious Liberty Task Force!" Sprinkled throughout is the chant, "I ain't afraid of no gays!"

Colbert goes on to critique Sessions's remarks not just for its culture war themes but also its uneven treatment of religions. Colbert calls Sessions an "attorney general and man who even he wants to punch," who made it clear his task force's priorities would be conservative Christian causes and battling laws against saying "Merry Christmas."

Daily Show alumnus Rob Corddry was featured with Colbert in the *The Late Show* segment on the Department of Justice's religious liberty event. He showed up in character as Liberty Task Force special agent, Tom Dockford.

> CORDDRY: Thank you for having me, Stephen. Merry Christmas.
>
> COLBERT: Thank you, but it is August.
>
> CORDDRY: You can't silence me, Colbert! It's always Christmas somewhere.
>
> CORDDRY: The RLTF is here to defend the religion of people of all faiths, Stephen, from Methodists to Baptists to orthodox Episcopalians.
>
> COLBERT: What about people who aren't Christian?
>
> CORDDRY: Eh, I'm pretty sure they're fine. We're focused on bigger problems, like nuns being forced to buy porn in a dream I had once.

As Colbert alluded to in his commentary, concerns about limits on sexual freedom are tied up with concerns that a particular religion, or particular brand of a religion, is being favored by the government. A few months after Sessions's talk, during the Supreme Court confirmation hearings for Judge Brett Kavanaugh, author Katherine Stewart penned a piece for the *New York Times*, "Whose Religious Liberty Is It Anyway?" She noted that throughout the preceding week of hearings, Senator Ted Cruz of Texas identified Kavanaugh as someone who would uphold "religious liberty." In Stewart's view, Cruz and other conservatives define the term in a way that actually means "its opposite." She argued that "if the Senate confirms Brett Kavanaugh, it will be declaring that the United States is a nation in which one brand of religion enjoys a place of privilege; that we are a nation of laws—except in cases where the law offends those who subscribe to our preferred religion; and that we recognize the dignity of all people unless they belong to specific groups our national religion views with disapproval." Stewart then goes on to provide examples, all of them related to the clash between conservative Christians and gay rights or access to abortion or contraception.

In a later op-ed, Stewart offered a direr warning: "I have attended dozens of Christian nationalist conferences and events over the past two years . . . This isn't the religious right we thought we knew. The Christian nationalist movement today is authoritarian, paranoid and patriarchal at its core. They aren't fighting a culture war. They're making a direct attack on democracy itself."

The media also raised concerns when the Department of Health and Human Services opened its new Conscience and Religious Freedom Division in January 2018. The division was meant to "protect doctors, nurses and other health care workers who refuse to take part in procedures like abortion or treat certain people because of moral or religious objections." Critics interpreted this as a "trampling over patients' civil rights"—especially the civil rights of "pregnant women and transgender individuals."

The idea that conservatives are using religious liberty simply as a tool to roll back protections for women and LGBTQ individuals has become so entrenched that even the ACLU has formally renounced its support of RFRA—a jarring development, given its key role in the law's enactment. In 1993, when the US Supreme Court watered down religious liberty protections in *Employment Division v. Smith*, the ACLU's then-president, Nadine Strossen, appeared before Congress to argue that RFRA was urgently needed, calling the *Smith* decision the "*Dred Scott* of First Amendment Law." Her position was within the mainstream of liberal thought at the time, leading to RFRA's near unanimous passage.

In striking contrast, Louise Melling, the ACLU's deputy legal director wrote an op-ed in the *Washington Post* in June 2015, "ACLU: Why We Can No Longer Support the Federal 'Religious Freedom' Law." Even the title reflected the author's cynicism about religious freedom, with the very phrase appearing in scare quotes.

The scare quotes phenomenon has become pandemic. Martin R. Castro, chair of the United States Commission on Civil Rights, identified the trend in one the commission's 2016 "Peaceful Coexistence" report, where he lamented that:

> The phrases 'religious liberty' and 'religious freedom' will stand for nothing except hypocrisy so long as they remain code words for discrimination, intolerance, racism, sexism, homophobia, Islamophobia, Christian supremacy or any form of intolerance.

Like Stewart's piece in the *New York Times*, Castro argues that conservatives are using religious liberty to enact Christian nationalism and "give one religion dominion over other religions, or a veto power over the civil rights and civil liberties of others."

Critics are wrestling to rewrite RFRA. On July 13, 2017, the Human Rights Campaign, ACLU, Center for American Progress,

Planned Parenthood, and other organizations introduced the Do No Harm Act, which seeks to amend RFRA by "specifically exempting areas of law where RFRA has been used to bypass federal protections" that "protect our most vulnerable populations." The purpose of the act is to "ensure that religious freedom is used as a shield to protect the Constitutional right to free exercise of religion and not a sword to discriminate."

Given this increasingly deep-seated perception of RFRA as a tool for (and not against) discrimination, several scholars of religious liberty jurisprudence have dug into the cases to see which claims RFRA tends to protect. My former colleague, Luke Goodrich, and Rachel Busick reviewed over 10,000 court opinions for religious freedom wins in the last five and in some cases ten years. They found that "religious minorities are significantly overrepresented in the cases relative to their population, while Christians are significantly underrepresented . . . RFRA has been underenforced. There were no cases involving a clash between gay rights and religious liberty."

Legal scholar, Christopher Lund, has also noted that the majority of RFRA cases have little to do with sexual morality or the culture wars: "Whatever else can be said of them, RFRA and state RFRAs have been valuable for religious minorities, who often have no other recourse when the law conflicts with their most basic religious obligations."

That's not to say that religious liberty doesn't ever raise issues relevant to gay rights. At the time this book went to press, the most recent outcry over religious liberty involved the Miracle Hill Ministries, a Christian charity that provides a number of services, including foster care support. In January 2019, the Trump administration permitted the agency to limit its services to prospective parents who shared its religious beliefs—including its beliefs about marriage and sexuality. What this meant in practice was that Miracle Hill could turn away non-Christians and same-sex couples. Social media and news sites were ablaze with headlines about religious freedom covering for intolerance.

Americans of opposing politics are locked in a fight about the scope and nature of religious freedom. But what exactly is this fight about —and how does it affect the rights of American Muslims?

||||||||||||||||||||||||||||||||||||||||||||||||||||||||||||||||||||||||||||||||||||||||||||||||||||||||||||||||||||||||

"WHEN CONSERVATIVES OPPOSE 'RELIGIOUS FREEDOM'"
Peter Beinart, *The Atlantic*

||||||||||||||||||||||||||||||||||||||||||||||||||||||||||||||||||||||||||||||||||||||||||||||||||||||||||||||||||||||||

The saga, in my view, began in earnest with a case involving Hobby Lobby Stores, Inc., a chain of American arts and crafts stores that is owned and operated by the Green family. The stores began out of founder David Green's garage and has grown from one 300-square-foot store to more than 550 stores across the country, becoming one of the nation's leading arts and crafts retailers.

Devout Christians, the Green family believes that "It is by God's grace and provision that Hobby Lobby has endured." The Greens therefore run their company in a manner they feel is consistent with biblical principles. For example, the stores are closed on Sundays and only operate sixty-six hours per week, based on the Greens' religious beliefs that their employees should have the opportunity to spend Sundays with their families. Similarly, they have applied Christian teachings on respect and fairness by increasing their employee wages for several consecutive years and starting fulltime workers at 90 percent above the federal minimum wage. Christian teachings have also prevented the Greens from engaging in certain conduct—for example, the Greens interpret their religious teachings as prohibiting consumption of alcohol, and they cannot facilitate someone else's consumption either. So, they have turned down requests from other businesses to rent the Hobby Lobby trucks to transport alcohol.

The Greens' religious beliefs against abortion also prevented them from complying with a small part of the Affordable Care Act—the part that required them to pay for two drugs in their employee health insurance that the Greens considered abortion-causing drugs. Those drugs were Plan B and Ella, the so-called morning-after pill and the week-after pill. Paying for these drugs would have violated the Greens' deeply held religious belief that life begins at the moment of conception, when an egg is fertilized.

But the Affordable Care Act required the Greens to pay for these drugs on pain of penalty, forcing the Greens to choose between violating their conscience and paying hefty fines to the government. The Greens decided to instead bring suit to demand the right to run their business in line with their religious principles.

On June 30, 2014, the US Supreme Court ruled five to four in favor of the Greens and Hobby Lobby. It struck down the part of the Affordable Care Act that required closely held corporations with religious objections to comply with the law in violation of its conscience (because the ruling was limited to "closely held" corporations, the conscience referred to is that of the owners). The court did not minimize the importance of women's access to birth control but said that the Affordable Care Act's requirements weren't the best way to get women these drugs—instead, it pointed to a number of other ways women can have access without the government also forcing the Greens to violate their conscience. This sort of balance, where the government achieves its purpose without unnecessarily restricting religious liberty, is required by the law, the court said, pointing specifically to RFRA.

The Greens' and Hobby Lobby's victory ignited a firestorm. Critics viewed the case not as a win for religious liberty but as a war on women and, because Hobby Lobby as a corporation won the suit, as an unprecedented broadening of corporate rights. To this day, many Americans remain appalled by the Supreme Court's willingness, as they see it, to empower the Greens to interfere with their female employees' personal lives and to subordinate those employees' right to birth control to their own religious preferences. They became even more worried as dozens of Catholic nonprofits also filed lawsuits against the Affordable Care Act's birth control provisions, claiming a religious exemption from the law.

More recently, similar concerns about special privileges for religious individuals came up in the *Masterpiece Cakeshop* case. Masterpiece Cakeshop is a bakery in Lakewood, Colorado, owned by the baker, Jack Phillips. The case involved Phillips's refusal to create a custom wedding cake for a gay couple, Charlie Craig and David Mullins. He was fine with selling the couple a premade cake, but he felt that making a custom cake for them would involve him in the celebration of their union—which Phillips, whose religious beliefs dictate that marriage can only be between one man and one woman, could not participate in.

In response to Phillips's refusal, Craig and Mullins filed a complaint with the Colorado Civil Rights Commission under the Colorado Anti-Discrimination Act. Under the act, a business serving the public cannot discriminate against its customers on the basis of race, religion, gender, or sexual orientation. The commission ruled in favor of the gay couple and not only ordered Masterpiece to make a cake for them, but to also change its policies in line with the anti-discrimination law, train its staff, and provide quarterly reports to the commission that it was complying with the law.

Phillips fought back. In his case, he argued that the commission violated his rights to free speech and religious liberty when it punished him for refusing to make a cake that he could not make without violating his conscience. On free speech, he said that "custom-designed wedding cakes constitute artistic expression" that deserve protection under the Free Speech Clause of the First Amendment. Speech doesn't just include written or spoken words; it also includes artistic expression, which American courts have defined pretty broadly. And, in Phillips's view, his custom wedding cakes are his artistic expression because he "communicate[s] through them." His cakes "announce a basic message: that this event is a wedding and the couple's union is a marriage." And they "declare an opinion too: that the couple's wedding 'should be celebrated.'"

On religious liberty, he admitted that in certain cases, the government has the duty to "prevent discrimination that 'deprives persons of their individual dignity.'" But in his case, the court could not prevent discrimination if it meant depriving Phillips of his constitutional rights. As his lawyers explained in their brief, Phillips is not a bad person. He doesn't discriminate against people because of their race, religion, or sexual orientation. He's happy to "create his custom art for everyone, including LGBT patrons, but he declines all requests (regardless of the requester's identity) to create custom artistic expression that conflicts with his faith." Making a custom wedding cake fits the narrow category of services that violate his faith, and that is why he refused to make the cake.

The Supreme Court decided the case on June 4, 2018. In the highly anticipated opinion, the Court avoided the complicated issues at the intersection of religious liberty and gay rights. It didn't answer whether services that involve speech or expression—such as making custom wedding cakes—can be refused to gay couples based on the service-provider's religious beliefs. In fact, the court didn't say much at all on the free speech claim. It instead looked at the religious liberty question and emphasized that whatever the balance may be between religious liberty and anti-discrimination laws, one thing that is not permitted is overt hostility to religion and the second-class treatment of "religious beliefs and persons." The court was concerned by some of the background facts in the case, namely that the commission had refused the Christian baker's request for accommodation while permitting another baker in the state to refuse to make cakes with messages condemning homosexuality. The court admitted that there may be good reasons for treating these two separate bakers differently, but it found evidence that the commission treated Phillips the way it did only because it found his religious views "offensive." The court said that wasn't right—the government couldn't decide which view is offensive and which one isn't and then punish the one it thinks is offensive.

The opinion did not resolve the open question of whether a religious business owner can refuse services to a same-sex couple. But the very existence of the case has occupied the minds of many Americans, who see it as a continuation of a pattern where conservative Christians are using their religious beliefs to impose their own sexual mores on other Americans. Conservative Christians see themselves as under attack, but other Americans see this group as wielding tremendous power and influence and are genuinely confused as to how any group this powerful can feel like victims.

But the despair is real. First, consider the demographic shift. A 2017 study by the Public Religion Research Institute (PRRI) found that white Christians are now a minority in America. (As noted in the introduction, I recognize that not all conservatives are white Christians and vice versa, but there is significant overlap between these groups.) The "end of White Christian America," is what Robert P. Jones, the founder of PRRI, calls it. He explains, "the anger, anxiety and insecurity many contemporary white evangelicals feel are better understood as a response to an internal identity crisis precipitated by the recent demise of 'white Christian America,' the cultural and institutional world built primarily by white Protestants that dominated American culture until the last decade."

Whereas a 2007 study by the Harvard sociologist Robert Putnam is often cited to explain racial tension in America today, Jones says Putnam's study doesn't extend to interreligious tensions. Based on interviews with almost 30,000 Americans, Putnam found that the more racially and ethnically diverse a community is, the less likely people are to trust each other. In fact, they trust "one another about half as much as they do in the most homogenous settings." But Jones points out that non-Christian religions constitute only 6 percent of the US population, and if you take Jews out of that mix as an already-accepted group, religious minorities constitute only 4 percent. The Muslim population might be growing, but it's growing much more slowly than it is in Europe, and it'll be decades before Muslims overtake Jews as the largest non-Christian group in the US. "This analysis points to a critical insight for the challenge of religious diversity in America. Today anxieties and resistance stem not primarily from increasing *diversity* but rather from a sense of *displacement*" among many white Christians.

Concurrent to this demographic shift, religious conservatives have lost important cases related to same-sex marriage, most fundamentally *Obergefell v. Hodges*, which established a constitutional right to same-sex marriage. As legal scholar, Nelson Tebbe, explained to *Vox*, these losses, along with the broader cultural shifts that are tied up with them, makes this "sector of the population . . . feel beleaguered on account of their religious beliefs, as well as [on account of] a constellation of other sorts of cultural and social characteristics and preferences."

But even as they experience this existential threat, liberals, and American culture in general, have not taken their concerns seriously. "Call it the Kim Davis test," Michelle Boorstein wrote in the *Washington Post*, referring to the county clerk in Kentucky who refused to issue marriage licenses to same-sex couples because she had a moral objection to same-sex marriage. Either you thought Davis "had a legitimate concern about being connected to gay marriage licenses," or you thought "her cause was a joke" and that she was way out of line for refusing to fulfill the duties of her office. That Davis, who became a hero for the Christian Right, was widely ridiculed in the media and even "slut-shamed" and "'hillbilly' shamed," made it clear which side America chose.

The Christian Right's despair (or, as liberals see it, frustrated entitlement), feeds into its opposition against Muslims. Here, it's worth noting that political conservatives weren't always contemptuous of Muslims, and Muslims, for their part, used to lean Republican, too. The immigrant parts of the Muslim community in particular consistently supported the Republican Party throughout the 1980s and 1990s, even as the party gradually Christianized. As one writer explains, Muslim immigrants who left their homes many miles away to start anew were drawn to the "Republican message of self-reliance and entrepreneurship, the exaltation of small business owners, the emphasis on cutting taxes to encourage industriousness." Even as late as 2001, a Zogby poll found that 42 percent of Muslims voted for George W. Bush and 31 percent for Al Gore; another poll found much larger percentages of support for Bush. But egregious post-9/11 violations of Muslims' rights that began under then-president Bush turned the tide in favor of Democrats. Today, there are "virtually no Muslims . . . among self-identified Republicans."

Conservative Christian views of Muslims have also taken a sharp turn. As Peter Beinart wrote in *The Atlantic*, "During George W. Bush's presidency, Christian conservatives often described Muslims as ideological allies." Even "after 9/11 . . . a review of responses to the attacks noted that the Christian right is 'refusing to vilify Islam after Sept. 11 and remains committed to an alliance of 'orthodox believers.'" A 2015 piece in *The Guardian* catalogues past Islamophilia among conservative commentators who today espouse a virulent Islamophobia. In the early years of the "war on terror," some prominent social conservatives openly admired the sexual mores they associated with Islam. Pat Buchanan said in 2004 that "conservative Americans have more in common with devout Muslims than with liberal Democrats." Three years later, conservative writer Dinesh D'Souza extended that theory in his book, *The Enemy at Home: The Cultural Left and Its Responsibility for 9/11.*

Where did all the love go? For one, as conservatives' own religious concerns are being devalued, conservatives also see vehement support for Muslims' rights, and suddenly religious liberty is no longer a defense of religious values but about Christian values specifically. Muslims, already the darlings of the Left, cannot benefit from the efforts of the Christian Right.

The Right also perceives a double standard in the Left's treatment of Christianity versus Islam. Many conservative Christians believe that the Left would support religious liberty claims made by Muslims, but object to the same claims made by Christians. In a widely-circulated video, conservative comedian Steven Crowder enters a Muslim bread bakery in Dearborn, Michigan. Crowder poses as a gay man looking for a wedding cake for his upcoming wedding and tries to place the cake order, but the baker declines the request. Crowder's point with the video is to show that while Christian bakers like Jack Phillips are excoriated by liberals, Muslim bakers with the same objections as Phillips' are left alone. As one person explained it to me, "The Left hates Christianity and opposes our religious claims because they want to rub our faces in the dirt. Meanwhile, for the Left, Islam is the better—the *best*—religion."

There is no real evidence, however, that the Left embraces such a double standard and that it would, for example, support a Muslim cake baker who refuses service on the basis of his or her religious beliefs. Even the Crowder video proves nothing; the baker who turned down Crowder's cake request did so because his bakery only bakes bread. The video is verifiably "fake news." But its patent falsity does little to shake conservatives' belief that the Left supports Muslims unequivocally.

The Right's tribal opposition to the political Left multiplies the Right's hostility toward Muslim religious rights. Think of it in terms of the ancient proverb "the enemy of my enemy is my friend." In the Right's view of Muslims, it's "the friend of my enemy is also my enemy." As I noted in chapter 2, there isn't even room to acknowledge that Muslims are actually facing religious discrimination in the

US—many of the same commentators who claim Christians are "persecuted" in America decry a "false" Muslim "victimhood."

Consider, for example, Senator Marco Rubio's comments on Obama's first mosque visit. Rubio dismissed Obama's statements about Islamophobia, stating that if Obama really wanted to talk about religious discrimination in America, he should have addressed Christian groups whose "traditional values . . . are being discriminated against." Rubio's comments are part of a broader narrative that pits Muslim and Christian rights against each other; Muslims and Christians cannot be in a mutual struggle for religious liberty.

This phenomenon fits a general pattern that sociologists have discovered in countries across the world. As I noted in chapter 6, a 2009 Pew Research Center study on global restrictions on religion found a correlation between government restrictions on religion and social hostilities: the more a government limited religious beliefs and practices, the more social unrest there was. The study defined "social hostilities" as "acts of violence and intimidation by private individuals, organizations or social groups," including for example, "mob or sectarian violence, crimes motivated by religious bias . . . harassment over attire for religious reasons, and other religion-related intimidation and violence." The theory may not be fully applicable to the US context, and it certainly does not explain the entire history of anti-Muslim sentiment in this country, but it does give us insight into our current state.

Some Americans—here, conservative Christians—find that the government is restricting their right to live out their faith freely, whether it's human rights commissions like the Colorado Human Rights Commission in *Masterpiece* or the Obama administration in its attempt to force religious employers to pay for their employees' birth control. I once moderated a panel discussion that included Brian Grim, one of the authors of the Pew study, and an audience member asked him directly whether he would count restrictions on Christian wedding vendors as a "government restriction"—Grim said yes. So, government restrictions are on the rise, or at least many conservatives view it that way, and in turn social hostilities are also on the rise. In the US context, Muslims end up facing the brunt of those hostilities. The Muslim-liberal alliance further feeds into this hostility.

This sociological pattern helps explain a June 2018 poll by Morning Consult. The poll found that white evangelicals are more likely to support religious business owners refusing services to LGBTQ individuals if the business owner is a Christian, Jew, or Mormon—but less so if the business owner is a Muslim. Regardless of what the religious liberty claim is and how passionately religious conservatives may support it, some Americans are adamant about cutting Muslims out.

It's a trend we have seen throughout this book. We started with the story of the Islamic Center of Murfreesboro and the attempts by the local antimosque opposition to carve out an exception to federal and local religious land use law. Suddenly, the Religious Land Use and Institutionalized Persons Act, a law that was passed unanimously and with broad bipartisan support, was no longer applicable to an entire faith community, and the best way the opposition could explain this was by denying that Islam was a religion.

We saw the same process in the way religious arbitration that is available to all faith communities becomes controversial when it is used by American Muslims. Other religious Americans can wear religious garb in the workplace, but Muslim women seeking accommodations for the headscarf are rejected as wanting to impose Islam on the secular workplace. So are Muslim truck drivers who ask to be exempt from delivering alcohol for their employer because doing so would violate their religious beliefs; Pamela Geller calls the drivers' request "Islamic supremacism in action."

The issue here isn't whether American law should or should not offer these accommodations. The issue is equal treatment; if American law does offer these accommodations, it should offer them equally, not selectively. It cannot be that when Christians seek religious accommodations, religious liberty is a right to be free from state coercion in matters of faith and practice—but when it is a near-identical Muslim issue, religious liberty is a means of facilitating Islam's takeover of America.

Yet this is exactly the position of many opponents of the Muslim community. When I called out the hypocrisy in my September 2018 *New York Times* opinion-editorial, "A Religious Double Standard," Geller responded on her website that Christian religious liberty is "not part of a larger effort to establish and reinforce the principle that wherever Christian belief and practice conflict with American law, it is American law that must give way"—whereas, in Geller's view, every time a Muslim human decides to exercise his or her fundamental human right to religious liberty, he or she is part of a nefarious attempt at world domination.

Geller's argument is absurd, but it has traction. As the Park 51 fiasco engulfed the nation in 2010, some legal experts foretold that many Americans may even stop supporting religious accommodations altogether if it means Muslims get to benefit, too. Professor Richard Schragger of the University of Virginia Law School wrote, "Conservative evangelicals, in particular, might back away from blanket religion-favoring exemptions once mosques begin springing up in Indiana or Tennessee." Even government subsidies may be questioned: "After enough stories of government subsidizing the speech or social service activities of Muslims, the political culture's solicitude towards government church support might wane." Schragger's conclusion: "In the post 9/11 world there will . . . be some soul searching about religion-favoring legislation if it has to apply equally to all faiths—even those that seem hostile to American values." Judges, too, are not immune to politics and may become wary of treating religion with favor if that means extending those favors to Muslims.

Schragger's predictions when he wrote them in 2010 may have seemed far-fetched then, but his prescience has become clear. The false claim that "Islam is not a religion" is on the rise, in both implicit and explicit forms, and it is specifically aimed at eroding religious liberty for American Muslims. If proponents do not succeed in applying the law selectively, they may resort to opposing religious accommodations entirely.

It should come as no surprise then that many American Muslims have in recent years refused to support conservative Christians in their religious claims against abortion, contraception, and same-sex marriage. There are numerous reasons for this refusal, but the simplest, most pragmatic reason is a fear of empowering exactly those who want to disempower Muslims.

||||||||||||||||||||||||||||||||||||||||||||||||||||||||||||||||||||||||||||||||||||||||||||||||||||||||||||||||||||||||||||

"WHAT BINDS MUSLIMS TO THE DEMOCRATIC PARTY?"
Jacob Lupfer, Religion News Service

||||||||||||||||||||||||||||||||||||||||||||||||||||||||||||||||||||||||||||||||||||||||||||||||||||||||||||||||||||||||||||

According to the Pew Research Center, Muslim support for same-sex marriage is growing, particularly among Muslim millennials (who include those people who were "born from 1981 to 1999 and generally came of age after 9/11"). Only three in ten Muslim millennials believe that society should discourage homosexuality. Even among older American Muslims, almost half (44 percent) say that society should accept homosexuality. Overall, 52 percent of Muslims believe that society should accept homosexuality—compared to only 34 percent of white evangelicals who say the same thing.

Generally, this openness doesn't arise from any religious basis. Traditional Islamic law won't punish homosexual desire, but it will punish homosexual behavior. According to Islamic law, "all sexual contact between unmarried men and women is forbidden," and marital intercourse is defined specifically as vaginal intercourse. The Qur'an tells the story of Sodom and condemns "its people's overall immorality . . . specifically criticizing its men for 'going to men out of desire instead of to women.' Sodomy, understood as anal sex, was thus prohibited by the consensus of Muslim scholars . . ." Lesbian sex, while not sodomy, is also prohibited under the general rule against non-marital sexual contact.

That said, a number of Muslim scholars in America are reinterpreting Islamic sources on same-sex relations and a few Muslim organizations, such as Muslims for Progressive Values and the Muslim Alliance for Sexual and Gender Diversity, are creating opportunities for gay Muslims to worship and engage meaningfully in the community. These initiatives, along with changing attitudes among Americans generally, help explain the broad acceptance by American Muslims of homosexuality and same-sex marriage.

But Muslim acceptance is also grounded largely in the shared experience of marginalization for Muslims and LGBTQ individuals. When looking at the *Masterpiece* scenario, Muslims see a conservative Christian refusing service on the basis of his beliefs. The baker is conflated with all of the vocal conservative Christians who have time and again expressed overt hostility and contempt for Muslims. It is very easy for a Muslim to hypothesize a slippery slope scenario where a Christian baker or service-provider of any type is given leeway with respect to an LGBTQ customer and then turns around and uses that against a Muslim customer.

Justice Ruth Bader Ginsburg presented this precise hypothetical to the lawyers for the baker. During the oral arguments in *Masterpiece Cakeshop*, Ginsburg asked one of Phillips's lawyers whether, under his legal theory, Phillips should also be able to refuse a custom cake for people of a certain religion (or gender or national origin). The lawyer replied, "I think pretty much everything but race would fall in the same category." (The argument is that refusing service to someone based on his or her race is different because it involves objecting to the person rather than to an action, like a same-sex wedding. Race is also different because of its unique place in American history and the role of racial discrimination in the "racial caste system that was sanctioned by law . . . and that in many respects continues today.") Phillips's other lawyer also confirmed as much; she said that a baker should be able to refuse a custom cake for an interreligious wedding if the baker "object[ed] to the message being conveyed in that expression." When Muslims, in this context, hear "interreligious wedding" they hear "Muslim-Christian wedding."

This line of argument, coupled with the explicit statements of many influential conservatives that their religious liberty wins are for Christians, not for Muslims, sends a clear message to American Muslims: we are not interested in working with you, we are interested in working only *against* you. Seen through this lens, conservative religious liberty wins begin to look less about protecting religious believers who have been wronged by an overbearing government and more about empowering an unjust and unfriendly foe.

It's a worry that mirrors the concerns of many progressives about the ends of freedom. A 2018 study commissioned by the *New York Times* examined over six decades of freedom of expression (including free speech and religious liberty) at the US Supreme Court. A key finding of the study was that the court under the current chief justice, John Roberts, "more than any modern Court . . . has trained its sights on speech promoting conservative values." While the Roberts court does not decide more free speech cases than previous courts, when it does decide these cases, it tends to hold in favor of conservative speech and against liberal speech. What this means in practical terms is that the more frequent beneficiaries of free speech in recent years are parties thought of as powerful, such as corporations, employers, or religious majorities, instead of parties without power, like employees and minorities.

For example, the court's 2014 decision in *Hobby Lobby* clarified the rights of closely held corporations to religious liberty, which these corporations can now use to deny federally mandated benefits to their employees. Critics are also wary that the only reason the Greens' and Hobby Lobby's concerns were taken seriously by the conservative justices of the Supreme Court is that the Greens were Christians. In other words, if the Greens had been Muslims, they would have surely lost.

This shift from protecting the powerless to the powerful worries liberals. A June 2018 piece in the *New York Times*, "How Conservatives Weaponized the First Amendment," quotes several progressive legal scholars who regret their past "absolutist commitment to free speech." They no longer see free speech as indispensable to a just society; instead, the scholars argue, free speech amplifies injustice.

American Muslims experience that injustice, in heightened form, every day. And discrimination has convinced them that it is simply stupid to support their avowed enemies. The view is that if Christian conservatives have power, Muslims will inevitably suffer. And regardless of whether Christians score significant religious liberty victories, they will find a way to deny those same rights to Muslims.

With conservatives turning Muslims away, the Left becomes the obvious other choice for partnerships and coalitions. Between the two sides, the Left seems like a surer bet when it comes to the long-term protection of Muslims' rights.

Yet Muslim coalition-building with liberals is not always and only about self-interest. There is a genuine sense of solidarity. Many religious, civic, and popular leaders in the Muslim community remind their constituents time and again that regardless of Islamic law positions on homosexuality, Muslims in America should band together with other oppressed minorities. Muslims and LGBTQ individuals are both fighting for their civil rights, and to succeed, they must form alliances and support each other's causes.

After the US Supreme Court ruled in *Obergefell v. Hodges* that the fundamental right to marry is guaranteed to same-sex couples, Muslim comedian, Hasan Minhaj, and the well-known religion scholar and public commentator, Reza Aslan, cowrote "An Open Letter to American Muslims on Same-Sex Marriage." In their piece, Minhaj and Aslan, explained:

> When you are an underrepresented minority—whether Muslim, African American, female, etc.—democracy is an all or nothing business. You fight for everyone's rights (and the operative word here is "fight"), or you get none for yourself. Democracy isn't a buffet. You can't pick and choose which civil liberties apply to which people. Either we are all equal, or the whole thing is just a sham.

Later, some Muslim activists extended this logic to *Masterpiece*. Ilhan Calgri, the senior policy fellow for religious freedom at the Muslim Public Affairs Council wrote in *Religion News Service*, "American Muslims understand that religious liberty should be interpreted in ways that are equality-enhancing, not equality-denying, and that in order for America's values of freedom and equality to prevail, our religious freedoms cannot come at the cost of another's civil liberty."

As with many progressives opposed to conservative religious liberty claims, for many American Muslims, the slippery slope scenario is always front and center: if Phillips can turn away a gay couple, who else can he turn away? How do we even function in a world where discriminatory practices are permitted? An amicus brief filed in *Masterpiece* by the Muslim advocacy group, Muslim Advocates, said the Christian baker could not win because if we let conservative Christians discriminate, they will use that to deny not just services, but also housing and employment, to vulnerable religious minorities. In other words: it is necessary to limit religious liberty for the majority to protect it for minorities.

The brief also raised concerns about dignitary, or psychological, harm suffered by people who are discriminated against in public accommodations. Citing mostly studies and scenarios about people who were refused services because of their race or religion, the brief extends its point about psychological harm to the case of a gay couple refused services for their wedding. This harm, the brief argues, is real and should not be minimized. It's a concern that Muslim Advocates and its Muslim constituency share with many American progressives. For example, the Center for American Progress, a progressive public policy research and advocacy organization, has made the argument verbatim: "Service refusals, including the kind Craig and Mullins faced at Masterpiece Cakeshop, cause dignitary harm to LGBTQ people and can manifest in increased mental health disparities."

Finally, the alliance between Muslims and progressives can also be attributed in part to the politicization of Muslim identity. Muslim religious expression for many Muslims has taken on clear political import. In chapter 7, I quoted a piece from *TIME* that proclaimed the hijab a political symbol. That piece explained:

> While it seems counter-intuitive to wear hijab in a world that increasingly has a negative perception of Muslims . . . there is a significant presence of American Muslim women wearing the hijab as a strong sense of identity. As one of these women, I know and have insight to a representation of hijab that is rarely portrayed—a representation that I call the American hijab, the antithesis and retaliation to whiteness and the American media, and a nod of solidarity to other people of color . . . In this sense, hijab, rather than strictly being a religious decision, is also a sociopolitical choice and representation.

In this fight against "whiteness," "the American media," and symbols of oppression more generally, the seemingly natural alliance is with other groups fighting the same forces.

That is not to say that this politicization of Muslim identity—and the alliances with progressive groups—has not been rejected or criticized by other parts of the community. While the large, national Muslim organizations may be the most vocal and widely heard on social justice issues, including matters of sexual freedom, they do not always represent the views of vast swaths of the American Muslim community. In fact, Crescent Foods, a Muslim-owned food company, signed onto a brief in support of Hobby Lobby in its Supreme Court case. As the leadership team explained to me on the phone, Hobby Lobby's desire to run its business according to its religious values was something that really resonated with them.

And the alliance between the Left and Americans Muslims is not without its contradictions. When conservative Christians win contentious religious liberty cases, some liberals fight back by generating fear about Muslims using the court victory to their advantage. For example, a trending hashtag on Twitter the day of the *Hobby Lobby* ruling was #ScaliaLaw, a play on the name of Justice Scalia, who voted with the conservative majority, and "sharia"—the implication being, as many publications made clear, that the *Hobby Lobby* decision paved the way for Muslim-owned companies to force their employees to follow Islamic edicts. A common scaremongering technique: conjuring images of Muslim employers enforcing the burqa, or face veil, on their female employees. As one person commented on an article in *The Economist*, "I eagerly await the first instance of a closely-held Muslim-controlled corporation requiring that all its female employees wear a burqa." In *The New Yorker*, Steve Coll, the dean of Columbia University's journalism school, even drew a comparison to the "Pakistani Taliban . . . a closely held, profit-making enterprise organized on religious principles." What better way to make conservatives regret the court decision than to use their own favorite bogeyman? The *Daily Kos* put it this way: "How would conservatives and their agents respond if a company with Islamic beliefs (however defined) decided to impose its religious values on white, Christian, American employees?"

These comments reveal the fragility of Muslim alliances with the Left. They also suggest that the relationship is based on a tacit agreement that Muslims, as religious believers, will never challenge any of the rights championed by the Left, such as a progressive vision of gender or sexual equality. Much as the Right fails to see religious liberty as a universal right afforded to everyone regardless of their politics, the Left's advocacy of Muslims' rights is conditioned on Muslim participation in and support for the Left's political goals.

Some Muslim scholars and commentators have tried to tease out these complexities. The answer isn't to choose conservatives over liberals, because the alliances will never line up perfectly. The answer, as these scholars have identified it, is for Muslim social justice activists to engage in ways that are authentic to their religious identity.

Dozens of Muslim religious thinkers and community leaders signed onto a piece on the conservative web-magazine, *MuslimMatters*, called "Counsel to Muslim Social Justice Activists." In it, they urged Muslim activists to "preserve all that is special about being Muslim" by prioritizing "the non-negotiable teachings of Islam." They also cautioned against forming alliances with "special interest groups" that would "unduly alienate large swaths of the demographic that activists and/or religious scholars themselves claim to represent." Importantly, the letter did not frame proper Muslim activism in liberal or conservative terms; instead, it said "the way forward in the US political arena requires a synthesis of the best that both liberals and conservatives have to offer." And Islamic values should guide who we work with and on which issues: "Our main desire is that Islam and the preservation of its values be given priority and not sacrificed on the altar of political opportunism . . . Islamic mores [are] worth showcasing . . . even if they clash with those of our allies at times." An influential Muslim leader, Dawud Walid, captured this approach in his book, *Towards Sacred Activism*.

Some conservative scholars have negotiated Islamic values and gay rights advocacy by taking a noncompromising position on the morality of homosexual relations, but still advocating for full legal rights for gay couples. For example, a leading conservative Muslim scholar wrote a scathing critique of progressive Muslim activists who reinterpret Islamic law to support homosexual relations. In a Facebook post for his almost 900,000 Facebook followers, the scholar, Yasir Qadhi, said "there is very little Islam" in what these activists advocate:

> Of late, one of their main points is the claim that same-sex unions are Islamically permissible—a claim that has absolutely no precedent in the entire history of our religion amongst all of the sects and trends of the Ummah [Muslim community], despite the diversity of Islamic thought.

Yet, in his commentary on the *Obergefell* decision, he made a similarly forceful argument that the Supreme Court had decided correctly in establishing the constitutional right to same-sex marriage. That the US does not derive its law from theology is a good that also benefits Muslims, Qadhi argues, because if the "dominant majority" gets to ban "alternative lifestyles," it would ban "our lifestyle," too. He also urges his listeners to treat LGBTQ people with love and respect.

The politics and political causes of the American Muslim community are complex. In the mix we have theology, Islamic law, political and pragmatic calculations, experiences of oppression, and a rancorous relationship with conservatives who denigrate Muslims at every turn. In the process of negotiating it all, some American Muslims have chosen to elevate politics, others look mostly to theology as a source of guidance. Given my unique experiences as an American Muslim devoted to her faith and also immersed in religious liberty law and philosophy, I've carved out a position uniquely my own.

"RELIGIOUS LIBERTY IS NOT A LIBERAL
OR CONSERVATIVE POLITICAL IDEA"
Don Byrd, Blog for the Baptist Joint Committee for Religious Liberty

Advocates like myself who promote religious liberty across political and religious lines, representing conservative Christian clients and a range of religious minorities, Sikhs, Muslims, Jews, Native Americans included, find America's cynicism about religious freedom exceedingly worrying. My expansive approach has been informed by my international advocacy in countries where religious liberty is literally a matter of life and death. Those experiences have given me pretty sobering insight into what a society looks like when the fundamental human right to religious liberty is threatened. Say the wrong thing and you'll find yourself in prison. Interpret your religion differently than the mainstream does and find yourself on death row. I've seen firsthand what the ramifications would be if Americans, too, started carving out broad exceptions to religious liberty because we failed to see the importance of a particular belief or found that that belief offended our liberal sensibilities.

It's this type of vigilance that has motivated my own approach to religious liberty claims that I don't agree with. One of the hallmarks of religious liberty is that it protects people of all faiths, even if their beliefs seem unfounded, flawed, implausible, or downright silly. It's not that religious liberty requires relativism or indifference to truth. Instead, it's based on an understanding of the religious quest—humans searching for answers to their ultimate questions and living in accordance with their authentic beliefs.

That journey is different for everyone, both among religious communities and among members of the same community. We may think that another's belief is wrong, but the premise behind religious freedom is that people have the *right to be wrong*. It's a concept that I first learned from the founder of my former law firm, Seamus Hasson. He emphasized the need for intellectual and moral coherence in the way we advocate for religious liberty across a wide diversity of beliefs and practices. This principle of "the right to be wrong" is the foundation of all of my religious liberty work.

Of course, in today's polarized climate, it is far easier to embrace this diversity in my advocacy when the belief or religious practice at issue pertains to a religious minority. It's a relief to be able to step away from culture war–centric topics and instead advocate for a Native American's religious access to eagle feathers or a Santeran's right to animal sacrifice or a Sikh American's right to carry a *kirpan*. At least when it comes to non-Muslim minorities, Americans on both sides of the political aisle generally seem to find it fairly easy to support religious liberty.

It's a lot harder when the religious claim you're protecting has to do with abortion, contraception, and same-sex marriage, as in the *Hobby Lobby* and *Masterpiece Cakeshop* cases. I was part of the legal team that represented Hobby Lobby, and I have spoken publicly in favor of the *Masterpiece* ruling. In these cases, I have managed to persist despite the political backlash, relying on my unshaken belief that Americans are better off when the government stays out of their religious affairs.

The conflict between sexual freedom and religious liberty—and especially between LGBTQ rights and religious liberty—is no doubt real. And the fact patterns in these cases can be quite difficult as courts try to balance competing rights. But too often, Americans are swayed by fear when they decide which side to support. We fear what others may do if we let them have rights. It's what many conservatives argue about Muslims: If you give Muslims rights, they will take over America! And it's what many liberals, their Muslim allies included, argue about conservatives: If you empower them, they will oppress all the rest of us!

Granted, these statements are not both backed by evidence—the supposed Muslim threat in the US isn't supported by actual evidence, whereas many prominent conservatives *have* made explicit claims about wanting a Christian nation and have tried to institute policies that would favor Christian values. Christian groups also hold far more power and influence in America than Muslims do.

But in both cases—the real and the imagined threat—I push back with the same warning: We cannot let our fear reign because it will only endanger the long-term health of our human rights. If we start weakening the legal protections for religious freedom because we think religious freedom is protecting all the wrong beliefs, we'll soon enough find ourselves in a place where the law fails to protect much at all. To prevent this, we have to be careful to protect the "right to be wrong."

This long-term outlook on religious liberty is the foundation for this book—it's the reason I think all Americans, and not just Muslims, should be concerned about what is happening with American Muslims' rights today. It's also the reason I show up to support conservative Christians in many of their religious claims. The focus of the law should always be on negotiating differences in a way that best protects everyone's fundamental rights.

In making this argument, I am like the many other American Muslims who argue for a coherent approach to civil rights. I agree with Reza Aslan and Hasan Minhaj that "democracy isn't a buffet. You can't pick and choose which civil liberties apply to which people. Either we are all equal, or the whole thing is just a sham." Their argument is incontrovertible. But the way it's argued implies that "civil rights" are only for minorities. The conservative Christian religious claims being rejected are not claims for "civil rights."

Aslan and Minhaj seem to share the concern liberal free-speech scholars have about the use (or "weaponization") of free speech to protect groups seen as powerful. Their concern echoes the concept of "repressive tolerance" first developed in 1965 by Herbert Marcuse, the "'father' of the New Left," whose ideas are seeing a resurgence among many scholars today. In Marcuse's view, indiscriminate "tolerance only empowers the already powerful and makes it easier for them to domi-nate." What's needed instead is a "liberating tolerance" that "favors the weak and restrains the strong." Some people get rights, others don't.

Aslan and Minhaj's approach also implicitly diminishes the impor-tance of religious liberty in the "buffet" of rights, at least in cases where religious liberty protects beliefs they don't agree with. In con-trast to this approach, I advocate for coherence across majority and minority claims (that is, for "indiscriminate tolerance," not tolerance applied selectively), including religious claims.

I am alarmed, for example, when US senators question Cath-olic nominees to the federal bench about their religious beliefs. In December 2018, senators Mazie Hirono and Kamala Harris asked Brian Buescher, a nominee for the federal court in Nebraska, to resign from the Knights of Columbus. They feared his membership in the Catholic organization would impede his ability to "fairly judge mat-ters relating to reproductive rights." In 2017, Senator Dianne Feinstein grilled another Catholic nominee Amy Coney Barrett, asking Barrett whether "the dogma lives loudly within you," that, is, whether her Catholics beliefs would affect her ability to rule impartially. The insin-uation was not unlike claims during John F. Kennedy's presidential campaigns: would his allegiance lie with the Pope or with America? Those biases may seem remote for many Americans, a thing of the past—but they are rearing their heads in new ways today.

We can have a hard time pinpointing the phenomenon, or even rec-ognizing these sorts of biases as problematic. Many Americans may dismiss religious liberty as less important than other human rights, like free speech or sexual freedom, because when we think of religious liberty, we think of religious beliefs—and especially those religious beliefs we find "backward" or incomprehensible. But religious liberty isn't any "less liberal" than any of our other rights. It protects human autonomy and gives us the freedom to make our own choices in how we pursue meaning in our lives. It's not our beliefs that religious liberty protects—it protects us, the humans who hold those beliefs. Put another way, religious liberty protects believers, not beliefs.

In today's fraught politics, it can be helpful to see religious liberty (including conservative religious claims) through the prism of human autonomy, to locate the human at the center of the story. Once we've centered our perspective on a person, the conflict between religious liberty and other rights may seem less impenetrable. The discourse may become less about a political agenda and more about the individual human raising a religious freedom claim—and from there, we may be able to negotiate coexistence.

Consider, for example, the view of Chai Feldblum, a Georgetown law professor and "the first out lesbian EEOC Commissioner." She agrees with the *Masterpiece* ruling in favor of the Christian baker. In her view, Justice Kennedy's opinion was "permeated with respect, dignity and nuance" and in no way pitted LGBTQ rights against religious liberty. In fact, Kennedy's opinion explicitly noted that "gay persons and gay couples cannot be treated as social outcasts or as inferior in dignity and worth." But, Feldblum notes, the nuance of his approach is sorely lacking among advocates on either end of the spectrum.

> Many progressive LGBT advocates decried the outcome in the case and vowed to fight on against religious "bigotry" and "prejudice." Many conservative religious advocates declared that the baker had won in the face-off against the "radical homosexual agenda" to eliminate any vestige of religious freedom in America—a fight they would continue to wage.

Feldblum finds in both approaches a failure to see the "deeper point of our constitutional democracy"—to live in a pluralistic society where people with different beliefs can co-exist with peace and dignity. This pluralism requires that both LGBTQ and religious individuals and organizations be able to express themselves authentically. "The government should work to ensure that" religious "organizations can thrive and flourish even if they hold and teach views that others may find offensive." Even when religious beliefs conflict with anti-discrimination laws, the government should respect the religious believer and exempt him or her from the law. In order to move forward as a country, Americans must "acknowledge the full and complex reality of those who are different from us and then find the generosity of spirit to reach across divides and come together in thoughtful and respectful dialogue."

We can't come together in this "thoughtful and respectful dialogue" if we don't have freedom to think about and discuss our religious faith freely—that is, if we don't have religious freedom. Progressive religious groups like Muslims for Progressive Values wouldn't be able to develop new interpretations of Islamic scriptures if they didn't have religious freedom. Similarly, traditional religious believers wouldn't be able to carve out a position on sexual freedom that is authentic to their religious identity if they didn't have religious freedom. To break the impasse, we have to extend freedom to everyone, including those we disagree with.

Importantly, Feldblum roots her perspective in her deep appreciation of religion. "Respect for religion is a paramount and lifelong value for me," she tells us. "I grew up in a home in which religion and God were the defining aspects of our daily lives." A basic appreciation for religion and its central role in the lives of humans is critical to finding solutions.

For example, a number of states acknowledged the importance of religious claims when they passed same-sex marriage laws that also provided religious exemptions. In Maryland, where I live now, the same-sex marriage law prohibits the state from coercing religious officials to solemnize same-sex marriage; guarantees that "certain religious entities have exclusive control over their own theological doctrine, policy teachings, or beliefs regarding who may marry within that faith"; and protects "certain officials from being subject to any fine or penalty for failing or refusing to join individuals in Marriage." It also says the government cannot require "certain religious entities . . . to provide services, accommodations, advantages, facilities, goods, or privileges to an individual under certain circumstances." By respecting the role of religion in people's lives, laws like this bring us closer to mutual agreement.

Of course, there will be times when we can't find a solution. In those limited cases where the conflict between religious liberty and sexual freedom is intractable, the courts should apply the law objectively and evenhandedly. Religious liberty as a constitutional right has the means to facilitate coexistence among tremendous diversity. We've seen the legal test throughout this book: the court looks at the government's compelling interest (for example, its interest in the equal treatment of citizens) and determines whether there is a way to serve that interest without violating a religious believer's constitutional right to live according to his or her faith. If there is a better way, the religious believer wins. If there isn't, the religious believer loses.

||||||||||||||||||||||||||||||||||||||||||||||||||||||||||||||||||||||||||||||||||||||||||||||||||||||||||||||||||||||||||||||||||||||||||

"INVITATION TO A DIALOGUE: AMERICA'S FUTURE"
New York Times

||||||||||||||||||||||||||||||||||||||||||||||||||||||||||||||||||||||||||||||||||||||||||||||||||||||||||||||||||||||||||||||||||||||||||

Religious freedom may stop us from coercing others to agree with us, but it doesn't stop us from persuading others to agree with us. Too often, we over-rely on legislators and the courts to figure out for us what we should be figuring out for ourselves: how do we create a society where we can co-exist with people whose views are drastically different from our own?

I have grappled with this question on a personal level, and on numerous fronts. For one, I am an American Muslim woman, which means I have dealt with stereotypes about my faith and my personal independence and autonomy. For as long as I can remember, the dominant narrative in the news has been that Muslim women are oppressed by their religion and by Muslim men. When many Americans think about Islam, certain stereotypes immediately come to mind—first, violence and terrorism, and second, violence inflicted upon women by their coreligionists. The images are sensational: harems; honor killings; women covered head-to-toe in burqas, beaten by the Taliban with sticks. These were the images that enlivened the national discourse in the immediate aftermath of the September 11, 2001 attacks and spurred our country to wage a "war on terrorism."

This is one level at which I have experienced vulnerability. On a parallel plane is my experience within my community. For example, many Muslim women feel unwelcome in their local mosques or feel second-class to the male members of the congregation. Men and women are segregated in the mosque, and there are countless narratives of how decrepit the women's sections are or how women are always expected to keep young children in their section—implying that men's concentration in prayer is more important than women's, that men's spirituality trumps women's.

These matters are, of course, not as black-and-white as they often appear, and I have for years teased out the complexities on this and many other issues through my web-magazine, altmuslimah.com. In the last chapter, I described some of the discussions on the site about headscarves and dehijabization. The website in fact covers a lot more than that, mostly focusing on issues pertinent to gender roles and rights in the American Muslim community. Over the course of altmuslimah.com's decade of publishing and programming, hundreds of Muslim women and men have come there to share their concerns, discuss solutions, and pave the way to change through this dialogue and discourse. We have covered everything from women's leadership in the Muslim community to the lack of female presence on public panel discussions to problematic gender roles in marriage to judgments about women's dress choices to struggles with courtship to the connection between Muslim masculinity and politics. This discussion has borne fruit: Muslim organizations are becoming more cognizant of Muslim women's needs; conversations originally happening on my website are now happening on stage at national Muslim conventions; more and more women are stepping up to lead workshops, write opinion pieces, or deliver public lectures on the issues altmuslimah .com covers.

On altmuslimah.com, we also feature groundbreaking scholarship, often by female scholars of Islamic texts, that offers new interpretations of verses and traditions relevant to gender and gender roles. This scholarship points to a third alternative in the "social" versus "traditional" Muslim dichotomy described in Chapter 7—when traditionally excluded groups advocate from religious texts for broader rights, they are not breaking away from the sacred but in fact rooting their arguments in it.

This process of internal dialogue, debate, and change isn't unique to the Muslim community. Soon after I launched altmuslimah.com, one of my Catholic friends started a sister site (appropriately titled, "altcatholicah") to explore women's issues in the conservative Catholic community. She wasn't interested in defying the boundaries set by the church; instead, she wanted to talk about women's issues in a way that was fresh but still authentic to traditional beliefs. Meanwhile, other Christians are having conversations on whether their churches will perform gay marriages or ordain female ministers. Still others are tackling sexism more broadly; one Black minister wrote in the *New York Times*, "It's on Men to End Sexism in the Black

Church": "In my classes, speeches and sermons, I tell white people that if they fail to speak up when confronted with anti-blackness, they are giving space to hate . . . The same is true of patriarchy and misogynoir in the black church. It would be morally inconsistent for me to demand that white people confront their privilege while I let black men off the hook."

My experience of change through social engagement has colored my approach to religious liberty just as much as my legal training has. American Muslims, like all religious Americans, have the freedom to negotiate their issues internally without the government interfering or regulating the process. And the result has been far better than if the government had gotten involved by, say, penalizing mosques that treated women unequally. No one is forcing us to change under threat of penalty. The change is organic and meaningful because it is what the community wants and how it thinks it can best embrace its religious values and ideals. That sort of authenticity is what makes for real and lasting progress.

It is also the type of process that many religious liberty advocates envision for a society torn by culture wars. The best way to heal from the wars and find common ground is not by getting the government involved, fining or firing people who disagree with our positions. Instead, we need to figure it out on our own. The US Supreme Court helped lay the groundwork for that negotiation by noting in *Obergefell* that "many who deem same-sex marriage to be wrong reach that conclusion based on decent and honorable religious or philosophical premises, and neither they nor their beliefs are disparaged here, nor should they be disparaged in a pluralistic society." The court continued to model respect for tolerance and diversity in *Masterpiece*, where it did not set itself out as a "champion for one or another faction, but rather" encouraged Americans "to respect and reconcile the vital, longstanding policies and commitments expressed in various laws that sometimes come into tension."

What might that negotiation entail? One model is the Tolerance Means Dialogues happening at universities across the nation. A small group of experts on either religious liberty or LGBTQ rights advocacy have organized these dialogues because, as they explain:

> We have three choices: we can continue to avoid [the hard issues] and remain in our echo-chambers; we can shout each other down, convinced we're right; or we can approach each other with a spirit of humility, believing that we can grow together toward a better future.

The evangelical Christian university, Biola, offered similar guidance in its interview with Caleb Kaltenbach, an alumnus and the author of *Messy Grace: How a Pastor with Gay Parents Learned to Love Others without Sacrificing Conviction*. Kaltenbach encouraged readers to move past mere "tolerance" of LGBTQ people and "engage in meaningful relationships." Treat people as "actual people," and "embrace the tension by developing friendships over meals, coffee and more. Engage in conversations. Try to understand who they are as a person (experiences, hopes, dreams, fears, etc.)." Kaltenbach goes on to offer advice for specific occasions, like what to do if someone with a same-sex attraction confides in you or how to decide whether to attend a same-sex wedding.

Importantly, Kaltenbach approaches these matters with due respect to the real spiritual questions and struggles that evangelicals face in these scenarios. He does not discount or dismiss those concerns as illegitimate or bigoted. The Tolerance Means Dialogues similarly honor religious beliefs. Mutual respect is the foundation; seeing the other as a real human is the starting point.

These fundamental points hold true for all of our religious liberty culture wars—including the one that pits Muslims against conservatives. Each side needs to see the other as "actual people." To quote

Kaltenbach again, "embrace the tension by developing friendships over meals, coffee and more. Engage in conversations. Try to understand who they are as a person (experiences, hopes, dreams, fears, etc.)."

This book was my attempt at starting that conversation, and I welcome the opportunity to continue it.

|||||||||||||||||||||||||||||||||||||||||||||||||||||||||||||||||||||||||||||||||||||||||||||||||||||||||||||||||||||||||||||||||||||||||

"EVANGELICAL, MUSLIM, JEWISH. IT'S TIME WE ALL RENEW OUR COMMITMENT TO RELIGIOUS FREEDOM"

Oliver Thomas and Charles C. Haynes, *USA Today*

|||||||||||||||||||||||||||||||||||||||||||||||||||||||||||||||||||||||||||||||||||||||||||||||||||||||||||||||||||||||||||||||||||||||||

The biggest question in religious liberty today is: Does it apply to everyone equally?

Are we going to vie endlessly to win rights for our own religious communities but make sure to deny it to everyone we think will "abuse" the right? Are we comfortable with letting freedom reign, even if it means letting people express their religious beliefs in ways that we find deeply objectionable?

With Justice Brett Kavanaugh on the US Supreme Court, there is now a solid five to four conservative majority—which likely means that the protection of religious liberty as championed by conservative Americans is going to be front and center for years to come. The decision for both conservatives and liberals is whether we'll continue to fight about who and what religious liberty applies to, or if we'll protect the broadest scope of that right for all, and not some, Americans.

Religious liberty has the capacity to protect a wide range of religious practices. It protects against government interference with religious associational practices, such as the ability of religious believers to form organizations that maintain and advance religious objectives. It protects the rights of those organizations to determine their own rules for hiring, firing, and dispute resolution. Religious liberty also gives religious believers the "right not to kill" by supporting exemptions from abortion, assisted suicide, military service, and capital punishment. And it protects a far-ranging list of ways to express and propagate our faith, and to infuse our public lives with religious purpose.

The philosophy behind this broad protection is, again, the protection of personal autonomy. Religion is central to the lives of many humans. For those humans, religion adds meaning to their lives and compels them to be positive forces for society. It is in all of our interests to keep this freedom as broad as it can be.

ACKNOWLEDGMENTS

I set out at the beginning of 2018 to write this book, having no idea what it would entail and how to even begin to navigate the process. But I did find my way, with the careful and generous guidance of my friends, family, and colleagues. My husband, Shabbir, has been the key to all of my successes in the thirteen years of our marriage, and he was the key to this one, too. He gave me the space and the support I needed to bring this book to fruition.

My children are so excited that I wrote about them and made them "famous"! My au pair, Abbie Llewellyn, kept the kids busy and happy and allowed me peace of mind to finish this project. And then there were my cheerleaders: my siblings, Shan, Lubna, and Sarah, my sisters-in-law, Hina, Nabiha, and Sumiya, and my mother, Naseem, who is overjoyed that I captured, in these pages, at least a small part of my father's tremendous story.

My agent, Leslie Meredith of Mary Evans, Inc., championed my ideas, edited my drafts, and helped me stay on top of a fast-moving news cycle. Jessica Case at Pegasus Books from our very first conversation understood me in a way few people do. My comrade, Montse Alvarado, told me "you will definitely be successful!"—the confident way she said (and says) that made all the difference.

Sofia Ali-Khan, Emilie Kao, and Ben Marcus gave generously of their time in reviewing multiple drafts of multiple chapters. Thank you to Eboo Patel, Michael Frandsen, Tim Schultz, Luke Goodrich, Sana Saeed, Mariam Ahmed, and Butheina Hamdah for their careful review and feedback on one or several chapters. Thank you also to the man whose work and ethos have inspired my career on religious liberty, Seamus Hasson.

Amina Chaudhary helped me formulate my book topic; Azeem Ibrahim and Emily Hardman gave me important feedback on my book proposal; Rabia Chaudry offered helpful guidance to get me started. David Snyder, Trice Jacobson, Abby Skeans, and Ali Ahmed stewarded critical resources my way. Guthrie Graves-Fitzsimmons and the team at ReThink Media have been with me from the start. Haroon Azar at the UCLA Initiative on Security and Religious Freedom, and my colleagues at the Religious Freedom Center of the Freedom Forum Institute gave me the research tools I needed. My interns, Nicole Fauster, Rebecca and Caroline Deucher, and Pooya Safarzadeh assisted with research, interviews, and drafting. Special thanks to Nicole for her probing insight, and to Caroline for adding color to this book by helping me with the storytelling.

The storytelling would have been wholly impossible without the characters, my interviewees: Daoud Abudiab, Dr. Ossama Bahloul, Oz Sultan, Zahra Billoo, Abed Awad, Muneer Awad, Dr. Muhammad Farouk, and Naveed Anjum. My favorite character of all: my father, to whom I dedicate this book.

Thank you also to my experts on speed-dial: Dalia Mogahed, Ismail Ali, Tannaz Haddadi, Qasim Rashid, Janan Delgado, Faisal Kutty, and Travis Wussow, who all responded immediately (and helpfully) to my urgent calls and texts. I also benefited from conversations with Sahar Aziz, Nathan Lean, Zareena Grewal, and Jordan Denari Duffner. And finally, thank you to Jenée Desmond-Harris at the *New York Times* for first publishing my ideas in op-ed form, which in turn generated an online conversation that has informed so much of what's in this book.

ABOUT THE AUTHOR

Asma T. Uddin is a religious liberty lawyer and scholar working for the protection of religious expression for people of all faiths in the US and abroad. She is an expert in American law on church-state relations and international human rights law on religious freedom. Uddin is an active lecturer to diverse religious groups in the US and overseas on the importance of religious liberty, and she is widely published on the topic by law reviews, university presses, and national and international newspapers.

Uddin has worked on religious liberty cases at the US Supreme Court and in federal appellate and trial courts. She has defended religious claimants as diverse as evangelicals, Sikhs, Muslims, Native Americans, Jews, Catholics, and members of the Nation of Islam. Her legal, academic, and policy work focuses on freedom of expression such as religious garb, land use, access to religious materials in prison, rights of parochial schools, religious arbitration, etc. Uddin worked with the US Department of State on advocacy against the UN Defamation of Religions Resolution. She received a State Department grant to develop the Legal Training Institute in the Middle East and North Africa and Southeast Asian countries.

In addition to her legal work, Uddin writes and speaks on Muslims and gender. As the founding editor-in-chief of altmuslimah.com, she has managed the web-magazine, and organized vigorous debates and conferences on the multifaceted issues of gender, politics, and religion. Uddin has advised numerous media projects on American Muslims, including most recently as producer and advisor for the Emmy- and Peabody-nominated docuseries, *The Secret Life of Muslims*.

After graduating from The University of Chicago Law School, Uddin served as Counsel for the Becket Fund for Religious Liberty and as director of strategy for the Center for Islam and Religious Freedom in Washington, DC. She is an expert advisor on religious liberty to the Organization for Security and Cooperation in Europe (OSCE), a senior scholar at the Newseum's Religious Freedom Center, a fellow with the Initiative on Security and Religious Freedom at the UCLA Burkle Center for International Relations, and a Fellow at Georgetown University's Berkley Center for Religion, Peace, and World Affairs. She is also a term-member with the Council on Foreign Relations.

APPENDIX

||||||||||||||||||||||||||||||||||||||||||||||||||||||||||||||||||||||||||||||||||||||||||||||||||||||||||||||||||||||||||||||||||||||||||||

KEY SUPREME COURT CASES ON RELIGIOUS LIBERTY

Reynolds v. United States (1879)
An anti-bigamy statute did not violate the Free Exercise Clause, even though plural marriage was part of religious practice, because governments have the right to punish activity that is considered criminal, regardless of whether someone is engaging in that activity based on their religious beliefs.

United States v. Ballard (1944)
Whether a religious belief is true or false is irrelevant to a religious liberty claim, as long as the belief was sincerely held.

Torcaso v. Watkins (1961)
Maryland violated the Establishment Clause when it required that a candidate for public office declare a belief in God to be eligible for the position.

Sherbert v. Verner (1963)
South Carolina violated the Free Exercise Clause when it denied unemployment benefits to a person for turning down a job that required the person to work on the Sabbath.

United States v. Seeger (1965)
A person can have conscientious objector status based on a belief that holds a similar position in their life to that of a belief in God.

Welsh v. United States (1970)
A person can have conscientious objector status based on a belief that is held with the same strength that traditional religious believers hold their religious convictions.

Wisconsin v. Yoder (1972)

Amish students were permitted to stop attending school at the age of 14 instead of 16, as required by state law, because the state's interest in having students attend two additional years of school did not outweigh the individual's right to religious freedom.

Serbian Orthodox Diocese v. Milivojevich (1976)

The lower court violated the First Amendment when it adjudicated "quintessentially religious controversies" instead of leaving those determinations to the church tribunals.

Larson v. Valente (1982)

The Free Exercise and Establishment Clauses prohibit the government from making "explicit and deliberate distinctions between different religious organizations."

Employment Division v. Smith (1990)

The Free Exercise Clause permitted the state of Oregon to deny unemployment benefits to someone fired from a job for smoking peyote as part of a religious ceremony because the law criminalizing the possession of peyote is "valid and neutral" and does not target religious acts.

Church of the Lukumi Babalu Aye v. City of Hialeah (1993)

The city ordinances passed by Hialeah, Florida, banning animal sacrifice violated the Free Exercise Clause. The texts of the laws clearly targeted the Santería religion, and laws that are designed to oppress a religion or its practices violate the Free Exercise Clause.

Gonzales v. O Centro Espírita Beneficente União do Vegetal (2006)

Adherents of a small religious group can continue to import and use an illegal drug in their worship services because the government did not adequately demonstrate that it had a compelling interest in banning this particular group from using the drug. In satisfying the strict scrutiny standard, the government must show that its interest is compelling when its law is applied "to the person."

Hosanna-Tabor Evangelical Lutheran Church
v. Equal Employment Opportunity Commission (2012)
The Establishment and Free Exercise Clauses bar lawsuits brought on behalf of ministers against their churches, claiming termination in violation of employment discrimination laws.

Burwell v. Hobby Lobby (2014)
Regulations promulgated by the Department of Health and Human Services, as applied to closely held corporations, requiring employers to provide employees with no-cost access to contraception violates the Religious Freedom Restoration Act.

Holt v. Hobbs (2015)
Arkansas prison policy that prevented a Muslim prisoner from growing a half-inch beard in accordance with his religious beliefs violates the Religious Land Use and Institutionalized Persons Act.

Equal Employment Opportunity Commission
v. Abercrombie & Fitch Stores (2015)
Title VII of the Civil Rights Act of 1964 requires only that applicants show that their need for a religious accommodation motivated the employer's decision not to hire them.

Masterpiece Cakeshop v. Colorado Civil Rights Commission (2018)
The Colorado Civil Rights Commission's hostility toward a cakeshop owner's religious reasons for declining to make a cake for a gay wedding violated the Free Exercise Clause.

Trump v. Hawaii (2018)
In implementing the travel ban, President Trump lawfully exercised the broad discretion granted to him under the law to suspend the entry of aliens into the United States.

NOTES

INTRODUCTION

Beinart, Peter. 2017. "The Denationalization of American Muslims." *The Atlantic*, March 19, 2017. https://www.theatlantic.com/politics/archive/2017/03/frank-gaffney-donald -trump-and-the-denationalization-of-american-muslims/519954/

Dewey, John. 1934. *A Common Faith*. New Haven: Yale University Press.

Durkeim, Émile. 1995. *The Elementary Forms of Religious Life*. Translated by Karen E. Fields. New York: The Free Press.

Engage. n.d. Homepage. Accessed February 11, 2019. http://engagepakistan.com/engage/

English Oxford Living Dictionaries. "Islamophobia." Accessed February 11, 2019. https:// en.oxforddictionaries.com/definition/islamophobia

Freeman v. State, 2003 WL 21338619 (2003)

French, David. 2017. "Some Arguments for Muslim Religious Liberty Are More Compelling than Others." *National Review*, April 13, 2017. https://www.nationalreview. com/2017/04/religious-liberty-muslims-deserve-protection-liberal-allies-still-wrong/

Greeley, Andrew and Michael Hout. 2006. *The Truth about Conservative Christians: What They Think and What They Believe*. Chicago: University of Chicago Press.

Green, Emma. 2016. "When 'Religious Freedom' Leaves Children Dead." *The Atlantic*. October 6, 2016. https://www.theatlantic.com/politics/archive/2016/10/child-abuse -religious-exemptions-tennessee/503063/

Grogan, Courtney. 2018. "Ambassador Brownback: 'Religious freedom is the most important foreign relations topic today.'" *Catholic News Agency*, February 6, 2018. https://www.catholicnewsagency.com/news/ambassador-brownback-religious-freedom -is-the-most-important-foreign-relations-topic-today-76831

Kamali, Mohammad Hashim. 1997. *Freedom of Expression in Islam (Fundamental Rights and Liberties in Islam series)*. Cambridge: The Islamic Texts Society.

Manseau, Peter. 2018. "Why Thomas Jefferson Owned a Qur'an." *Smithsonian*, January 31, 2018. https://www.smithsonianmag.com/smithsonian-institution/why-thomas -jefferson-owned-qur-1-180967997/

Marrakesh Declaration. 2016. "The Rights of Religious Minorities in Predominantly Muslim Majority Countries." http://www.marrakeshdeclaration.org

Merriam-Webster Dictionary. "Islamophobia." Accessed February 11, 2019. https://www .merriam-webster.com/dictionary/Islamophobia

Merriam-Webster Dictionary. "Religion." Accessed February 11, 2019. https://www. merriam-webster.com/dictionary/religion

Nuyen, A.T. 1998. "Is Kant a Divine Command Theorist?" *History of Philosophy Quarterly*. Vol. 15, No. 4 (Oct): 441–453

Online Etymology Dictionary. "Religion." Accessed February 11, 2019. https://www
    .etymonline.com/word/religion. Religion is "conduct indicating a belief in divine power,
    from Anglo-French *religiun* (11c.)," Old French *religion* "piety, devotion; religious
    community," and directly from Latin *religionem* . . . "respect for what is sacred,
    reverence for the gods; conscientiousness, sense of right, moral obligation; fear of the
    gods; divine service; religious observance; a religion, a faith, a mode of worship, cult;
    sanctity, holiness.

Petty, Aaron R. 2016. "Accommodating 'Religion.'" Tennessee Law Review. 83: 529–574.

Pew Research Center. 2013. "The World's Muslims: Religion, Politics and Society." http://
    www.pewforum.org/2013/04/30/the-worlds-muslims-religion-politics-society-overview/

Philpott, Daniel. 2015. "Are Muslim countries really unreceptive to religious freedom?"
    Washington Post, July 10, 2015. https://www.washingtonpost.com/news/monkey-cage/
    wp/2015/07/10/are-muslim-countries-really-unreceptive-to-religious
    -freedom/?noredirect=on&utm_term=.8316a14c5c1f

Philpott, Daniel. 2016. "Religious Freedom in Islam Today: A Survey of Regimes." Filmed
    April 29, 2016 at Religious Freedom in Islam?: Intervening in a Culture War, Princeton, NJ.
    Video. https://jmp.princeton.edu/events/religious-freedom-islam-intervening-culture-war

Resnick, Brian. 2017. "All Muslims are often blamed for single acts of terror. Psychology
    explains how to stop it." *Vox*, November 30, 2017. https://www.vox.com/science-and
    -health/2017/11/30/16645024/collective-blame-psychology-muslim

Russell-Kraft, Stephanie. 2016. "'Freedom vs. Liberty': Why Religious Conservatives Have
    Begun to Favor One Over the Other." Religion Dispatches, October 12, 2016. http://
    religiondispatches.org/freedom-vs-liberty-why-religious-conservatives-have-begun-to
    -favor-one-over-the-other/

Spellberg, Denise. 2013. *Thomas Jefferson's Qur'an: Islam and the Founders*. New York:
    Alfred A. Knopf.

Stanek, Steven. 2007. "Egypt hindering religious freedom, human rights groups say."
    SFGate, November 16, 2007. https://www.sfgate.com/news/article/Egypt-hindering
    -religious-freedom-human-rights-3235896.php

Stanley-Becker, Isaac. 2018. "Anti-vaccination stronghold in N.C. hit with state's worst
    chickenpox outbreak in 2 decades." *Washington Post*, November 19, 2018
    . https://www.washingtonpost.com/nation/2018/11/19/anti-vaccination-stronghold-
    nc-hit-with-states-worst-chickenpox-outbreak-decades/?noredirect=on&utm_
    term=.4c8bcd1d5bec&wpisrc=nl_most&wpmm=1

Stetzer, Ed. "A Muslim Declaration on Religious Minorities: An Interview w/ Pastor Bob
    Roberts in Marrakesh, Morocco." *Christianity Today*, January 28, 2016. https://www
    .christianitytoday.com/edstetzer/2016/january/marrakesh-morocco-interview-w-pastor
    .html

The American Heritage Dictionary of the English Language. "Religion." Accessed
    February 11, 2019. https://www.ahdictionary.com/word/search.html?q=religion.
    Religion is "the belief in and reverence for a supernatural power or powers, regarded
    as creating and governing the universe: respect for religion; A particular variety of such
    belief, especially when organized into a system of doctrine and practice: the world's
    many religions; A set of beliefs, values, and practices based on the teachings of a
    spiritual leader; . . . A cause, principle, or activity pursued with zeal or conscientious
    devotion: a person for whom art became a religion."

The New York Times Archives. 1991. "Court Says Ill Child's Interests Outweigh

Religion." https://www.nytimes.com/1991/01/16/us/court-says-ill-child-s-interests
-outweigh-religion.html

Uddin, Asma. 2010. "My Take: Most victims of Muslim religious persecution are other
Muslims." *CNN Belief Blog*, May 21, 2010. http://religion.blogs.cnn.com/2010/05/21/
my-take-most-victims-of-muslim-religious-persecution-are-other-muslims/

Van Wyk, Tanya. 2015. "Political theology as critical theology." HTS Teologiese Studies/
Theological Studies 71(3), Art #3026, 8 pages. http://www.scielo.org.za/pdf/hts/
v71n3/64.pdf

Walsh, Declan. 2007. "Blood and Guts." *The Guardian*, July 20, 2007. https://www
.theguardian.com/world/2007/jul/21/pakistan.declanwalsh

Wikipedia. "Allah." Accessed February 11, 2019. https://en.wikipedia.org/wiki/
Allah#Pronunciation_of_the_word_Allah

CHAPTER 1

Alyahya, Mohammed. 2016. "Don't Blame 'Wahhabism' for Terrorism." *New York
Times*, October 19, 2016. https://www.nytimes.com/2016/10/20/opinion/dont-blame
-wahhabism-for-terrorism.html

Annenberg Public Policy Center. 2017. "Americans Are Poorly Informed About Basic
Constitutional Provisions." https://www.annenbergpublicpolicycenter.org/americans-are
-poorly-informed-about-basic-constitutional-provisions/

Barry, John M. 2012. "God, Government and Roger Williams' Big Idea." *Smithsonian
Magazine*, January 2012. https://www.smithsonianmag.com/history/god-government
-and-roger-williams-big-idea-6291280/

Bauman, Chad. 2018. "Conservative Christians: Think Twice Before Claiming 'Islam Is
Not a Religion.'" *Rewire News*, October 26, 2018.
https://rewire.news/religion-dispatches/2018/10/26/conservative-christians-think-twice
-before-claiming-islam-is-not-a-religion/

BBC. "CAR cannibal 'ate man as revenge.'" Last modified January 13, 2014. https://www
.bbc.com/news/av/world-africa-25714233/car-cannibal-ate-man-as-revenge

Beinart, Peter. 2017. "The Denationalization of American Muslims." *The Atlantic*, March
19, 2017. https://www.theatlantic.com/politics/archive/2017/03/frank-gaffney-donald
-trump-and-the-denationalization-of-american-muslims/519954/

Beinart, Peter. 2017. "When Conservatives Oppose 'Religious Freedom.'" *The Atlantic*,
April 11, 2017. https://www.theatlantic.com/politics/archive/2017/04/when-
conservatives-oppose-religious-freedom/522567/

Benjamin, Zaid (@zaidbenjamin). 2016. "#Trump Choice for National Security
Adviser Michael Flynn: Islam is a political ideology that hides itself behind what
they call a religion." Tweet, November 18, 2016. https://twitter.com/zaidbenjamin/
status/799696968071016448/video/1

Beydoun, Khaled A. 2018. "US liberal Islamophobia is rising— and more insidious than
rightwing bigotry." *The Guardian*, May 26, 2018. https://www.theguardian.com/
commentisfree/2018/may/26/us-liberal-islamophobia-rising-more-insidious

Blackburn, Bradley. 2010. "Plan for Mosque in Tennessee Town Draws Criticism from
Residents." *ABC News*, June 18, 2010. http://abcnews.go.com/WN/murfreesboro-
tennessee-mosque-plan-draws-criticism-residents/story?id=10956381

Boorstein, Michelle. 2015. "When Muslims are the target, prominent religious freedom advocates largely go quiet." *Washington Post*, December 30, 2015. https://www. washingtonpost.com/news/acts-of-faith/wp/2015/12/10/when-muslims-are-the-target-prominent-religious-freedom-advocates-largely-go-quiet/?utm_term=.121c2176d2e8

Branch, Chris. 2014. "State Rep. John Bennett Stands by Anti-Islam Comments: 'Islam Is Not Even A Religion.'" *The Huffington Post*, September 22, 2014. https://www .huffingtonpost.com/2014/09/22/oklahoma-john-bennett-islam_n_5863084.html

Brown, Robbie and Christine Hauser. 2012. "After Attacks and Threats, Tennessee Mosque Opens." *New York Times*, August 10, 2012. https://thelede.blogs.nytimes .com/2012/08/10/after-attacks-and-threats-tennessee-mosque-opens/

Burke, Daniel. 2017. "Anti-Muslim hate crimes: Ignorance in action?" *CNN*, January 30, 2017. https://www.cnn.com/2017/01/30/us/islamerica-excerpt-hate-crimes/index.html

Carmichael, Leigh. n.d. "American Christians' Perceptions of Muslims and its Implications for Ministry." Zwemer Center for Muslim Studies. Accessed February 13, 2019. http:// www.zwemercenter.com/items/american-christians-perception-of-muslims-and-its -implications-for-ministry/

CBS News. "Fire at Tenn. Mosque Building Site Ruled Arson." *CBS News*, August 30, 2010. https://www.cbsnews.com/news/fire-at-tenn-mosque-building-site-ruled-arson/

Church, William Farr. 1972. *Richelieu and Reason of State*. Princeton: Princeton University Press.

Dart, Tom and Oliver Laughland. 2018. "Three Kansas men convicted over mass 'slaughter' plot targeting Muslims." *The Guardian*, April 18, 2018. https://www. theguardian.com/us-news/2018/apr/18/kansas-terror-plot-kill-muslims-conviction

"Divine Deception of Islam." *Study-Grow-Know*, November 28, 2011. https:// studygrowknowblog.com/2011/11/28/divine-deception-of-islam/

FBI. n.d. "What We Investigate." Accessed February 11, 2019. https://www.fbi.gov/ investigate/civil-rights/hate-crimes

Flowers, Larry. 2018. "Two men apologize for allegedly vandalizing Murfreesboro mosque." *WKRN.com*, March 9, 2018. https://www.wkrn.com/news/local-news /two-men-apologize-for-allegedly-vandalizing-murfreesboro-mosque_201803260352 31168/1077209030

French, David. 2017. "Some Arguments for Muslim Religious Liberty Are More Compelling than Others." *National Review*, April 13, 2017. https://www. nationalreview.com/2017/04/religious-liberty-muslims-deserve-protection-liberal-allies -still-wrong/

Gallup. 2008. "Do Muslims Want Democracy and Theocracy?" Last modified March 8, 2008. https://news.gallup.com/poll/104731/muslims-want-democracy-theocracy.aspx

Gallup. n.d. "Views of Violence." Accessed February 13, 2019. https://news.gallup.com/ poll/157067/views-violence.aspx

George, Robert. 2014. "Muslims, Our Natural Allies." *First Things*, February 2, 2014. https://www.firstthings.com/blogs/firstthoughts/2014/02/muslims-our-natural-allies

Gjelten, Tom. 2015. "Conservatives Call For 'Religious Freedom,' But for Whom?" NPR, December 11, 2015. https://www.npr.org/2015/12/11/458969192/conservatives-call-for-religious-freedom-but-for-whom

Gilsinan, Kathy. 2015. "Could ISIS Exist Without Islam?" *The Atlantic*, July 3, 2015. https://www.theatlantic.com/international/archive/2015/07/isis-islam/397661/

Golla, Rajiv. 2016. "A Mosque, A Fire, and A Lesson." *Roads and Kingdoms*, July 11, 2016. http://roadsandkingdoms.com/2016/a-mosque-a-fire-and-a-lesson/

Haas, Brian. 2013. "Texas man pleads guilty to bomb threat at Tenn. Mosque." *USA Today*, June 4, 2013. https://www.usatoday.com/story/news/nation/2013/06/04/guilty -plea-in-tennessee-mosque-threat/2390285/

Harney, John. 2016. "How Do Sunni and Shia Islam Differ?" *New York Times*, January 3, 2016. https://www.nytimes.com/2016/01/04/world/middleeast/q-and-a-how-do-sunni -and-shia-islam-differ.html

Harriot, Michael. 2018. "Are White Men America's Biggest Terror Threat? We Checked." *The Root*, November 2, 2018. https://www.theroot.com/are-white-men-americas- biggest-terror-threat-we-checke-1830175112

Harvard Divinity School Religious Literacy Project. n.d. "Catholicism in France." Accessed February 13, 2019. https://rlp.hds.harvard.edu/faq/catholicism-france

Henderson, Alex. 2015. "6 modern-day Christian terrorist groups our media conveniently ignores." *Salon*, April 7, 2015. https://www.salon.com/2015/04/07/6_modern_day_ christian_terrorist_groups_our_media_conveniently_ignores_partner/

Institute for Social Policy and Understanding. 2016. "ISPU American Muslim Poll Key Findings." https://www.ispu.org/wp-content/uploads/2016/08/ampkeyfindings-2.pdf

Isaacs, Arnold R. 2016. "Meet the radical anti-Islam conspiracy theorists advising Ted Cruz." *Washington Post*, April 14, 2016. https://www.washingtonpost.com/ posteverything/wp/2016/04/14/meet-the-radical-anti-islam-conspiracy-theorists-advising -ted-cruz/?noredirect=on&utm_term=.fe16a2b655e6

Kaleem, Jaweed. 2018. "Attacks on religious and racial minorities fueled sharp rise in hate crimes in 2017, FBI says. *Los Angeles Times*, November 13, 2018. http://www.latimes .com/nation/la-na-fbi-hate-crimes-20181113-story.html

Kemph, Marie. 2012. "Man indicted for Murfreesboro mosque bomb threat." *Murfreesboro Post*, June 22, 2012. https://www.murfreesboropost.com/news/man- indicted-for-murfreesboro-mosque-bomb-threat/article_52ca63b7-84d7-5dbe-af61 -aa5925e0890d.html

Kimbriel, Samuel. 2017. "Christianity is political. But America's politically active Christians seem to be forgetting that." Washington Post, November 21, 2017. https:// www.washingtonpost.com/news/posteverything/wp/2017/11/21/christianity-is- political-but-americas-politically-active-christians-seem-to-be-forgetting-that/?utm_ term=.5989117bf2a8

Merritt, Jonathan. 2014. "How Religious-Freedom Laws Could Come Back to Hurt the Faithful." *The Atlantic*, March 3, 2014. https://www.theatlantic.com/politics/ archive/2014/03/how-religious-freedom-laws-could-come-back-to-hurt-the -faithful/284164/

Lichtblau, Eric. 2016. "Hate Crimes Against American Muslims Most Since Post-9/11 Era." *The New York Times*, September 17, 2016. https://www.nytimes.com/2016/09/18/ us/politics/hate-crimes-american-muslims-rise.html

Lipka, Michael. 2015. "The most and least racially diverse U.S. religious groups." Pew Research Center, July 27, 2015. http://www.pewresearch.org/fact-tank/2015/07/27/ the-most-and-least-racially-diverse-u-s-religious-groups/

Marzouki, Nadia. 2017. *Islam: An American Religion*. New York: Columbia University Press.

McCarthy, Andrew C. 2015. "Ben Carson and Islam." *National Review*, September 21, 2015. http://www.nationalreview.com/corner/424379

McGreal, Chris. 2010. "Muslims in America increasingly alienated as hatred grows in Bible belt." *The Guardian*, September 10, 2010. https://www.theguardian.com/world/2010/sep/10/us-muslims-america-alienated-hatred

Ochieng, Akinyi. 2017. "Muslim Schoolchildren Bullied by Fellow Students And Teachers." NPR, March 29, 2017. https://www.npr.org/sections/codeswitch/2017/03/29/515451746/muslim-schoolchildren-bullied-by-fellow-students-and-teachers

Oxford Islamic Studies Online. n.d. "Sufism." Accessed February 11, 2019. http://www.oxfordislamicstudies.com/article/opr/t125/e2260

Peterson, Jordan. 2017. "Why ISLAM is not a Religion of Peace. Explained by Jordan Peterson." Last modified December 20, 2017. https://youtu.be/wCIMOncHfTA

Pew Research Center. 2010. "Growing Number of Americans Say Obama is a Muslim." http://www.pewforum.org/2010/08/18/growing-number-of-americans-say-obama-is-a-muslim/

Pew Research Center. 2017. "How the U.S. general public views Muslims and Islam." http://www.pewforum.org/2017/07/26/how-the-u-s-general-public-views-muslims-and-islam/

Pew Research Center. 2017. "Religious Beliefs and Practices." http://www.pewforum.org/2017/07/26/religious-beliefs-and-practices/

Pew Research Center. 2016. "Republicans Prefer Blunt Talk About Islamic Extremism, Democrats Favor Caution." http://www.pewforum.org/2016/02/03/republicans-prefer-blunt-talk-about-islamic-extremism-democrats-favor-caution/

Pew Research Center. 2017. "Terrorism and concerns about extremism." Last modified July 26, 2017. http://www.pewforum.org/2017/07/26/terrorism-and-concerns-about-extremism/

Political Islam. n.d. "What is Islam?" Accessed February 13, 2019. https://www.politicalislam.com/author/

Saletan, William. 2014. "The Muslim Taxi Driver." *Slate*, February 27, 2014. https://slate.com/news-and-politics/2014/02/arizonas-antigay-bill-did-warnings-about-muslim-religious-freedom-help-prompt-a-veto.html

Schelzig, Erik. 2010. "Tenn. gov hopeful questions if Islam is a 'cult.'" *Seattle Times*, July 27, 2010. https://www.seattletimes.com/seattle-news/politics/tenn-gov-hopeful-questions-if-islam-is-a-cult/

Schragger, Richard. 2011. "The Politics of Free Exercise After Employment Division v. Smith: Same-Sex Marriage, the 'War on Terror, and Religious Freedom." *Cardozo Law Review*. 32: 2009-2031.

Smith, David. 2014. "Christian militias take bloody revenge on Muslims in Central African Republic." *The Guardian*, March 10, 2014. https://www.theguardian.com/world/2014/mar/10/central-african-republic-christian-militias-revenge Southern Poverty Law Center. n.d. "Tony Perkins." Accessed February 13, 2019. https://www.splcenter.org/fighting-hate/extremist-files/individual/tony-perkins

Spencer, Robert. 2014. "Why Robert George Is the Chris Christie of Conservative Intellectuals." *PJ Media*, December 25, 2014. https://pjmedia.com/blog/why-robert -george-is-the-chris-christie-of-conservative-intellectuals/6/

Stark, Rodney. 1996. *The Rise of Christianity*. Princeton: Princeton University Press.

Stewart, Katherine. 2018. "Why Trump Reigns as King Cyrus." *The New York Times*, December 31, 2018. https://www.nytimes.com/2018/12/31/opinion/trump-evangelicals -cyrus-king.html

Street, Paul and Anthony R, Dimaggio. 2016. *Crashing the Tea Party: Mass Media and the Campaign to Remake American Politics*. New York: Routledge.

Stockard, Sam. 2010. "Mosque lawsuit boils down to dislike of Islam." *The Daily News Journal*, November 23, 2010. http://web.archive.org/web/20101126075717/ http://www.dnj.com/article/20101123/OPINION02/11230308/1014/OPINION/ STOCKARD++Mosque+lawsuit+boils+down+to+dislike+of+Islam

Stolberg, Sheryl Gay. 2010. "In Defining Obama, Misperceptions Stick." *New York Times*, August 18, 2010. http://www.nytimes.com/2010/08/19/us/politics/19memo.html

Study Quran. n.d. "Siin." Accessed February 13, 2019. http://www.studyquran.co.uk/20_ SIIN.htm.

Suebsaeng, Asawin. 2016. "Allen West's Muslim Hate Goes Well Beyond a Genocide Meme." *Daily Beast*, December 12, 2016. https://www.thedailybeast.com/allen-wests -muslim-hate-goes-well-beyond-a-genocide-meme

Tackett, Del. n.d. "What's a Christian Worldview?" Focus on the Family. Accessed February 13, 2019. https://www.focusonthefamily.com/faith/christian-worldview/whats -a-christian-worldview/whats-a-worldview-anyway

Timm, Jane C. 2014. "GOP candidate Jody Hice in 2011: 'Most people think Islam is a religion, it's not.'" MSNBC, June 24, 2014. http://www.msnbc.com/msnbc/gop-jody -hice-islam-doesnt-deserve-first-amendment-protections

The Church of Jesus Christ of the Latter-day Saints. n.d. "Church Points to Joseph Smith's Statements on Religious Freedom, Pluralism." Accessed February 13, 2019. https://www.mormonnewsroom.org/article/church-statement -religious-freedom-pluralism

Tupper, Seth. 2018. "Tapio questions religious freedom for Muslims." Rapid City Journal, January 21, 2018. http://rapidcityjournal.com/news/local/tapio-questions-religious- freedom-for-muslims/article_a4e4532f-1b69-5b4d-9400-a70fb5028caa.html#tracking- source=home-top-story-1

Uddin, Asma. 2018. "What Islamophobic Politicians Can Learn from Mormons." *New York Times*, May 22, 2018. https://www.nytimes.com/2018/05/22/opinion/mormons -islamophobia-utah.html

Volokh, Eugene. 2014. "'Islam is not even a religion; it is a social, political system that uses a deity to advance its agenda of global conquest.'" *Washington Post*, September 22, 2014. https://www.washingtonpost.com/news/volokh-conspiracy/wp/2014/09/22/islam- is-not-even-a-religion-it-is-a-social-political-system-that-uses-a-deity-to-advance -its-agenda-of-global-conquest/?utm_term=.99b03dff7e2b

Waldman, Steven. 2016. "'Islam Is Not a Religion': The Real Reason Michael Flynn's Appointment is Ominous." *Washington Monthly*, November 25, 2016. https:// washingtonmonthly.com/2016/11/25/the-real-reason-michael-flynns-appointment-is -ominous-islam-is-not-a-religion/

Warren, Rick. 2014. "Religious Liberty is America's First Freedom." *Washington Post*, March 21, 2014. https://www.washingtonpost.com/opinions/religious-liberty-is -americas-first-freedom/2014/03/21/498c0048-b128-11e3-a49e-76adc9210f19_story .html?noredirect=on&utm_term=.09fbafa682f8

Wildman, Sarah. 2017. "A top White House aide was asked if Trump thought Islam was a religion. He refused to answer." *Vox*, March 1, 2017. https://www.vox.com/ world/2017/3/1/14778756/white-house-trump-sebastian-gorka-islam-religion-anti-semitism

YouTube. 2012. "CNN's Unwelcome - Muslims Next Door - Soledad O'Brien." Last modified January 24, 2012. https://www.youtube.com/watch?v=4JRzeZMw6LM

Zakaria, Fareed. 2014. "Let's be honest, Islam has a problem right now." *Washington Post*, October 9, 2014. https://www.washingtonpost.com/opinions/fareed-zakaria-islam -has-a-problem-right-now-but-heres-why-bill-maher-is-wrong/2014/10/09/b6302a14 -4fe6-11e4-aa5e-7153e466a02d_story.html?noredirect=on&utm_term=.06dc2ca9cedc

Zoll, Rachel. 2015. "AP-NORC Poll: Christian-Muslim split on religious freedom." *Associated Press*, December 30, 2015. https://apnews.com/de486b3d64154d0baae9 f04fba0a4094/ap-norc-poll-religious-rights-us-christians-most-valued

CHAPTER 2

Ali, Wajahat, Eli Clifton, Matthew Duss, Lee Fang, Scott Keyes, and Faiz Shakir. 2011. "The Roots of the Islamophobia Network in America." Last modified August 26, 2011. https://www.americanprogress.org/issues/religion/reports/2011/08/26/10165/fear-inc/

Allam, Hannah and Talal Ansari. 2018. "State and Local Republican Officials Have Been Bashing Muslims. We Counted." *Buzzfeed News*, April 10, 2018. https://www.buzzfeed .com/hannahallam/trump-republicans-bashing-muslims-without-repercussions?utm_ term=.vt8k3q3b3d#.prN3dmdOdG

Amos, Deborah. 2018. "Those Affected by Trump's Travel Ban Hope For End To 'Chaos' After Supreme Court Case." *National Public Radio*, April 24, 2018. https://www.npr .org/sections/parallels/2018/04/24/605260314/those-affected-by-trumps-travel-ban -hope-for-end-to-chaos-after-supreme-court-ca

Barnes, Robert. "In travel ban case, Supreme Court considers 'the president' vs. 'this president.'" *Washington Post*, April 22, 2018. https://www.washingtonpost.com/ politics/courts_law/in-travel-ban-case-supreme-court-considers-the-president-vs-this -president/2018/04/22/f33f1edc-44cb-11e8-8569-26fda6b404c7_story.html

Beinart, Peter. 2017. "The Denationalization of American Muslims." *The Atlantic*, March 19, 2017. https://www.theatlantic.com/politics/archive/2017/03/frank-gaffney-donald -trump-and-the-denationalization-of-american-muslims/519954/

Bever, Lindsey. 2015. "Pamela Geller, the incendiary organizer of Texas 'prophet Muhammad cartoon contest.'" *Washington Post*, May 4, 2015. https://www .washingtonpost.com/news/morning-mix/wp/2015/05/04/why-a-woman-named-pamela -geller-organized-a-prophet-muhammad-cartoon-contest/?utm_term=.8560d0682dc3

Blackman, Josh. 2018. "The Travel Bans." *Cato Supreme Court Review*. https://object .cato.org/sites/cato.org/files/serials/files/supreme-court-review/2018/9/2018-cato -supreme-court-review-2.pdf

Blythe, Anne. 2017. "Judge orders FBI notes turned over to man accused of shooting three Muslim students." *News & Observer*, March 14, 2017. https://www.newsobserver.com/ news/local/crime/article138457408.html#storylink=cpy

Boorstein, Michelle. 2018. "Why many religious liberty groups are silent about the

Supreme Court's decision on Trump's travel ban." *Washington Post*, June 28, 2018
.https://www.washingtonpost.com/news/acts-of-faith/wp/2018/06/26/why-many
-religious-liberty-groups-are-silent-on-the-supreme-courts-decision-to-uphold-trumps
-travel-ban/?noredirect=on&utm_term=.e34ef54ad48a

Bosniak, Linda. 2000. "Citizenship Denationalized." *Indiana Journal of Global Legal Studies*. 7: 447-509.

Brittain, Amy and Abigail Hauslohner. 2017. "Anti-sharia group offers donors a private tour and cocktails at Trump hotel." *Washington Post*, June 20, 2017. https://www.washingtonpost.com/politics/anti-sharia-group-offers-donors-a-private-tour-and-cocktails-at-trump-hotel/2017/06/20/0b758b86-5138-11e7-be25-3a519335381c_story.html

Brown, Jonathan A.C. 2014. *Misquoting Muhammad: The Challenge and Choices of Interpreting the Prophet's Legacy*. London: Oneworld Publications.

Burke, Daniel. 2017. "Trump says US will prioritize Christian refugees." CNN, January 30, 2017. https://www.cnn.com/2017/01/27/politics/trump-christian-refugees/index.html

Bump, Philip. 2016. "Marco Rubio downplays Muslim discrimination. So do many Republicans." *Washington Post*, February 7, 2016. https://www.washingtonpost.com/news/the-fix/wp/2016/02/07/marco-rubio-downplays-muslim-discrimination-as-do-many-republicans/?utm_term=.24c288805fc1

CBS Local. 2018. "Police Arrest Man Suspected of Pulling Wigs Off Orthodox Jewish Women." Last modified November 7, 2018. https://losangeles.cbslocal.com/2018/11/07/hate-crime-wigs-orthodox-jewish-women/

Daniel M. Filler. 2003. "Terrorism, Panic, and Pedophilia." *Virginia Journal of Social Policy and the Law*. 10: 345-382.

Desmond-Harris, Jenée. 2017. "'Crying is an everyday thing': life after Trump's 'Muslim ban' at a majority-immigrant school." *Vox*, February 16, 2017. https://www.vox.com/identities/2017/2/16/14584228/muslim-ban-trump-immigration-ban-children-kids-schools-anxiety

Diamant, Jeff. 2017. "American Muslims are concerned—but also satisfied with their lives." Pew Research Center, July 26, 2017. http://www.pewresearch.org/fact-tank/2017/07/26/american-muslims-are-concerned-but-also-satisfied-with-their-lives/

Diamond, Jeremy. 2016. "Trump doubles down on calls for mosque surveillance." *CNN*, June 15, 2016. http://www.cnn.com/2016/06/15/politics/donald-trump-muslims-mosque-surveillance.

Elsheikh, Elsadig, Basima Sisemore, and Natalia Ramirez Lee. 2017. "Legalizing Othering: The United States of Islamophobia." Last modified September 2017. http://haasinstitute.berkeley.edu/sites/default/files/haas_institute_legalizing_othering_the_united_states_of_islamophobia.pdf

Estepa, Jessica. 2017. "'Preventing Muslim immigration' statement disappears from Trump's campaign site." *USA Today*, May 9, 2017. https://www.usatoday.com/story/news/politics/onpolitics/2017/05/08/preventing-muslim-immigration-statement-disappears-donald-trump-campaign-site/101436780/

Fantz, Ashley, Steve Almasy, and AnneClaire Stapleton. 2015. "Muslim teen Ahmed Mohamed creates clock, shows teachers, gets arrested." *CNN*, September 16, 2015. https://www.cnn.com/2015/09/16/us/texas-student-ahmed-muslim-clock-bomb/index.html

Fisher, Max. 2016. "Marco Rubio's comments about Muslims are getting to be almost as

frightening as Trump's." *Vox*, February 6, 2016. https://www.vox
.com/2016/2/4/10918372/marco-rubio-muslims-media

Greenberg, David. 2018. "America's Forgotten Pogroms." *Politico*, November 2, 2018.
https://www.politico.com/magazine/story/2018/11/02/americas-forgotten
-pogroms-222181

Friedman, Richard A. 2018. "The Neuroscience of Hate Speech." *New York Times*,
October 31, 2018. https://www.nytimes.com/2018/10/31/opinion/caravan-hate-speech
-bowers-sayoc.html

Fox News. 2017. "Ex-IU student gets probation for Muslim woman attack." Last modified
January 23, 2017. https://www.foxnews.com/us/ex-indiana-u-student-gets-probation
-for-muslim-woman-attack

Gass, Nick. 2015. "Trump: 'Absolutely no choice' but to close mosques." *Politico*, November
18, 2015. http://www.politico.com/story/ 2015/11/trump-close-mosques-216008.

George, Michael. 2017. "Police Probe Threats Made to Brooklyn Nun as Possible Hate
Crime." NBC, July 5, 2017. https://www.nbcnewyork.com/news/local/NYC-Police
-Probe-Threats-Made-to-Brooklyn-Nun-as-Hate-Crime--432790873.html

GhaneaBassiri, Kambiz. 2013. "Islamophobia and American History: Religious
Stereotyping and Out-grouping of Muslims in the United States." In *Islamophobia in
America: The Anatomy of Intolerance*, edited by Carl W. Ernst, 53-74. New York:
Palgrave MacMillan.

Greene, Leonard. 2017. "Gadfly Pamela Geller wins bid to post transit ads for film critical
of Muslims." *New York Daily News*, September 5, 2017. http://www.nydailynews.com/
new-york/pamela-geller-wins-bid-post-transit-ads-anti-muslim-film-article-1.3471936

Goodstein, Laurie. 2003. "Seeing Islam as 'Evil' Faith, Evangelicals Seek Converts." *New
York Times*, May 27, 2003. http://www.nytimes.com/2003/05/27/us/seeing-islam-as-evil
-faith-evangelicals-seek-converts.html

Gomez, Mark. 2016. "Hijab-wearing woman describes San Jose State attack." *Mercury
News*, November 9, 2016. https://www.mercurynews.com/2016/11/09/woman-wearing
-hijab-attacked-at-san-jose-state/

Goth, Brenna and Jim Walsh. 2015. "A clash of freedoms during Phoenix mosque
protest." *AZ Central*, May 28, 2015. https://www.azcentral.com/story/news/local/
phoenix/2015/05/29/law-enforcement-prepares-protest-outside-phoenix
-mosque/28136557/

Hauslohner, Abigail. 2018. "New NSC chief of staff is from group that believes Muslims
are plotting to take over U.S." *Washington Post*, May 30, 2018. https://www
.washingtonpost.com/news/post-nation/wp/2018/05/30/new-national-security-council
-chief-of-staff-comes-from-a-group-that-believes-muslims-are-plotting-to-take-over
-america/?noredirect=on&utm_term=.5f0b3debbed1

Hauslohner, Abigail. 2018. "'What's next?' Muslims grapple with Supreme Court ruling
that they believe redefines their place in America." *Washington Post*, June 26, 2018.
https://www.washingtonpost.com/national/whats-next-muslims-grapple-with-supreme
-court-ruling-that-they-believe-redefines-their-place-in-america/2018/06/26/ce322d14
-7969-11e8-aeee-4d04c8ac6158_story.html?noredirect=on&utm_term=.dc96c3ff52f6

Hernandez, Miriam. 2015. "Trump cites history to defend Muslim immigration ban."
ABC 7, December 9, 2015. http://abc7.com/politics/trump-cites-history-to-defend
-muslim-immigration-ban/111 6396.

Hillyard, Vaughn. 2015. "Donald Trump's Plan for a Muslim Database Draws
Comparison to Nazi Germany." *NBC News*, November 20, 2015. http://www
.nbcnews.com/politics/2016-election/trump-says-he-would-certainly-implement-muslim
- database-n466716.

Hitchens, Christopher. 2007. "Facing the Islamist Menace." Review of *America Alone:
The End of the World as We Know It*, by Mark Steyn. *City Journal*, Winter 2007,
https://www.city-journal.org/html/facing-islamist-menace-12993.html

Hofstadter, Richard. 1965. *The Paranoid Style in American Politics*. New York: Vintage
Books.

Hussein, Shakira. 2015. "The Myth of the Lying Muslim: 'Taqiyya' and the Racialization
of Muslim Identity." *ABC Religion and Ethics*, May 28, 2015. http://www.abc.net.au/
religion/articles/2015/05/28/4244447.htm

Ian Shin, *"Scoot – Smoot – Scoot": The Seating Trial of Senator Reed*, https://web.archive.
org/web/20080309131303/http://gainesjunction.tamu.edu/issues/vol3num1/ishin/ishin.pdf

Izadl, Elahe and Lindsey Bever. 2015. "The history of anti-Islam controversy in Ahmed
Mohamed's Texas city." *Washington Post*, September 16, 2015. https://www
.washingtonpost.com/news/acts-of-faith/wp/2015/09/16/the-history-of-anti-islam
-controversy-in-ahmed-mohameds-texas-city/?utm_term=.f87b936fd264

John F. Kennedy Presidential Library and Museum. n.d. "John F. Kennedy and Religion."
Accessed February 14, 2019. https://www.jfklibrary.org/learn/about-jfk/jfk-in-history/
john-f-kennedy-and-religion

Jones, Katie. 2017. "Taqiyya Alert: Manchester Bombing Imam Deception." *Geller
Report*, June 18, 2017. https://gellerreport.com/2017/06/taquiyya-alert-manchester
-bombing-imam-deception.html/

Kane, Alex. 2017. "Even Muslim-American Citizens Have Been Caught in the Net of
Trump's Travel Ban." *The Nation*, March 23, 2017. https://www.thenation.com/article/
even-muslim-american-citizens-have-been-caught-in-the-net-of-trumps-travel-ban/

Kazem, Halima and Tom Dart. 2015. "US Muslim leaders brace for protests with
potentially armed demonstrators." *The Guardian*, October 9, 2015. https://www
.theguardian.com/world/2015/oct/09/us-muslim-community-phoenix-oklahoma-city
-protests-mosques

Kearns, Erin and Betus, Allison and Lemieux, Anthony, "Why Do Some Terrorist Attacks
Receive More Media Attention Than Others?" (April 2, 2018). Kearns, E.M., Betus,
A. & Lemieux, A. "Why Do Some Terrorist Attacks Receive More Media Attention
Than Others?" Justice Quarterly, Forthcoming. Available at SSRN: https://ssrn.com/
abstract=2928138 or http://dx.doi.org/10.2139/ssrn.2928138

Kessler, Glenn. 2015. "Trump's outrageous claim that 'thousands' of New Jersey Muslims
celebrated the 9/11 attacks." *Washington Post*, November 22, 2015. https://www
.washingtonpost.com/news/fact-checker/wp/2015/11/22/donald-trumps
-outrageous-claim-that-thousands-of-new-jersey-muslims-celebrated-the-911-
attacks/?noredirect=on&utm_term=.c6efbf058cfb.

Khan, Aysha. 2018. "For American Muslims, family border separations are personal."
Religion News Service, July 18, 2018. https://religionnews.com/2018/07/18/for
-american-muslims-family-separation-at-the-border-is-personal/

Khan, Uzra. 2015. "Yes, Senator Rubio, there's plenty of evidence of discrimination
against Muslim Americans." *QZ*, December 8, 2015. https://qz.com/568054/yes
-senator-rubio-theres-plenty-of-evidence-of-discrimination-against-muslim-americans/

Kirkpatrick, David D. 2012. "Anger Over a Film Fuels Anti-American Attacks in Libya and Egypt." *New York Times*, September 11, 2012. http://www.nytimes .com/2012/09/12/world/middleeast/anger-over-film-fuels-anti-american-attacks-in-libya -and-egypt.html

Kniffin, Eric N. 2011. "Are American Muslims Entitled to the Same Free Exercise Rights as Other Americans?" *Huffington Post*, May 31, 2011. https://www.huffingtonpost .com/eric-n-kniffin/are-american-muslims-enti_b_867777.html

Larimer, Sarah. 2015. "Why Franklin Graham says Donald Trump is right about stopping Muslim immigration." *Washington Post*, December 10, 2015. https://www .washingtonpost.com/news/acts-of-faith/wp/2015/12/10/why-franklin-graham-says -donald-trump-is-right-about-stopping-muslim-immigration/?utm_term=.2126b96321d4

Leon, Melissa. 2015. "Bill Maher and Richard Dawkins Slam Muslims: 'To Hell with Their Culture.'" *Daily Beast*, October 3, 2015. https://www.thedailybeast.com/bill -maher-and-richard-dawkins-slam-muslims-to-hell-with-their-culture

Lewin, Lyric. 2017. "These are the faces of Trump's ban." *CNN*, January 2017. https:// www.cnn.com/interactive/2017/01/politics/immigration-ban-stories/

Linddara, Dara. 2018. "The Trump administration's separation of families at the border, explained." *Vox*, August 14, 2018. https://www.vox.com/2018/6/11/17443198/children -immigrant-families-separated-parents

Lugo, Karen. 2016. *Mosques in America: A Guide to Accountable Permit Hearings and Continuing Citizen Oversight*. Washington, DC: Center for Security Policy Press. http:// www.centerforsecuritypolicy.org/wp-content/uploads/2016/12/Mosque_in_America.pdf

Mai-Duc, Christine. 2015. "Texas cartoon contest shooting: Why Images of Muhammad are Offensive to Muslims." *Los Angeles Times*, May 4, 2015. http://www.latimes.com/ nation/nationnow/la-na-nn-texas-cartoon-why-muhammad-images-offensive-20150504 -htmlstory.html

Malkin, Michelle. 2017. "Never Forget: Muslim Hate Crime Hoaxes." *National Review*, September 13, 2017. https://www.nationalreview.com/2017/09/muslim-hate-crime- hoaxes-retrospective/

Marzouki, Nadia. 2017. *Islam: An American Religion*. New York: Columbia University Press.

Masterpiece Cakeshop, Ltd. v. Colorado Civil Rights Comm'n, 138 S. Ct. 1719 (2018). https://www.supremecourt.gov/opinions/17pdf/16-111_j4el.pdf

Mathias, Christopher. "A Pastor Who Said Islam Is 'Evil' Is Speaking at Trump's Inauguration." *Huffington Post*, January 18, 2017. https://www.huffingtonpost .com/entry/franklin-graham-islamophobia-trump-inauguration_us_587e3ea5e 4b0aaa369429373

McCammon, Sarah. 2016. "Conservative Christians Grapple with Whether 'Religious Freedom' Includes Muslims." *NPR*, June 29, 2016. https://www.npr.org/2016/06/ 29/483901761/conservative-christians-grapple-with-what-religious-freedom-means-for -muslims

McLaughlin, Eliott C. 2018. "Yemeni mother wins visa fight to see her dying child in a California hospital." *CNN*, December 18, 2018. https://www.cnn.com/2018/12/18/us/ oakland-child-life-support-yemeni-mother-travel-ban/index.html

Missouri Digital Heritage. n.d. "The Missouri Mormon War." Accessed February 17, 2019. https://www.sos.mo.gov/archives/resources/mormon.asp

Missouri Government. n.d. "Extermination Order." Accessed February 22, 2019
    .https://www.sos.mo.gov/cmsimages/archives/resources/findingaids/miscMormRecs/
    eo/18381027_ExtermOrder.pdf

Mohammad, Niala. 2016. "I didn't realize how often Muslims get kicked off planes, until
    it happened to me." *The Guardian*, September 8, 2016. https://www.theguardian.com/
    world/2016/sep/08/muslim-woman-kicked-off-american-airlines-flight-islamophobia;
    Revesz, Rachael. 2016. "Muslim woman kicked off plane as flight attendant said she
    'did not feel comfortable' with the passenger." *Independent*, April 15, 2016. https://
    www.independent.co.uk/news/world/americas/muslim-woman-kicked-off-plane-as
    -flight-attendant-said-she-did-not-feel-comfortable-with-the-a6986661.html

Moore, Tina. 2016. "Muslim woman in religious garb set on fire while shopping." *New
    York Post*, September 12, 2016. https://nypost.com/2016/09/12/muslim-woman-in
    -religious-garb-set-on-fire-while-shopping/

Mulder, William. n.d. "Immigration and the "Mormon Question": An International
    Episode." Accessed February 17, 2019. http://files.lib.byu.edu/mormonmigration/
    articles/ImmigrationAndTheMormonQuestionAnInternationalEpisode.pdf

New America Muslim Diaspora Initiative. n.d. "Anti-Muslim Activities in the United States."
    Accessed February 14, 2019. https://www.newamerica.org/in-depth/anti-muslim-activity/

Ortega, Hannah. 2018. "Protestors Across Dallas-Fort Worth Hope Rallies Against
    Immigration Separation Will Bring Change." *Dallas News*, June 26, 2018. https://www
    .dallasnews.com/news/immigration/2018/06/26/protesters-across-dallas-fort-worth
    -hope-rallies-immigrant-separation-will-bring-change

Pew Research Center. 2017."Americans Express Increasingly Warm Feelings Toward
    Religious Groups." Last modified February 15, 2017. http://www.pewforum
    .org/2017/02/15/americans-express-increasingly-warm-feelings-toward-religious-groups/

Phillips, Amber. 2018. "A brief rundown of the long legal history of Trump's travel ban."
    Washington Post, June 26, 2018. https://www.washingtonpost.com/amphtml/news/
    the-fix/wp/2018/06/26/a-brief-rundown-of-the-long-legal-history-of-trumps-travel
    -ban/?noredirect=on

Pilkington, Ed. "Anti-sharia laws proliferate as Trump strikes hostile tone toward
    Muslims." *The Guardian*, December 30, 2017. https://www.theguardian.com/
    us-news/2017/dec/30/anti-sharia-laws-trump-muslims

Power, Carla. 2015. "What Ayaan Hirsi Ali Doesn't Get About Islam." TIME, April 17,
    2015. http://time.com/3825345/what-ayaan-hirsi-ali-doesnt-get-about-islam/

Revesz, Rachael. 2016. "Southwest Airlines kicks Muslim off a plane for saying
    'inshallah', meaning 'God willing' in Arabic." *Independent*, October 5, 2016. https://
    www.independent.co.uk/news/world/americas/muslim-passenger-southwest-airlines
    -khairuldeen-makhzoom-arabic-phone-uncle-baghdad-cair-statement-a7347311.html

Schleifer, Theodore. 2016. "Donald Trump: 'I think Islam hates us.'" *CNN*, March 9,
    2016. https://www.cnn.com/2016/03/09/politics/donald-trump-islam-hates-us/index.html

Schwarz, Hunter. 2017. "138 years ago, the controversy over travel bans and religion was
    about Mormons from Europe." *CNN*, January 30, 2017. https://www.cnn.com/
    2017/01/30/politics/1879-mormon-travel-ban/index.html

Selk, Avi. 2015. "Ahmed Mohamed swept up, 'hoax bomb' charges swept away as Irving
    teen's story." *Dallas News*, September 15, 2015. https://www.dallasnews.com/news/
    dallas-county/2015/09/15/ahmed-mohamed-swept-up-hoax-bomb-charges-swept-away
    -as-irving-teen-s-story-floods-social-media

Settembre, Jeanette. 2017. "How a hate crime empowered this Muslim millennial to start a self-defense movement." *Market Watch*, November 6, 2017. https://moneyish.com/ heart/how-a-hate-crime-empowered-this-muslim-millennial-to-start-a-self-defense -movement/

Solis, George, 2017. "Maryland 5-Year-Old Detained at Airport Reunited With Mom." *CBS Baltimore*, January 30, 2017. https://baltimore.cbslocal.com/2017/01/30/maryland -5-year-old-detained-at-airport-reunited-with-mom/

Tai, Hina and Winn Periyasamy. 2016. "Trump's Islamophobia rhetoric means a public health crisis for Muslims." *The Guardian*, November 30, 2016. https://www .theguardian.com/world/2016/nov/30/donald-trump-muslims-public-health-crisis

Talbot, Margaret. 2015. "The Story of a Hate Crime." *New Yorker*, June 22, 2015. https://www.newyorker.com/magazine/2015/06/22/the-story-of-a-hate-crime

The Guardian. "Two-year-old son of Yemeni woman who sued to enter US dies in California." Last modified December 29, 2018. https://www.theguardian.com/ us-news/2018/dec/29/two-year-old-son-yemeni-woman-sued-enter-us-dies-california

Tomlinson, Zac. 2017. "Rana Abdelhamid, Founder of (IM)WISE, On Community Building & Gender-based Violence." *Medium*, November 8, 2017. https://medium.com/ muslim-women-speak/rana-697c69829013

Toobin, Jeffrey. 2019. "The Supreme Court is Quietly Changing the Status of Religion in American Life." *The New Yorker*, March 6, 2019. https://www.newyorker.com/news/ daily-comment/the-supreme-court-is-quietly-changing-the-status-of-religion-in-american-life?utm_campaign=aud-dev&utm_source=nl&utm_brand=tny&utm_mailing=TNY_ Daily_030719&utm_medium=email&bxid=5bd67dcc24c17c104802cd4a&user_ id=48821338&esrc=&utm_term=TNY_Daily

Trefethen, Sarah and Tina Moore. 2016. "Woman arrested for allegedly attacking two Muslim women." *New York Post*, September 9, 2016. https://nypost.com/2016/09/09/ woman-arrested-for-allegedly-attacking-two-muslim-women/

Trump v. Hawaii, 138 S. Ct. 2392 (2018). "Brief *Amicus Curiae* of The Becket Fund for Religious Liberty in Support of Neither Party." March 2018. https://s3.amazonaws.com/ becketnewsite/Becket-Amicus-Trump-v-Hawaii-amicus-v3.pdf

Trump v. Hawaii, 138 S. Ct. 2392 (2018). https://www.supremecourt.gov/opinions/ 17pdf/17-965_h315.pdf

Trump v. Hawaii, 138 S. Ct. 2392 (2018). "Brief for *Amici Curiae* National Association of Muslim Lawyers and Other Muslim Bar Associations in Support of Respondents." March 30, 2018. https://www.supremecourt.gov/DocketPDF/17/17-965/41848/201803 30171806891_17-965%20Trump%20v%20Hawaii%20Amicus%20Brief%20of%20 National%20Association%20of%20Muslim%20Lawyers.pdf

Uddin, Asma. 2018. "It's Time We Talk About the 'Trump Effect' On Kids." *Teen Vogue*, January 19, 2018. https://www.teenvogue.com/story/its-time-we-talk-about-the-trump -effect-on-kids

Uddin, Asma. 2016. "Religious Freedom and Discrimination in America— Then and Now." Accessed February 14, 2019. http://www.ispu.org/wp-content/uploads/2016/08/ ISPU_Relgious_Freedom4.pdf

Wang, Amy B. 2017. "Trump asked for a 'Muslim ban,' Giuliani says—and ordered a commission to do it 'legally.'" *Washington Post*, January 29, 2017. https://www .washingtonpost.com/news/the-fix/wp/2017/01/29/trump-asked-for-a-muslim-ban -giuliani-says-and-ordered-a-commission-to-do-it-legally/?utm_term=.84671a 57ed2c.

Warikoo, Niraj. 2015. "Anti-Islam rallies across USA making Muslims wary." *USA Today*, October 9, 2015. https://www.usatoday.com/story/news/.../anti-islam...across-usa ...muslims.../73672674/

Wiki Islam. n.d. "Islam and Pedophilia." Accessed February 14, 2019. https://wikiislam ..net/wiki/Islam_and_Pedophilia

Witte, John and Joel E. Nichols. 2010. "Faith-Based Family Laws in Western Democracies?" *Fides et Libertas: The Journal of the International Religious Liberty Association.* 119–132. https://papers.ssrn.com/sol3/papers.cfm?abstract_id=1805304

YouTube. 2017. "Muslim woman teaches the 'hijab-grab' technique for self-defense I New York Post." Last modified August 10, 2017. https://www.youtube.com/ watch?v=RSLvfXZvSgw

YouTube. 2019. "Mehdi Hasan expose media hypocrisy on New Zealand Mass shooting." Last modified March 19, 2019. https://www.youtube.com/watch?v=K8QFeOydWYc

YouTube. 2015. "Robert Spencer on Why ISIS is Islamic." Last modified March 14, 2015. https://www.youtube.com/watch?v=Dw9lG83lr0s#t=24m07s

Zombie Time. n.d. "The *Jyllands-Posten* Cartoons." Accessed February 14, 2019. http:// www.zombietime.com/mohammed_image_archive/jyllands-posten_cartoons/

CHAPTER 3

A.A. ex rel. Betenbaugh v. Needville Indep. Sch. Dist., 611 F.3d 248, 253 (5th Cir. 2010).

Akyol, Mustafa. 2018. "Why Do Muslims Slaughter Animals for God?" *New York Times*, August 21, 2018. https://www.nytimes.com/2018/08/21/opinion/eid-al-adha-sacrifice -isaac.html

BBC Religions. 2009. "Sacrifice." Last modified September 15, 2009. http://www.bbc .co.uk/religion/religions/santeria/ritesrituals/sacrifice.shtml

Bessard v. California Community Colleges, 867 F. Supp. 1454, 1456 (E.D.Cal. 1994).

Beydoun, Khaled A. 2016. "Islam Incarcerated: Religious Accommodation of Muslim Prisoners Before Holt v. Hobbs." *University of Cincinnati Law Review.* 84: 99–151.

Bryan, Susannah. 2011. "Sunrise commissioner blocks Muslim sacrifice of goats and lambs." *Sun Sentinel,* November 2, 2011. http://articles.sun-sentinel.com/2011-11-02/ news/fl-sunrise-politician-blocks-muslim-fest-20111102_1_sunrise-commissioner-sheila -alu-animal-sacrifices-sacrifices-for-religious-purposes

Cavanaugh v. Bartelt, 178 F.Supp.3d 819 (2016).

Cheema v. Thompson, 67 F.3d 883, 884 (9th Cir. 1995).

Church of the Flying Spaghetti Monster. n.d. "About." Accessed February 17, 2019. https://www.venganza.org/about/

Church of the Flying Spaghetti Monster. n.d. "Open Letter to Kansas School Board." Accessed February 17, 2019. https://www.venganza.org/about/open-letter/

Data USA. n.d. "Hialeah, FL." Accessed February 15, 2019. https://datausa.io/profile/geo/ hialeah-fl/

Dolovich, Sharon. 2013. "Forms of Judicial Deference in Prison Law." Prison Legal News,

January 15, 2013. https://www.prisonlegalnews.org/news/2013/jan/15/forms-of-judicial
-deference-in-prison-law/

Dowdy, Daniel. 2018. "Absurdity, Sincerity, Truth, and the Church of the Flying Spaghetti
Monster: Title VII Religious Protections and Perceived Satire." *Rutgers Journal of Law
and Religion.* 19: 175–211.

Editorial Board. 2019. "Is Religious Freedom for Christians Only?" *The New York Times,*
February 9, 2019. https://www.nytimes.com/2019/02/09/opinion/supreme-court
-alabama-execution.html

Epps, Garrett. 2014. "Elegy for a Hero of Religious Freedom" *The Atlantic,* December 9,
2014. https://www.theatlantic.com/politics/archive/2014/12/elegy-for-an-american-hero
-al-smith-smith-employment-division-supreme-court/383582/

Feldman, Stephen M. 2006. "Empiricism, Religion, and Judicial Decision-Making."
William & Mary Bill of Rights Journal. 15: 43–57.

Gilsinan, Kathy. 2016. "Big in Europe: The Church of the Flying Spaghetti Monster." *The
Atlantic,* November 2016. https://www.theatlantic.com/magazine/archive/2016/11/big
-in-europe/501131/

Gonzales v. Centro Espirita Beneficente Uniao do Vegetal, 546 U.S. 418 (2006).

Haines, Lester. 2016. "Russian Pastafarian wins right to bear colander." The Register,
January 15, 2016. https://www.theregister.co.uk/2016/01/15/russian_pastafarian/

Henley, Jon. 2018. "Spaghetti injunction: Pastafarianism is not a religion, Dutch court
rules." *The Guardian,* August 16, 2018. https://www.theguardian.com/world/2018/
aug/16/pastafarianism-is-not-a-religion-dutch-court-rules

Henry, John. 2018. "Northern Virginia town ends blockade of Muslim business." WUSA9,
August 20, 2018. https://www.wusa9.com/article/news/local/virginia/northern-virginia
-town-ends-blockade-of-muslim-business/65-585893586

Holt v. Hobbs, 135 S. Ct. 853 (2015). "Brief of *Amici Curiae* The Sikh Coalition And
Muslim Public Affairs Council In Support Of Petitioner." http://www.scotusblog.com/
wp-content/uploads/2017/08/13-6827tsacSikhCoalition.pdf

Holt v. Hobbs, 135 S. Ct. 853 (2015). https://www.supremecourt.gov/opinions/14pdf/13
-6827_5h26.pdf

http://www.nbcnews.com/id/7162088/ns/us_news-crime_and_courts/t/report-prison-staff
-mistreated-muslims/#.W-0CMi_MxUM

Humphrey, Sara. 2015. "North Texas residents react to traditional Muslim ritual." KXII
Fox News 12, September 24, 2015. https://www.kxii.com/home/headlines/North-Texas
-residents-react-to-traditional-Muslim-ritual-329381801.html

Klein, Konstantin. 2017. "German courts take on the Flying Spaghetti Monster." *DW,*
February 8, 2017. https://www.dw.com/en/german-courts-take-on-the-flying-spaghetti
-monster/a-39943249

Lund, Christopher C. 2016. "RFRA, State RFRA, and Religious Minorities." *San Diego
Law Review.* 53: 163-184.

Office of the Inspector General. 2003. "Report to Congress on Implementation
of Section 1001 of the USA PATRIOT Act." https://oig.justice.gov/special/0307/index.htm

O'Grady, Siobhan. 2018. "Sorry, Dutch Pastafarians, but you still can't wear a colander on your government ID . . . yet." *Washington Post*, August 17, 2018.https://www
.washingtonpost.com/world/2018/08/17/sorry-dutch-pastafarians-you-still-cant-wear
-colander-your-government-id-yet/?utm_term=.6d935b0eb84c

Ovalle, David. 2017. "How ritual chicken sacrifices in Miami helped halt Trump's travel ban." *Miami Herald*, February 11, 2017. https://www.miamiherald.com/news/local/
community/miami-dade/article131983429.html

Religious Freedom Restoration Act, 42 U.S.C § 2000bb.

Roy, Eleanor Ainge. 2016. "World's first Pastafarian wedding takes place in New Zealand." *The Guardian*, April 17, 2016. https://www.theguardian.com/world/2016/
apr/18/worlds-first-pastafarian-wedding-takes-place-in-new-zealand

Schragger, Richard. 2011. "The Politics of Free Exercise After Employment Division v. Smith: Same-Sex Marriage, the 'War on Terror,' and Religious Freedom." *Cardozo Law Review*. 32: 2009–2031.

Serbian Eastern Orthodox Church v. Milivojevich, 426 U.S. 696 (1976).

Sewell v. Pegelow, 291 F.2d 196 (1961)

Sisk, Gregory C. and Michael Heise. 2012. "Muslims and Religious Liberty in the Era of 9/11: Empirical Evidence from the Federal Courts." *Iowa Law Review*. 98: 231-291.

Smith, Christopher. 2016. *The Supreme Court and the Development of Law: Through the Prism of Prisoners Rights*. New York: Palgrave Macmillan.

Thorpe, Kimberly. 2009. "A court case forced a Santeria priest to reveal some of his religion's secrets. Its ritual of animal sacrifice, he revealed on his own." *Dallas Observer*, October 22, 2009. http://www.dallasobserver.com/content/printView/6406316

U.S. v. Ballard, 322 U.S. 78 (1944).

U.S. v. Kuch, 288 F. Supp. 439, 442 (D.D.C 1968).

U.S. v. Lee, 455 U.S. 252 (1982).

U.S. v. Meyers, 95 F.3d 1475 (10th Cir. 1996).

U.S. v. Seeger, 380 U.S. 163 (1965).

Welsh v. U.S., 398 U.S. 333 (1970).

White, Kaila. 2017. "Arizona man wears colander in driver's license photo in name of religious freedom." *AZ Central*, June 1, 2017.
https://www.azcentral.com/story/news/local/chandler/2017/06/01/arizona-man-wears
-colander-drivers-license-photo-name-religious-freedom/362732001/

Willingham, AJ. 2018. "By 2040, Islam could be the second-largest religion in the US." CNN, January 10, 2018. https://www.cnn.com/2018/01/10/politics/muslim-population
-growth-second-religious-group-trnd/index.html

Wybraniec, John and Roger Finke. 2004. "Religious Regulation and the Courts: The Judiciary's Changing Role in Protecting Minority Religions from Majoritarian Rule." In *Regulating Religion: Case Studies from Around the Globe*, edited by James T. Richardson, 535-553. New York: Kluwer Academic/Plenum Publishers.

CHAPTER 4

Abudiab, Daoud. 2012. "My Faith: After my mosque was torched." *CNN Belief Blog*, August 7, 2012. http://religion.blogs.cnn.com/2012/08/07/my-faith-after-my-mosque -was-torched/

ACLU. 2018. "Nationwide anti-mosque activity." Last modified May 2018. https://www .aclu.org/issues/national-security/discriminatory-profiling/nationwide-anti-mosque-activity

Bahloul, Ossama. Interview by Rebecca Deucher. Phone call. October 2018.

Berger, Eric. 2018. "Florissant man confesses to Chesed Shel Emeth vandalism." STL Jewish Light, April 25, 2018. http://www.stljewishlight.com/news/local/florissant -man-confesses-to-chesed-shel-emeth-vandalism/article_63f2a41e-48c3-11e8-820e -434bb20ac29d.html

Berlinger, Joshua and Rob Frehse. 2017. "Jewish cemetery vandalized in New York, third case in recent weeks." CNN, March 3, 2017. https://www.cnn.com/2017/03/03/us/ jewish-cemetery-vandalized-headstones-new-york/index.html

Blumenthal, Ralph and Sharaf Mowjood. 2009. "Muslim Prayers and Renewal Near Ground Zero." *New York Times*, December 8, 2009. https://www.nytimes .com/2009/12/09/nyregion/09mosque.html

Broden, Scott. 2016. "Imam leaving Murfreesboro mosque." *Daily News Journal*, January 26, 2016. https://www.dnj.com/story/news/2016/01/26/imam-leaving-murfreesboro -mosque/79339044/

CBS Miami. 2015. "Miami Muslim Congregation on Edge Over Mosque Vandal(s)." Last modified September 25, 2015. https://miami.cbslocal.com/2015/09/25/miami-muslim -community-on-edge-over-mosque-vandals/

CBS News. "Fire at Tenn. Mosque Building Site Ruled Arson." *CBS News*, August 30, 2010. https://www.cbsnews.com/news/fire-at-tenn-mosque-building-site-ruled-arson

Chalmers, Robert. 2011. "Pamela Geller: American patriot or extremist firebrand?" *Independent*, May 15, 2011. https://www.independent.co.uk/news/world/americas/ pamela-geller-american-patriot-or-extremist-firebrand-2282486.html

CNN. 2010. "Protesters descend on Ground Zero for anti-mosque demonstration." Last modified June 7, 2010. http://www.cnn.com/2010/US/06/06/new.york.ground.zero .mosque/index.html

CNN Presents Transcripts. 2012. "Unwelcome: The Muslims Next Door." Last modified August 12, 2012. http://transcripts.cnn.com/TRANSCRIPTS/1208/12/cp.01.html

De Gennaro, Nancy. 2017. "Murfreesboro mosque vandalism: Residents rally around Muslim community." *Daily News Journal*, July 13, 2017. https://www.dnj.com/story/ news/2017/07/12/murfreesboro-mosque-vandalism-residents-rally-around-muslim -community/465891001/

Dreher, Rod. 2015. "Texas Town to Muslims: 'We Won't Bury You.'" *The American Conservative*, August 6, 2015. https://www.theamericanconservative.com/dreher/texas -town-to-muslims-we-wont-bury-you/

Foley, Kathleen E. "Not in Our Neighborhood: Managing Opposition to Mosque Construction." Washington, DC: Institute for Social Policy and Understanding, 2010. http://www.ispu.org/wp-content/uploads/2016/08/ISPU_Not_In_Our_Neighborhood_ Kathleen_Foley-3.pdf

Geller, Pamela. 2015. "It's Official: Ground Zero Mosque Defeated!" *Breitbart*, September 26, 2015. http://www.breitbart.com/big-government/2015/09/26/its-official-ground-zero-mosque-defeated/

Golla, Rajiv. 2016. "A Mosque, A Fire, and A Lesson." *Roads and Kingdoms*, July 11, 2016. http://roadsandkingdoms.com/2016/a-mosque-a-fire-and-a-lesson/

Grant, Tobin. 2011. "Richard Land Leaves Interfaith Coalition on Mosques." *Christianity Today*, January 25, 2011. https://www.christianitytoday.com/news/2011/january/richard-land-leaves-interfaith-coalition-on-mosques.html

Gryboski, Michael. 2016. "Russell Moore Takes on Critics at SBC for Supporting Religious Freedom for Muslims to Build Mosques." *Christian Post*, June 16, 2016. https://www.christianpost.com/news/erlcs-russell-moore-takes-heat-sbc-supporting-religious-freedom-muslims-build-mosque-165299/#Iuox1i6Gc0LE7BbW.99

Haag, Matthew. 2018. *"Muslim Groups Raise Thousands for Pittsburgh Synagogue Shooting Victims." New York Times*, October 29, 2018.https://www.nytimes.com/2018/10/29/us/muslims-raise-money-pittsburgh-synagogue.html

Hamacher, Brian. 2009. "Two Teens Busted for Miami Mosque Smash-Up." NBC6, July 14, 2009. https://www.nbcmiami.com/news/local/Two-Teens-Busted-for-Miami-Mosque-Smash-Up.html

Hayden, Jonathan. 2009. "Islamic Center of Columbia Attack–One Year Later." Journey Into America, February 2, 2009. https://journeyintoamerica.wordpress.com/2009/02/02/columcia-islamic-center-attack-one-year-later/

Holley, Joe. 2015. "Dispute over Islamic cemetery splits N. Texas community." *Houston Chronicle*, July 24, 2015. https://www.houstonchronicle.com/news/columnists/native-texan/article/Dispute-over-Islamic-cemetery-splits-N-Texas-6402572.php

Jordan, Guy. n.d. "The Politics of (Mere) Presence: The Islamic Center of Murfreesboro, Tennessee." Yale Mavcor Center for the Study of Material & Visual Cultures of Religion. Accessed February 18, 2019. https://mavcor.yale.edu/conversations/essays/politics-mere-presence-islamic-center-murfreesboro-tennessee

Kamper, Deni. 2019. "Hundreds help 'paint away the hate' at vandalized Hindu temple." WLKY, February 2, 2019. https://www.wlky.com/article/hundreds-help-paint-away-the-hate-at-vandalized-hindu-temple/26121488

Krijestorac, Mirsad. "Mapping Muslim Communities in 'Hispanicized' South Florida." In *Crescent over Another Horizon: Islam in Latin America, the Caribbean, and Latino USA*, edited by Maria del Mar Logroño Narbona and Paulo G. Pinto, 276–303. Austin: University of Texas Press.

Kuruvilla, Carol. 2017. "Muslims Raised Over $100,000 To Help Rebuild Black Churches in The South." *Huffington Post*, January 5, 2017. https://www.huffingtonpost.com/entry/muslims-raise-over-100000-to-help-rebuild-black-churches-in-the-south_us_5 5ad4be7e4b0d2ded39fac57?fbclid=IwAR27AUkzvZq752Jbli3ZIrefXK2K-Cz8Q_ RW-LnsTEx1lAdLAs_bQifW5WU

Lavoie, Denise. 2016. "Backlash greets plans for Muslim cemeteries across US." Associated Press, April 25, 2016. https://apnews.com/58d4287818d94658ac52db51ddd94f36

Laycock, Douglas and Luke W. Goodrich. 2012. "RLUIPA: Necessary, Modest, and Under-Enforced." *Fordham Urban Law Journal*. 39: 1021–1072.

Lee, Jessica and Sara Jean Green. 2018. "Fire ravages Bellevue mosque—for second

time." Seattle Times, June 12, 2018. https://www.seattletimes.com/seattle-news/
firefighters-battling-blaze-at-bellevue-mosque/

Local10. 2015. "Police Baker Act man accused of vandalizing Islamic School of Miami."
Last modified, September 29, 2015. https://www.local10.com/news/police-baker-act
-man-accused-of-vandalizing-islamic-school-of-miami

Lugo, Karen. 2016. *Mosques in America: A Guide to Accountable Permit Hearings and
Continuing Citizen Oversight.* Washington, DC: Center for Security Policy Press. http://
www.centerforsecuritypolicy.org/wp-content/uploads/2016/12/Mosque_in_America.pdf

May, Ashley and Hafner, Josh. 2018. "Pittsburgh synagogue shooting: What we know,
questions that remain." *USA Today*, October 29, 2018. https://www.usatoday.com/
story/news/nation-now/2018/10/29/pittsburgh-synagogue-shooting-what-we
-know/1804878002/

Meador, Jonathan. 2011. "A Murfreesboro paper and a Smyrna citizen do battle over
Islam." *Nashville Scene*, September 29, 2011. https://www.nashvillescene.com/news/
article/13040040/a-murfreesboro-paper-and-a-smyrna-citizen-do-battle-over-islam

Michel, Martin. 2010.
"Planned Tennessee Mosque Also Gets Mixed Reaction." NPR, August 20, 2010. https://
www.npr.org/templates/story/story.php?storyId=129324342

Misra, Tanvi. 2017. "Mosque NIMBYism: The Neighborhood Muslim Ban." City Lab,
April 5, 2017. https://www.citylab.com/equity/2017/04/a-short-history-of-zoning
-obstructionism-against-mosques/521829/

"Mohammad Ali Chaudry, Ph.D." Accessed February 18, 2019. Chaundry_Ali_Bio_short
-082416.pdf

Montgomery, David, Christopher Mele, and Manny Fernandez. 2017. "Gunman Kills
at Least 26 in Attack on Rural Texas Church." *New York Times*, November 5, 2017.
https://www.nytimes.com/2017/11/05/us/church-shooting-texas.html

Moore, Rowan. 2010. "Why Park51 is much more than the 'mosque at Ground Zero.'"
The Guardian, November 7, 2010. https://www.theguardian.com/world/2010/nov/07/
ground-zero-park51-new-york

Noriega, David. 2016. "Muslims Used to Love Living In Tennessee—Now It's A
Nightmare." BuzzFeed News, April 3, 2016. https://www.buzzfeednews.com/article/
davidnoriega/muslims-used-to-love-living-in-tennessee-now-its-a-nightmare

Oak and Laurel. 2018. "The Year in Cemetery Vandalism: 2017." Last modified January
7, 2018. http://www.oakandlaurel.com/blog/the-year-in-cemetery-vandalism-2017

O'Connor, Brendan. 2015. "The Sad, True Story of the Ground Zero Mosque." *The
Awl*, October 1, 2015. https://www.theawl.com/2015/10/the-sad-true-story-of-the
-ground-zero-mosque/

Peretz, Martin. 2010. "The New York Times Laments 'A Sadly Wary Misunderstanding of
Muslim-Americans.' But Really Is It 'Sadly Wary' Or A 'Misunderstanding' At All?" *The
New Republic*, September 4, 2010. https://newrepublic.com/article/77475/the-new-york
-times-laments-sadly-wary-misunderstanding-muslim-americans-really-it-sadly-w

Pink, Aiden. 2018. "Muslims Give Crowdfunded $238K to Jewish Pittsburgh as
Conspiracy Theories Swirl." *Forward*, November 28, 2018. https://forward.com/news/
breaking-news/414957/muslims-give-crowdfunded-238k-to-jewish-pittsburgh-as
-conspiracy-theories/

Rawlins, John. 2017. "Mount Carmel cemetery restored after vandalism spree."
    ABC 6 Action News, October 24, 2017. https://6abc.com/mt--carmel-cemetery-restored
    -after-vandalism-spree/2563037/

Rice, Andrew. 2018. "The fight for the right to be a Muslim in America." *The Guardian*,
    February 8, 2018. https://www.theguardian.com/news/2018/feb/08/how-to-stop-a
    -mosque-the-new-playbook-of-the-right

Romell, Rick. 2012."Shooter's odd behavior did not go unnoticed." *The Journal Sentinel*,
    August 6, 2012. http://archive.jsonline.com/news/crime/shooter-wade-page-was-army
    -vet-white-supremacist-856cn28-165123946.html/

Salazar, Christian. 2010. "Building damaged in 9/11 to be mosque for NYC Muslims."
    USA Today, May 7, 2010. https://usatoday30.usatoday.com/news/religion/2010-05-07
    -mosque-ground-zero_N.htm

Schragger, Richard. 2011. "The Politics of Free Exercise After Employment Division v.
    Smith: Same-Sex Marriage, the 'War on Terror,' and Religious Freedom." *Cardozo Law
    Review*. 32: 2009–2031.

SOP Newswire. 2009. "Two Teens Arrested for Vandalizing an Islamic School." Last
    modified July 7, 2009. http://thesop.org/story/law/2009/07/07/two-teens-arrested-for
    -vandalizing-an-islamic-school.php

Staletovich, Jenny. 2015. "After vandalism, Miami mosque leaders call for unity."
    Miami Herald, September 25, 2015. https://www.miamiherald.com/news/local/crime/
    article36633666.html

Tharoor, Ishaan. 2010. "Mosque Protests Add Note of Discord to 9/11 Remembrances."
    TIME, September 11, 2010. http://content.time.com/time/nation/
    article/0,8599,2017674,00.html

The Guardian. 2015. "Proposed Muslim cemetery raises concern about 'radical Islam'
    in Texas." Last modified July 19, 2015. https://www.theguardian.com/us-news/2015/
    jul/19/muslim-cemetery-texas-farmersville

Treene, Eric. 2012. "RLUIPA and Mosques: Enforcing A Fundamental Right in
    Challenging Times." *First Amendment Law Review*. 10: 330–362.

W.W. 2010. "Park51 and the shame of American skittishness." *Economist*, August 21,
    2010. https://www.economist.com/democracy-in-america/2010/08/21/park51-and-the
    -shame-of-american-skittishness

Yan, Holly and Eric Levenson, 2017. "Empathy and action: Muslims unite to help fix
    vandalized Jewish cemeteries." CNN, March 1, 2017. https://www.cnn.com/2017/02/28/
    us/jewish-cemetery-muslim-help-trnd/index.html

YouTube. 2010. "Religious Freedom Under Fire: Murfreesboro Tennessee Mosque Arson."
    Last modified September 13, 2010. https://www.youtube.com/watch?v=s4S6egZYzqQ
    at 1:27

YouTube. 2012. "CNN's Unwelcome - Muslims Next Door - Soledad O'Brien." Last
    modified January 24, 2012. https://www.youtube.com/watch?v=4JRzeZMw6LM

YouTube. 2012. "Rising Above Hate | Next Door Neighbors Storytellers | NPT."
    Last modified January 10, 2012. https://www.youtube.com/watch?v=Vtfvi3yLTM4

CHAPTER 5

Abd-Allah, Umar Faruq. 2004. "Islam and the Cultural Imperative." Accessed February 19, 2019. http://www.artsrn.ualberta.ca/amcdouga/Hist347/additional%20rdgs/ article%20culture%20imperative.pdf

Ali, M. Mansur. n.d. "They Are Your Garments and You Are Theirs: Marital Relation and the Metaphor of the Garment, Reflections on Surat al-Baqarah." Accessed February 19, 2019. https://www.ilmgate.org/they-are-your-garments-and-you-are-theirs-marital -relation-and-the-metaphor-of-the-garment-reflections-on-surat-al-baqarah-they-are -your-garments-and-you-are-theirs-marital-relation-and-the-metapho/

Ali, Wajahat, Eli Clifton, Matthew Duss, Lee Fang, Scott Keyes, and Faiz Shakir. 2011. "The Roots of the Islamophobia Network in America." Last modified August 26, 2011. https://www.americanprogress.org/issues/religion/reports/2011/08/26/10165/fear-inc/

Associated Press. 2018. "GOP leaders in Texas consider removal of Muslim member." Last modified November 28, 2018. https://apnews.com/d86baecc49ce44e5a77d7 780fcf466ce; Tinsley, Anna M. 2018. "Tarrant Republicans who want to remove Muslim are targeting others in party." *Star-Telegram*, November 29, 2018. https://www.star-telegram.com/news/state/texas/article222209090.html

Awad v. Ziriax, 670 F.3d 1111 (10th Cir. 2012).

Badr, Gamal Moursi. 1978. "Islamic Law: Its Relation to Other Legal Systems." *The American Journal of Comparative Law* 26, Spring. 187–198.

Bernstein, Maxine. 2017. "Man accused in MAX attack confessed to stabbing, said, 'I'm happy now. I'm happy now.'" *The Oregonian*, May 2017. https://www.oregonlive.com/ portland/index.ssf/2017/05/man_accused_in_max_attack_cont.html

Beth Din of America. n.d. "About Us." Accessed February 19, 2019. https://bethdin.org/ about/

Broyde, Michael J. 2017. *Sharia Tribunals, Rabbinical Courts, and Christian Panels*. New York: Oxford University Press.

Broyde, Michael. 2017. "Sharia in America." *Washington Post*, June 30, 2017. https:// www.washingtonpost.com/news/volokh-conspiracy/wp/2017/06/30/sharia-in-america/ ?utm_term=.ec2cc85bd582

Campbell, Kay. 2014. "Amendment One to outlaw 'foreign law' in Alabama? Not such a good idea, some Christians say." AL, October 30, 2014. https://www.al.com/news/ huntsville/index.ssf/2014/10/how_will_you_vote_on_amendment.html

Commack Self-Serv. Kosher Meats, Inc. v. Hooker, 680 F.3d 194 (2d Cir. 2012).

Cruz, Ted. (@tedcruz). 2018. "Discrimination against Dr. Shafi b/c he's Muslim is wrong. The Constitution prohibits any religious test for public office & the First Amendment protects religious liberty for every faith. The Party of Lincoln should welcome everybody & celebrate Liberty." Tweet, December 7, 2018. https://twitter.com/tedcruz/status/1071179810968399874?ref_src=twsrc% 5Etfw%7Ctwcamp%5Etweetembed%7Ctwterm%5E1071179810968399874&ref_ url=https%3A%2F%2Fwww.usatoday.com%2Fstory%2Fnews%2Fpolitics%2F201 9%2F01%2F10%2Ftexas-governor-backs-muslim-vice-chair-gop-faction-seeks-his- ouster%2F2534938002%2F

Culp-Ressler, Tara. 2014. "Christians Blast Ballot Initiative Banning Sharia Law in Alabama." *Think Progress*, November 2, 2014. https://thinkprogress.org/christians -blast-ballot-initiative-banning-sharia-law-in-alabama-7166c97ae507/

Dreher, Rod. 2018. "Muslim Discipleship In Post-Christian America." *The American Conservative*, December 19, 2018. https://www.theamericanconservative.com/dreher/muslim-discipleship-post-christian-america/

Elliott, Andrea. 2011. "The Man Behind the Anti-Shariah Movement." *New York Times*, July 30, 2011. https://www.nytimes.com/2011/07/31/us/31shariah.html

Elsheikh, Elsadig, Basima Sisemore, Natalia Ramirez Lee. 2017. "Legalizing Othering: The United States of Islamophobia." Last modified September 2017. http://haasinstitute .berkeley.edu/sites/default/files/haas_institute_legalizing_othering_the_united_states_of_islamophobia.pdf

Family Research Council. n.d. "Tony Perkins' Washington Update: How Do You Solve a Problem like Sharia?" Accessed February 19, 2019. https://www.frc.org/washingtonupdate/20151209/how-do-you

Feldman, Noah. 2008. "Why Shariah?" *New York Times*, March 16, 2008. https://www.nytimes.com/2008/03/16/magazine/16Shariah-t.html

Feldman, Noah. 2016. "A Lesson for Newt Gingrich: What Shariah Is (and Isn't)." *New York Times*, July 15, 2016. https://www.nytimes.com/2016/07/17/opinion/sunday/a-lesson-for-newt-gingrich-what-shariah-is-and-isnt.html

French, David. 2017. "Some Arguments for Muslim Religious Liberty Are More Compelling than Others." *National Review*, April 13, 2017. https://www.nationalreview.com/2017/04/religious-liberty-muslims-deserve-protection-liberal-allies-still-wrong/

Franklin Graham said on ABC's Town Hall: "Muslims 'want to build as many mosques and cultural centers as they possibly can so they can convert as many Americans as they can to Islam. I understand that.'" Ali, Wajahat, Eli Clifton, Matthew Duss, Lee Fang, Scott Keyes, and Faiz Shakir. 2011. "The Roots of the Islamophobia Network in America." Last modified August 26, 2011. https://www.americanprogress.org/issues/religion/reports/2011/08/26/10165/fear-inc/

Fried, Joseph P. 2000. "Court Ruling Highlights Divergences On 'Kosher.'" *New York Times*, August 5, 2000. https://www.nytimes.com/2000/08/05/nyregion/court-ruling-highlights-divergences-on-kosher.html

Furber, Musa. 2018. "Husbands must inform wives they are not obligated to cook and clean." Last modified June 26, 2018. http://musafurber.com/2018/06/26/husband-must-inform-wives-are-not-obligated-to-cook-and-clean/

Gaudiosi, Monica M. 1988. "The Influence of the Islamic Law of Waqf on the Development of the Trust in England: The Case of Merton College." *University of Pennsylvania Law Review*. 136: 1231–1261.

Goodstein, Laurie and Sharon Otterman. 2018. "Catholic Priests Abused 1,000 Children in Pennsylvania, Report Says." *New York Times*, August 14, 2018. https://www.nytimes.com/2018/08/14/us/catholic-church-sex-abuse-pennsylvania.html

H.B. 1060, 54th Leg., 1st Sess. (Okl. 2013). http://webserver1.lsb.state.ok.us/cf_pdf/2013-14%20INT/hB/HB1060%20INT.PDF

Hena Khan. n.d. "It's Ramadan, Curious George." Accessed February 19, 2019. https://www.henakhan.com/ircg

Hosanna-Tabor Evangelical Lutheran Church & Sch. v. E.E.O.C., 565 U.S. 171 (2012).

H.R. 597, 2011 Leg., 1st Reg. Sess. (Ala. 2011) (Constitutional Amendment)

H.R. 1056; 52d Leg., 2d Reg Sess. (Okla. 2010); H.R. 4769, 96th Leg., Reg. Sess. (Mich. 2011).

H.R. 2582, 15th Leg., 1st Reg. Sess. (Ariz. 2011), http://www.azleg.gov/legtext/50leg/1r/ bills/hb2582p.pdf.

Hursh, John. 2014. "The role of culture in the creation of Islamic Law." In *Islamic Legal Theory: Volume 1*, edited by Mashood Baderin, 1401-23. New York: Routledge.

Islam Question & Answer. 2001. "If a woman works, does she have to pay the household expenses?" Last modified August 7, 2001. https://islamqa.info/en/answers/2686/if-a -woman-works-does-she-have-to-pay-the-household-expenses

Kampeas, Ron. 2011. "Anti-sharia laws stir concerns that halachah could be next." *Jewish Telegraph Agency*, April 28, 2011. https://www.jta.org/2011/04/28/life-religion/anti -sharia-laws-stir-concerns-that-halachah-could-be-next

Katz, Basil. 2012. "New York kosher law is kosher, court rules." *Reuters*, May 11, 2012. https://www.reuters.com/article/usa-religion-kosher/new-york-kosher-law-is-kosher -court-rules-idUSL1E8GBOXE20120511

Keller, Nuh Ha Mim. 1997. *Reliance of the Traveller: A Classic Manual of Islamic Sacred Law*. Beltsville: Amana Publications.

Kennett, Wendy. 2016. "It's Arbitration, But Not as We Know It: Reflections on Family Law Dispute Resolution." *International Journal of Law, Policy and the Family* 30, no. 1–31. https://doi.org/10.1093/lawfam/ebv017

Kutty, Faisal. 2014. "Islamic Law" in "US Courts: Judicial Jihad or Constitutional Imperative?" *Pepperdine Law Review*. 41: 1059-1090.

Lipka, Michael. 2017. "Muslims and Islam: Key findings in the U.S. and around the world." Pew Research Center, August 9, 2017. http://www.pewresearch.org/fact -tank/2017/08/09/muslims-and-islam-key-findings-in-the-u-s-and-around-the-world/

Mendes, Muhammed. 2016. "Resources About Women and the Sacred Feminine in the Qur'anic Worldview." Last modified October 26, 2016. https://muhammadmendes .wordpress.com/2016/10/26/books-about-women-and-the-sacred-feminine-in-the -quranic-worldview/

McGrath, Kara. 2018. "Lisa Vogl Is the First Woman To Sell Hijabs In A U.S. Department Store." *Bustle*, February 19, 2018. https://www.bustle.com/p/lisa-vogl-is-the-first -woman-to-sell-hijabs-in-a-us-department-store-8099073

Mills, Rabia. n.d. "Women's Rights in the Islamic Prenuptial Agreement: Use Them or Lose Them." Accessed February 19, 2019. http://muslimcanada.org/prenuptial.pdf

Nasr, Seyyed Hossein, Caner K. Dagli, Maria Massi Dakake, Joseph E.B. Lumbard, Mohammed Rustom. 2015. *The Study Quran: A New Translation and Commentary*. New York: Harper One.

Okwodu, Janelle and Mickalene Thomas. 2018. "Ms. Marvelous." *Vogue*, March 8, 2018. https://www.vogue.com/projects/13541583/sana-amanat-vogue-american- women-marvel-comics/ Penguin Random House. n.d. "Amal Unbound by Aisha Saeed." Accessed February 19, 2019. https://www.penguinrandomhouse.com/books/533523/ amal-unbound-by-aisha-saeed/9780399544682/

Pilkington, Ed. "Anti-sharia laws proliferate as Trump strikes hostile tone toward Muslims." *The Guardian*, December 30, 2017. https://www.theguardian.com/ us-news/2017/dec/30/anti-sharia-laws-trump-muslims

Polo, Susana. 2018. "Ms. Marvel's G. Willow Wilson reflects on the political side of Wonder Woman." *Polygon*, November 13, 2018. https://www.polygon.com/comics/2018/11/13/18092090/wonder-woman-58-g-willow-wilson-interview

Quraishi-Landes, Asifa. 2011. "Understanding Sharia in an American Context." Last modified July 26, 2011. https://www.ispu.org/understanding-sharia-in-an-american -context/

Quraishi-Landes, Asifa. 2015. "The Sharia Problem with Sharia Legislation." *Ohio Northern University Law Review*. 41: 545–566.

Rao, Mallika. 2018."Hasan Minhaj Invites You to Take Off Your Shoes." The Atlantic, December 2, 2018. https://www.theatlantic.com/amp/article/577048/?fbclid=IwAR0h GaB7DwU7T3cmAmBVOZaSefIDBrLKV5GpOOO0AA3s8ZyS7s6drpBFVFc

Salaam Reads. n.d. Accessed February 19, 2019. http://salaamreads.com

Samuels, Alex. 2019. "Tarrant County GOP's vice-chairman survives recall vote over his religion." *Texas Tribune*, January 10, 2019. https://www.texastribune.org/2019/01/10/tarrant-county-gop-shahid-shafi-vote-muslim/

S.B. 1028 (Tenn. 2011). http://www.capitol.tn.gov/Bills/107/Bill/SB1028.pdf

Schwinn, Steven. 2015. "Anti-Sharia Laws: A Solution in Search of a Problem." *Jurist*, March 18, 2015. https://www.jurist.org/commentary/2015/03/steven-schwinn -sharia-law/

Shapiro, Ben. 2017. "Why the Left Protects Islam." Daily Wire, July 26, 2017. https://www.dailywire.com/news/18993/why-left-protects-islam-ben-shapiro

Sisemore, Basima and Rhonda Itaoui. 2018. "Trump's travel ban is just one of many US policies that legalize discrimination against Muslims." Last modified January 30, 2018. https://haasinstitute.berkeley.edu/trump's-travel-ban-just-one-many-us-policies-legalize -discrimination-against-muslims.

Southern Poverty Law Center. n.d. "Tony Perkins." Accessed February 13, 2019. https://www.splcenter.org/fighting-hate/extremist-files/individual/tony-perkins

Stone, Michael. 2017. "Alabama Official: Bible Justifies Roy Moore's Sex Abuse of Teen Girls." *Patheos*, November 9, 2017. https://www.patheos.com/blogs/progressivesecularhumanist/2017/11/alabama-official-bible-justifies-roy-moores-sex -abuse-teen-girls/

The Noble Qur'an. n.d. Accessed February 19, 2019. https://quran.com

Uddin, Asma. 2013. "The First Amendment: Religious Freedom for All, Including Muslims." *Washington and Lee Journal of Civil Rights and Social Justice*. 20: 73-81.

Uddin, Asma. 2018. "The Latest Attack on Islam: It's Not a Religion." *New York Times*, September 26, 2018. https://www.nytimes.com/2018/09/26/opinion/islamophobia -muslim-religion-politics.html

Volokh, Eugene. 2014. "Foreign Law in American Courts." *Oklahoma Law Review*. 66: 227–243.

Volokh, Eugene. 2014. "Religious Law (Especially Islamic Law) in American Courts." *Oklahoma Law Review*. 66: 431-458.

Wills, Garry. 2017. *What the Qur'an Meant: And Why It Matters*. New York: Viking.

Yam, Kimberly. 2018. "Bill Clinton's Remarks to Muslims Prompted Hasan Minhaj To Create 'Patriot Act.'" *Huffington Post*, November 8, 2018. https://www.huffingtonpost .com/entry/bill-clinton-hasan-minhaj_us_5be4a123e4b0dbe871a8cd01

YouTube. 2010. "Oklahoma Rep Rex Duncan proposes Law Against Judges using Sharia Law in state." Last modified June 13, 2010. https://www.youtube.com/watch?v =-LxwPN-2pYw&feature=youtu.be

YouTube. 2012. "Jerry Agar & Pamela Geller On Oklahoma's Sharia Setback." Last modified January 13, 2012. https://www.youtube.com/watch?v=UdAAX3Ui_QA

Younis, Mohamed. 2009."Muslim Americans Exemplify Diversity, Potential." Gallup, March 2, 2009. https://news.gallup.com/poll/116260/muslim-americans-exemplify -diversity-potential.aspx

Yusuf, Hamza. "The Rights and Responsibilities of Marriage." Recorded lecture series. Alhambra Productions, 2002. 14 compact discs.

Zakaria, Rafia. 2013. "Sharia law ban and Muslim wives." *Al Jazeera*, February 16, 2013. https://www.aljazeera.com/indepth/opinion/2013/02/201321174724878286.html

CHAPTER 6

According to the Brennan Center for Justice, CVE under President Trump operates on the "assumption that diversity and the experience of discrimination in America are suggestive of a national security threat— and that Muslim, immigrant, black, or LGBTQ Americans, from kindergarten on, must be surveilled to keep our country safe."

Alhassen, Maytha. 2018. "Haqq & Hollywood: Illuminating 100 years of Muslim Tropes and How to Transform Them." Last modified October 2018. http://popcollab.org/ wp-content/uploads/2018/10/HaqqAndHollywood_Report.pdf

Apuzzo, Matt and Joseph Goldstein. 2014. "New York Drops Unit That Spied on Muslims." *The New York Times,* April 15, 2014. https://www.nytimes.com/2014/04/16/ nyregion/police-unit-that-spied-on-muslims-is-disbanded.html

Apuzzo, Matt and Adam Goldman. 2016. "Judge Rejects Settlement Over Surveillance of Muslims by New York Police Department." *New York Times,* November 1, 2016. https://www.nytimes.com/2016/11/01/nyregion/nypd-muslim-lawsuit-settlement. html?module=inline

Apuzzo, Matt and Adam Goldman. 2017. "After Spying on Muslims, New York Police Agree to Greater Oversight." *New York Times*, March 6, 2017. https://www.nytimes .com/2017/03/06/nyregion/nypd-spying-muslims-surveillance-lawsuit.html

Apuzzo, Matt and Al Baker. 2016. "New York to Appoint Civilian to Monitor Police's Counterterrorism Activity." *New York Times*, January 8, 2016. https://www .nytimes.com/2016/01/08/nyregion/new-york-to-appoint-monitor-to-review-polices -counterterrorism-activity.html?_r=0&module=inline

Ariosto, David. 2012. "Surveillance unit produced no terrorism leads, NYPD says." CNN, August 22, 2012. https://www.cnn.com/2012/08/21/justice/new-york-nypd-surveillance -no-leads/index.html

Aziz, Sahar F. 2012. "Protecting Rights as a Counterterrorism Tool: The Case of American Muslims." http://dx.doi.org/10.2139/ssrn.2144299

Basu, Moni. 2016. "15 years after 9/11, Sikhs still victims of anti-Muslim hate crimes." CNN, September 15, 2016. https://www.cnn.com/2016/09/15/us/sikh-hate-crime -victims/index.html

BBC News. 2016. "Who was Capt Humayun Khan?" Last modified August 1, 2016. https://www.bbc.com/news/election-us-2016-36945318

Brennan Center for Justice. 2015. "Countering Violent Extremism (CVE): A Resource Page." Last modified October 4, 2018. https://www.brennancenter.org/analysis/cve-programs-resource-page.

Brown, Hayes. 2013. "America: Choosing Security Over Liberty Since 1798." *Foreign Policy*, June 11, 2013. https://foreignpolicy.com/2013/06/11/america-choosing-security-over-liberty-since-1798/

CBS News. 2012. "Information: NYPD paid me to 'bait' Muslims." Last modified October 23, 2012. https://www.cbsnews.com/news/informant-nypd-paid-me-to-bait-muslims/

Center for Constitutional Rights. 2018. "Settlement Reached in NYPD Muslim Surveillance Lawsuit." Last modified April 9, 2018. https://ccrjustice.org/home/press-center/press-releases/settlement-reached-nypd-muslim-surveillance-lawsuit

Chaudry, Zainab. 2016. "Flying While Muslim or Arab: Know Your Rights as An Airline Passenger. InshAllah." *Huffington Post*, April 20, 2017. https://www.huffpost.com/entry/flying-while-muslim-or-ar_b_9717596

City University of New York Law School. n.d. "Mapping Muslims: NYPD Spying and Its Impact on American Muslims." Accessed February 20, 2019. http://www.law.cuny.edu/academics/clinics/immigration/clear/Mapping-Muslims.pdf

Clinton, Hillary Rodham. 2017. *What Happened*. New York: Simon & Schuster.

Doherty, Carroll. 2013. "Balancing Act: National Security and Civil Liberties in Post-9/11 Era." Last modified June 7, 2013. http://www.pewresearch.org/fact-tank/2013/06/07/balancing-act-national-security-and-civil-liberties-in-post-911-era/

Friedersdorf, Conor. 2013. "The Horrifying Effects of NYPD Ethnic Profiling on Innocent Muslim Americans." *The Atlantic*, March 28, 2013. https://www.theatlantic.com/politics/archive/2013/03/the-horrifying-effects-of-nypd-ethnic-profiling-on-innocent-muslim-americans/274434/

Gallup. n.d. "Views of Violence." Accessed February 20, 2019. https://news.gallup.com/poll/157067/views-violence.aspx

Gast, Phil. 2012. "Wisconsin temple shooting victims: Putting others first." CNN, August 7, 2012. https://www.cnn.com/2012/08/06/us/wisconsin-shooting-victims/index.html

Greenberg, Karen J. 2016. "Liberty is Security." The American Conservative, October 3, 2016. https://www.theamericanconservative.com/articles/liberty-is-security/

Greenberg, Michael. 2012. "New York: The Police and the Protesters." *New York Review of Books*, October 11, 2012. https://www.nybooks.com/articles/2012/10/11/new-york-police-and-protesters/

Grewal, Zareena. 2014. *Islam Is a Foreign Country: American Muslims and the Global Crisis of Authority*. New York: New York University Press.

Hassan v. City of New York, 804 F.3d 277 (3d Cir. 2015).

Hassan v. City of New York, 2014 WL 654604 (D.N.J. Feb. 20, 2014).

Hassan v. City of New York, 2014 WL 654604 (D.N.J. Feb. 20, 2014). "First Amended Complaint." October 3, 2012. https://ccrjustice.org/sites/default/files/assets/10_First%20Amended%20Complaint.10.3.2012.pdf

Hayed, Michael Edison. 2017. "Muslims 'absolutely' the group most victimized by global terrorism, researchers say." ABC News, June 20, 2017. https://abcnews.go.com/Politics/muslims-absolutely-group-victimized-global-terrorism-researchers/story?id=48131273

Huq, Aziz Z. 2011. "Private Religious Discrimination, National Security, and the First Amendment." *Harvard Law & Policy Review*. 5: 347–374.

Ibrahim, Nagwa. 2009. "The Origins of Muslim Racialization in U.S. Law." *UCLA Journal of Islamic and Near Eastern Law*. 7: 121–155.

Legacy.com. n.d. "Paramjit Kaur Obituary." Accessed February 20, 2019. http://www.legacy.com/ns/paramjit-kaur-obituary/159013929

Lewin, Tamar. 2001. "Sikh Owner of Gas Station Is Fatally Shot In Rampage." *New York Times*, September 17, 2001. https://www.nytimes.com/2001/09/17/us/sikh-owner-of-gas-station-is-fatally-shot-in-rampage.html

Kundnani, Arun. 2014. *The Muslims Are Coming! Islamophobia, Extremism, and the Domestic War on Terror*. Brooklyn: Verso.

Kurzman, Charles. 2014. "Muslim American Terrorism in 2013." Last modified February 5, 2014. https://sites.duke.edu/tcths/files/2013/06/Kurzman_Muslim-American_Terrorism_in_20131.pdf

Mohammad, Niala. 2016. "I didn't realize how often Muslims get kicked off planes, until it happened to me." *The Guardian*, September 8, 2016. https://www.theguardian.com/world/2016/sep/08/muslim-woman-kicked-off-american-airlines-flight-islamophobia

Moynihan, Colin. 2018. "Last Suit Accusing N.Y.P.D. of Spying on Muslims Is Settled." *New York Times*, April 5, 2018. https://www.nytimes.com/2018/04/05/nyregion/last-suit-accusing-nypd-of-spying-on-muslims-is-settled.html

Muslim Justice League. n.d. "What is Countering Violent Extremism (CVE)?" Accessed February 20, 2019. https://www.muslimjusticeleague.org/cve/

Muslim Justice League. n.d. "Countering Violent Extremism: Community Perspectives and Concerns." Accessed February 20, 2019. https://www.scribd.com/doc/296645135/Countering-Violent-Extremism-Community-Perspectives-and-Concerns "MJL does not provide mental health counseling or social services of any kind. Yet individuals with whom we work—including those experiencing distress as a result of discrimination—occasionally share with us that they are suffering from a mental health problem and would like to seek counseling or treatment but feel unsafe doing so given an inability to know which providers may now or in future be collaborating in CVE. MJL believes mental health services benefit many individuals invaluably, and we would like to offer unqualified assurances that seeking help is safe. However, given known instances of CVE recruitment of mental health providers, and the reality that CVE is being deployed in a non-transparent manner, we cannot ethically, and do not, give such assurances." Muslim Justice League. 2017. Letter to the Honorable Chair DeSantis and Members of the National Security Subcommittee regarding National Security Subcommittee Hearing on Combatting Homegrown Terrorism." https://www.muslimjusticeleague.org/wp-content/uploads/2017/07/MJL-Letter-for-Hearing-on-22Combatting-Homegrown-Terrorism22.pdf

Myers, Alexis. 2016. "Muslim family kicked off flight demands apology from United Airlines." *Chicago Tribune*, April 2, 2016. https://www.chicagotribune.com/news/local/breaking/ct-united-airlines-removes-muslim-family-met-20160401-story.html

National Security Adviser, John Bolton, presided over an anti-Muslim think tank, Gatestone, that peddles culturalist views of Islam. Przybyla, Heidi. 2018. "John Bolton presided over anti-Muslim think tank." NBC News, April 23, 2018. https://

www.nbcnews.com/politics/white-house/john-bolton-chaired-anti-muslim-think-tank-n868171; Former national security adviser, Michael Flynn, and former White House Deputy Assistant to the President, Sebastian Gorka, are two other examples, as is Gorka's wife, Katharine, who is still an adviser to the secretary of homeland security, Beinart, Peter. 2018. "Trump Shut Programs to Counter Violent Extremism." *The Atlantic*, October 29, 2018. https://www.theatlantic.com/ideas/archive/2018/10/trump-shut-countering-violent-extremism-program/574237/; Hudson, John. 2017. "The Gorka That Matters Isn't Leaving The Trump Administration." *BuzzFeed News*, August 29, 2017. https://www.buzzfeednews.com/article/johnhudson/the-gorka-that-matters-isnt-leaving-the-trump-administration

New America Foundation. n.d. "Part IV. What is the Threat to the United States Today?" Accessed February 20, 2019. https://www.newamerica.org/in-depth/terrorism-in-america/what-threat-united-states-today/

New York Daily News. 2011. "NYPD keeps secret files on Muslims who change their names to sound more American: report." Last modified October 26, 2011. https://www.nydailynews.com/new-york/nypd-secret-files-muslims-change-names-sound-american-report-article-1.968327

PermaRecord. 2017. "2011 National Counterterrorism Center Report on Terrorism." Accessed February 20, 2019. https://perma.cc/SE3U-5C2P Pew Research Center. 2009. "Global Restrictions on Religion." Last modified December 17, 2009. http://www.pewforum.org/2009/12/17/global-restrictions-on-religion/

Philpott, Daniel. 2018. "Religious Freedom: A Strategy for Security." Last modified October 31, 2018. https://www.religiousfreedominstitute.org/blog/religious-freedom-a-strategy-for-security

Privacy and Civil Liberties Oversight Board. 2014. "Report on the Telephone Records Program." Last modified January 23, 2014. https://fas.org/irp/offdocs/pclob-215.pdf

Revesz, Rachael. 2016. "Muslim couple kicked off Delta flight for 'sweating', saying 'Allah' and texting." *Independent*, August 4, 2016. https://www.independent.co.uk/news/world/americas/muslim-couple-kicked-off-delta-air-lines-plane-flight-attendant-uncomfortable-allah-sweating-texting-a7172591.html

Revesz, Rachael. 2016. "Muslim passenger kicked off American Airlines flight after attendant announces: 'I'll be watching you.'" *Independent*, July 20, 2016. https://www.independent.co.uk/news/world/americas/muslim-kicked-off-plane-american-airlines-racial-discrimination-cair-uncomfortable-a7147311.html

Revesz, Rachael. 2016. "Muslim woman kicked off plane as flight attendant said she 'did not feel comfortable' with the passenger." *Independent*, April 15, 2016. https://www.independent.co.uk/news/world/americas/muslim-woman-kicked-off-plane-as-flight-attendant-said-she-did-not-feel-comfortable-with-the-a6986661.html

Ryan, Missy. 2016. "Capt. Humayun Khan, whose grieving parents have been criticized by Trump, was 'a soldier's officer.'" *Washington Post*, August 2, 2016. https://www.washingtonpost.com/news/checkpoint/wp/2016/08/02/slain-army-captain-at-center-of-political-storm-was-a-soldiers-officer/?noredirect=on&utm_term=.c0fd37b95738

Saiya, Nilay and Anthony Scime. 2014. "Explaining religious terrorism: A data-mined analysis." *Conflict Management and Peace Science*. 32, no. 5: 487–512. https://doi.org/10.1177/0738894214559667

Salinger, Tobias. 2016. "Muslim prayer on Massachusetts railway platform prompts police alert, heavily armed response." *New York Daily News*, June 17, 2016. https://www.nydailynews.com/news/national/muslim-prayer-mass-subway-platform-prompts-police-alert-article-1.2678045

Sinnar, Shirin. 2018. "Procedural Experimentation and National Security in the Courts." *California Law Review*. 106: 991–1060.

Somin, Ilya. 2017. "The case against special judicial deference in immigration and national security cases." *Washington Post*, October 22, 2017. https://www.washingtonpost.com/amphtml/news/volokh-conspiracy/wp/2017/10/22/the-case-against-special-judicial-deference-in-immigration-and-national-security-cases/

Spellberg, Claire. 2018. "Bill Clinton's Tone-Deaf Request to Muslims Inspired Hasan Minhaj's 'Patriot Act.'" *Decider*, November 8, 2018. https://decider.com/2018/11/08/bill-clinton-inspired-hasan-minhaj-patriot-act/amp/

Stack, Liam. 2016. "College Student Is Removed from Flight After Speaking Arabic on Plane." *New York Times*, April 17, 2016. https://www.nytimes.com/2016/04/17/us/student-speaking-arabic-removed-southwest-airlines-plane.html

The Economist. 2019. "Third-generation Muslims in the West are devising a new Islam for themselves." Last modified February 16, 2019. https://www.economist.com/special-report/2019/02/14/third-generation-muslims-in-the-west-are-devising-a-new-islam-for-themselves.

The Pulitzer Prizes. 2012. "Matt Apuzzo, Adam Goldman, Eileen Sullivan and Chris Hawley of *the Associated Press*." Accessed February 20, 2019. https://www.pulitzer.org/winners/matt-apuzzo-adam-goldman-eileen-sullivan-and-chris-hawley

The Washington Institute. n.d. "Shaarik H. Zafar." Accessed February 20, 2019. https://www.washingtoninstitute.org/experts/view/shaarik-h.-zafar

The White House. 2014. "Remarks by Assistant to the President for Homeland Security and Counterterrorism Lisa O. Monaco." Last modified April 15, 2014. https://obamawhitehouse.archives.gov/the-press-office/2014/04/16/remarks-assistant-president-homeland-security-and-counterterrorism-lisa-

The White House Fellows and Foundation. n.d. "Samar Ali." Accessed February 20, 2019. https://www.whff.org/announcements/samar-ali-2010-11-receives-the-2018-impact-award/

Trump v. Hawaii, 138 S. Ct. 2392 (2018). "Brief of *Amici Curiae* Former National Security Officials in Support ff Respondents." September 18, 2017. https://www.americanbar.org/content/dam/aba/publications/supreme_court_preview/briefs-2017-2018/16-1436-16-1540-amicus-resp-former-national-security-officials.authcheckdam.pdf

UCLA Burkle Center. n.d. "Haroon Azar." Accessed February 20, 2019. https://law.ucla.edu/faculty/faculty-profiles/haroon-azar/

Uddin, Asma. 2016. "When a Swimsuit Is a Security Threat." *New York Times*, August 24, 2016. https://www.nytimes.com/2016/08/24/opinion/when-a-swimsuit-is-a-security-threat.html

US State Department. n.d. "Tajikistan 2016 International Religious Freedom Report." Accessed February 20, 2019. https://www.state.gov/documents/organization/269188.pdf

Winter, Jana. 2017. "FBI and DHS Warned of Growing Threat from White Supremacists Months Ago." Foreign Policy, August 14, 2017. https://foreignpolicy.com/2017/08/14/fbi-and-dhs-warned-of-growing-threat-from-white-supremacists-months-ago/

Women in the World. 2016. "American Muslim women removed from plane for making flight attendant feel 'unsafe.'" Last modified August 5, 2016. https://womenintheworld.com/2016/08/05/american-muslim-women-removed-from-plane-for-making-flight-attendant-feel-unsafe/

Yaccino, Steven, Michael Schwirtz, and Marc Santora. "Gunman Kills 6 at a Sikh Temple Near Milwaukee." *New York Times*, August 5, 2012. https://www.nytimes .com/2012/08/06/us/shooting-reported-at-temple-in-wisconsin.html

YouTube. 2018. "U.S. Commitment to International Religious Freedom." Last modified February 9, 2018. https://www.youtube.com/watch?v=UKSrEbGjtAs&feature=youtu .be&t=10m13s

CHAPTER 7

Abou-Sabe, Kenzi. 2016. "Somali-American Legislator Says DC Taxi Driver Called Her ISIS." NBC News, December 8, 2016. https://www.nbcnews.com/news/nbcblk/somali -american-%20legislator-says-dc-taxi-driver-called-her-isis-n693681

ACLU. n.d. "Discrimination Against Muslim Women—Fact Sheet." Accessed February 20, 2019. https://www.aclu.org/other/discrimination-against-muslim-women-fact-sheet#9

ACLU Southern California. 2012. "Muslim Former Employee Sues Disney For Discrimination." Last modified August 13, 2012. https://www.aclusocal.org/en/press -releases/muslim-former-employee-sues-disney-discrimination

Akyol, Mustafa. 2019. "The Creeping Liberalism in American Islam." *The New York Times*, February 18, 2019. https://www.nytimes.com/2019/02/18/opinion/america-islam.html

Al-Khatahtbeh, Amani. 2016. "On Being the Media's Token Muslim Girl." *The Cut*, October 19, 2016. https://www.thecut.com/2016/10/amani-al-khatahtbeh-on-being-the -medias-token-muslim-girl.html

Ali, Saba. 2018. "I've worn a hijab for decades. Here's why I took it off." *Washington Post*, August 16, 2018. https://www.washingtonpost.com/outlook/ive-worn-a-hijab-for -decades-heres-why-i-took-it-off/2018/08/16/96cace1e-a095-11e8-93e3-

Ali-Khan, Sofia. 2016. "Bandaging My Wounds: A Spiritual Journey Through Hijab." altmuslimah, February 24, 2016. http://www.altmuslimah.com/2016/02/10879/

Aziz, Sahar F. 2012. "From the Oppressed to the Terrorist: Muslim American Women Caught in the Crosshairs of Intersectionality." *Hastings Race & Poverty Law Journal*. 9: 191–263.

Aziz, Sahar F. 2014. "Coercive Assimilationism: The Perils of Muslim Women's Identity Performance in the Workplace." Michigan Journal of Race and Law. 20: 1–64.

Basatneh, Alaa. 2016. "It's not safe to wear my hijab now that Trump will be president." *Splinter*, November 15, 2016. https://splinternews.com/its-not-safe-to-wear-my-hijab -now-that-trump-will-be-pr-1793863762

Beydoun, Khaled A. 2018. "Acting Muslim." Harvard Civil Rights-Civil Liberties Law Review. 53: 1–64.

Chaudhry, Rabea. 2015. "Part 1: Dr. Umar Faruq Abd-Allah on Hijabs and Headscarves." altmuslimah, December 11, 2015. http://www.altmuslimah.com/2015/12/dr-_umar_ faruq_abd-allah_on_hijabs_and_headscarves/

Chung, Frank. 2017. "Target hijab pic sparks debate." News.com.au, January 12, 2017. https://www.news.com.au/finance/business/retail/target-hijab-pic-sparks-debate/news-sto ry/8226e82f739b76bb10c0fb624ace2e1b

Clinton, Hillary (@HillaryClinton). 2016. "In Rio, Olympic fencer Ibtihaj Muhammad became the first American Muslim athlete to compete while wearing a hijab." Tweet, August 8, 2016. https://twitter.com/hillaryclinton/status/762675570937298944?lang=en

Cooney, Samantha. 2016. "A Muslim Woman Made History for Appearing in *Playboy*." *TIME*, September 28, 2016. http://time.com/4511338/noor-tagouri-hijab-playboy/; Baharir, Ruth Perl. 2016. "In First, Playboy Features Journalist Noor Tagouri in a Hijab–Stirring Up an Islamic Storm." *Haaretz*, September 30, 2016. https://www.haaretz.com/israel-news/culture/journalist-noor-tagouri-first-woman-to-wear-hijab-in-playboy-1.5444208

del Gaizo, Anna. 2016. "Media Wunderkind Noor Tagouri Makes a Forceful Case for Modesty." *Playboy*, September 22, 2016. https://www.playboy.com/read/renegades-noor-tagouri

E.E.O.C. v. Abercrombie & Fitch Stores, Inc., 135 S. Ct. 2028 (2015). "Brief Amicus Curiae of The Becket Fund for Religious Liberty In Support Of Petitioner." December 2014. https://s3.amazonaws.com/becketpdf/Amicus-Brief-FINAL.pdf

Ellison, Keith. 2016. "Ibtihaj Muhammad." *TIME*, April 20, 2016. http://time.com/4301357/ibtihaj-muhammad-2016-time-100/

Eltahir, Nafisa. 2016. "Muslim Americans Should Reject the Politics of Normalcy." *The Atlantic*, September 25, 2016. https://www.theatlantic.com/politics/archive/2016/09/muslim-americans-should-reject-respectability-politics/501452/

Essma Bengabsia's Facebook post is reprinted here with permission.

Euceph, Misha. 2017. "How Progressives Tokenize the Hijab." *Wall Street Journal*, February 2, 2017. https://www.wsj.com/articles/how-progressives-tokenize-the-hijab-1486081260

Ghumman, S., and Ryan, A. M. (2013). "Not welcome here: Discrimination towards women who wear the Muslim headscarf." *Human Relations, 66*, no. 5, 671–698. http://dx.doi.org/10.1177/0018726712469540

Geller, Pamela. 2016."Pamela Geller: Muslim Woman Demands Workplace Accommodate Her Hijab." *Breitbart*, August 5, 2016. https://www.breitbart.com/politics/2016/08/05/pamela-geller-muslim-woman-demands-workplace-accommodate-her-hijab/

Gomaa, Mariam. 2014. "American Hijab: Why My Scarf is a Sociopolitical Statement, Not a Symbol of My Religiosity." TIME, November 11, 2014. http://time.com/3576827/enums/

Gouveia, Alexandria. 2016. "Hijabi News Presenter Sparks Controversy After Posing in Playboy." *Emirates Woman*, September 29, 2016. http://emirateswoman.com/hijabi-news-presenter-sparks-controversy-signing-playboy-contract/

Haddad, Y.Y.; Jane, I.S.; Kathleen, M. 2006. *Muslim Women in America: The Challenge of Islamic Identity Today.* New York: Oxford University Press.

Hafiz, Yasmine. 2017. "'Mipsterz' 'Somewhere in America' Video Showcases Muslim Hipster Swag; Sparks A Passionate Discussion."

Huffington Post, December 6, 2017. https://www.huffingtonpost.com/2013/12/02/mipsterz-somewhere-in-america-video_n_4374182.html

Hamdah, Butheina. 2018. "American Culture and the Liberalization of Hijab." *Muftah*, July 9, 2018. https://muftah.org/american-culture-and-the-liberalization-of-hijab/#.XHApcy3MwUG

Hamid, Shadi. 2018. "The Difficulty with Diversity." *Cardus*, December 13, 2018. https://www.cardus.ca/comment/article/the-difficulty-with-diversity/

Hansen, Zachary. 2018. "DoorDash driver allegedly attacked, choked with own head scarf by customer." AJC, May 8, 2018. https://www.ajc.com/news/crime--law /doordash-driver-allegedly-attacked-choked-with-own-head-scarf-customer/ NPbpPlxO0WRc1JBjtiYe0O/

Harris, Paul. 2011. "Living with 9/11: the Muslim American." The Guardian, September 5, 2011. https://www.theguardian.com/world/2011/sep/05/living-with-911-muslim -american

Hauser, Christine. 2017. "New Barbie Is Modeled After American Olympian Who Wears a Hijab." New York Times, November 14, 2017. https://www.nytimes.com/2017/11/14/ business/barbie-hijab-ibtihaj-muhammad.html

Hussain, Murtaza. 2016. "U.S. Military White Paper Describes Wearing Hijab As 'Passive Terrorism.'" The Intercept, February 23, 2016. https://theintercept.com/2016/02/23/ department-of-defense-white-paper-describes-wearing-hijab-as-passive-terrorism/

Independent. n.d. "New York woman 'tries to rip off Muslim mother's hijab and pushes over her child in buggy.'" Accessed February 20, 2019. https://www.independent.co.uk/ news/world/americas/attacker-tries-to-rip-off-muslim-mothers-hijab-pushes-over-her -child-in-buggy-a7237856.html

Khalid, Asma. 2011.
"Lifting the Veil: Muslim Women Explain Their Choice." NPR, April 21, 2011. https:// www.npr.org/2011/04/21/135523680/lifting-the-veil-muslim-women-explain-their -choice

Kotz, Pete. 2018. "As Rep. Ilhan Omar is introduced to America, the religious right freaks out." City Pages, December 10, 2018. http://www.citypages.com/news/as-rep-ilhan -omar-is-introduced-to-america-the-religious-right-freaks-out/502294551

Koura, Fatima. "Hijab in the Western Workplace: Exploring Islamic Psychotherapeutic Approaches to Discrimination." Journal of Psychology and Behavioral Science 4, no. 2: 80–88. http://jpbsnet.com/journals/jpbs/Vol_4_No_2_December_2016/7.pdf

Koura, F. 2018. "Navigating Islam: The Hijab and the American Workplace." Societies 8, 125. https://www.mdpi.com/2075-4698/8/4/12524d1703d2a7a_story.html?nore direct=on&utm_term=.a66d482d4c67

Kumar, Rashmee. 2018. "Marketing the Muslim Woman: Hijabs and Modest Fashion Are the New Corporate Trend in The Trump Era." The Intercept, December 29, 2018. https://theintercept.com/2018/12/29/muslim-women-hijab-fashion-capitalism/

Lewis, Reina and Asma T. Uddin. 2016. "What the Modest Movement Can Teach Every Woman About Choice." Refinery29, November 10, 2016. https://www.refinery29.com/ en-us/2016/11/129291/modest-dress-choice-muslim-women-clothing

Lowe, Lindsay. 2018. "Meet the first American TV reporter to wear a hijab on the air." Today, March 8, 2018. https://www.today.com/style/tahera-rahman-first-air-tv-reporter -wear-hijab-t124701

Malik, Nesrine. 2018. "Thanks, L'Oréal, but I'm growing weary of this hijab fetish." The Guardian, January 25, 2018. https://www.theguardian.com/commentisfree/2018/jan/25/ oreal-hijab-fetish-amena-khan-muslim-women

Mandviwala, Tasneem. 2017. "Same Circus, Different Performers: Problems of Mainstreaming Muslim Women in Western Media." altmuslimah, January 1, 2017. http://www.altmuslimah.com/2017/01/circus-different-performers-problems -mainstreaming-muslim-women-western-media/

Mazziotta, Julie. 2016. "Some Muslim Women Say They're 'Scared to Wear the Hijab' After Trump's Win." *People*, November 9, 2016. http://people.com/bodies/muslim -women-scared-wear-hijab-trump-win/

Mintz, Howard. 2010. "Abercrombie & Fitch hit with bias lawsuit from Muslim job applicant." *East Bay Times*, September 1, 2010. https://www.eastbaytimes .com/2010/09/01/abercrombie-fitch-hit-with-bias-lawsuit-from-muslim-job-applicant-2/

Mipsterz in America. n.d. "Meet the Mipsterz: Somewhere in America." Accessed February 21, 2019. https://mipsterzinamerica.com/somewhere-in-america/

Mogahed, Dalia and Youssef Chouhoud. 2017. "American Muslim Poll 2017: Muslims at the Crossroads." Last modified March 2017. https://www.ispu.org/wp-content/ uploads/2017/03/American-Muslim-Poll-2017-Report.pdf

Myers, Anthony. 2011. "Muslim woman sues Abercrombie & Fitch over hijab." *East Bay Times*, June 27, 2011. https://www.eastbaytimes.com/2011/06/27/muslim-woman-sues -abercrombie-fitch-over-hijab/

NBC 4 New York. 2017. "Group of Teenage Girls Spit on, Beat Hijab-Wearing Woman in Downtown Brooklyn, Call Her 'Terrorist': Police." Last modified December 29, 2017. https://www.nbcnewyork.com/news/local/Bias-Crime-Muslim-Woman-Attack-Brooklyn -New-York-Adams-Street-467128133.html

New York Post. 2015. "Porn star performs while wearing hijab, sparking controversy." Last modified January 7, 2015. https://nypost.com/2015/01/07/porn-star-performs -while-wearing-hijab-sparking-controversy/

Nike. n.d. "Women's Hijab Nike Pro." Accessed February 21, 2019. https://www.nike .com/us/en_us/c/women/nike-pro-hijab

Patel, Eboo. 2018. *Out of Many Faiths: Religious Diversity and the American Promise*. Princeton: Princeton University Press.

Pescaro, Mike. 2018. "Police: Man Pulled on Woman's Hijab in NH Restaurant." NECN, July 2, 2018. https://www.necn.com/news/new-england/Police-Man-Pulled-on-Womans -Hijab-in-NH-Restaurant-487164341.html

Pew Research Center. 2017. "Similar shares of U.S. Muslim women say they always wear hijab in public, never wear hijab-06-08." Last modified July 26, 2017. http:// www.pewforum.org/2017/07/26/religious-beliefs-and-practices/pf_2017-06-26_ muslimamericans-06-08/

Pixlee. n.d. "What Is a Social Media Influencer?" Accessed February 21, 2019. https:// www.pixlee.com/definitions/definition-social-media-influencer

Prisco, Joanna. 2018. "Girl Proudly Models Her Hijab in Gap's Inclusive Back-to-School Ad." *Global Citizen*, August 9, 2018. https://www.globalcitizen.org/en/content/girl -hijab-model-gap-ad/

Rateb, Darah M. 2009. "The Dehijabization Phenomenon." altmuslimah, March 30, 2009. http://www.altmuslimah.com/2009/03/the_dehijabization_phenomenon/

Saeed, Sana. 2013. "Somewhere in America, Muslim Women Are 'Cool.'" The Islamic Monthly, December 2, 2013. https://www.theislamicmonthly.com/somewhere-in -america-muslim-women-are-cool/

Sakuma, Amanda. 2016. "Muslim Women Wearing Hijabs Assaulted Just Hours After Trump Win." NBC News, November 10, 2016. https://www.nbcnews.com/politics/2016 -election/muslim-women-wearing-hijabs-assaulted-just-hours-after-trump-win-n681936

Salaam Global Islamic Economy Gateway. 2017. "Report: State of the Global Islamic Economy 2017/18." Last modified November 27, 2017. https://www.slideshare.net/ EzzedineGHLAMALLAH/state-of-the-global-islamic-economy-20172018

Sarkar, Monica. 2016. "H&M's latest look: Hijab-wearing Muslim model stirs." CNN, August 26, 2016. https://www.cnn.com/style/article/hm-hijab-model/index.html

Sarsour, Linda. 2016. "Thoughts on the Controversy Surrounding Noor Tagouri's Interview." Ilmfeed, September 25, 2016. https://ilmfeed.com/my-thoughts-on-the-controversy -surrounding-nour-tagouris-interview-with-playboy/; Al-Khatahtbeh, Amani. 2016. "I Turned Down Playboy and Still Support Women's Choice to Do It." *Muslim Girl*, 2016. http://muslimgirl.com/30936/turned-playboy-still-support-womens-choice/

Sartwell, Crispin. 2019. "The Oscars and the Illusion of Perfect Representation." *The New York Times*, February 25, 2019. https://www.nytimes.com/2019/02/25/opinion/oscars -2019-diversity.html

Sheikh, Aminah. 2013. "Why I Participated in the 'Somewhere in America' #Mipsterz Video." *Patheos*, December 4, 2013. https://www.patheos.com/blogs/altmuslim/ 2013/12/why-i-participated-in-the-somewhere-in-america-mipsterz-video/

Shields, Lauren. 2013. "My Year of Modesty." *Salon*, July 2, 2013. https://www.salon .com/2013/07/02/my_year_of_modesty/

Smith, Samuel. 2017. "Robert P. George Warns: Militant Secularists 'Want Your Kids.'" *Christian Post*, October 25, 2017. https://www.christianpost.com/news/robert-p-george -warns-militant-secularists-want-your-kids.html

Uddin, Asma. 2016. "When a Swimsuit Is a Security Threat." *The New York Times*, August 24, 2016. https://www.nytimes.com/2016/08/24/opinion/when-a-swimsuit-is-a -security-threat.html

Uddin, Asma T. and Inas Younis. 2016. "Playboy's Interview with a Muslim Woman Mocks Modesty and Offends Women." *Washington Post*, September 28, 2016. https:// www.washingtonpost.com/news/acts-of-faith/wp/2016/09/28/playboys-interview-with-a -muslim-woman-mocks-modesty-and-offends-women/?utm_term=.81622ce2b57d

US Equal Employment Opportunity Commission. n.d. "Religion-Based Charges Filed from 10/01/2000 through 9/30/2011 Showing Percentage Filed on the Basis of Religion-Muslim." https://www.eeoc.gov/eeoc/events/9-11-11_religion_charges.cfm. These numbers can be explained by both the rise in prejudice post-9/11 and, as one study found, "the possibility of increased enforcement of Title VII by EEOC on behalf of Muslims." Goodrich, Luke W. and Rachel N. Busick. 2018. "Sex, Drugs, and Eagle Feathers: An Empirical Study of Federal Religious Freedom Cases." *Seton Hall Law Review*. 48 353–401.

US Equal Employment Opportunity Commission. n.d. "What You Should Know about the EEOC and Religious and National Origin Discrimination Involving the Muslim, Sikh, Arab, Middle Eastern and South Asian Communities." Accessed February 20, 2019. https://www.eeoc.gov/eeoc/newsroom/wysk/religion_national_origin_9-11.cfm

CHAPTER 8

Aslan, Reza and Hasan Minhaj. 2015. "An Open Letter to American Muslims on Same-Sex Marriage." *Religion Dispatches*, July 7, 2015. http://religiondispatches.org/ an-open-letter-to-american-muslims-on-same-sex-marriage/

Beinart, Peter. 2017. "When Conservatives Oppose 'Religious Freedom.'" *The Atlantic*, April 11, 2017. https://www.theatlantic.com/politics/archive/2017/04/when-conservatives-oppose-religious-freedom/522567/

Biola Magazine. 2016. "How Should Christians Respond to Gay Friends or Family Members?" Last modified Winter 2016. http://magazine.biola.edu/article/16-winter/how-should-christians-respond-to-gay-friends-or-fa/

Boorstein, Michelle. 2015. "When Muslims are the target, prominent religious freedom advocates largely go quiet." *Washington Post*, December 30, 2015. https://www.washingtonpost.com/news/acts-of-faith/wp/2015/12/10/when-muslims-are-the-target-prominent-religious-freedom-advocates-largely-go-quiet/?utm_term=.121c2176d2e8

Brown, Jonathan AC. 2015. "Muslim Scholar on How Islam Really Views Homosexuality." *Variety*, June 30, 2015. https://variety.com/2015/voices/opinion/islam-gay-marriage-beliefs-muslim-religion-1201531047/

Buncombe, Andrew. 2015. "Kim Davis: Court clerk has become a hero of America's Christian right by refusing gay people the right to wed." *Independent*, September 1, 2015. https://www.independent.co.uk/news/world/americas/kim-davis-court-clerk-has-become-a-hero-of-americas-christian-right-by-refusing-gay-people-the-right-10481399.html

Burwell v. Hobby Lobby Stores, Inc., 573 U.S. 682 (2014). "Brief of Church of The Lukumi Babalu Aye, Inc., The International Society for Krishna Consciousness, Inc., Ave Maria University, Colorado Christian University, East Texas Baptist University, Crescent Foods, The Institutional Religious Freedom Alliance, and The Queens Federation Of Churches As Amicus Curiae In Support Of Hobby Lobby And Conestoga, Et Al." January 28, 2014. https://www.americanbar.org/content/dam/aba/publications/supreme_court_preview/briefs-v3/13-354-13-356_amcu_clba-etal.authcheckdam.pdf

C-SPAN. 2017. "Muslim Public Affairs Council, Religious Liberty." Last modified November 5, 2017. https://www.c-span.org/video/?436394-3/muslim-public-affairs-council-religious-liberty

Calgri, Ilhan. 2017. "A Muslim perspective on the Masterpiece Cakeshop case." Religion News Service, December 6, 2017. https://religionnews.com/2017/12/06/a-muslim-perspective-on-the-masterpiece-cakeshop-case/

Coll, Steve. 2014. "When the Taliban Meets Hobby Lobby." *The New Yorker*, July 1, 2014. https://www.newyorker.com/news/daily-comment/when-the-taliban-meets-hobby-lobby

Cox, Daniel and Robert P. Jones. 2017. "America's Changing Religious Identity." PRRI, September 6, 2017. https://www.prri.org/research/american-religious-landscape-christian-religiously-unaffiliated/

Daley, Kevin. 2018. "Democrats Question Judicial Nominee About Membership in Catholic Association." *Daily Signal*, December 23, 2018. https://www.dailysignal.com/2018/12/23/democrats-question-judicial-nominee-about-membership-in-catholic-association/

DeVega, Chauncey. 2014. "What if a Muslim Company Used the 'Hobby Lobby' Decision to Impose Its Values on White Christians?" *Daily Kos*, June 30, 2014. https://www.dailykos.com/stories/2014/06/30/1310729/-What-if-a-Muslim-Company-Used-the-Hobby-Lobby-Decision-to-Impose-Its-Values-on-White-Christians

Diamant, Jeff and Claire Gecewicz. 2017. "5 facts about Muslim Millennials in the U.S." Last modified October 26, 2017. http://www.pewresearch.org/fact-tank/2017/10/26/5-facts-about-muslim-millennials-us/

Epstein, Lee, Andrew D. Martin and Kevin Quinn. 2018. "6+ Decades of Freedom of Expression in the U.S. Supreme Court." Last modified June 30, 2018. http://epstein.wustl.edu/research/FreedomOfExpression.pdf

Feldblum, Chai. 2018. "What I Really Believe About Religious Liberty and LGBT Rights."
Medium, August 1, 2018. https://medium.com/@chaifeldblum/what-i-really-believe
-about-religious-liberty-and-lgbt-rights-2cc64ade95a2

Fisher, Max. 2016. "Marco Rubio's comments about Muslims are getting to be almost as
frightening as Trump's." *Vox*, February 6, 2016. https://www.vox.com/2016/
2/4/10918372/marco-rubio-muslims-media

Geller, Pamela. 2016. "Pamela Geller: Muslim Woman Demands Workplace Accommodate
Her Hijab." *Breitbart*, August 5, 2016. https://www.breitbart.com/politics/2016/08/05/
pamela-geller-muslim-woman-demands-workplace-accommodate-her-hijab/

Geller, Pamela. 2016. "Illinois: Two Muslim truck drivers awarded $240,000 for refusing
to deliver alcohol." Freedom Outpost, 2016. https://freedomoutpost.com/illinois-two
-muslim-truck-drivers-awarded-240000-for-refusing-to-deliver-alcohol/

Geller, Pamela. 2018. "New York Times hits 'disturbing trend' of seeing Islam as 'not a
religion.'" Geller Report, September 27, 2018. https://gellerreport.com/2018/09/times
-trend-religion.html/

Gomaa, Mariam. 2014. "American Hijab: Why My Scarf is a Sociopolitical Statement, Not a
Symbol of My Religiosity." *TIME*, November 11, 2014. http://time.com/3576827/enums/

Goodrich, Luke W. and Rachel N. Busick. 2018. "Sex, Drugs, and Eagle Feathers: An
Empirical Study of Federal Religious Freedom Cases." *Seton Hall Law Review*. 48
353–401. This study was limited to cases in the Tenth Circuit.

Graham, David A. 2015. "How Republicans Won and Then Lost the Muslim Vote." *The
Atlantic*, December 9, 2015. https://www.theatlantic.com/politics/archive/2015/12/
republicans-muslim-vote-george-w-bush-donald-trump/419481/

Greenhouse, Linda. 2018. "How the Supreme Court Grasps Religions." *New York Times*,
May 10, 2018. https://www.nytimes.com/2018/05/10/opinion/supreme-court-religion
.html. The *Masterpiece* and travel ban cases "will tell us a lot about how the current
court thinks about religion—specifically, how it defines religious discrimination and who
it thinks needs the court's protection."

HHS.gov. 2018. "HHS Announces New Conscience and Religious Freedom Division."
Last modified January 18, 2018. https://www.hhs.gov/about/news/2018/01/18/hhs-ocr
-announces-new-conscience-and-religious-freedom-division.html

Hasson, Kevin Seamus. 2005. *The Right to Be Wrong: Ending the Culture War Over
Religion in America*. New York: Crown Publishing Group.

H.B. 438. (Maryland 2012) http://mlis.state.md.us/2012rs/bills/hb/hb0438t.pdf

Huetteman, Emmarie. 2018. "Critics say conservative Trump Health and Human Services
appointee is trampling over patients' civil rights." *USA Today*, March 5, 2018. https://
www.usatoday.com/story/news/nation/2018/03/05/critics-say-conservative-trump-health
-and-human-services-appointee-trampling-over-patients-civil-rig/394542002/

Human Rights Campaign. 2018. "Do No Harm Act." Last modified December 21, 2018.
https://www.hrc.org/resources/do-no-harm-act

Human Rights Campaign. n.d. "Stances of Faiths on LGBTQ Issues: Islam—Sunni and
Shi'a." Accessed February 22, 2019. https://www.hrc.org/resources/stances-of-faiths-on
-lgbt-issues-islam

Ifill, Sherrilyn. 2018. "Symposium: The First Amendment protects speech and religion,
not discrimination in public spaces." SCOTUSBlog, June 5, 2018. http://www

.scotusblog.com/2018/06/symposium-the-first-amendment-protects-speech-and-religion
-not-discrimination-in-public-spaces/

Jazayerll, Rany. 2012. "Essay: How the Republican Party alienated the once reliable
Muslim voting bloc." *Washington Post*, November 16, 2012. https://www
.washingtonpost.com/local/essay-how-the-republican-party-alienated-the-once-reliable
-muslim-voting-bloc/2012/11/15/23e2af70-2da5-11e2-9ac2-1c61452669c3_story
.html?noredirect=on&utm_term=.6cc54a9e6b99

Jonas, Michael. 2007. "The Downside of Diversity." *New York Times*, August 5, 2007.
http://archive.boston.com/news/globe/ideas/articles/2007/08/05/the_downside_of_
diversity/

Jones, Robert P. 2016. "The Evangelicals and the Great Trump Hope." *New York Times*,
July 11, 2016. https://www.nytimes.com/2016/07/11/opinion/campaign-stops/the
-evangelicals-and-the-great-trump-hope.html?ref=opinion&_r=1

Jones, Robert P. 2018. "Pluralism After White Christian America." In *Out of Many Faiths:
Religious Diversity and the American Promise*. Princeton: Princeton University Press.

Kodjak, Alison. 2018. "Trump Admin Will Protect Health Workers Who Refuse Services
on Religious Grounds." NPR, January 18, 2018. https://www.npr.org/sections/health
-shots/2018/01/18/578811426/trump-will-protect-health-workers-who-reject-patients
-on-religious-grounds

Kuruvilla, Carol. 2017. "American Muslims Are Now More Accepting of Homosexuality
Than White Evangelicals." *Huffington Post*, August 1, 2017. https://www
.huffingtonpost.com/entry/american-muslims-are-now-more-accepting-of-homosexuality
-than-white-evangelicals_us_597f3d8de4b02a4ebb76ea3d

Lund, Christopher C. 2016. "RFRA, State RFRA, and Religious Minorities." *San Diego
Law Review*. 53: 163-184.

Leonard, Robert. 2015. "The many (unfair) shamings of Kim Davis." *The Hill*, October 6,
2015. https://thehill.com/blogs/pundits-blog/uncategorized/256014-the-many-unfair
-shamings-of-kim-davis

Liptak, Adam. 2018. "How Conservatives Weaponized the First Amendment." *New York
Times*, June 30, 2018. https://www.nytimes.com/2018/06/30/us/politics/first
-amendment-conservatives-supreme-court.html

Lukianoff, Greg and Jonathan Haidt. 2018. *The Coddling of the American Mind: How
Good Intentions and Bad Ideas Are Setting Up a Generation for Failure*. New York:
Penguin Press.

Markham, Claire. 2017. "Tales and Truth in the *Masterpiece Cakeshop* Arguments."
Center for American Progress, December 7, 2017.
https://www.americanprogress.org/issues/religion/news/2017/12/07/443911/tales-truth-
masterpiece-cakeshop-arguments/

Masterpiece Cakeshop v. Colorado Civil Rights Commission, 138 S.Ct. 1719 (2018).
"Brief for Petitioners." August 31, 2017. http://www.scotusblog.com/wp-content/
uploads/2017/09/16-111-ts.pdf

Masterpiece Cakeshop, Ltd. v. Colorado Civil Rights Comm'n, 138 S. Ct. 1719 (2018).
"Brief of *Amici Curiae* 15 Faith and Civil Rights Organizations in Support Of
Respondents." October 30, 2017. https://www.muslimadvocates.org/files/AmicusBrief_
MasterpieceCakeshop-1.pdf

Masterpiece Cakeshop, Ltd. v. Colorado Civil Rights Comm'n, 138 S. Ct. 1719

(2018). Oral Arguments. https://www.supremecourt.gov/oral_arguments/argument_transcripts/2017/16-111_f314.pdf

Melling, Louise. 2015. "ACLU: Why we can no longer support the federal 'religious freedom' law." *Washington Post*, June 25, 2016. https://www.washingtonpost.com/opinions/congress-should-amend-the-abused-religious-freedom-restoration-act/2015/06/25/ee6aaa46-19d8-11e5-ab92-c75ae6ab94b5_story.html?postshare=6371435345896586&utm_term=.d13f8c3a062b

Masterpiece Cakeshop, Ltd. v. Colorado Civil Rights Comm'n, 138 S. Ct. 1719 (2018). "Brief of *Amici Curiae* 34 Legal Scholars in Support Of Petitioners." September 7, 2017. http://www.scotusblog.com/wp-content/uploads/2017/09/16-111_tsac_34_legal_scholars.pdf

Miller, Emily McFarlan and Yonat Shimron. 2018. "Why is Jeff Sessions quoting Romans 13 and why is the bible verse so often invoked?" *USA Today*, June 16, 2018. https://www.usatoday.com/story/news/2018/06/16/jeff-sessions-bible-romans-13-trump-immigration-policy/707749002/

MuslimMatters. 2017. "Counsel to Muslim Social Justice Activists." Last modified February 10, 2017. https://muslimmatters.org/2017/02/10/counsel-to-muslim-social-justice-activists/

Noble, Alex. 2014. "The Evangelical Persecution Complex." *The Atlantic*, August 4, 2014. https://www.theatlantic.com/national/archive/2014/08/the-evangelical-persecution-complex/375506/

Obergefell v. Hodges, 135 S. Ct. 2584 (2015).

Pew Research Center. 2009. "Global Restrictions on Religion: Social Hostilities Index (SHI)." Last modified December 17, 2009. http://www.pewforum.org/2009/12/17/global-restrictions-on-religion/

Pew Research Center. 2009. "Global Restrictions on Religion." Last modified December 17, 2009. http://www.pewforum.org/2009/12/17/global-restrictions-on-religion/

Pew Research Center. 2017. "Political and Social Views: Like Americans overall, Muslims now more accepting of homosexuality." Last modified July 25, 2017. http://www.pewforum.org/2017/07/26/political-and-social-views/pf_2017-06-26_muslimamericans-04new-06/

Pew Research Center. n.d. "Religious Landscape Study: Who oppose or strongly oppose gay marriage who are Muslim." Accessed February 22, 2019. http://www.pewforum.org/religious-landscape-study/religious-tradition/muslim/views-about-same-sex-marriage/opposestrongly-oppose/

Piacenza, Joanna. 2018. "Christians, White Evangelicals Have Contrasting Views on Issues in Cake Case." Morning Consult, June 4, 2018. https://morningconsult.com/2018/06/04/christians-white-evangelicals-have-contrasting-views-issues-cake-case/

Real Clear Politics. 2015. "Steven Crowder: Gay Wedding Cakes at Muslim Bakeries?" Last modified April 4, 2015. https://www.realclearpolitics.com/video/2015/04/04/steven_crowder_gay_wedding_cakes_at_muslim_bakeries.html

Rienzi, Mark L. 2012. "The Constitutional Right Not to Kill." *Emory Law Journal*. 62:121–178.

Rusin, David J. 2013. "Hate-Crime Stats Deflate 'Islamophobia' Myth." *National Review*, January 11, 2013. https://www.nationalreview.com/2013/01/hate-crime-stats-deflate-islamophobia-myth-david-j-rusin/

Schultz, Tim. 2017. "Where the ACLU went wrong on religious freedom." *The Hill*, November 14, 2017. https://thehill.com/opinion/civil-rights/360165-where-the-aclu-went-wrong-on-religious-freedom

Shea, Christopher. 2018. "Why Jeff Sessions thinks Christians are under siege in America." *Vox*, August 1, 2018. https://www.vox.com/the-big-idea/2018/8/1/17638706/religious -liberty-sessions-task-force-masterpiece-scalia-constitution

Sparrow, Jeff. 2015. "Conservatives' yearning for Islam is the love that dare not speak its name." *The Guardian*, November 19, 2015. https://www.theguardian.com/world/ commentisfree/2015/nov/19/conservatives-yearning-for-islam-is-the-love-that-dare-not -speak-its-name

Stern, Mark Joseph. 2019. "The Trump Administration Will Let Adoption Agencies Turn Away Jews and Same-Sex Couples. Thank SCOTUS." *Slate*, January 24, 2019. https:// slate.com/news-and-politics/2019/01/trump-adoption-same-sex-couples-jews-miracle -mill.html; Lacy, Akela. 2018. "South Carolina Is Lobbying to Allow Discrimination Against Jewish Parents." *The Intercept*, October 19, 2018. https://theintercept .com/2018/10/19/south-carolina-foster-parent-discrimination-miracle-hill-ministries/

Stewart, Katherine. 2018. "Whose Religious Liberty Is It Anyway?" *New York Times*, September 8, 2018. https://www.nytimes.com/2018/09/08/opinion/kavanaugh-supreme -court-religious-liberty.html

Stewart, Katherine. 2018. "Why Trump Reigns as King Cyrus." *New York Times*, December 31, 2018. https://www.nytimes.com/2018/12/31/opinion/trump-evangelicals -cyrus-king.html

Stone, Brian. 2015. "Rush Limbaugh, Dearborn and the Muslim Baker Bigotry Myth." *The Huffington Post*, April 6, 2015. https://www.huffingtonpost.com/brian-stone/rush -limbaugh-dearborn-an_b_7002854.html

The Economist. 2014. "The Hobby Lobby ruling: Disingenuous." Comments. Accessed February 22, 2019. https://www.economist.com/node/21606232/all-comments

Tolerance Means Dialogues. n.d. "About." Accessed February 22, 2019. https://www .tolerancemeans.com/about/

Tushnet, Mark. 2018. "Is it anti-Catholic to ask a Supreme Court nominee how her religion affects her decisions?" *Vox*, July 5, 2018. The author notes that Barrett had explored in a legal academic article how Catholic judges should handle death penalty cases. While questioning a nominee about his or her legal arguments is legitimate, questioning his or her religiosity or religious affiliations is not. Feinstein's question veered into the latter.

Uddin, Asma. 2018. "Sessions's (and My) Remarks at the DOJ Religious Liberty Summit." Religious Freedom Center, August 10, 2018. http://www.religiousfreedomcenter.org/ sessionss-and-my-remarks-at-the-doj-religious-liberty-summit/

Uddin, Asma T. 2018. "The Latest Attack on Islam: It's Not a Religion." *New York Times*, September 26, 2018. https://www.nytimes.com/2018/09/26/opinion/islamophobia -muslim-religion-politics.html.

US Commission on Civil Rights. 2016. "Peaceful Coexistence: Reconciling Nondiscrimination Principles with Civil Liberties." Last modified September 7, 2016. http://www.newamericancivilrightsproject.org/wp-content/uploads/2016/09/Peaceful -Coexistence-09-07-16-6.pdf

Ware, Lawrence. 2018. "It's on Men to End Sexism in the Black Church." *The New York Times*, December 1, 2018. https://www.nytimes.com/2018/12/01/opinion/sunday/its-on -men-to-end-sexism-in-the-black-church.html

YouTube. 2018. "Who Ya Gonna Call? Religious Liberty Task Force!" https://www .youtube.com/watch?v=L0rTGcI1rK8. Last modified August 1, 2018.